Based on extensive fieldwork that involved interviewing women and policy-makers, this book offers innovative insights on the design and implementation of transitional justice in Timor-Leste (East Timor). Dr Perez Vasquez offers a masterful and critical overview of transitional justice laws and policies and the extent to which these are impacted by community and family relationships. A unique guide for academics and policy-makers wanting to understand the unfolding of transitional justice in local contexts as well as women's experiences in conflict and post-conflict situations.

Professor Gentian Zyberi, Norwegian Centre for Human Rights, University of Oslo. Member of the UN Human Rights Committee (CCPR)

In telling the transitional justice process through the words of women and placing this in conversation with postcolonial feminist research on transitional justice, Perez Vasquez has crafted an important and enduring contribution to international understandings of transitional justice, of gender and conflict and of the persistent blindspots in international and legal campaigns for justice. The Blind Letters is both timely and timeless. In reading the book the reader is given insight into what the next generation of transitional justice scholarship and activism must be centering: local voices and expertise, the persistence and diversity of gender and the importance of women's participation as a process toward justice and away from the continuation of harm.

Gina Heathcote, Professor of Gender Studies and International Law, School of Law, SOAS University of London

While raising Timorese women's voices and reaching to the deepest of our hidden experiences during the conflict against Indonesia, Dr Pérez Vásquez has superbly managed to demonstrate how the package of justice given after the war was after all only for the benefit a few men leaders, none for the women.

Bella Galhos
A survivor of sexual violence and Timorese human rights defender

WOMEN'S ACCESS TO TRANSITIONAL JUSTICE IN TIMOR-LESTE

Seeing the role of transitional justice an area of contestation, this book focuses on the principle of equality guaranteed in the access to transitional justice mechanisms. By raising women's experiences in dealing with the law and policies as well as the implications of community and family practices during post-conflict situations, the book shows how these mechanisms may have been implemented mechanically, without considering the different intersections of discrimination, the public and private divides that exist in the local context or the stereotypes and values of international and national actors.

The book argues that without unpacking the barriers in the administration of transitional justice, the different mechanisms that are implemented in a post-conflict situation may set a higher threshold for the participation of women. Moreover, by taking into account women's perceptions of justice, it argues that scholars have paid insufficient attention to the welfare structures that are produced after a conflict, particularly the pensions of veterans. Going beyond the focus on sexual violence, a relationship between the violations and post-conflict economic justice may have longer-term consequences for women since it perpetuates their inequality and lack of recognition in times of peace. The use of transitional justice may thus exacerbate the invisibility of and discrimination against certain sections of the population.

Inspired by the work of Hannah Arendt and based on extensive field research in Timor-Leste, the book has larger implications for the overarching debate on the social consequences of transitional justice.

Women's Access to Transitional Justice in Timor-Leste

The Blind Letters

Noemí Pérez Vásquez

•HART•
OXFORD • LONDON • NEW YORK • NEW DELHI • SYDNEY

HART PUBLISHING

Bloomsbury Publishing Plc

Kemp House, Chawley Park, Cumnor Hill, Oxford, OX2 9PH, UK

1385 Broadway, New York, NY 10018, USA

29 Earlsfort Terrace, Dublin 2, Ireland

HART PUBLISHING, the Hart/Stag logo, BLOOMSBURY and the Diana logo are trademarks of Bloomsbury Publishing Plc

First published in Great Britain 2022

The views expressed herein are those of the author and do not necessarily reflect the views of the United Nations.

A catalogue record for this book is available from the British Library.

A catalogue record for this book is available from the Library of Congress.

ISBN: HB: 978-1-50995-763-7
ePDF: 978-1-50995-765-1
ePub: 978-1-50995-764-4

Typeset by Compuscript Ltd, Shannon

To find out more about our authors and books visit www.hartpublishing.co.uk. Here you will find extracts, author information, details of forthcoming events and the option to sign up for our newsletters.

Acknowledgements

I WOULD LIKE to express my heartfelt thanks to all the women I interviewed, particularly those who are survivors of violence. These women, whether they carried a gun or not, are heroines, and the Timorese state owes them recognition for the evil and for the sacrifices they experienced under Indonesian rule. I would also like to thank ACbit and its director, Manuela Leong Pereira, who has been working tirelessly for the recognition of the women whose rights were gravely violated before 1999. While living in Timor-Leste, I was also a Visiting Researcher at the Universidade Nacional Timor Lorosa'e (UNTL), a university of reference in Timor-Leste. I will always be deeply grateful to all the professors and administrative personnel I met for all the intellectual and material support. As part of this research, I also spent six months at the Dili District Court, where the serious crimes case files of the Special Panels are located. I sat in an office surrounded by Timorese justice officers and I cannot thank each of them enough for their patience and friendship.

I would like to say a special thank you to Marfiano Manuel 'Titiso' for being my research assistant. He not only translated the interviews and efficiently organised our trips to each of the municipalities that we visited in Timor-Leste, but also helped me understand the way in which Timorese people think and behave. Some of the photos for this book were taken by Dr Carlos Oviedo, a Colombian friend and anthropologist himself whom I met in Dili while we were both doing our doctoral field research. After seeing his photographic skills, I invited him on some of my trips.

I also wish to express my thanks to the following:

To the Parliament of Timor-Leste, the Prosecutor's Office, Belun, La'o Hamutuk think tank, the Centro Audiovisual Max Stahl, the United Nations, and all the people whom I interviewed and talked to, including Alvaro Vasconcellos, Anacleto Ribeiro, Aniceto Guterres, Anildo da Cruz, Anjet Lanting, Anna Lisa Picone, Antonio Helder do Carmo, Antonio Sampaio, Arsenio Pereira, Barbara Oliveira, Bella Galhos, Benicia Magno, Bruno Lencastre, David Ximenes, Dora Martins, Fernanda Borges, Fidelis Magalhães, Flaviano Lemos, Fily Gandi, Flavio Simões, Florencio Gonzaga, Francesco Flori, Gabriel Sá, Gabriela Soares, Gianna Bonis-Profumo, Helen Hill, Hugo Fernandes, José Guerra, José Teixeira, Juvenal Dias, Kerry Brogan, Laleke de Araújo, Leigh-Ashley Lipscomb, Louis Gentile, Mara Bernardes de Sá, Maria Natércia Gusmão Pereira, Niall Almond, Nísia Magalhães, Nuno Rodrigues, Pat Walsh, Rebecca Engel, Riovaldi Saldanha, Rosario de Araújo and Sandra Silva. And to all the others who are not on this list but who provided me with different angles from which to see my research. I did not visit a single institution in Timor-Leste without receiving people's kind support.

To my PhD supervisors, Phil Clark and Fareda Banda, who were both an ideal combination and saw very different aspects of me. Phil Clark gave me confidence and calm along this journey, stepped in when I needed to organise my ideas and made me reflect on my research from a wider perspective. I also cannot thank him enough for the teaching opportunities that he offered me. Fareda transmitted strength, and with her attention to detail not only did she expose me to many authors and PhD opportunities, but more importantly, helped me to refine my arguments. She also gave me one of the best pieces of advice that I ever received: 'make sure to have time to think.' I was so lucky to have them as my supervisors.

To Matei Negrescu, who has been a long-time mentor and the greatest supporter through many years. To my dear friend Liiri Oja, who was also doing a PhD on women's rights in parallel with me. We both teamed up during this journey and supported, and in a way, influenced each other. To Merryl Lawry-White and Juliette Clancy for providing me strength when I despaired. To John Taggart for his kind support and to Justin Hicks, Jo Choulerton and Tom Adams, because with their dedicated and kind support, they made this book possible.

Finally, on a very personal note, when I was in Timor-Leste, I could not stop thinking about my own country, Venezuela. Because of oil, the rural generations of my beloved grandparents saw themselves suddenly overrun by foreigners, who were soon the managers of the main national industry – until a new Venezuelan generation was trained. In the meantime, life stories crossed and were framed by those changing times and people's own private limitations. I therefore dedicate this book to the women who preceded me in my family, who insisted on offering to their offspring the best education they could afford. To my great-grandmother Josefa, who was illiterate, clever and resilient, to my adored grandmother Noemí, briefly a secretary and later housewife, who used to wake me up at 4am so I could double check my notes before my elementary school tests, and to my mother, María, a professor who has worked hard and sacrificed her own life for the well-being of her daughters.

Noemí Pérez Vásquez

Interview of a survivor of sexual violence in Aileu, Timor-Leste. © Carlos Oviedo.

Table of Contents

Abbreviations

AMP	Aliansa Mudansa ba Progresu/ Alliance of Change for Progress.
API and APII	Additional Protocols I and II to the Geneva Conventions.
APODETI	Associação Popular Democrática Timorense/ Popular Democratic Association of Timor.
Bapa	Catch-all term for any Indonesian male used by Timorese people.
CAT	Convention against Torture and Other Cruel, Inhuman or Degrading Treatment or Punishment.
CAVR	Commission for Reception, Truth and Reconciliation in East Timor.
CEDAW	Convention on the Elimination of all Forms of Discrimination Against Women.
CERD	The Committee on the Elimination of Racial Discrimination.
CHEGA!	The title of the CAVR Report, which means in Portuguese 'no more, stop, enough'.
CNC	Centro Nacional Chega!/ Chega! National Centre.
CNRT	Congresso Nacional de Reconstrução de Timor/ National Congress for Timorese Reconstruction (political party).
CTF	Commission for Truth and Friendship between Indonesia and Timor-Leste.
DDR	Disarmament, Demobilisation and Reintegration programme.
Falintil	Forças Armadas da Libertação Nacional de Timor-Leste/ The Armed Forces for the National Liberation of East Timor.
Fretilin	Frente Revolucionária de Timor-Leste Independente/ The Revolutionary Front for an Independent East Timor.
GA	UN General Assembly.

GC	The Geneva Conventions.
Hansip	A local security officer, member of Indonesian Civil Defence Force in a village.
IAC	International Armed Conflict.
IACHR	Inter-American Commission on Human Rights.
IACtHR	Inter-American Court of Human Rights.
ICC	International Criminal Court.
ICCPR	International Covenant on Civil and Political Rights.
ICESCR	International Covenant on Economic, Social and Cultural Rights.
ICPPED	International Convention for the Protection of All Persons from Enforced Disappearance.
ICTJ	International Center for Transitional Justice.
ICTR	International Criminal Tribunal for Rwanda.
ICTY	International Criminal Tribunal for the former Yugoslavia.
INTERFET	International Force East Timor.
KHUNTO	Kmanek Haburas Unidade Nasional Timor Oan/ Party of the Enhancement of Timorese National Unity.
KLA	Kosovo Liberation Army.
Komnas HAM	Komisi Nasional Hak Asasi Manusia/ Indonesian National Commission on Human Rights.
KUHP	Kitab Undang-Undang Hukum Pidana/ Indonesian Penal Code.
MP	Member of Parliament.
NAP	National Action Plan.
NIAC	Non-International Armed Conflict.
OHCHR	Office of the United Nations High Commissioner for Human Rights.
OPMT	Organização Popular de Mulher Timorense/ Popular Organisation of East Timorese Women.
PLP	Partidu Libertasaun Popular/ People Liberation Party.
POLRI	Indonesian National Police.

PSVI	The Preventing Sexual Violence in Conflict Initiative.
SCSL	Special Court for Sierra Leone.
SDGs	Sustainable Development Goals.
SGBV	Sexual and gender-based violence.
SR	(UN) Special Rapporteur.
SRSG	Special Representative of the UN Secretary-General.
Suco	Municipalities, larger villages.
TNI	Tentara Nasional Indonesia/ Indonesian National Armed Forces.
TRC	Truth and Reconciliation Commission.
UDHR	Universal Declaration of Human Rights.
UDT	União Democrática Timoresense/ Timorese Democratic Union.
UNGAR	United Nations General Assembly Resolution.
UNMIK	United Nations Mission in Kosovo.
UNMISET	United Nations Mission of Support to East Timor.
UNSCR	UN Security Council Resolution.
UNTAET	United Nations Transitional Administration in East Timor.
WPS	Women, Peace and Security agenda.

TIMOR-LESTE
Banda Sea
INDONESIA
Atauro
Island
Straight of Wetar
Dili
Baucau
Liquica
Manatuto
Lospalos
Savu Sea
Gleno
Aileu
Ainaro
Viqueque
Pante
Macasar
Maliana
Same
Suai
INDONESIA
Timor Sea
25 km

Timor-Leste

1

Introduction: 'The Blind Letters'

DURING INTERVIEWS WITH 77 women in Timor-Leste, I asked each at the beginning if they knew how to read and write. Tia Kasian, a famous veteran who runs a children's school in Liquiçá, gave a beautiful answer: 'Yes, I went to the school of blind letters.'[1] This took my research assistant by surprise, who was expecting a simple 'yes or no' answer. Tia Kasian meant that the school was there, but that she could not see the letters, so she could not learn how to read and write. I thought that her folk poetic answer was a rich and perfect metaphor for explaining that transitional justice may also be there, but that due to intersectional forms of discrimination it is only accessible for a few.

Transitional justice has been generally defined as the process of justice implemented after serious violations of international law and concerned with dealing with the past (Teitel 2002). It has been applied lately not only to armed conflicts but also to periods of civil strife and/or state repression, in which grave human rights violations such as summary executions, enforced disappearances, torture and arbitrary detentions have taken place (Olsen, Payne and Reiter 2010: 805). The literature on transitional justice has focused largely on which mechanisms or combination of mechanisms are best for society; on the tensions between retributive justice and restorative justice; and on the greater importance of local contexts and actors over international impositions. Within this last debate, the political discourse about the importance of national appropriation and local participation has ensured that the specificities of context are considered in transitional justice (Corradi and Schotsmans 2012). As this book will show, this may, however, be insufficient to ensure protection to all those who were affected during a conflict situation.

Scholars have also reflected on the impact of transitional justice. Skaar and Gianella Malca (2015: 20), for instance, identify the increased respect for human rights as one of the common areas on which transitional justice is expected to have an impact, whereas Duggan (2010: 320) notes the formation of new national identities through history education reform. Ainley (2015: 241–42) observes that although there is little agreement on what constitutes the 'success' of transitional justice and how it should be measured and judged, factors that

[1] Interview with Participant 52, Liquiçá, Liquiçá, Timor-Leste, 25 January 2017.

are commonly cited include outcomes; mandates, processes and functioning of institutions; involvement of, and reaction from, victims and affected populations; adherence to universal normative standards; and cost-effectiveness. While the list of elements of impact may be extensive, a justice system that should be blind and accessible to everyone may not in reality consider structural conditions and contextual barriers that impact the accessibility of transitional justice. Seeing the role of transitional justice as a site of contestation, this book contributes to the analysis and evaluation of post-conflict justice by questioning the principle of equality allegedly guaranteed in the local access to transitional justice.

Because of the intersections of different forms of marginalisation, women may suffer more intense societal exclusion (Charlesworth and Chinkin 2000: 19). Therefore, to presume an apparent neutrality of a justice system that has been appropriated locally may be, on the contrary, used to obscure the gendered nature of rights as well as 'the fact that society is unequal with certain social groups having suffered historical disadvantage …' (WLSA 1999: 54). By unpacking the barriers and layers of discrimination in the administration of transitional justice, we can see how the different mechanisms that are implemented in a post-conflict situation may be blind to the violations committed against women. Based on extensive field research in Timor-Leste, I conduct such an unpacking by raising the experiences of Timorese women in dealing with the laws and policies of transitional justice as well as the implications of community and family practices. More specifically, I uncover women's experiences in dealing with the different transitional justice mechanisms that were available to them, including trials, truth commissions and reparations, to show how transitional laws and policies may protect those in power and exacerbate the invisibility of and discrimination against certain groups of the population who are in a more vulnerable situation.

The aim of this book is therefore to interrogate how women navigate justice after a conflict and what justice, in terms of transitional justice, means for women. Going beyond the focus on sexual violence, I argue that transitional justice mechanisms may be implemented mechanically, without considering either different intersections of discrimination, the public and private divides that exist in the local context, or the stereotypes and patriarchal values of international and national actors. In this regard, my fieldwork experience researching on women's access to transitional justice made me reflect on Fraser's tri-dimensional model of gender justice concerning the political, the sociocultural and the economic. More specifically, she advocates for (1) the need for better political representation of women and their interests in public decision-making concerning rules and procedures designed to claim justice and in terms of individual and collective access to claims for recognition and redistribution; (2) understanding the cultural dimension of recognition, meaning 'revaluating disrespected identities and the cultural products of maligned groups'; and (3) highlighting the economic dimension of redistribution of income and the re-organisation of the division of labour (Fraser 2008; 1997: 15). Based on the interviews with Timorese women, I reflect more in depth on the participation and recognition of women through their access to transitional justice mechanisms, and how because of intersectionality, their invisibility and discrimination against them in these processes have an aftereffect in their access to redistribution.

Without unpacking the barriers in the administration of transitional justice, the different mechanisms implemented in a post-conflict situation may therefore set higher thresholds – meaning additional layers – that limit women's participation and the recognition of their experiences. Moreover, by engaging with different concepts of justice, I argue that when considering women's opinions concerning the justice received, scholars have paid insufficient attention to the welfare structures that are created after a conflict, particularly the systems providing pensions for veterans. Women's perceptions of both justice and contributions during a conflict are deliberately excluded, neglecting the fact that the relationship between violations and post-economic justice may have long-term consequences for women since it perpetuates their silence, inequality and lack of recognition in the aftermath of a conflict. The book also draws on comparative materials from other jurisdictions to illustrate in a global context the structural barriers that women face when accessing transitional justice and its impact on them in times of peace.

I. TRANSITIONAL JUSTICE: A BRIEF OVERVIEW

While transitional justice may be traced back to cases such as the restoration of democracy in Athens in 405 and 411 BC (Elster 2004: 4), the modern understanding of its concept re-emerged after the Nuremberg and Tokyo trials of the Second World War. Decades later, transitional justice was brought once again to the fore with the fall of several authoritarian governments in Latin America during the 1980s, with the subsequent extinction of communist regimes in Central and Eastern Europe, and in response to the ethnic cleansing committed during the armed conflicts in the former Yugoslavia and in Rwanda in the early 1990s (Leebaw 2008: 98–99; Arthur 2009: 322–23). With its rapid and widespread application to the promotion of truth, accountability, reparation and reconciliation, the normative framework of transitional justice has unquestionably become one of the central policy options currently advocated to societies affected by conflict and/or serious abuses.

There are, nevertheless, still ambiguities regarding transitional justice as a concept and field of knowledge. According to the UN (2004: 4), transitional justice 'comprises the full range of processes and mechanisms associated with a society's attempts to come to terms with a legacy of large-scale past abuses, in order to ensure accountability, serve justice and achieve reconciliation'. It is considered that transitional justice is based on international human rights law, international humanitarian law, international criminal law and international refugee law and that five pillars frame its process: truth, justice, reparations, the guarantees of non-repetition and more recently memorialisation (UN 2020: para 2; OHCHR 2014a: 5). Bell (2009), on the other hand, notes three conceptions of transitional justice, including the fight against impunity through human rights, conflict resolution related to constitution making, and state-building in the aftermath of mass atrocity. In practice, transitional justice manifests itself through the provision of specific mechanisms. The Office of the High Commissioner for Human Rights (OHCHR) regards transitional justice as including both judicial and non-judicial mechanisms, such as prosecution initiatives; truth commissions; mapping the justice sector; monitoring legal systems; institutional reforms; vetting and reparations (OHCHR 2008, 2006, 2005). Transitional justice may also include community-based practices and amnesties. These mechanisms can be used in any combination and the ones that require prosecutions for perpetrators are classed as retributive justice, while those aimed at ensuring the participation of different actors, healing victims, and bringing reconciliation to societies are commonly referred to as restorative justice (Braithwaite 2002: 11–12; Olsen, Payne and Reiter 2010: 805).

Transitional justice has not escaped criticism. Some critics have highlighted that attention has focused on the accountability of perpetrators established by the codification of international criminal law rather than on redress and reparations for victims and the responsibility of the state (Evans 2012: 3). Moreover, there may be a tendency for international actors to apply one-size-fits-all justice policies to many post-conflict environments, suggesting an ideological approach rather than one based on national interests and needs. Questions of legitimacy have also arisen where international versions of justice are imposed in place of local conceptions and ideas of what constitutes justice. For instance, the involvement of international tribunals in seeking justice for victims has been mainly based on a Western approach to retributive justice, ignoring other forms or components of justice, such as traditional mechanisms (Okello and Hovil 2007). There has been further criticism concerning the exclusion of local communities as active participants in the design and implementation of transitional justice mechanisms, raising fundamental questions of empowerment and local ownership (Lundy and McGovern 2008: 266, 274). As a result, international pressure in the implementation of transitional justice mechanisms has meant in many cases an interference in domestic and sovereign affairs, imposing an external version of justice and questioning local culture, civil society and authority structures (Friedman 2015: 55, 61).

African scholars have also called for a greater recognition of the role of local traditions within transitional justice processes and for efforts to be grounded in the experiences and sensibilities of local communities (Komakech 2012; Ndahinda and Muleefu 2012). In this regard, the UN Secretary General's report on transitional justice affirmed that 'due regard must be given to indigenous and informal tradition for administering justice or settling disputes, to help them to continue their vital role and to do so in conformity with both international standards and local tradition' (UN 2004: para 36). This focus on the local context, however, reflected broader discussions of humanitarian and human rights programmes around the world. Kennedy (2004: 131) warned that policy makers 'think of their techniques as having shape, potential, potency abstracted from the context of their application, and precisely to overlook the specificity of context'. An homogenised local context, however, cannot be the only issue taken into account in the implementation of the mechanisms of transitional justice. Based on the participation and recognition of Timorese women throughout the mechanisms of transitional justice, I show that there must also be a focus on the interaction of the diverse social groups and their public and private dynamics during the design and implementation phases. This would also be more aligned with the core of the 1979 Convention on the Elimination of all Forms of Discrimination Against Women (CEDAW), which reaffirms that discrimination occurs not only in direct instances, such as legislation, but also in culture and traditions, customs, practices and through gender stereotyping. In the next section, I provide an overview of the protection of women's rights through the interventions of transitional justice. Taking into account a gender dimension across the different mechanisms has been historically full of challenges.

II. WOMEN'S RIGHTS WITHIN TRANSITIONAL JUSTICE

A. Retributive Justice

Typically manifested through trials, retributive justice holds that perpetrators must be brought to account, punished and given what they 'deserve' (Clark 2008: 197–98). Because this justice, it is argued, has a deterrent effect, others do not commit the same crime. Although courts and tribunals have been the main model used since the Second World War, they have had a poor record of dealing with cases concerning women. For instance, despite the fact there were accounts of the use of rape during the Second World War, rape and sexual violence were not explicitly listed as examples of war crimes or crimes against humanity in Article 6 of the Nuremberg Charter (1945), and as result, they did not feature in the Nuremberg trials – they were not perceived as significant (UN 2021a: para 37; Reilly 2009: 100–101).[2] Rape and sexual violence also received limited attention in the International Military Tribunal for the Far East, also known as the Tokyo Trials (Reilly 2009: 100–101). Rape, for instance, was also not listed as a war crime or crime against humanity in its Charter, although in its judgment the Tribunal 'recorded that approximately 20,000 cases of rape had occurred in the city of Nanking during the first month of its occupation' (UN 2021a: para 37). Only after women started to break their silence did new

[2] The Nuremburg Charter (1945) established the core concepts used in the prosecution of war crimes after the Second World War.

accounts begin to surface, revealing not only the scale of these crimes but also how they were sidelined by political alliances and the justice system implemented at that time.[3]

The first explicit reference to rape and sexual assault was later included in the definitions of 'grave breach' of the 1949 Geneva Conventions, the core instruments of international humanitarian law that regulate the conduct of armed conflicts. More specifically, through Article 27 of the IV Geneva Convention which focuses on the protection of civilians, states are obliged to protect women in an international armed conflict 'against any attack on their honour, in particular against rape, enforced prostitution, or any form of indecent assault'. This was also criticised, since by defining rape as an offence against honour, there were misconceptions that women should be protected from men rather than indicating that women have rights of their own and that rape is an attack against their lives; that sexual violence is a breach of social mores, including damaging a woman's reputation and her value from the perspective of men, but not an expressly prohibited war crime that demands prosecution; that by not calling rape a crime of violence, the provision presents women as male and family property; and that sexual violence is a lesser crime rather than an offence of a distinctly violent and sexual nature (Charlesworth and Chinkin 2000: 314; Reilly 2009: 101).

As a result, 'sexual crimes against women have been historically excluded from legal prohibition under the laws of war, but when included they have been facets of a male status violation' (Ní Aoláin 1997: 888). Although not a grave breach provision, Article 27 of the Geneva Convention IV – which applies in international armed conflicts (IACs) – is the article that refers explicitly to SGBV against women, but when it does, it focuses on women's honour. Whereas Common Article 3 of the four Geneva Conventions – which applies in non-international armed conflicts (NIACs) – gets closest to referencing crimes of sexual and gender-based violence (SGBV), by expressly prohibiting acts against non-combatants, including murder of all kinds, violence to life and person, torture, the taking of hostages, and what can be related to crimes of a sexual and gender nature, 'outrages upon personal dignity, in particular humiliating and degrading treatment' (Reilly 2009: 101).[4] Moreover, one Article across the

[3] *cf* the book 'A Woman in Berlin' (Anonymous 2005 [1954]).

[4] Gender-based violence is 'any harmful act directed against individuals or groups of individuals on the basis of their gender' (eg sexual violence, domestic violence, trafficking, forced/early marriage and harmful traditional practices) (OHCHR 2014b). Sexual violence is a form of gender-based violence and it is defined as 'any sexual act, attempt to obtain a sexual act, unwanted sexual comments or advances, or acts to traffic, or otherwise directed against a person's sexuality using coercion, by any person regardless of their relationship to the victim, in any setting' (eg rape, sexual abuse, forced pregnancy, forced sterilisation, forced abortion, forced prostitution, trafficking, sexual enslavement, forced circumcision, castration and forced nudity) (OHCHR 2014b). *cf* CEDAW GR 19, 1992: para 6; CEDAW GR 30, 2013 and GR 35, 2017: para 1. The OHCHR (2018: 30) has also stated that gender-based violence, including sexual violence, is a human rights violation (eg violation of the right to physical integrity, the right to be free from torture, cruel,

four Geneva Conventions, lists among the crimes of grave breaches willful killing, torture or inhuman treatment, and 'willfully causing great suffering or serious injury to body or health' (Reilly 2009: 101). In practice, not only wartime rape and sexual violence were not sufficiently explicitly enumerated, but these provisions were also not interpreted to include the commission of these acts as war crimes and/or crimes against humanity.

It took until the International Criminal Tribunal for the former Yugoslavia (ICTY) in 1993, the International Criminal Tribunal for Rwanda (ICTR) in 1994 and the Special Court for Sierra Leone (SCSL) in 2002, for a jurisprudential acknowledgment of the use and extent of sexual violence in armed conflict. This was unavoidable. Estimates of the use of rape against women as a tool of war were alarming in the main conflicts of the 1990s: up to 60,000 cases in the former Yugoslavia (1992–95), between 100,000 and 250,000 cases during the three months of genocide in Rwanda (1994), and more than 60,000 cases during the conflict in Sierra Leone (UN 2014).[5] Consequently, these tribunals started dealing with rape and other forms of SGBV as an international crime, if committed within the categories of war crimes, crimes against humanity and/or genocide, showing how their infliction is not about sex but about power, domination and violence (Hayes 2016: 369–71). Chinkin and Kaldor (2013) argue that the increase in the incidence of systematic rape as a weapon of war was a central component of 'New Wars', which are fought by men in the name of a political identity that usually has a significant gender dimension and are financed by predatory economic activities that tend to affect women more than men. In contrast to the heroic warrior of the 'old wars', they conclude that the construction of masculinity in these new wars is much more contradictory and insecure.

In the 1990s, because trials were intended to help the state sustain the rule of law, to provide justice to the victims and to deter future atrocities, women's campaigns started focusing on the field of international humanitarian law and international criminal law, particularly on the inclusion of gender-sensitive provisions both in the Rome Statute and in the procedures of the International Criminal Court (ICC). As a result, the Rome Statute, adopted in 1998, became

inhuman or degrading treatment or punishment, the right to be free from slavery; the right to equality and non-discrimination) that can be committed by a variety of perpetrators, including state and non-state actors and/or individuals. I am aware that conflict-related sexual violence (CRSV) is a defined term used by the UN, however, I opted for the use of SGBV because transitional justice is also applicable to situations that do not involve conflict. See UN Secretary-General, *The Report of the UN Secretary General on Conflict Related Sexual Violence for 2018*, UN Doc S/2019/280, 29 March 2019, para 4.

[5] Graybill cites a higher number of cases of sexual violence in Rwanda. According to her, Human Rights Watch established that virtually every Tutsi woman and adolescent girl who survived the genocide had been raped, while the UN Special Rapporteur in Rwanda, extrapolating from the number of unwanted pregnancies after the genocide (with 100 cases of rape resulting in one pregnancy), estimated that the total number of women raped was between 250,000 and 500,000 (Graybill 2012: 211–14).

the first instrument of international criminal law to expressly include crimes of sexual violence and to acknowledge SGBV as constitutive acts for genocide, crimes against humanity and war crimes, eliminating 'allegedly' the ambiguity that had blocked the prosecution of crimes against women in previous post-war trials (Women's Initiatives for Gender Justice 2018: 8; Reilly 2009: 102–3). More specifically, when the Rome Statute deals with sexual violence as a crime against humanity (Article 7) and/or as a war crime (Article 8), it expressly includes rape, sexual slavery, enforced prostitution, forced pregnancy, enforced sterilisation, or any other form of sexual violence of comparable gravity such as forced marriage, insertion of foreign objects into genital or anal openings, abduction and forced nudity. At the procedural level, the ICC also established a Victims and Witnesses Unit to ensure the safety of victims and witnesses and to provide counselling and other necessary services, especially for cases of sexual violence; rules of evidence to prevent attacks on the credibility of victims or witnesses based on past sexual behaviour; the appointment of a legal advisor with expertise on violence against women; and the need for gender balance among judges and ICC personnel (Reilly 2009: 103).

Although this was an important step, in practice the Statute and procedural policies of the ICC may have positioned men and women differently, leading to different gender justice outcomes (Chappell 2016: 36). The focus on women and sexual violence in conflict, particularly rape, has generated criticism surrounding the sexualisation and passivity of the experience of women in conflict. There is indeed a significant imbalance between women testifying to sexual violence and women testifying to non-gender related crimes in international trials (Chappell 2016; Campbell 2007). Nesiah (2011: 143) claims that the dominant story of the international criminal tribunals addressing war crimes has transformed women's subjectivity as a 'victim' of international crimes. As a result, the emphasis on stereotyping women as victims of sexual violence, particularly rape, may have sexualised the experience of women in conflict. The effect of this is to ignore that women can also participate in other ways during conflicts, including as perpetrators, combatants and collaborators. But even in cases of sexual violence, there are complaints that judges have not taken into account victims' testimonies and that these cases have been insufficiently reflected during sentencing (Chappell 2016: 88). Chappell (2016: 110–14) claims that the further a sexual violence case progresses at the ICC, the more likely it is to be withdrawn by the Prosecutor or dismissed by the bench. Famously, in the Lubanga case, although sexual violence violations were known by the Office of the Prosecutor (OTP) to be pervasive in the conflict, he was only indicted for child soldier war crimes (Chappell 2016: 110–14).[6] When questioned about the lack of attention to sexual crimes, the Prosecutor initially stated that he lacked both the time and the evidence to link Thomas Lubanga

[6] Lubanga, a former Commander in Chief of the *Forces Patriotiques pour la Libération du Congo* (UPC/FPLC), was arrested in March 2006 for having been involved in the conflict in the Democratic Republic of Congo.

to other crimes, but after some time, he suggested that the crimes did not meet the crimes against humanity threshold test because they were not 'systematic' (Chappell 2016: 110–14).[7]

It was only with the Bemba case in March 2016 that the ICC saw its first conviction on the basis of command responsibility for SGBV.[8] His case also showed a progressive dropping of charges concerning SGBV crimes. Although his arrest warrant initially included crimes against humanity (rape, rape as a torture, and other forms of sexual violence) and war crimes (rape, rape as a torture, outrages upon personal dignity, and other forms of sexual violence), many of these charges were later dropped at the confirmation-of-charges stage, owing to alleged poor evidence presented by the OTP (Chappell 2016: 117–19). Moreover, contrary to the jurisprudence of other international tribunals, the ICC Pre-Trial Chamber did not regard the gravity of forced nudity as sufficient to constitute 'other forms of sexual violence' within the definition of crimes against humanity and war crimes (Chappell 2016: 117–19). As a result, Jean-Pierre Bemba was initially convicted on two counts of crimes against humanity (murder and rape), as well as on three counts of war crimes (murder, rape and pillaging) (*The Guardian* 2016). He was eventually acquitted by the ICC Appeals Chamber in June 2018 (Women's Initiatives for Gender Justice 2018). In July 2019, the ICC Trial Chamber declared Bosco Ntaganda guilty of rape and sexual slavery as war crimes and crimes against humanity committed in 2002 and 2003 (ICC 2019).[9] Although this conviction is still subject to appeal, this is the first case at the ICC where an individual has been found guilty of the crime of sexual slavery (UN Women 2019). Moreover, the ICC found that 'a person's status as a combatant or victim of illegal recruitment does not nullify protections against sexual violence under international humanitarian law' (Women's Link Worldwide 2019). This all means that although women continue to be targeted in armed conflicts and women's groups have strongly advocated the recognition of their specificities in the ICC system, since the Rome Statute entered into force, only one individual has been convicted for crimes of SGBV. On top of that, there are concerns about the distanced approach and the impact of the ICC on domestic affairs. In fact, Clark (2018: 150–86, 268–301) argues that there has been limited development of positive complementarity, ie as a cooperative partner to domestic

[7] Article 7 of the Rome Statute defines the acts of 'crimes against humanity' when committed as part of a widespread **or** systematic attack directed against any civilian population. The judges have decided that it is not necessary to establish both conditions. *Prosecutor v Thomas Lubango Dyilo* ICC-01/04-01/06.

[8] Jean-Pierre Bemba was a president and Commander in Chief of the *Mouvement de Libération du Congo*, arrested in May 2008 for crimes committed in the Central African Republic between 2002 and 2003. *The Prosecutor v Jean-Pierre Bemba Gombo* ICC-01/05-01/08.

[9] The former leader of the *Forces Patriotiques pour la Libération du Congo* (UPC/FPLC) was found guilty on 13 counts of war crimes and 5 counts of crimes against humanity, including rape, sexual slavery, displacement of civilians, and enlisting and conscripting child soldiers under the age of 15 and using them to participate actively in hostilities (UN Women 2019). *The Prosecutor v Bosco Ntaganda* ICC-01/04-02/06.

judiciaries, and by relying mainly on distanced sources of evidence, such as the use of video footage during the one-week trial of Ahmad Al Faqi al Mahdi in 2016, the lack of extensive on-the-ground evidence has also affected the pursuit of SGBV charges.

With the increasingly negative perception in the 2000s of the ad hoc tribunals and in parallel to the creation of the ICC, the international community started to support judicial alternatives such as hybrid tribunals. These tribunals – defined by their mix of international and local staff and by the use of international and national substantive and procedural law – were established by the UN in numerous countries, including Iraq, Sierra Leone, Kosovo, Bosnia and Herzegovina, Cambodia, and Timor-Leste (Sikkink and Booth 2007: 7). However, there was criticism that because of time constraints and limited resources and capacity to deal with thousands of cases and/or perpetrators, international and hybrid tribunals focused their efforts only on those who bear greatest responsibility for the crimes and/or those who are responsible for notorious crimes (Hollis 2015: 21). As a result, only a handful of people are ever prosecuted. Finally, there has also been criticism of how victims and witnesses are treated during hearings at international tribunals, and how this treatment can deepen their trauma and lead to their re-victimisation. Although I will expand in Chapter five on the implications of the use of consent by the defence during proceedings, victims may also face constant interruption during their testimony, be asked inappropriate questions – even in cases of sexual violence – or simply be forced to remain silent about a certain crime and be asked to elaborate on another one. In the *Akayesu* case, although there were allegations of sexual violence and the victims wanted to talk about their experiences, the ICTR prosecutor's strategy was based on demanding that the witnesses focus on other grievances that were easier to prove in order to make winning the case more straightforward, thus contributing to the continued silencing of the victims.[10] Only the dissenting opinion of the female judge Pillay referred to sexual violence, which showed the lack of judicial sensitivity to the significance of gender crimes (Kelsall and Stepakoff 2007).[11] The ICC and other international tribunals therefore have a difficult and complex record in women's participation and recognition of their crimes.

B. Restorative Justice

This model of justice focuses on the rebuilding of relationships between perpetrators and victims, for example by requiring perpetrators to provide reparations to victims (Clark 2008: 197–98). Consequently, it is interested in 'restoring

[10] In 1998, the ICTR Chamber in *Akayesu* held that sexual violence, including rape and forced nudity, could constitute the crimes of genocide, crimes against humanity, and war crimes under the ICTR Statute. *The Prosecutor v Jean-Paul Akayesu* ICTR-96-4-A.

[11] The South African jurist served as the UN High Commissioner for Human Rights from 2008 to 2014.

property loss, restoring injury, restoring a sense of security, restoring dignity, restoring a sense of empowerment, restoring deliberative democracy, restoring harmony based on a feeling that justice has been done, and restoring social support' (Braithwaite 2002: 12). In this book, I will focus on truth commissions and reparations. Initially chosen by Latin American countries and South Africa to deal with former atrocities, the use of truth commissions has since proliferated. They are considered to be non-judicial temporary fact-finding bodies that investigate widespread human rights or humanitarian law violations in order to promote a general understanding of what happened and the reasons why those violations occurred, with the ultimate goal of ensuring the nation does not experience these again (UN 2004: para 50). In contrast to trials, truth commissions have a different participation balance: on the one hand they are considered to be a victim-participatory process as the survivors can share their stories of injustices. On the other hand, there is a lesser focus on the agency of perpetrators per se and a larger one on the factors that forced them to participate in a specific conflict. Although truth commissions typically conclude their work with a final report that contains findings of facts and recommendations, the challenge lies in their implementation.

Gender mainstreaming has permeated the design and implementations of truth commissions over time: policy makers ensure a gender-balanced composition; that gender justice is made part of the commissions' mandates; and that commissioners receive gender training (Rubio-Marín 2006: 46–47). This in practice means organising thematic hearings (eg South Africa, Peru, Sierra Leone and Timor-Leste), special research teams (eg Timor-Leste) and chapters of their final reports all focused on women (eg Peru, Timor-Leste) (Rubio-Marín 2006: 46–47). Citing the experiences of Timor-Leste and Colombia, the Special Rapporteur (SR) on transitional justice also suggested combining a special gender unit (with specialists) and the incorporation of specialised members into the other teams (UN 2020: para 13). The SR also observes the need of proper gender-training processes, particularly for teams that collect statements, because sometimes they are the only point of contact with victims (UN 2020: para 15). In general, Rubio-Marín (2006: 46–47) writes that these commissions 'seem to have offered wonderful opportunities to give women voice but also to ensure that this voice transcends and reaches the public'. However, based on her grounded study of women's participation at the South African Truth and Reconciliation Commission (TRC), Ross (2003: 50) highlights the complexities of women's participation when observing that we need to be careful of these processes, as 'diverse ways of telling have different qualities, and silences are not neutral or homogenous or uniform in their effects'.

When it comes to reparations programmes, they are widely considered to be at the core of restorative justice because they seek to address the damage suffered by victims of human rights abuses, such as physical violations and property destruction. According to The Basic Principles on the right to reparation (2005), they can be provided in the forms of restitution (reinstatement), compensation (eg money, goods or services), rehabilitation (eg medical and psychological care), satisfaction (eg public apologies and public memorials) and guarantees of non-repetition (The Basic Principles 2005; CEDAW GR 33 2015: para 19). Reparations can be ordered by national or international courts or by administrative reparations programmes and they can be provided on a case-by-case basis in proportion to the harm caused by the violation or benefit a wider number of victims who suffered different types of violations (Rubio-Marín and de Greiff 2007: 321). While the first reparations programmes did not address women's particular experiences, there has been increasing attention to reparations for SGBV, such as the Nairobi Declaration (2007) and the Guidance Note of the UN Secretary General on Reparations for Conflict-Related Sexual Violence (2014) (Gilmore, Guillerot and Sandoval 2020: 5; UN 2020: para 27). Consequently, today the incorporation of a gender perspective in reparations programmes assumes that reparations should be provided for crimes concerning SGBV (UN 2020: para 27).

Since reparations are usually conceived as a mechanism for restoring the status quo prior to the violence or abuse, from a gender perspective, reparations are expected to transform structural inequalities and address the various disadvantages that women suffer before an armed conflict, prevent their re-occurrence and respond to women's specific needs (CEDAW GR 30 2013: para 79). However, in practice cases of SGBV may be disregarded and be taken into account as 'collateral damage', limiting women's access to reparations (Duggan and Abusharaf 2006: 626). The provision of reparations is also highly dependent on the political will, domestic law and, perhaps more importantly, the availability of resources; host states do not usually welcome their duty to direct their local resources towards redressing the violations committed by other states and/or international actors. As the SR on transitional justice mentions, an obstacle to reparations is that they would suggest a recognition of legal responsibility and therefore a precedent (UN 2021b: para 59). Moreover, social and institutional behaviour may also prevent women from seeking redress. As a result of these elements, reparations for victims, particularly women, have the tendency to be greatly affected.

C. Other Initiatives on Transitional Justice

Women's advocacy has also focused on other international initiatives, such as the UN Security Council Resolution (UNSCR) 1325 on Women, Peace and Security (WPS). Adopted in 2000, the resolution aims to understand women's experiences in conflict – it represented the first occasion on which women rights and leadership were acknowledged as vital components in peacebuilding and post-conflict reconstruction (Chinkin and Kaldor 2013: 179; Bafo 2019).[12]

[12] UNSCR 1325 was incorporated into CEDAW GR 30 on women in conflict prevention, conflict and post-conflict situations (2013).

The WPS agenda is articulated around four pillars of implementation, namely participation, protection, prevention, and relief and recovery, and between 2000 and 2019, 10 resolutions were adopted, recognising the need to include women in all aspects of peacemaking, post-conflict reconstruction and peacebuilding, including in the design, implementation and evaluation of transitional justice processes. For instance, UNSCR 2122 (2013) emphasises that more must be done to ensure that transitional justice measures address the full range of violations and abuses of women's human rights, and the differentiated impacts of these violations and abuses on women and girls. The resolutions further require States to draft National Action Plans (NAPs) which set the commitments and review the progress of the policy implementation concerning the four pillars of the agenda.

However, the large number of UN resolutions involving women in conflict reflect political tensions between those states which, on the one hand, promote greater protection of women against sexual violence in conflict, and those, on the other hand, which prefer to focus on women's participation in public life, including peace negotiations and in peace-keeping missions, ie military observers, civilian police, human rights and humanitarian personnel. The WPS agenda may additionally have progressively left aside other fundamental issues for women who experience the transition between conflict and peace. For instance, in Resolution 2467 of April 2019, references concerning the connection between the WPS agenda and the ICC as well as the connection to 'sexual and reproductive health' were removed because of the US veto threat, as the US argued that reference to reproductive health included abortion (Leimbach 2019; Chinkin and Rees 2019: 15). The Security Council resolutions may thus not only lack binding legal force, but also instead of proposing a transformative agenda, they may lack a gender vision based on principles of equality of outcomes and autonomy for women (Ní Aoláin, Haynes and Cahn 2011: 16; *cf* Chinkin and Rees 2019). The resolutions may thus have a limited impact in addressing the discrimination that contributes to women's vulnerability in situations of armed conflict. As such, their efficacy remains highly contested (Heathcote 2018).

Gready and Robins have also made a call for a transformative justice defined as a 'transformative change that emphasizes local agency and resources, the prioritization of process rather than preconceived outcomes, and the challenging of unequal and intersecting power relationships and structures of exclusion at both local and global levels' (Gready 2019: 2). Transformative justice deals with issues of process and context (eg the causes of conflict, political obstacles to justice and equal treatment, histories of social exclusion and poverty) and the impacts that are felt at the local and national levels (Gready 2019: 8; Robins 2019: 307–8). Because this justice entails a shift in focus from the legal to the social and political, and from the state and institutions to communities and everyday concerns, they argue that it is not the result of top-down impositions, but of a more bottom-up understanding and analysis of the lives and needs of populations (Gready and Robins 2019: 31–56). Rather than a focus on individual grievances and traditional mechanisms such as time-framed courts and truth commissions, their proposal is more preoccupied with the collective concerns of a society: they conceive as tools of transformation a range of policies and approaches that can have a longer-term impact on the social, political, and economic status of a large range of stakeholders (Gready 2019: 22; Gready and Robins 2019: 31–56).

Within these transformative justice discussions, Ní Aoláin (2019: 153, 171) suggests that rather than adopting a mainstreaming approach, foregrounding gender orders – how people live and act, meaning the day-to-day of men's and women's lives – and consistently surfacing the exercise of social, economic, political, and communal power are the essential steps to centralising gender relations in transitional and transformative justice. Why is this so? Because gendered orders normalise the 'marginalization, subordination, and exploitation of feminized practices or persons such that routinized feminization can be associated with routinized devalorization' (Ní Aoláin 2019: 153). As such, for transformative gender justice, 'the starting point is subjecting every practice, mechanism, and reform activity to intense gender analysis, viewing every single practice (and the change that is sought around it) as gendered activity' (Ní Aoláin 2019: 153–54). I concur with the argument that processes and practices are important and I am also concerned about power relations and the exclusion cycles that women face between past and future. The devil is indeed in the details. As Kouvo (2011: 175) shows with the case of women in Afghanistan, naive and poorly constructed strategies have resulted in inadequate attention to ensuring that women's rights and discourses are Afghan-owned, in inadequate attention to differences among Afghan women and the shortcomings of women's schemes in family and community-based systems, and in a failure to understand how the politically-active women operate.

Embedded within a 'one-size-fits-all' approach in the delivery of transitional justice systems is what I call a mechanical design and implementation of transitional justice packages that are sold as a quick solution to conflicts.[13] As my contribution to the discussions of women's experiences after conflict and the social consequences of transitional justice, I will demonstrate how the gender blindness in the design and process of transitional justice may indeed lead to the perpetuation of women's invisibility and discrimination, as shown not only in the case of Timor-Leste – the focal case study of this book – but also in other post-conflict countries. In Kosovo, for instance, despite the transitional justice implemented in this other UN administered transition – ie the UN is mandated to act and perform the role of a government – perpetrators of widespread and systematic conflict-related sexual violence were not brought to justice. It was almost two decades after the end of the war, in January 2018, that legislative changes in Kosovo recognised survivors of war-time rape by allowing

[13] In his first report on the rule of law and transitional justice, the UN Secretary General made a call to avoid one-size-fits-all formulas and the importation of foreign models that do not take into account national assessments, local participation and people's needs and aspirations (UN 2004).

them to receive reparations (Amnesty International 2017). In the case of Bosnia and Herzegovina, Chinkin and Paradine (2001: 112, 177) argue that while the General Framework Agreement (GFA) recognised ethnic identity, gender was totally absent, forgetting that the war was not only fought along ethnic lines but also that gender-based violence targeted women. This gender blindness may reflect the tensions generated during the negotiations concerning transitional justice. As was shown in Colombia, one of the reasons for rejecting the referendum for the peace agreement was the inclusion of what certain politicians and religious leaders called the 'gender ideology' which, they argued, undermined Colombian family values (*BBC Mundo* 2016). Reflecting on how women's treatment remains elusive in both transitional and transformative justice processes, Ní Aoláin (2019: 150) observes that 'only when the analysis and reality of patriarchy is intrinsically integrated into justice discourses will gendered change be possible'.

III. A FEMINIST RESEARCH

This book is designed to critically examine how transitional justice laws and policies evolved in a particular context; in other words, to study how the transitional justice process unfolds in social life. It is framed within a post-colonial feminist approach defined by Reilly (2009: 167) as an 'interest in addressing the implications of postcolonial legacies and related global disparities in the articulation of feminist perspectives and analysis'. Such ideas examine norms that view western ideals as true and universal and call into question any knowledge that arises elsewhere (Schömer 2013: 250). Although transitional justice has been widely applied, because of legalist approaches inherited by international actors, the way to address justice has been mainly through the drafting of laws and regulations (*cf* McEvoy 2007). Nesiah (2011: 155) also observes a mechanical implementation of transitional justice: 'like an Ikea furniture piece, the selling point of transitional justice institutions is that they come in flat packages that are easily shipped, unpacked and set up in new terrain'. She continues:

> wrapped in self-doubt at 'home' (whatever 'home' is – be it an academic discipline, a place, a social movement), it can become simplified when taken overseas – it rediscovers a new terrain for redemption, where feminism can once again be an emancipatory project (Nesiah 2011: 155).

Transitional justice in this regard is profoundly connected to the position of women within their societies. Moyo (2012: 240), for instance, highlights that based on 'claims to universality by Eurocentric, masculine, elitist and peremptory accounts which dominate the legal scholarship that form the normative basis for transitional justice', it can be seen as a masculine human rights strategy that is reminiscent of imperial intervention in the lives of post-colonial subjects. It is not by chance that the human rights violations that often dominate transitional justice mechanisms include forced disappearances, extrajudicial killings and torture, while other human rights violations that are faced by women, such as internal displacement, loss of a family member and violations of economic, social and cultural rights, are not addressed (Moyo 2012: 252). With this project, I therefore explore women's experiences through justice mechanisms that were designed abroad and examine how their implementation was adjusted in a local context. Moreover, I engaged with empirical knowledge about gender relations and local practices and procedures concerning women's access to transitional justice and elucidated the needs and priorities of Timorese women as opposed to top-down impositions (*cf* Bentzon et al 1998: 25). Although I refer to 'women', my book uses the concept of gender to understand the social construction of women's inequality, the structures of power, domination and disadvantage, and how masculinity is embedded within these structures (Cohn 2013: 5; Oakley 1998: 135–36; Cock 1991: 26; CEDAW GR 25 2004: fn 2). In this regard, I provide unique insights into how affected groups of women view and make sense of their experiences, which in turn provides sharper focus on the efficacy of post-conflict initiatives exported globally.

To reflect on the discrimination entrenched in the administration of transitional justice, I also examined various forms of intersectionality. This term was introduced by Kimberlé Crenshaw (1989: 139) to raise the invisibility of discrimination against black women as a result of treating race and gender as mutually exclusive categories. Intersectionality is thus an analytical tool for analysing the discrimination of subordinate groups by explaining the ways in which other factors, including race, ethnicity, religion, health, age, marital and socio-economic status, urban/rural location, illiteracy, sexual orientation and gender identity, among others, can, in concert or together, affect women (CEDAW GR 28 2010: para 18).[14] The Committee of the International Convention on the Elimination of All Forms of Racial Discrimination (CERD) also suggests as working methods of intersectionality an analysis of the form and manifestation of the discrimination, its circumstances, context and consequences, as well as the availability and accessibility of remedies and complaint mechanisms (GR 25 2000: para 5). The Committee on the Rights of Persons with Disabilities (CRPD) has also stated that:

> Intersectional discrimination recognizes that individuals do not experience discrimination as members of a homogenous group but rather, as individuals with multidimensional layers of identities, statuses and life circumstances. It acknowledges the lived realities and experiences of heightened disadvantage of individuals caused by multiple and intersecting forms of discrimination, which requires targeted measures to be taken with respect to disaggregated data collection, consultation, policymaking, the enforceability of non-discrimination policies and the provision of effective remedies (CRPD GC 3 2016: para 16).

[14] See CEDAW GR 30 (2013: paras 6–7).

As I will show, unless we foresee and reform discriminatory processes, entrenched gender norms (or racial, class, ethnic norms, and so on) and power relations within international institutions and local communities will continue to disrupt projects of post-conflict justice and/or render them meaningless. In this connection, this book touches upon the neoliberal component of the human rights discourse and shows that discrimination against women throughout post-conflict justice frameworks is part of larger dimensions of power.

Because I explore different layers of transitional justice, this book also incorporates the theory of legal pluralism. Legal pluralism considers that

> besides the state law or accessing formal structures, there are other social formations that generate binding laws and norms on members of those formations and because of this, it is necessary to find out women's real-life experiences and their views as to where they get justice and what they mean by justice (WLSA 1999: 28).

When it comes to post-conflict justice, this legal plurality has also permeated the development of transitional justice (Palmer 2015: 8). In her book about the three criminal courts of post-genocide Rwanda, Palmer (2015: 3, 9) analyses the participants' understanding of the practices of the ICTR, Rwandan national courts and gacaca (a community-led process) and how their views shape each institution's legal culture and objectives. In contrast to Palmer who, among a variety of participants, focuses mainly on judges and lawyers and their rational competition, I explore the plurality of transitional justice firstly as experienced by women, to then navigate and analyse the public and private factors that intervened in these processes. Finally, in addition to international human rights law, disciplines such as political theory and legal anthropology helped me to analyse my field material. In particular, I have been inspired by the work of Hannah Arendt, who reflected on politics, people's rights, truth and trials after the Second World War. Arendt (1971: 423) maintained that we should not theorise without looking at and understanding experience, and in my research women's experiences enabled me to understand the complexities of accessing transitional justice.

A. Data Collection

I chose Timor-Leste as the focal case study for several reasons. A key motivator was the role of the international community in the design and implementation of the transitional justice mechanisms in that country. The level of UN intervention in transitional justice processes around the world has varied from direct involvement – being in charge of designing all the mechanisms and providing funding and personnel – to cases of more limited participation, mainly relying on different means of persuasion and depending on the cooperation of governments. Along with Kosovo, in Timor-Leste the UN is considered to have had unprecedented power in the process of transitional administration (McAuliffe 2011: 106–7). Moreover, while not all peace operations are mandated to address transitional justice, in Timor-Leste the UN was directly responsible for the administration of the trials of serious crimes and also had a significant role in the development of the truth and reconciliation commission and the draft law on reparations for victims (*cf* UN 2004: 5, 17). Another reason for focusing on the Timorese case was the wide variety of justice initiatives and mechanisms used: a UN Commission of Inquiry (1999); a special Indonesian investigative commission (1999–2000);[15] a Serious Crimes Unit (SCU) and Special Panels (court) for Serious Crimes (2000–2005); an Indonesian Ad Hoc Human Rights Court for East Timor (2003); a Commission of Experts (CoE) appointed by the UN Secretary General to assess progress of judicial mechanisms in Indonesia and Timor-Leste for bringing to justice perpetrators of gross human rights violations (February–May 2005);[16] the Commission for Reception, Truth and Reconciliation in East Timor (CAVR); and a Commission for Truth and Friendship between Indonesia and Timor-Leste (CTF) (Wandita, Campbell-Nelson and Pereira 2006: 287).[17] This meant a large number of initiatives with which women could have interacted. Furthermore, because transitional justice in Timor-Leste is relatively recent, it allows for access to the main participants as well as the examination of the social consequences of its implementation.

In addition to consulting secondary sources, such as transitional justice laws and policies, this book is based on the field research I carried out in Timor-Leste in 2016–17. There, my study involved in-depth semi-structured interviews with 123 individuals, of whom 77 were women affected by the Timorese conflict and 46 were policy makers, politicians, UN and NGO employees. Interviews were conducted with Timorese women on the gap between their experiences during the conflict and the justice received and their evaluation of their contributions and the institutional failure to recognise those. Women may not have known the laws and regulations but they were aware of certain incongruities and issues in the system that were not fair and affected them disproportionately. Hence, by listening to women's narratives about their experiences of trying to access justice, I was able to learn their location within the legal and social frameworks and the barriers they faced. I also interviewed government officials, UN employees, civil society activists and other officials who had a role in the design and implementation of transitional justice mechanisms or who have an extensive expertise in women's rights and/or experience of access to justice in Timor-Leste. Interviewing both women victims and policy makers allowed me to triangulate the data and to understand transitional justice in

[15] This was Indonesia's National Commission on Human Rights (Komnas HAM), which released a report on 31 January 2000 listing the names of Indonesian and East Timorese officials that it recommended be investigated.

[16] Gross violations of human rights include torture and similar cruel, inhuman or degrading treatment; extrajudicial summary or arbitrary execution; slavery; enforced disappearances; and rape and other forms of sexual violence of comparable gravity (OHCHR 2009).

[17] *cf* Ostowar (2020).

Timor-Leste from different angles, to dig deeper into the barriers in its system, and to analyse the causes and effects of women's lack of participation and recognition.

Because data comes in different forms, I was also attentive to informal discussions and personal comments when I navigated everyday as well as elite networks. Observing both personal values of international and local actors as well as organisational values entrenched in institutions helped me to highlight that transitional justice is a non-neutral process, influencing and influenced by the interaction between gendered human actors within a complex interplay of local and international systems of law (*cf* Bentzon et al 1998: 27). Finally, with prior authorisation given by a senior judge and officer-in-charge (OIC), I conducted archival research at the Dili District Court for six months. There I examined the court records of the Special Panels for Serious Crimes, the hybrid tribunal created by the UN to try serious criminal offences, in order to provide a feminist revision of their legal cases and unveil women's participation.

B. The Interviews and Research Process

I lived in Dili for 16 months and I travelled around Timor-Leste to carry out interviews with women living in rural and urban areas, visiting 10 of the 13 Timorese municipalities, including Dili, Bobonaro, Viqueque, Lautém, Baucau, Aileu, Ainaro, Ermera, Liquiçá and Manufahi. Regarding the policy makers, I interviewed former personnel of the UN Transitional Administration, international and local judges, Timorese Truth Commission personnel, staff at the President's and Prime Minister's Offices, members of Parliament and Parliamentary officials, members of the Commission of Veterans, and staff at the following institutions and bodies: the Prosecutor's Office, the Ministry of Justice, the Ministry of Solidarity, OHCHR, UN Women, Centro Nacional Chega!, the Museum of the Resistance, and several NGOs, such as ACbit, La'o Hamutuk and Belun.

While Timorese people are multilingual, Portuguese and Tetum are the two official languages of the country. I had the advantage of being fluent in Portuguese before my arrival in August 2016. I also started learning Tetum as soon as I arrived because this language was more broadly spoken by the Timorese population and I wanted to immerse myself in the community. I wanted to learn as much as possible from their culture and to be able to better communicate with the broadest range of people in the language in which they felt most comfortable. I wanted to show respect for their culture. To ensure accuracy and to navigate cultural codes in my interviews with women, I was also supported by a research assistant. I hired him after choosing from 10 candidates. Although in the beginning I was looking for a female research assistant, I was impressed when he told me that he came from Los Palos, a village far from Dili, and how through a scholarship he managed to study for his Bachelor's degree in Sociology and Women and Gender Studies in the United States. During the interview process, he proudly raised his commitment to women's rights: 'I was in a class of 30 students, of which we were only two men, and I was the only heterosexual one'.[18] Before we started the interviews with the women, I gave him instructions on interviewing techniques, including to keep to the exact words used by them (OHCHR 2011a: 12). By the time I was conducting my last interviews with the women, I was able to introduce my research, ask the questions myself and to understand their stories in Tetum. During my interviews with policy makers I spoke English or Portuguese – in my three last interviews we found that me conducting the interviews in Tetum was the easiest.

There were three stages to my interview data collection. During the first stage, when I arrived in Timor-Leste, I interviewed through a process of snowballing, UN workers, civil society activists and other officials. During these interviews, ACbit, a local non-governmental organisation that seeks to empower women survivors of the violence during the Indonesian occupation in Timor-Leste, from 1975 to 1999, was repeatedly suggested to me as a key source for my research. When I approached the organisation's director, she gave me an overview of the situation of women in the country and agreed to introduce me to women in the above-mentioned villages. Thus, with ACbit's support, for the second stage of my interviews, I organised meetings with women in a large number of locations to ensure a diverse sample of women from urban and rural areas. During these interviews, besides learning about the barriers and the different ways women were discriminated against in their access to transitional justice, I also greatly deepened my knowledge of community and family dynamics. In the third and final stage, I interviewed specific policy makers and participants in the prosecutions, the CAVR, the veterans' pensions and the UN system. During these interviews, I could explain barriers mentioned to me by the women, follow the justice system as explained to me by the policy makers and understand the legal and policy issues that greatly affected women's participation and recognition.

Through my interviews with women victims of the conflict, I soon discovered that the majority of women had never shared their stories before their participation in the activities led by ACbit, which mostly occurred from 2012 onwards. This meant that cases concerning serious human rights violations against women had never been dealt with by any of the different transitional justice mechanisms. There was also a tendency for women to ask for an apology for the violations they endured, talk about the lack of recognition of these violations and their participation during the Indonesian occupation and, as I will explain later, make a connection of justice to the veterans' pensions. Consequently, I adjusted my research and focused on women's lack of

[18] I am confident of my decision: Marfiano Manuel always made everyone around him feel comfortable and calm and I never felt that his gender intimidated women.

participation and recognition as the two central themes of my book. Hearing the multiple reasons that women did not participate in the transitional justice mechanisms allowed me to identify, describe and analyse the patterns of irregularities that impeded women's participation in the justice process, including a temporal selectivity of the crimes considered, a hierarchy of murder over SGBV in terms of the gravity of crimes, a concept of torture that only applies to men, a local selection of participants that favoured males and their experiences, and a distinction between victims and reparations vs resistance and pensions. Women's experiences in conflict may therefore be silenced by the mechanisms put in place to provide justice and this leads to women's lack of recognition. This also explains why I included the veterans' pensions as part of transitional justice mechanisms, even though it has largely been unexplored in the post-conflict justice literature. There were also other elements of intersectionality that interfered in the delivery of transitional justice, such as rural and urban accessibility, literacy and personal connections, as well as corruption and private elements, including the fact that women may decide to sacrifice themselves for their family. All of these elements showed a lack of attention to the real implementation of transitional justice.

In this book I opted therefore to provide a critical assessment of each of these mechanisms through which Timorese women interacted – namely, trials, truth commissions, reparations and the veterans' pensions – and to carry out my research from different angles. As such, I examined the laws and policies as well as the community and family practices, all of which may have interfered in the delivery of transitional justice mechanisms. By adopting this approach, it was also possible to map and reflect on how a transitional justice system, implemented first by the UN Administration and later by the Timorese government, considered women's experiences and guaranteed their participation and recognition. I included comparative materials from other jurisdictions to show and verify larger trends in the structural barriers that women face in transitional justice and the logic behind their socio-economic exclusion in peace time. Although this book does not attempt to argue that women's experiences in dealing with transitional justice are the same in Timor-Leste and beyond, this research helps scholars and policy makers to reflect on the importance of international and local dynamics and on the need to design flexible processes to correct discriminatory threats.

C. Research Questions

For the interviews with women, we adopted the following modus operandi: ACbit would contact the women's cooperatives first to notify them of the aim of my research. When we arrived, women received us with Timorese coffee and we chatted about life in general, following Timorese traditions. After some time, we would start the interviews. Because they were semi-structured interviews, I used interview guides (see appendix) and expanded on relevant points raised so that the content of the answers determined the next question, before continuing with the general guideline of the interviews (OHCHR 2011a). A first set of questions concerned interviewees' personal data, including name, clan, age, marital status, place of living and level of education. This allowed me to reflect on the intersections and dimensions of power concerning their experiences of access to transitional justice. The interviews were then divided into three parts: the first focused on women's experiences under Indonesian rule, including the circumstances and the type of human rights violations they suffered (if any were perceived), who was responsible (the alleged perpetrator) and their participation in the conflict and resistance movement (*cf* OHCHR 2011a: 10). During the second part, we discussed their interactions with the transitional justice processes. Although before my interviews I had not expected to explore women's access to veterans' pensions, this emerged organically as part of the post-conflict justice framework. The third part of the interviews focused on the women's post-transitional justice situation, including whether participating in transitional justice had a positive effect on their lives, the meaning of justice for them, whether they were satisfied with what they had received, and, if not, what they would have liked to receive following what they suffered. Being semi-structured interviews, questions were not always asked in the same way and because responses were open, women narrated their experiences in their own words and talked about what was important to them.

In my discussions with policy makers, politicians, UN representatives and NGO employees, my questions centred on the process of the transitional justice mechanisms, to understand their implementation and the complexities of women's access to them. I asked open questions about the law and process of the specific mechanism in which the policy maker participated, about their role, the challenges that they perceived and I checked with them the barriers raised by the women in the villages. I found it easy to secure access to all of the policy makers. On many occasions I heard that the Timorese wanted to help researchers as a way of helping to keep the history of their young country alive.

IV. ETHICS OF THE RESEARCH UNDERTAKEN

Examining the justice that women received after suffering from human rights violations in a conflict is a sensitive research area that requires extra assurances to minimise risks to women's lives and the generation of secondary trauma and/or other reactions, such as depression and anxiety (OHCHR 2011a: 25–26; OHCHR 2001b: 9; Lee 1993). Issues, however, of mental health and trauma after a conflict have been contested. On the one hand, research from more than two decades ago 'suggested that describing one's traumatic experiences in a detailed one-session manner, as often required for legal documentation, increased the risk of chronic post-traumatic stress disorder (PTSD)' (Meffert et al 2016: 1). On the other hand, Bistoen (2016: 3) argues that there is a Western assumption – which has permeated research – in which all those who experience a violent conflict have a self-evident and universal PTSD. He continues, 'the individual inhabitants of violent crises are seen as fundamentally at risk of traumatization ...' and there is 'the desire to prevent or attenuate the impact of horrific events on the fragile human mind' (Bistoen 2016: 17). The OHCHR (2011b: 6–7) has stated that while some survivors may develop long-term problems, we should avoid assuming that all will be traumatised, debilitated or extremely emotional in the aftermath of trauma and that in fact, 'many survivors of traumatic events regain their emotional control relatively quickly'. When conducting human rights investigations, the OHCHR (2018: 25) has further stated that:

> Respect of the 'Do No Harm' principle requires a proper assessment of gender dynamics and cultural norms that may result in victims and witnesses being exposed to further harm, including re-traumatization or stigma, violence and marginalization at the hands of alleged perpetrators or the victims' families and communities. At the same time, it is important not to make assumptions about victims' needs or condition based on stereotypical views. For example, it should not be assumed that all victims of sexual violence would find the process of recounting their experience traumatizing. If well conducted, such process could in fact be healing and empowering.

Mannell et al (2018: 95) also argue that 'in a context where women are often blamed for the violence they have experienced, acceptance of their story without judgment from those in their surrounding environment plays an important role in their recovery from trauma'. Based on their study of survivors of GBV in Afghanistan, they concluded that in order for the storytelling process to act as a positive therapeutic encounter, there should be two enabling factors: a sympathetic listener and a supportive social environment (Mannell et al 2018: 96). In this connection, here I describe how I took informed decisions and extra care to ensure I complied with all ethical requirements to undertake research of this kind, and most importantly, that I did not harm or jeopardise the safety of any victim.

Before I went to Timor-Leste, my field research and interviews had been approved in accordance with the ethical standards of SOAS, University of London. More specifically, as part of the doctoral requirements at SOAS, I first successfully completed the course Research Integrity – Social and Behavioural Sciences on April 2016. My research also received ethical clearance by the SOAS Research Ethics Panel (REP). Through this process, I had a First-Stage Ethical Review. Given that my research project entailed more than a minimal risk given the sensitivity of my topic and the gathering of personal information, I was also required to complete a full ethics review prior to starting the research. As such, as part of a Second-Stage Ethical Review, my research was examined by the REP. In order to mitigate potential risks, I specified the actions that were going to be taken during my field research, such as consent, an appropriate translation so women could understand the implications of being subjects of an academic research project, and a careful consideration the use of anonymity for each case. I also anticipated interviewing the women in a second stage of my overall interview schedule to make sure I understood well the context and was familiar with their culture before approaching them (OHCHR 2011a: 9). My overseas fieldwork was approved on September 2016.

Interviewing victims, including those of SGBV, was not new to me. I had the advantage of more than 11 years of experience working in human rights and victims' rights protection through my work at the UN and non-governmental organisations, including in zones affected by conflict such as Eastern Democratic Republic of Congo (DRC) and South Sudan. I am also a certified member of the Justice Rapid Response initiative, which deploys investigators of mass atrocities, as well as of NORDEM, a Norwegian civilian capacity provider specialising in human rights. I have also been trained in interviewing techniques by NORDEM in Norway and by the Institute for International Criminal Investigations (IICI) in The Hague. As part of my preparation, I also constantly referred to specialist guides, such as the International Protocol on the Documentation and Investigation of Sexual Violence in Conflict (2014).

In the beginning of each interview, I ensured that I had the informed consent of the participants.

> Informed consent is at heart an interpersonal process between researcher and participant, where the prospective participant comes to an understanding of what the research project is about and what participation would involve and makes his or her own free decision about whether, and on what terms, to participate (Guillemin and Gillan 2004: 272).

In the women's own local language I first explained the purpose and content of my research and what it was going to be used for, and I clarified the terms and phases in which the interview was conducted. I also explained in advance to the women that when they talked about their human rights violations, they did not need to feel obliged to mention information that they did not want to – I was attentive that this did not happen during the interview process – and I clarified that I was not after the details because I was not collecting legal evidence or proving crimes – my research focuses on women's access to transitional justice (OHCHR 2011a: 25). I also explained to them that they could say no to my request. Women understood fully who I was and how I was going to use the information provided by them and that the information could be published. I also carried out the interviews as comfortably as possible and in a friendly environment, always trying to put participants at ease. After the interviews in the villages, which ended with women's ideas and dreams of justice, I thanked them in Tetum and we all ate local Timorese meals together, normally prepared by the women themselves. In Ainaro we all ate while we talked because the cooperative organised it that way. I made sure to cover all expenses the women incurred. At the end of our encounters women proudly showed me their local market space (Bobonaro) and their shelter (Ermera) and even made me wear their traditional female dress (Viqueque).

My Timorese interlocutors were always open to discussing my research. However, I heard politicians say that they did not want to talk about the years when Timor-Leste was under Indonesian rule and wanted to focus on the future. While interviewing women, the message was different. They wanted to give their views and to be heard. Groups of women living in more remote areas such as Lalerik Mutin, Viqueque showed an even greater eagerness to talk because they said that nobody goes to where they live, so they found it important that I was coming from far away to hear what they had to say. Coulter (2009: 149) recognises the challenge that 'victims of war may have been educated by humanitarian organisations about their suffering and rights attached to a discourse of material and social survival'. Some indeed may argue that women's discourse about transitional justice and women's rights may have been transplanted by external agents and that they are forced to talk about their violations in the hope of obtaining compensation. Coulter (2009: 19, 95) acknowledges that by compiling women's narratives, their 'war narratives reconstructed the war and their experiences of it in light of the present', so they are filtered through a variety of post-war experiences, including humanitarian discourse, responses from society, family situations, health and poverty. This is similar to what a current minister in the Timorese Government once told me: the memory of women may have been altered through the years, meaning that their narratives were modified. Narratives, however, are based on personal events and it may take years for the human being to express deep experiences. Moreover, this does not alter the fact that specific victims of gross human rights violations did not have access to transitional justice mechanisms.

I recognise that women initially agreed to talk to me because of their trust in ACbit. This widely known NGO organises activities such as story-telling and the creation of women's safe houses and cooperatives. I am grateful for their approval and support for my research. With the exception of five women (two in Viqueque and three in Dili), the rest of the 77 interviewed women were all participants of the ACbit's cooperatives and activities, which means they had already publicly shared their experiences. The two women in Viqueque were introduced to me by the coordinator of the women's cooperative in that region and I interviewed them alone in their houses. The three women in Dili worked on women's rights issues in Timor-Leste and did not hesitate to share with me their views and experiences. Again, this book does not argue that all Timorese women experience the same fate in the justice process that the women belonging to ACbit's activities did. However, the advantage is that by partnering with a local organisation, these women have had multiple experiences of telling their stories, including of SGBV.[19] They felt empowered enough to talk about human rights violations, their frustrations regarding the denial of justice and their current needs and expectations. The OHCHR (2011b: 7) has also recognised that one of the factors that contributes to a person recovering naturally from a traumatic event is counting on a strong social and emotional support as these women have.

Depending on the case, I exclude key information about the participants. Some of the statements from policy makers are anonymised at their own request or to avoid creating difficulties for them in the future. Following the standard practice of human rights investigations, the names of the victims are also anonymised, with the exception of some specific women, who are leaders in their communities, have participated and provided their testimonies in national and public fora and have been great advocates in their search for women's justice and recognition from the Timorese state (OHCHR 2015: 47). It is a mistake to think that all of these women are vulnerable and that they should be hidden for ethical reasons.[20] By hiding their names I felt I would be contributing to a silence that they are precisely trying to break (*cf* Bistoen 2016: 17). In this regard, the UN Special Rapporteur on the right to health has recently stated that good mental health 'must be defined by the social, psychosocial, political, economic and physical environment that enables individuals and populations to live a life of dignity, with full enjoyment of their rights and in the equitable pursuit of their potential' (UN 2019b: para 89). Hence, 'empowering persons in a vulnerable situation so that they can participate on equal terms is an important factor in the promotion of mental health' (UN 2019b: para 80).

V. STRUCTURE

The next chapter provides the background to and legal framework of the implementation of transitional justice in Timor-Leste. The chapter begins with the historical background of Timor-Leste and the international legal implications of the Indonesian intervention. Based on interviews carried out with Timorese women, the chapter then expands on the specificities of the violations committed against them between 1975 and 1999. It also provides an overview of the justice received by the participants. The chapter ends by exploring some international legal considerations pertinent to the concept of access to transitional justice and expands on women's participation in transitional justice mechanisms. The last section of the chapter focuses on the barriers faced by women when they try to access transitional justice.

[19] When gathering information on human rights violations, the OHCHR (2018: 25) suggests establishing contact with victims through local organisations and networks of women who have established trust within the communities.

[20] When we asked women if it was fine for them to be photographed, they always accepted without hesitation.

The third chapter focuses on silence and memory. Silence cuts across the whole process of access to transitional justice, affecting the invisibility of, and discrimination against women in the long-term. I start by reflecting on women's recognition in the aftermath of a conflict. As the case of Timor-Leste shows, the narrative of the new state silences and ignores women's violations, experiences and contributions to independence, while it promotes a hypermasculine warrior identity that exalts the veterans as the heroes of the past. I then expose the main human rights issues for Timorese women today and show how their violations are framed within a continuum from conflict to peace and how therefore there is a failure in the guarantees of non-repetition. The chapter ends by examining what women state they want from transitional justice: they have a broader perception of justice, which extends beyond courts and encompasses a sense of socio-economic justice.

The next chapters (Chapters four to seven) focus on the different barriers that affected Timorese women in their access to prosecutions, truth and reconciliation commissions, reparations and veterans' pensions. Women's participation and recognition are at the core of the examination of the laws, policies, community and family practices that interfere in their access to transitional justice.

Chapter four focuses on the prosecutions carried out in Timor-Leste after the conflict. I explore the factors of a public and private nature that have had an impact on the number of cases reported, leading to a reduced number of cases concerning women. Specifically, the chapter starts by providing contextual information from the Special Panels for Serious Crimes (Special Panels) and the Serious Crimes Unit (SCU). It then analyses the legislation that was drafted, and it provides an account of the different reports that denounced the commission of crimes against women at that time. I then explore the role of these legal institutions, from the investigation to their proceedings, and how their modus operandi and priorities affected women's participation and recognition. I also show how private dynamics mattered. The chapter ends with some reflections concerning the convictions and sentencing, and explores their follow-up.

The fifth chapter focuses on the truth commissions to which Timorese women were exposed and the ways in which various structural and institutional components downplayed their participation and recognition of their experiences. The chapter starts by analysing the Commission for Reception, Truth and Reconciliation in East Timor (CAVR), and its focus on women. It then explores the Commission for Truth and Friendship (CTF) between Indonesia and Timor-Leste and how cases concerning women were dealt with by this bi-national initiative. After exploring women's participation in these commissions, the chapter then elaborates on truth and women's healing and it ends with a section on women's recognition through this restorative process.

Chapter six deals with the different frameworks of reparations that appeared after the conflict and how the interplay between the public and private spheres obstructed the access of this right by women. The chapter begins by providing a background on the complexities of reparations. It then explores the reparations considered and provided by the different entities surrounding transitional justice: first, the UN, including the Special Panels for Serious Crimes; second, the truth commissions; and third, the Timorese government. Private interactions may have had an impact on the silencing of SGBV crimes committed against women. Based on the almost non-existent provision of reparations for women, I end with a section that discusses the way forward.

The seventh chapter examines women's access to veterans' pensions. Although this mechanism is not traditionally included as a mechanism of transitional justice, it was one of the most important elements raised in the interviews with Timorese women. This chapter starts with an explanation of the Disarmament, Demobilisation and Reintegration (DDR) and veterans' pension programmes, and it raises the complexities concerning the inclusion of women. I then explain how these programmes were implemented in the particular case of Timor-Leste. More specifically, the chapter discusses different elements of discrimination against women through the veterans' pension legislation and its implementation. When the private space is examined, culture and family relationships also have an effect on the effective access of women to the veterans' pensions. As a result of the interplay of all these factors, women may have been excluded from this post-conflict economic justice. The chapter then shows the effects of the implementation of veterans' pensions and how they are particular discriminatory against women in the foundation of new states. It ends with some reflections concerning the limits of the discourse on rights.

The final chapter summarises the main findings and presents some final reflections on women's access to transitional justice processes: women's participation and recognition; reparations vs. veterans' pensions; the continuum of violence against women; post-colonial elements and impositions on the concept of justice; and the policy ramifications of gender mainstreaming. Because transitional justice is not an innocent construction, the ultimate output should not simply be further drafts of legal and policy documents but a critical process that corrects both the public and private divides that impede women's equal access to its mechanisms.

At the end of our encounters women proudly showed their local market space and their shelters and even made me wear their traditional female dress. Photos from Lalerik Mutin, Viqueque. © Carlos Oviedo.

2

Transitional Justice in Timor-Leste: 'Loron Loron, Kalan Kalan'

THIS CHAPTER BEGINS by providing some historical context on Timor-Leste, before raising the international legal implications of the Indonesian intervention. Based on interviews with Timorese women, I analyse the specificities of the grave violations committed against them and provide a general overview of the justice received by the participants. Here I also deal with some international legal considerations regarding the concept of access to transitional justice and I reflect on the concept of participation. The chapter ends with an analysis of the barriers faced by women to access justice.

I. THE BACKGROUND: HISTORY OF TIMOR-LESTE

In 1974, while most of the former African colonies had regained their independence, the authoritarian regime of Portugal was still involved in colonial wars to hold on to them. When national discontent led to the 1974 Carnation Revolution in Lisbon and the fall of the Salazar and Caetano regimes, it was no surprise that Portugal focused on its own domestic situation. This fostered a process of de-colonisation, which for the first time permitted the establishment of political parties in Timor-Leste. However, their leaders soon found themselves embroiled in power competition marked by disagreement regarding how to bring about independence. The three groups held different views: the Timorese Democratic Union (UDT) advocated gradual independence from Portugal; the Revolutionary Front for an Independent East Timor (Fretilin) had a revolutionary discourse that called for a complete and rapid declaration of independence from Portugal; and the Popular Democratic Association of Timor (Apodeti) wanted Timor-Leste to be part of Indonesia (Walsh 2011: 57). By August 1975, as a result of the political tensions, the Timorese people found themselves embroiled in a civil war, in which crimes were committed by several factions of the political parties while fighting each other, forcing the Portuguese to withdraw from Dili to seek protection in the island of Ataúro (Post-CAVR 2008; Ronen 2012: 292). Between 1,500 and 3,000 people died and thousands were detained and displaced (Wandita, Campbell-Nelson and Pereira 2006: 285).

Fretilin prevailed and unilaterally declared the independence of East Timor on 28 November 1975.[1]

Only days later, on 7 December 1975, Indonesia employed the use of force, justifying its intervention on several grounds: that it was acting in self-defence, that it had been invited by the East Timorese, that it was necessary in order to maintain stability in Indonesia and Southeast Asia and that its intervention was for humanitarian reasons (Ronen 2012: 292). The fear of the establishment of what could be seen as a communist government in the context of the Cold War meant that the full-scale invasion by Indonesia had the tacit approval of the United States (Wandita, Campbell-Nelson and Pereira 2006: 285; *cf* Strating 2019). According to Ronen (2012: 293–94), 'few concrete measures were taken to sanction Indonesia's actions and no collective policy of non-recognition was ever expressly adopted'. On 12 December 1975, the UNGA Resolution 3485 called on Indonesia

> to desist from further violation of the territorial integrity of Portuguese Timor and to withdraw without delay its armed forces from the territory in order to enable the people of the Territory freely to exercise their right to self-determination and independence.[2]

In July 1976, nevertheless, Indonesia decided to annex Timor-Leste as its 27th province and apply Indonesian law to the territory (Ronen 2012: 292). Subsequent UN resolutions became more ambiguous with regard to the unlawfulness of the intervention, failing to condemn Indonesia (Ronen 2012: 293–94).[3] Timor-Leste would find itself under the effective control of Indonesia from December 1975 to September 1999.

During this period, the international community witnessed several events in which the Timorese population was subjected to gross violations of human rights law and serious violations of international humanitarian law, including the summary execution of five international journalists in Balibó in 1975, a severe humanitarian crisis in 1977–79 caused by the use of starvation as a war tactic, and the massacre of hundreds of people in the cemetery of Santa Cruz in 1992. This situation continued until 1998, when Suharto, who had ruled Indonesia since 1967, was forced to resign owing to a severe economic crisis in his own country. The instability in Indonesia together with work of the resistance and the international pressure led by Timorese in exile, certain governments and civil society, led in May 1999 to an agreement between Indonesia and Portugal: the UN

[1] After independence in 2002, the Timorese government decided to rename East Timor as Timor-Leste.

[2] UN General Assembly Resolution (UNGAR) 3485 (12 December 1975).

[3] UN Security Council Resolution (UNSCR) 384 (22 December 1975) (S/RES/384) (1975) and 389 (6 April 1976) (R/RES/389) (1976). UNGAR 31/53 (1 December 1976) (A/RES/31/53), 32/34 (28 November 1977) (A/RES/32/34), 33/39 (13 December 1978) (A/RES/33/39), 34/40 (21 November 1979) (A/RES/34/40), 35/27 (11 November 1980) (A/RES/35/27), 36/50 (24 November 1981) (A/RES/36/50) and 37/30 (23 November 1982).

would organise a referendum over independence or integration within Indonesia as an autonomous region.[4] The referendum took place in August 1999 and over 78.5 per cent of the voters chose to reject the proposal for special autonomy within Indonesia, meaning they wanted independence (CAVR 2005: 287).

Timorese militias – which had been formed at the beginning of 1999 with the support of Indonesia – revolted following the result of the popular consultation. Together with elements of the Indonesian security forces, these militias carried out a violent campaign in which pro-independence supporters were terrorised and killed (UN 1999b: para 20). As a result of the escalation of violence, there were between 1,500 and 2,000 deaths, 400,000 people were displaced, and 70 per cent of infrastructure, houses and buildings were destroyed (Strohmeyer 2001: 107–9; UN 1999a: para 20; CAVR 2005: 1328). Thousands of children were also taken from their families and sent to Indonesia between 1975 and 1999 (CAVR 2005: 2143). The CAVR would later determine that from 1974 to 1999, there were approximately 102,800 conflict-related deaths (an estimated 18,600 people killed or disappeared and 84,200 people who died due to hunger and illness in excess of what would be expected due to peacetime mortality), more than 11,000 allegations of torture and over 1,000 allegations of sexual violence, including rape and sexual slavery (CAVR 2005: 488; CAT 2017: para 8).

In response to the atrocities, the UN Security Council authorised the intervention of the Australian-led International Force East Timor (INTERFET), which arrived on 20 September 1999, causing Indonesian troops to leave Timor-Leste (Rothschild 2017: 446). The Security Council, acting under Chapter VII of the UN Charter, adopted Resolution 1272 in October 1999, to establish the UN Transitional Administration in East Timor (UNTAET). UNTAET, with a three-year mandate, temporarily assumed the powers of the state to design institutions of governance aimed at fostering political, social and economic stability and peace (McAuliffe 2011: 106–7). The resolution mandated a Special Representative of the Secretary-General (SRSG) to adopt regulations to administer the territory, including through the exercise of legislative, executive and judicial powers (Nouwen 2006: 196). Along with Kosovo, Timor-Leste constituted the first occasion on which 'UN peace operations exercised full judicial authority within a territory and were mandated specifically to establish a state justice system' (Bull 2008: 8).[5] The UNTAET mission took immediate steps to draft, promulgate, and enforce a range of regulations that had the force of law in the administered territories as well as to set up mechanisms for the investigation, prosecution, and trial of individuals suspected of serious violations of international law (Strohmeyer 2001: 110–11). As asserted by the UN SRSG in Timor-Leste, there was a need in the country 'to establish a system of firm democratic governance based on

[4] *cf* Fernandes (2021).

[5] Menon (2019: 9) argues that in contrast to Kosovo, the UN had a freer hand in Timor-Leste because of the total lack of infrastructure, any form of government and qualified human resources, which also required the organisation to experiment, improvise, and sometimes innovate.

principles such as the rule of law, respect for human rights, protection of vulnerable groups and accountability to the people' (Hasegawa 2006: 78).

The UNTAET and its exclusive power lasted for around two-and-a-half years, until 20 May 2002, when the country became an independent state and power was transferred to the leadership of a new elected Timorese government (Ronen 2012: 294–95). The mission was followed by several others, including the UN Mission of Support in East Timor (UNMISET), which from 2002 to 2005 was mandated to assist Timor-Leste with security and development programmes. The next section explores the applicable laws in the Timorese situation.

II. INTERNATIONAL LEGAL FRAMEWORK

International law prohibits the use of force, with the exception of its use by the Security Council under Chapter VII of the 1945 UN Charter and the right to self-defence in the event of an armed attack, as per Article 51 of the same instrument. When Indonesia intervened in Timor-Leste, it violated this prohibition and the obligation to respect the Timorese people's right to self-determination (Ronen 2012: 292). While the CAVR (2005: 7) in its Chega! report referred to the 'militarised foreign occupation', there has not been an agreement about the extent to which, in a strict international legal sense, there was a belligerent 'occupation' of Timor-Leste by Indonesia.[6] Although the UN, for instance, denounced the Indonesian intervention, it never declared the occupation to be either legitimate or illegal (Ronen 2012: 301; Chopra 2000: 29). Chopra (2000: 29) argues that during the planning for UNTAET, the question of sovereignty was avoided, and since only Australia recognised Indonesia's claim to East Timor, Portugal was treated as the lawful administering authority throughout Indonesia's intervention.[7]

Indonesia would also benefit from not being considered an occupying power. Koskenniemi (2008: 164) has argued that to declare occupation status would limit the liberty of action of the occupying state because it becomes 'accountable to the population and to the external world by reference to the specific rules and principles that govern occupation under international humanitarian law'. Therefore, Koskenniemi (2008: 164) continues, states have avoided the use of the concept of belligerent occupation, a status which, he argues, can only be applied to the West Bank and Gaza and the occupation of Iraq by the US-led coalition in 2003–04. Beyond this debate, the International Court of Justice (ICJ) has stated that 'physical control of territory and not sovereignty or legitimacy of title is the basis of State liability for acts affecting other States', so what is clear is that the relevant condition for the application of human rights is not formal sovereignty

[6] Chega! is the title of the CAVR report and it means in Portuguese 'enough, stop, never again.'

[7] Resolution 1272 was the instrument that gave sovereignty over Timor-Leste to the UN (Chopra 2000: 29).

but 'exercise of effective control' (Koskenniemi 2008: 168–69).[8] If we follow the ICJ's logic, although Indonesia may not be considered a belligerent occupier by some, by having effective control over Timor-Leste, it was obliged to protect the human rights of the Timorese people.

There was also the question of whether the armed conflict in Timor-Leste was international or non-international. International humanitarian law (IHL) is the area of public international law that regulates the means and methods of warfare in order to protect persons who are not or are no longer participating in the hostilities (ICRC 2014). This body of law, which comprises the four Geneva Conventions (GC) of 1949 and their two protocols of 1977, classifies a conflict as either international or non-international, and specifies the applicable laws and rules for combatants. More specifically, the regulations of the four Conventions and the Additional Protocol I (API) apply mainly to international armed conflicts (IACs), meaning international conflicts between two or more states, including wars of national liberation. They also deal with the methods and means of conducting warfare, such as the 'principle of distinction' as regards the civilian population. API further clarifies that an armed conflict against colonial domination and foreign occupation qualifies as an international conflict.

In contrast, the prohibitions of non-international armed conflicts (NIACs), which occur between governmental forces and non-governmental armed groups, or between such groups, are much less explicit as a result of the reluctance of states to limit their actions within their territories. They are regulated mainly by a simple common article (Article 3) – that appears throughout the four Geneva Conventions and which refers to a NIAC as an armed conflict in which one or more non-governmental armed groups are involved – together with the Additional Protocol II (APII), which provides a narrower definition by introducing requirements of (1) territorial control by the non-state actor, (2) with a certain level of organisation, including military command structure (ICRC 2008). The classification of a conflict matters because it determines the rules that apply in assessing the violations as grave breaches according to international humanitarian law. In Rwanda, for instance, by defining the genocide as a NIAC, the roles of other African countries, and even of France, were not considered, leading to an isolated examination of the conflict as being solely between Hutus and Tutsis. The issue is that, depending on the logic, if Timor-Leste were considered to be part of Indonesia, the conflict would be a NIAC, and if not, it would be considered an international armed conflict between two states, in which one was fighting for its national liberation against a foreign occupation.

[8] ICJ, Namibia case, [1971] ICJ Reps p 54 (para 118). *Advisory Opinion on the Legal Consequences for States of the Continued Presence of South Africa in Namibia*, International Court of Justice, 21 June 1971.

In any case, the Geneva Conventions and their Protocols establish that states have an obligation to train troops to avoid committing grave breaches, which are considered to include willful killing, torture and inhuman treatment, willfully causing great suffering or serious injury to body or health, the unlawful deportation, transfer, or confinement of civilians, as well as the extensive destruction and appropriation of property not justified by military necessity (ICRC 2004). They must also instruct their military commanders to prevent or put an end to such offences and to take steps against persons under their authority who have committed such crimes (Cameron 2008: 41). Although the prohibitions of a NIAC are less explicit, APII does deal with minimum duties of humane treatment (Cameron 2008: 43). For instance, concerning the protection of civilians, Article 13 of the APII provides that 'the civilian population as such, as well as individual civilians, shall not be the object of attack. Acts or threats of violence the primary purpose of which is to spread terror among the civilian population are prohibited'. This means that, even when one party is not a state in the conflict, there are minimum rules of war that apply. Moreover, for crimes against humanity, it does not matter if they happen within an IAC or a NIAC.

Focusing on the situation of women affected by armed conflict, the CEDAW Committee (GR 30 2013: para 20) has also made clear that under international humanitarian law, besides general protections that apply to both women and men, women are also entitled to some limited specific protections, such as:

> protection against rape, forced prostitution and any other form of indecent assault; priority in distribution of relief consignment to expectant mothers, maternity cases and nursing mothers in international armed conflict; detention in separate quarters from men and under the immediate supervision of women; and protection from the death penalty for pregnant women or mothers of dependent or young children.

The situation of Timor-Leste was not easy to classify, since Indonesia invaded the country several days after a unilateral declaration of independence from Portugal, allowing insufficient time for the consolidation and international acceptance of the newly independent state. The judges on the Special Panels, the hybrid tribunal, then determined in their first judgments in 2001 that there was at least an armed conflict beyond reasonable doubt during its jurisdictional timeframe, meaning the 1999 crisis, while refusing to comment on the classification of the conflict beforehand.[9] Hesitation regarding the classification of a conflict was not, however, a new situation for a tribunal dealing with grave violations of international human rights and international humanitarian law. When the ICTY had to classify a conflict in order to determine whether or not it had jurisdiction, the Appeals Chamber ruled in the *Tadić* case that the ICTY had jurisdiction to try the perpetrator as a violator of the 'laws and customs of war' (ICTY Statute Article 3), meaning they took into account those unwritten

[9] The CTF mentions an ongoing conflict from 1975 until 1999.

rules which, like international treaty law, are also recognised as a primary source of public international law (Cameron 2008: 48).[10] In other words, the ICTY, upon which the Special Panels relied in several of their judgments, ruled that customary law always applies in a conflict, whether it is international or non-international, a legal reasoning that can also be applied to the situation of Timor-Leste before 1999. Hence, forms of violence against women may constitute a crime against humanity, when committed as part of a widespread or systematic attack directed against any civilian population, within or outside an armed conflict, as prohibited under customary international law.

When it comes to international human rights law, a state can limit its obligation to protect certain rights because of the exceptional circumstances of war. Nevertheless, there are certain protected rights that are never restricted and that apply at all times, independently of whether there is conflict, and if there is, of its classification. One of these, for instance, is the freedom from torture, without exception, developed in the 1984 Convention against Torture and Other Cruel, Inhuman or Degrading Treatment or Punishment (CAT), which requires states to criminalise acts of torture and prosecute suspected offenders as well as permitting states to exercise jurisdiction over acts of torture (Cameron 2008: 43–44). This all means that where there is an armed conflict, whether international or non-international, human rights conventions and international humanitarian law apply in parallel and their different protections are complementary (CEDAW GR 30 2013: para 20). Moreover, when states exercise territorial or extraterritorial jurisdiction, whether by a unilateral military action or as members of international or intergovernmental organisations and coalitions, they are obliged to comply with both international human rights and international humanitarian law, both in conflict and post-conflict situations (CEDAW GR 30 2013: para 9).

Other actors such as the UN and non-state armed forces are also subjected to the rules of international law. The UN, as a legal person, is obliged by customary law to respect and protect human rights, even more so as an international administrator, as in the case of Timor-Leste, when it acts both as a subsidiary organ of an international agency and as a national authority (Sannerholm 2012: 231; Knoll 2008: 213; CEDAW GR 30 2013: para 9). Finally, as recently stated by the UN Special Rapporteur on transitional justice, not only is accountability for gross violations of human rights and international humanitarian law an obligation under international human rights law, but also customary international law establishes the obligation to investigate and punish genocide, war crimes and crimes against humanity (UN 2021b: para 22).

[10] ICTY, *Tadić Case*, Appeal Chamber, 1995, paras 97, 126–28.

III. HUMAN RIGHTS VIOLATIONS

The CAVR divides into three categories those women and girls who suffered from extrajudicial killings, disappearances, detention, torture, SGBV, forced displacement and other forms of violence by the Indonesian military: (1) those involved directly in resisting the Indonesian occupation, such as combatants, members of the Popular Organisation of East Timorese Women (OPMT) – the women's branch of Fretilin – and others from the clandestine networks; (2) those related to men involved in the resistance, or who were from communities suspected of being their collaborators; and (3) those with no clear connection to the resistance but who suffered as the result of large-scale military operations that targeted civilian populations (Wandita, Campbell-Nelson and Pereira 2006: 290). Out of all the 7,669 statements collected by the CAVR, more than 85,000 counts of violations were identified, including extrajudicial killings, forced disappearances, death by deprivation, illegal detention, torture, ill-treatment, forced displacement, forced recruitment, sexual violence, and property and economic violations (Wandita, Campbell-Nelson and Pereira 2006: 290–91). However, there were specificities concerning the violations inflicted on Timorese women because of their gender.

Indeed, an observation arising from many of the women interviewed is that under Indonesian rule, torture and ill-treatment, arbitrary detention and deprivation of liberty affected both men and women. However, while men were more often subject to extrajudicial killings, women suffered more from internal displacement and SGBV, including rape, sexual slavery, 'temporary' forced marriage and sexual harassment. The women interviewed also referred to violations of a reproductive nature, such as forced contraception, forced pregnancy and forced abortion. When they talked about torture, they referred to beatings, chairs being pressed over their toes and electric shocks, even when they were minors. Some of the women interviewed said they suffered sexual violence and/or torture while deprived of their liberty, usually while being kept on Indonesian military premises during the night, although this could also happen in other detention facilities.[11] Most women living in Bobonaro who participated in the interview process were family members, mainly spouses or sisters, of men who had been forcibly disappeared or summarily executed in the events related to a massacre at the Maliana police station in 1999.

Those women who went through 'temporary' forced marriage were usually forced to live with an Indonesian or a Hansip (a Timorese working for Indonesians as a local security officer in a village) and were expected to perform as housewives and engage in sexual activities. There were also those women

[11] When referring to SGBV, Timorese women used expressions such as 'they did wrong things to me', 'threats', 'play' and even 'they searched for guns' (*cf* OHCHR 2011a: 26).

who were gang-raped on a daily basis over long periods and whose violations may amount to sexual slavery. In fact, one of the first sentences in Tetum that I learnt during the interviews and that was often repeated by my informants was '*loron loron, kalan kalan*', which literally means 'every day, every night'. This was the typical answer when I asked some of these women about the frequency of the sexual violence committed against them. These women were known as the 'mistresses of the *bapas*' (Indonesians) and/or '*mulheres do mato*' (women of the mountains who could engage in sex everywhere). Many of these women present together in concert – perhaps, as Arendt would argue, because in concert they have more power in the public space. They were simply 'the women of the Indonesians'. Although the women did not mention enslavement, when, digging deeper, traits of sexual slavery could come to the surface.

Feminists have already discussed whether forced marriage and sexual slavery constitute different categories. Indeed, as Sellers (2011: 137) has pointed out, 'forced marriage linguistically seems analogous to other practices or institutions of slavery'. However, while sexual slavery means exercising rights of ownership over a person, forced marriage can be defined by

> the coerced nature of conjugality, the encroachment on private decision-making spaces, the role of military and political leaders instead of family and relatives in determining the marriages, the crushing of dignity and autonomy, the compulsory nature of parenthood, the linkage with the war effort, and the role of forced marriage in the terrorization of the general population (Denov and Drumbl 2020: 351; MacKinnon 2017: 177).

However, forced marriage as an international crime remains controversial because (i) it is not codified in any international criminal statute, (ii) it has been inconsistently defined, and (iii) it involves acts that can be assumed to be within crimes against humanity (Maloney 2021). Askin (2013: 53) argues that, in contrast to sexual slavery in which women are held in a location and raped by dozens of different men, in the crime of forced marriage women and girls are forced to cook, clean, provide sexual services and perform other so-called 'wifely duties' for a single male, including sexual intercourse, domestic labour and forced pregnancy (*cf* Denov and Drumbl 2020: 351).[12] In this regard two internationalised criminal tribunals – the SCSL in Sierra Leone and the Extraordinary Chambers in the Courts of Cambodia (ECCC) – pursued convictions for forced marriage as a crime against humanity under the category of 'other inhumane acts', recognising that, as distinct from sexual slavery, it was a new form of gendered harm that has an impact on women and girls

[12] For Askin (2013: 53), 'victims conscripted into "forced marriage" are often treated differently by society than victims of sexual slavery or rape, as those forced into so-called "marriage" are frequently rejected as collaborators', so if we want to treat 'forced marriage' as a serious crime to allow survivors their right to be a victim, forced marriage should be prosecuted under either 'sexual slavery' or 'other forms of sexual violence' instead of 'inhumane acts'.

during conflict (Denov and Drumbl 2020: 351; What Works 2018: 32).[13] The link between the two crimes has also been a subject of discussion at the ICC. Because the Rome Statute does not include the crime of forced marriage or forced conjugation, the ICC has adopted a flexible approach: depending on the circumstances, forced relationships may come within the ambit of both the crimes of slavery and other inhumane acts (Women's Initiatives for Gender Justice 2018: 155).[14]

Based on the interviews I carried out, although sexual slavery and forced marriage are considered different crimes, the lines between the two may sometimes be blurred. A large number of the Timorese women who introduced themselves as 'women of the Indonesians' indeed described having suffered the factual elements of the crime of enslavement: 'detention, physical control, forced housework, exchanges among perpetrators, psychological control, social alienation, and complete sexual access controlled by the perpetrators' (Sellers 2011: 126). In several interviews, stories of cases of forced marriage and sexual slavery were described as if they were not different. Many of the women involved were adolescents when they started being requested to go at night to be sexually assaulted in the battalion premises and/or forced into marriage. While their rights were violated, they were also said to have been stigmatised by the communities and perceived as traitors. Although the CAVR collected over 1,000 allegations of sexual violence from 1975 to 1999 and it is always difficult to prove the extent of these crimes, there are claims that sexual violence against women in Timor-Leste may have been in equal proportion to that of Rwanda and the former Yugoslavia (Corcoran-Nantes 2009: 85; CAVR 2005: 488).

The CAVR published its findings and recommendations in the 2005 Chega! report. One of its conclusions was that Indonesians committed widespread and systematic violations against the Timorese population. Many of my interviews exposed the commission of crimes, which were both organised in nature and

[13] *cf Prosecutor v Brima, Kamara and Kanu*, Case No SCSL-2004-16-A, Judgment, 202, February 22, 2008; the International Protocol on the Documentation and Investigation of Sexual Violence in Conflict (2014: 86). The *Sepur Zarco* case in Guatemala is also the first time that a domestic court prosecuted sexual slavery as an international crime (Martin and SáCouto 2020: 243).

[14] Women's Initiatives for Gender Justice (2018: 153) offers an account on how, while forced marriage was included under sexual slavery in the *Katanga and Ngudjolo* case, *Ongwen* and *Al Hassan* faced the explicit charge of forced marriage as 'an other inhumane act'. More specifically, the Pre-Trial Chamber in *Katanga and Ngudjolo* held that 'sexual slavery also encompasses situations where women and girls are forced into "marriage", domestic servitude or other forced labour involving compulsory sexual activity, including rape, by their captors' and in *Ongwen* considered that 'forced marriage may per se come within the ambit of the crime of other inhumane acts and is hence distinct from sexual slavery' (2018: 156). However, 'the Pre-Trial Chamber found that forced relationships in Uganda gave rise to both crimes. Similarly, the Pre-Trial Chamber in *Al Hassan* issued an arrest warrant for forced relationships, holding that they gave rise to both forced marriage as 'an other inhumane act' and 'sexual slavery' (2018: 156). *The Prosecutor v Germain Katanga and Mathieu Ngudjulo Chui* ICC-01/04-01/07; *The Prosecutor v Al Hassan Ag Abdoul Aziz Ag Mohamed Ag Mahmoud* ICC-01/12-01/18; *The Prosecutor v Dominic Ongwen* ICC-02/04-01/15.

perpetrated on a large scale over long periods, and which tended to occur at a number of locations. For instance, a considerable number of the women interviewed in Baucau and Viqueque were subjected to daily rape over more than 15 years during the Indonesian occupation. There were interviews that referred to daily rape in military facilities as well as to torture in police custody. To reflect on the commanders' superior responsibility, when I asked the women whether the Indonesian commanders knew about their violations, some replied that the there was no other possibility because of the location and the length of the violations, while others accused specific commanders of being participants in the commission of crimes.[15]

As concluded by the CAVR, women's stories suggest that human rights violations not only relate to the satisfaction of male sexual desires but may also have occurred as reprisals for the fact that some of the male family members of these women were part of the armed resistance, or simply occurred in retaliation for attacks by Timorese. Women described how, while many of their male family members went to the mountains to join the armed resistance, they usually stayed in the villages. When the Timorese resistance attacked, Indonesians could take reprisals against the civilian population, as happened in the villages of Mauchiga (Ainaro) in 1982 and Kraras (Viqueque) in 1983. Women were also targeted for having a family member who was fighting with the resistance in the mountains. If the Indonesians – or the Timorese supporting the Indonesians – did not see a male family member around, they assumed that he was in the mountains. Many of these women therefore may have suffered human rights violations as a reprisal for the attacks of the resistance or because of their personal connection to a man in the resistance. But because of women's work and support to the resistance, some of them would also be punished with torture, rape, and/or detention for short or long periods. When Indonesia invaded Timor-Leste, the Timorese resistance organised themselves on three fronts: the armed front with a military command structure living in the mountains, led by Xanana Gusmão; the diplomatic front in charge of international advocacy, led by José Ramos-Horta; and the clandestine movement, composed of those living in the cities and villages who were in charge of counter-intelligence against the Indonesians as well as collecting food and provisions for the subsistence of those in the mountains. The women interviewed participated mostly in the clandestine front.

[15] Cameron (2008: 49) observes that in the *Celebici case*, the ICTY defined the components of superior responsibility as: (1) a superior–subordinate relationship; (2) the command/Superior must have known or had reason to know that the subordinates were committing crimes; and (3) must have failed to take necessary and reasonable measures to prevent and punish them. The Trial Chamber also emphasised that the relationship must be one of 'effective control', suggesting that superiors may engage in criminal responsibility even in informal structures as long as there exists an effective command, and that superior responsibility may extend 'not only to military commanders but also to individuals in non-military positions of superior authority' (Cameron 2008: 49). Cameron cites *Prosecutor v Delalic et al*, Trial Chamber II, Case no IT-96-21, 16 November 1998, paras 355–363.

The Indonesians were not, however, the only actors who committed crimes against women. The Chega! report expands on the crimes committed by the Timorese against their own. There were the Timorese Hansips working under the orders of the Indonesians; there were the Pro-Indonesia Timorese militias, who were the main actors in the crimes during the 1999 crises; but there were also indications that the resistance groups committed human rights violations, although not in a widespread or systematic way, meaning that they did not amount to crimes against humanity (CAVR 2005: 1344). The role and responsibility of the resistance and the Timorese local authorities during and after the conflict are issues that are rarely discussed in Timor-Leste today. This is a fact that is of particular importance given that since independence in 2002, the country has been governed by the leaders of the Timorese resistance, many of whom were in the armed front. Moreover, during the interviews, women mentioned how several '*chefes de suco*' (village chiefs), who are local government representatives, worked as intermediaries for the Indonesians and facilitated the commission of the crimes against them. The village chiefs would later have an important role in the CAVR since the national authorities would rely on these community leaders to choose representative cases during local public hearings of the truth commission.

IV. ON JUSTICE RECEIVED

Most of the women interviewed mentioned that the violations against them occurred during the Indonesian occupation, whereas six cases concerning SGBV occurred or continued until the 1999 escalation of violence. However, five of those cases of human rights violations that occurred in 1999 were not considered for prosecution at the Special Panels for Serious Crimes, including the case of a girl who was 12 years old at the time and who was gang-raped on two consecutive days by a group of 10 militiamen – including the commander of the battalion – and was further taken as a sexual slave, until she managed to escape three months afterwards. When I first began collecting data, I asked myself why such cases were excluded from the trials. I also noticed that out of the 77 women interviewed only seven had participated in the Special Panels and of these, only one case specifically concerned a woman. This means that out of the 77 women participants in my data collection, only one case concerning a crime against a woman managed to reach the prosecutorial level of transitional justice. The story of low participation among the women interviewed is also reflected when it comes to the CAVR. Out of the 77 women, only 19 participated in the public hearings. In only one case concerning a woman were reparations granted. The case involved a woman working for the UN during the 1999 referendum who was raped and killed and whose reparation was provided by the UN, after the pursuit of an appeal and the persistent support of a particular UN international employee in Dili concerned with women rights.

The same case was taken to the Special Panels for Serious Crimes and to the CTF.

I also noticed that as part of the justice mechanisms that appear after the conflict, women conceive veterans' pensions to be part of transitional justice and, out of all such mechanisms, the one that has the longest-term – socio-economic – implications after the conflict. Some of these women were very shrewd when they mentioned the shortcomings of trials and truth commissions: 'trials were carried out in the capital and that is far away', 'the people who committed the crimes against us were not prosecuted', 'trials were for the bigger fish, people that we don't know and who did not commit the crimes against us', while regarding truth commissions, there was the opinion that 'they came, took information, and nothing else happened afterwards'. However, some of the women wanted to talk about what happened to them when they tried to access the veterans' pensions. They connect their experiences and human rights violations to this pension. Out of the 77 women interviewed, only 20 received a veterans' pension. Out of the 20 women that have received or continue to receive a pension, four pensions are related to their connection to men, mainly a husband or brother, rather than because of their own work in the resistance. In other words, out of the 77 women interviewed, only 16 have received a pension in recognition of their own work. On the other hand, 23 women who have applied for a pension are still waiting for an answer from the government. The veterans' pension was the post-conflict mechanism that women felt did not recognise their role and experience during the conflict and which is still generating a discriminatory effect against them. This all means that with the arrival of the UN administration in Timor-Leste and later under the Timorese leadership, although several mechanisms of transitional justice were implemented, the interviews suggested that there are question marks concerning women's equal access to post-conflict justice.

We already know that, according to the notion of citizenship in the Greek *polis*, women were excluded from military service and/or property, female slaves were used for reproductive purposes to increase the economic value of slavery, women's sexuality was regulated at the service of men, and all aspects of childbirth and child caring fell within the private sphere (Charlesworth and Chinkin 2000: 127–28). While it is true that human rights law, institutions and movements have brought more attention to a wide range of rights violations and therefore led to improvements in human well-being (Sikkink 2017: 14), the support for human rights entitlements and human rights institutions has been lately under the scrutiny of governments. Hopgood (2017: 297) argues that human rights have become contested concepts as a consequence of (geopolitical) power being more diffused, so the chances of a global consensus may recede. The post-1945 era and the alliances in favour of human rights were not exempt from criticisms either. Decades ago, Arendt (2017: 381–90) warned us about the ineffectiveness of the enforcement of human rights owing to the dependency on the identification of the citizen as a member of a state, rather than humanity itself. Arendt (2017: 387–88) further claims 'the fundamental deprivation of human rights is manifested first and above all in the deprivation of a place in the world which makes opinions significant and actions effective', in other words, being able to have a space in the community to express one's opinions and to take action. Arendt (2017: 390) invokes the concept of the 'right to have rights' as a human being, as a person. Whereas for Arendt (2017: 301), states ruled in reality over classes and not over individuals, I envisage a gender component in the recognition of women as full citizens and the subsequent effects on their participation in justice mechanisms and protection of their rights. In the next section, I will provide an overview of women's access to transitional justice.

V. ACCESS TO TRANSITIONAL JUSTICE

There is a plural understanding of justice. In a liberal setting of fundamental human rights and equal citizenship, justice has to do with a concept of fairness that is sustained by ensuring that law and procedures are applied uniformly and without arbitrary personal distinctions (WLSA 1999: 29). To put it simply justice is blind: neutral and balanced. Such a liberal conception of justice is closely related to the one used by the UN (2004: para 7) in its report on transitional justice and rule of law, when it defines justice as:

> an ideal of accountability and fairness in the protection and vindication of rights and the prevention and punishment of wrongs. Justice implies regard for the rights of the accused, for the interests of victims and for the well-being of society at large. It is a concept rooted in all national cultures and traditions and, while its administration usually implies formal judicial mechanisms, traditional dispute resolution mechanisms are equally relevant.[16]

Another conceptualisation – namely, distributive justice – recognises that laws, procedures and structures may be burdensome to some, so it emphasises the need for fair distribution of resources to enable people to satisfy their wants and needs (WLSA 1999: 29–30). Within this discussion of justice, Sen (2010) has reflected on an idea of justice that must take account of the lives people can actually lead and has pointed out how equality and a human capability – what individuals are able to do and their freedom of choice – are central features of participation in the life of a community. As I will explain later, these different conceptions have permeated transitional justice and generated some tensions.

[16] The UN Impunity Principles (2005) seem to take a broader definition of justice: Principle 1 states that 'Impunity arises from a failure by States to meet their obligations to investigate violations; to take appropriate measures in respect of the perpetrators, particularly in the area of justice, by ensuring that those suspected of criminal responsibility are prosecuted, tried and duly punished; to provide victims with effective remedies and to ensure that they receive reparation for the injuries suffered; to ensure the inalienable right to know the truth about violations; and to take other necessary steps to prevent a recurrence of violations.'

When it comes to the definition of access to transitional justice, it is important to first understand what is meant more broadly by access to justice, which even today has no exact legal definition. The term 'access to justice' has been used to describe a variety of provisions in international human rights instruments which promote and protect the right to a fair trial and the right to equal protection before the law. For instance, from Article 7 to Article 11, the UDHR protects the right of access to justice by recognising the right to an 'effective remedy', 'equality before the law', 'equal protection of the law', freedom from 'arbitrary arrest, detention or exile', and 'entitlement in full equality to a fair and public hearing by an independent and impartial trial' (Dias 2009: 22). As per the ICCPR, while Article 2 reiterates the right to an effective remedy, when a person's rights have been violated, by competent judicial, administrative or legislative authorities, Article 14 protects the principles of equal treatment, fair hearing and fair trial before competent courts and tribunals.[17] Article 2(1) of the ICESCR indirectly addresses the right to access to justice. Since individuals need to be able to challenge the state's failure to adopt all appropriate measures, states 'must put proper legal institutions and national legislation in place to ensure that citizens have a remedy for the breach of their fundamental rights' (Dias 2009: 23–24).

The CAT convention condemns the act of torture and also provides for access to justice when in its Article 14, it calls for states to 'ensure in their legal system that the victim of an act of torture obtains redress and has an enforceable right to fair and adequate compensation, including the means for as full rehabilitation as possible'. When it comes specifically to women's access to justice, Article 2 of CEDAW calls for states to 'adopt appropriate legislative and other measures, prohibiting all discrimination against women' and 'establish legal protection of the rights of women on an equal basis with men and ensure through competent national tribunals and other public institutions the effective protection of women against any act of discrimination'. Moreover, Article 15 requires states to 'accord to women equality with men before the law', and 'accord to women in civil matters, a legal capacity identical to that of men and the same opportunities to exercise that capacity'.

There are also non-binding international instruments that recognise the basic principles of access to justice and establish principles and guidelines for key players in the judicial system, including judges, lawyers, and prosecutors, such as, the Basic Principles on the Independence of the Judiciary (BPIJ) (1985), the Basic Principles on the Role of Lawyers (BPRL) (1990) and the Guidelines on the Role of Prosecutors (1990). The UN General Assembly Declaration of Basic Principles of Justice for Victims of Crime and Abuse of Power (1985) addresses the principles related to the protection of the rights of victims through

[17] See the HRC GC 13 (1984) Equality before the courts and the right to a fair and public hearing by an independent court established by law (Art 14) and GC 32 (2007) on Article 14: Right to equality before courts and tribunals and to a fair trial.

measures to improve access to justice and fair treatment, restitution, compensation and assistance in order to enable victims to obtain redress both in judicial and administrative mechanisms and in formal and informal procedures. Human rights treaties and non-binding instruments, therefore, condemn practices that have an impact on an individual's right to fair and equal treatment; seek to ensure their protection by laws, courts, and tribunals; and call for the provision of remedies to be guaranteed when rights are violated (Dias 2009: 25).

UN experts and entities have also provided their own concept of access to justice. The UN Special Rapporteur (SR) on Independence of Judges defined, for instance, access to justice as 'effective availability of institutional channels for the protection of rights and the resolution of various types of conflict in a timely manner and in accordance with the legal order' (UN 2008b: 6). In contrast, the United Nations Development Programme (UNDP) defines access to justice as 'the ability of people to seek and obtain a remedy through formal or informal institutions of justice, and in conformity with human rights standards' (UN 2018: 17). Access to justice, both formal and informal, is now considered to influence norms and shape societal structures and therefore can advance the wider development agenda (IDLO 2016). The nature and scope of a state's obligations concerning access to justice have been therefore broadened in subsequent jurisprudence of the core international human rights treaties, from being initially more linked to the right to fair trial and right to equality, to involving plural justice systems and administrative procedures. Access to justice thus came to be considered both a human right in itself and a means to achieve other human rights.

When it comes to women, the CEDAW Committee (GR 33 2015: paras 1, 3) not only indicates that the scope of the right to access to justice includes the plural justice systems that women may encounter when seeking to exercise this right, but also that this right is multidimensional and encompasses elements such as justiciability (unrestricted access to justice and claiming their rights), availability, accessibility, good-quality and accountability of justice systems, and provision of remedies for victims. More recently, women's access to justice has been defined in a UN report as:

> access by women, in particular, from poor and disadvantaged groups, to fair, effective, affordable and accountable mechanisms, for the protection of rights, control of abuse of power, and resolution of conflicts. This includes the ability of women to seek and obtain a fair and just remedy through formal and informal justice systems and the ability to influence and participate in law-making processes and institutions (UN 2018: 17).

The same report also explains how by emphasising the interconnection with development, conflict, post-conflict and other forms of crisis contexts, CEDAW General Recommendation (GR) 30 on Women in Conflict Prevention, Conflict and Post-Conflict Situations and CEDAW GR 33 on Women's Access to Justice provide a paradigm shift in justice for women (UN 2018: 18). Access to justice therefore refers to wider issues which go beyond the formal judicial system and which may have an impact on the ability of individuals to seek redress, not only from 'the establishment of institutions and procedural rules granting access to all, but also to the substantive laws themselves, and the empowerment of individuals to obtain justice' (Dias 2009: 5).

If we then think about plural justice systems provided after conflicts or situations where there have been grave violations of human rights, it becomes imperative to study the access to transitional justice mechanisms. The UN Report on the Rule of Law and Transitional Justice defines justice as

> an ideal of accountability and fairness in the protection and vindication of rights and the prevention and punishment of wrongs. Justice implies regard for the rights of the accused, for the interests of the victims and for the well-being of society at large (UN 2004: para 7).

In post-conflict countries, as showed by the case of Timor-Leste, victims currently interact not only with trials but also with truth commissions, reparations, and as has happened in many countries after they have been torn by war, veterans' pensions. To explore women's experiences of access to transitional justice, it is then crucial to reflect on the principle of equality, which asserts that human beings should be treated equally based on a common humanity (Habermas 2001; Okin 1999) and on the presumption that all human beings are 'potentially rational and responsible beings who have a genuine desire to be in control of their own lives' (Holtmaat 2013: 98). More specifically, whereas the UDHR simply states that 'all human beings are equal in rights and in dignity', the concept of equality has been expanded and today it is understood to have formal, substantive and transformative dimensions (CEDAW GR 25 2004). I now wish to expand on these dimensions.

While formal equality means that women have equal rights under the law, in the principle of substantive – or de facto – equality, it is recognised that in fact all human beings have different social, economic or other positions and possibilities in life so there is an idea that everyone 'should have equal opportunities to make something of their lives' (Holtmaat 2013: 98). In other words, more than being about legal guarantees of rights, substantive equality is about equal enjoyment of rights and equal opportunities and choices (Chinkin and Kaldor 2013: 178). Transformative equality, on the other hand, aims at social and cultural change by combating gender discrimination embedded in personal convictions, cultural practices and traditional values, as well as the systemic and structural discrimination that is ingrained in the country's legal, social and economic structures (Holtmaat 2013: 96, 111). Transformative equality requires states to take measures that challenge stereotypical views of men and women in both political economy (ie the division of labour and resources) and in cultural valuations (ie privileging masculinity and devaluing femininity) (Cook and Cusack 2010: 6). States are thus required to put in place non-stereotypical laws, policies, and practices that enable women to create their own roles and identities, and that eliminate wrongful, often patronising, treatment of women grounded in gender stereotypes (Cook and Cusack 2010: 6).

Finally, the more recent 2030 UN Agenda for Sustainable Development Goals (SDGs) defines a set of 17 goals on environmental, social, and economic development agreed in 2015 by all UN member states. While Goal 5 is about achieving gender equality, including ending all forms of discrimination, eliminating all forms of violence and undertaking reforms to equal rights to economic resources, Goal 16 is about the promotion of just, peaceful and inclusive societies, including by ensuring equal access to justice for all and the promotion and enforcement of non-discriminatory laws and policies. In this regard, transitional justice and development are assumed to be connected: while root causes of conflict can include violence and human rights violations, a lack of justice can itself fuel that violence and conflict, reversing gains achieved through development processes (OHCHR 2020). Transitional justice is seen thus as a tool of the state to ensure human rights, which is a central part of sustainable peace and development. Further guidance on Goal 16 establishes that in order to reach this goal, transitional justice will include measures such as 'victim-centric processes to deal with legacies of mass violations of human rights, incorporating victims' voices in peace and processes, returning property to people in the aftermath of conflict and investing in more broad-based, institutional reforms' (SDG16 Hub 2019: 42). In this project I will thus use the principles of both equality and access to justice to reflect on women's access to transitional justice mechanisms in general and not only in criminal trials. Based on the different dimensions of equality, in the next section I expand on the meaning of women's equal participation in their access to transitional justice.

VI. WOMEN'S PARTICIPATION IN TRANSITIONAL JUSTICE

Participation has been at the centre of international law and human rights. While the UN Charter is premised upon sovereignty and the rights of equal participation of all states, the first treaty sponsored and adopted at the behest of the UN Commission on the Status of Women (CSW) was the Convention on Political Participation of Women in 1952. The aim was to correct an ongoing discrimination against women through ensuring that women could participate in the political decision making within their states. Both the ICCPR and the ICESCR also anticipate that women should enjoy rights of participation in the political and economic life of a country without discrimination.[18] Participation as a fundamental human right was also recognised in the 1967 Declaration on

[18] *cf* HRC (2000) GC No 28: Article 3 (The Equality of Rights Between Men and Women); CESCR (2009) GC No 20 Non-discrimination in economic, social and cultural rights; and CESCR (2005) GC No 16 The Equal Right of Men and Women to the Enjoyment of All Economic, Social and Cultural Rights.

the Elimination of all Forms of Discrimination against Women (DEDAW), the precursor to what became CEDAW.

Consequently, the adoption of CEDAW in 1979 saw participation as key in several rights, including in the right to education and the right of rural women to participate in development planning, co-operatives and village councils – these were in addition to two free-standing provisions on the right to political participation in Article 7 and the right to participate at international levels in Article 8. In its GR 23 on Political and Public Life (1997), the CEDAW Committee reinforced the importance of women's voices and participation by advising states to ensure a core minimum of 30 per cent female representation as this was seen as the tipping point when women's presence would make a difference. The Committee again revisited women's participation in its GR 25 on Temporary Special Measures (TSMs) (2004) through increasing their representation and participation in public bodies. In the interim, there have been women's rights conferences; not least the 1995 Beijing Conference whose Platform and Declaration for Action reinforces the centrality of women's participation. All these international initiatives on women's participation were responding to a reality. In their groundbreaking article 'Feminist Approaches to International law', Charlesworth, Chinkin and Wright (1991) identified the under-representation of women in decision making as an example of the continuation of discrimination against women. The exclusion of women's voices means that their perspectives continue to be ignored in decision making resulting in policies that either ignore or embed existing structural inequalities.

In 1997, the UN then decided to adopt a global strategy called gender mainstreaming (also known as gender integration) for promoting gender equality (OHCHR 2011c: 4). This involved realising that there is a gender dimension to every occurrence of a human rights violation which required an increase in women's participation in the mechanisms dedicated to protecting and promoting human rights (UN 1998: para 9). More specifically, gender mainstreaming was defined as 'the process of assessing the implications for women, men and other gender identities of any planned action, including legislation, policies or programmes, in all areas and at all levels', such as in their design, implementation, monitoring and evaluation (OHCHR 2018: 8; 2011c: 4). Gender mainstreaming applied in transitional justice would thus mean integrating a gender perspective into human rights investigations, analysing the gender dimensions of human rights violations as well as the impacts of those violations, and ensuring that women's perspectives are reflected and not made invisible by non-gendered analysis (OHCHR 2018: 10, 37).[19]

While much has been written about participatory approaches to transitional justice, the impact of gender mainstreaming and the purpose or objectives of pushing for greater participation of women have, nevertheless, been put into question. Ní Aoláin (2019: 153) alerts that the mainstreaming approach has

[19] See also CEDAW GR No 33 on women's access to justice.

meant a process of adding women into regulatory frameworks, which in practice has done little to change the masculinity of institutions: to 'add and stir' women rarely transforms the gender codes and orders of transitional space. Tamale (1999) points out that it is limiting to expect women to speak for and about women's issues. Other scholars have argued that what is needed may not be more women but perhaps more gender-sensitive decision makers in order to facilitate the integration of a gendered approach to decision making. Evrard, Mejía Bonifazi and Destrooper (2021) also wisely observe that there is little evidence-based research on how to understand and evaluate victims' participation in transitional justice. In order to contribute to its understanding, they propose an analytical framework that acknowledges that multiple actors intervene at different times and in multiple spaces, and that is based on '(a) participants' identities and interests, (b) the spaces they navigate, (c) the relation between various interests, spaces and temporalities and (d) the open-ended nature of outcomes' (Evrard, Mejía Bonifazi and Destrooper 2021: 438, 447). As I will show, this book will contribute to understanding of the elements of women's participation in transitional justice by acknowledging that multiplicity of actors and spaces and showing that access to justice and women's participation are symbiotic – there cannot be access to justice without women's voices being heard.

The OHCHR (2018: 54) has indeed stated that women's participation in transitional justice processes can be conceived based on an adequate representation of women in relevant mechanisms to achieve reconciliation and accountability for human rights violations; it also entails equal access and participation by women and men during all stages of conflict prevention efforts, post-conflict transition and reconstruction processes. To put it simply, participation should mean that victims know their rights, share their views and influence outcomes of transitional justice (*cf* Gilmore, Guillerot and Sandoval 2020: 22).[20] Similarly, CEDAW GR 30 (2013) and the WPS resolutions usefully reinforce one another in their emphasis on women's equal access to transitional justice, including by calling for the rejection of amnesties for gender-based violations; ensuring the participation of women in the design, operation and monitoring of all the mechanisms; ensuring gender-sensitive investigations by security and justice sectors; and undertaking that post-conflict legal and judicial reform enhances women's access to justice (UN Women 2015: 14).

I thus envisage as key for women's participation in transitional justice, ensuring that their voices are heard in the investigations, that their violations are represented across the different mechanisms as well as guaranteeing their ability to gain redress for their violations compared to men. In this regard, reflecting on integrating a gender perspective into human rights investigations, the OHCHR (2018: 36) has observed the need to identify and address 'the prevailing challenges that might prevent or inhibit women's participation and

[20] Principle 34 of the UN Impunity Principles (2005) states that victims and civil society should play a meaningful role in the design and implementation of reparations programmes.

their voices to be heard (as men's voices generally tend to be overrepresented)' in order 'to enable and facilitate the disclosure of information on the violations women may have suffered or on the differentiated impact that the particular events, conflict or crisis has/had on women and girls'. As such, specific strategies to guarantee women's participation may include organising public hearings, including women only days; paying attention to the outreach and dissemination of information in order to reach out to a wide variety of women and other marginalised populations; ensuring that interviews are conducted in such a way that gender-specific questions are asked and that can illustrate and inform on the differentiated impact of the human rights violations on women, girls, men and boys; and ensuring that the information gathered also aims at documenting the violation of women and girls, beyond sexual violence, and documenting the differentiated impact of the violations against them (OHCHR 2018: 36).

Although a gender mainstreaming approach was taken into consideration in the transitional justice implemented in Timor-Leste, this book unpacks the barriers and discriminatory layers in the laws, policies, community and family practices that interfere in women's access to transitional justice mechanisms, excluding women from participating in processes that affect them.

VII. BARRIERS FACED BY WOMEN WHEN THEY ACCESS TRANSITIONAL JUSTICE

Article 1 of CEDAW defines discrimination as

> any distinction, exclusion or restriction made on the basis of sex which has the effect or purpose of impairing or nullifying the recognition, enjoyment or exercise by women, irrespective of their marital status, on a basis of equality of men and women, of human rights and fundamental freedoms in the political, economic, social, cultural, civil or any other field.

In other words, to satisfy a discrimination test against women, it must be shown that there is (1) a law, policy, or practice that makes a distinction, exclusion or restriction on women, and that (2) the difference in treatment is based on sex, and more broadly it is intended to cover gendered assumptions, practices and social structures (Byrnes 2012: 59; Cook and Cusack 2010: 107). Explaining the concept of discrimination against women on the basis of sex, the CEDAW Committee has observed that it includes those differences of treatment that exist 'because of stereotypical expectations, attitudes and behavior directed towards women which are based on the biological differences between women and men,' and that 'exist because of the existing subordination of women by men' (Cook and Cusack 2010: 104; CEDAW GR 25 2004; CEDAW GR 28 2010).

On this point, while CEDAW Article 2(f) requires states to 'take all appropriate measures, including legislation, to modify or abolish existing laws, regulations, customs and practices which constitute discrimination against women', Article 5(a) compels states

> to modify the social and cultural patterns of men and women, with a view to achieving the elimination of prejudices and customs and all other practices which are based on the idea of the inferiority or the superiority of either of the sexes or stereotyped roles for men and women.

The two articles are often cited in tandem, but while Article 2(f) is applicable upon showing that a law, regulation, custom, or practice constitutes discrimination against women, Article 5(a) is applicable just by showing that a prejudice or practice was based on a stereotype concerning 'the inferiority or superiority of either of the sexes', or on 'stereotyped roles for men and women' (Cook and Cusack 2010: 5). Cook and Cusack (2010: 9) define a stereotype as 'a generalized view or preconception of attributes or characteristics processed by, or the roles that are or should be performed by, members of a particular group', so 'all the dimensions of personality that make that individual unique are consequently filtered through the lens of a generalised view or preconception of the group with which the individual is identified'. These ideas of superiority and inferiority are intended to address thus 'how laws construct men as superior to women, and how laws construct certain subgroups of women as inferior to men, or vice versa, or other subgroups of women or men' (Cook and Cusack 2010: 73).

Because the interplay between the public and private spheres has been fundamental in understanding sex discrimination and injustice, the Convention also highlights the importance of addressing social structures. By using 'any other field' in Article 1, CEDAW means that the treaty is applicable to all spheres of both public and private life, from the law and policies to the community and family practices (Reilly 2009: 60–61). Article 3 also emphasises States parties' obligations to take positive steps to ensure the full development and advancement of women on a basis of equality with men in all fields, in particular in the political, social, economic and cultural fields. According to Chinkin (2012: 105), this is important because the denial of women's rights in all these fields contributes to their economic dependence, denial of personal autonomy and more generally to their lack of power. By linking the full development and advancement of women with the exercise and enjoyment of their human rights, this article provides the legal basis for structural – transformative – change in the lives of women: it requires positive and corrective action not only to achieve de facto equality, but also to ensure the elimination of structural inequalities that impede women's access to enjoyment of rights (Chinkin 2012: 102, 114). Some of the main issues the committee has mentioned under this article include, for example, investigating impediments to women's advancement, women and poverty, and equal access to justice and redress (Chinkin 2012: 121–22).

CEDAW then distinguishes between direct and indirect forms of discrimination. While direct discrimination means an explicit distinction of treatment between men and women on the basis of sex, indirect discrimination may occur when a law, policy, or practice seems to be sex- or gender-neutral but in reality has a detrimental effect on women when implemented (CEDAW GR 28, 2010: para 16). Discrimination against women can thus be manifested in diverse forms, for example:

> exclusion from or limited rights to participate in the political and public spheres of community life, economic marginalization and dependence, the prevalence of stereotypes that limited life opportunities or valued predominantly 'male' activities and characteristics over 'female' ones, inequality in the family, and violence against women in the community and in the family (Byrnes 2012: 52).

All of these examples were to some extent reflected in my conversations with the Timorese women when they referred to their experience in dealing with transitional justice. Indeed, positive obligations under international law do not necessarily guarantee equality and non-discrimination against women. The list is long, but when it comes to the administration of justice, women can be particularly affected by barriers such as discriminatory laws, procedural and evidentiary practices; the non-availability of courts and quasi-judicial bodies in rural and remote regions; the time and money needed to access them; the complexity of proceedings; the deficiencies in the quality of justice systems and legal advice; corruption and lack of awareness of human rights (UN 2008b: 24–32; CEDAW GR 33 2015: para 13; Cusack 2014: ii). Based on their sex/gender, women also often face specific barriers in their efforts to access justice, including 'male guardianship laws, fear of stigma and reprisals and cultural perceptions of men (and not women) as rights-bearers' (Cusack 2014: ii).[21] Consequently, stereotyping and personal values are also barriers that have a decisive impact on women's access to justice. For instance, Cusack (2014: 2) uses the term 'judicial stereotyping' to refer to:

> the practice of judges ascribing to an individual specific attributes, characteristics or roles by reason only of her or his membership in a particular social group (eg women). It is used, also, to refer to the practice of judges perpetuating harmful stereotypes through their failure to challenge stereotyping, for example by lower courts or parties to legal proceedings.

Thinking about the roles of judges – and also of other law enforcement officials – stereotyping can compromise the impartiality of decisions, influence understanding of the nature of the criminal offence, affect views about witness credibility and legal capacity, prevent offenders from being held legally accountable while blaming the victim/survivor, and impede access to legal rights and protections against SGBV (Cusack 2014: 2, 22). Based on preconceived beliefs, stereotyping may thus distort judges' perception of the facts, leading to miscarriages of justice and the re-victimisation of complainants (Cusack 2014: ii). Women face negative or prejudicial attitudes by those working in the

[21] While many rural women and girls live in communities where informal justice mechanisms are used to resolve disputes, eg village councils, women are excluded from them (CEDAW GR 34 2016).

legal system and in legal institutions, as has been widely documented from the *Vertido v Philippines* case,[22] where a state court erred about rape and consent, relying on gendered stereotypes, to the *Jallow v Bulgaria* case,[23] where authorities disregarded domestic violence, based on stereotyping concerning the roles of men and women in marriage.[24]

The stereotyping, however, may also come from well-intentioned legal actors, human rights activists and feminists. Sexual violence against women has been, for instance, a key issue within transitional justice. Nesiah (2011: 143) explains that 'if the "victim" or the privileged subject of transitional justice is the one whose rights to bodily integrity are violated, then the raped victim becomes the privileged subject of feminist transitional justice'. As with Nesiah's concern about stereotyping women as only victims of sexual violence, Ross (2003: 75–76) observes how the TRC's findings on women focused on an idea of passivity and bodily violation and did not give the correct account of the challenges faced by them in their opposition to the Apartheid state. Gender mainstreaming in transitional justice may thus have enforced the 'engendered' victim by not recognising the full complexity of women's violations and experiences and by ignoring other categories that do not necessarily equate justice with the rule of law (Nesiah 2011: 154, 157).

In this connection, despite the liberal idea that women's access to justice will be improved by promoting legal empowerment, there is today a recognition that women's access to justice is not only affected by their disempowerment and lack of knowledge of laws and legal procedures, but also by economic, social and cultural practices that perpetuate their inequality in society (IDLO 2013: 8–9).[25] Fraser (2008: 16; 2007: 27) argues that dealing with women's injustice means dismantling structural and institutionalised barriers that prevent them from participating with others as full partners in society. Moreover, as Dias and Welch (2009: 637) claim, 'effective access to justice must deal with both issues of process and issues of power since the power-holders are often able to misuse and abuse both legal and judicial processes'. Judicial process must therefore address not only the symptoms but also the causes of denial of justice, and this concerns the abuse of the power by the privileged ones (Dias and Welch 2009: 637). One of the conclusions after carrying out the interviews in Timor-Leste, for instance, is that scholars and policy makers working

[22] CEDAW, *Vertido v Philippines*, Communication No 18/2008, UN Doc CEDAW/C/46/D/18/2008, 16 July 2010.

[23] CEDAW, *Jallow v Bulgaria*, Communication No 32/2011, UN Doc CEDAW/C/52/D/32/2011, 28 August 2012.

[24] See *MC v Bulgaria*, Application No 39272/98, European Court of Human Rights, 3 December 2003.

[25] Legal empowerment is defined as 'using the law to enable disadvantaged groups to access justice and realize basic rights. This includes legal education; legal aid services; support for non-discriminatory dispute-resolution fora to complement or supplement informal systems; training of paralegals; and rights awareness' (IDLO 2013: 7).

on transitional justice should not leave aside those socio-economic structures that are heightened after a conflict, and which affect women's recognition and the guarantee of their equal rights as compared with men.

In this regard, Nesiah (2011: 144) has criticised how transitional justice institutions rely mainly on legalistic institutions, practices and discourses as if the 'fair application of legal rules to assess evidence and pass sanction represents the triumph of the rule of law over the abuse of power'. She further explains that

> tailored as they are to establishing facts regarding the culpability of individual defendants … court processes may offer victims little room to discuss the personal and social context of the violation; focused on justiciable indicators of harm, court processes and judicialised truth commission processes may not allow victims to convey the personal impact of the violation (Nesiah 2011: 146).

Engle (2015: 1071) also argues that there is today a turn of human rights towards individual criminal accountability that gives the impression that justice came to mean 'criminal justice' and that ends by reinforcing an individualised and de-contextualised understanding of the harms those rights aim to address. In other words, justice came to mean courts. Clarke (2009: 235–36) also warns that:

> A wide range of conceptions of justice exist alongside a notion of the individual and selfhood through which liberalist views of agency and free will thrive in particular moral and institutional economies and through which the language of the tribunal as triumphant and morally shaped takes shape, while the intelligibility of other trajectories or rationalities is negated.

But feminists may have also had a role in that turn toward individual criminal accountability. Reflecting on how feminism interacts with international and domestic governance, Halley (2018: 29) recounts that 'for many feminisms on many issues, punishment became the remedy of choice for any social wrong that they could describe as coercive or as harm'. The danger is that this turn may relieve pressure on the state to attend to race, class, and gender biases and the structural issues of distribution (Engle 2015: 1069). In this regard, Rees and Chinkin (2016: 1219) also argue that transitional justice is limited by its focus on large-scale past abuses, understood as violations of civil and political rights, failing to recognise the need to address gross violations of economic, social, and cultural rights associated with conflict.

As we shall see, the diversity of power structures that come into play within the scope of the transitional justice system has created discrimination, including inadequate law and lack of protective policy measures, limiting Timorese women's access to transitional justice once the conflict was over. I therefore examine the barriers that women face when interacting with the administration of these justice mechanisms, which were formally offered to them but which were not necessarily easy to reach and navigate because these mechanisms are blind to the specificities of women's participation and recognition. More specifically, I explore the barriers to the laws and policies of implementation and also those connected to the community and family dynamics. This is important because, as Ellickson (1998: 540) argues, 'much of the glue of a society comes not from law enforcement, as the classicists would have it, but rather from the informal enforcement of social norms by acquaintances, bystanders, trading partners, and others'. The delivery of justice is indeed affected by issues such as gender, class, ethnicity, religion and so on, which are components of the socio-cultural identity of all those actors that are surrounding the law and its institutional properties, the latter described as 'social practices or repeated patterns of behavior which produce a sense of legality' (Banakar 2013: 30). But I also reflect on the concept of justice and how women's wishes and demands have been taken into account. The complexity of understanding justice increases when both international and domestic laws, actors and institutions, conflate, as happens in the case when an international administration interferes in a post-conflict society. The case of Timor-Leste therefore shows the existence of different barriers which, when acting together, may set a higher threshold both for the participation of women in transitional justice mechanisms and for the recognition of their violations and experiences.

VIII. CONCLUSIONS

Whereas in situations of peace, international human rights law applies, when there is an armed conflict, whether international or non-international, human rights conventions and international humanitarian law apply in parallel and their different protections are complementary. The issue is that while international actors have insisted on the incorporation of international laws and standards into national contexts and domestic legal frameworks, there is a lack of attention to the implementation of the norms and justice canons at the local level, even more so after periods of immense violence.

At the same time, this chapter has shown how the concept of access to justice has been expanded and how the principle of equality should be guaranteed within transitional justice processes. However, based on the data obtained through the interviews, Timorese women had limited participation in the trials organised by the Special Panels and truth commissions as well as in their access to the provision of reparations and veterans' pensions. While there has been significant discussion about the selection and availability of the mechanisms, the case of Timor-Leste shows that their implementation may have been mechanical, without taking into consideration either the specificities of women's rights violations or the power dynamics between and within international and local actors. This means that barriers in the laws and in the policies of its implementation as well as community and family dynamics have a great impact on women's lives and human rights protection, particularly during post-conflict situations. The implementation of transitional justice in Timor-Leste thus shows that because of the different barriers there is a higher threshold for women's access to and participation in the justice mechanisms, affecting women's recognition as citizens in the new state. The next chapter anticipates the silencing of women during the post-conflict transitional justice initiatives and the continuum of the violations committed against them in times of peace.

Women in Aileu. © Carlos Oviedo.

After the interviews with a group of women in Ermera. © Riovaldi Saldanha.

3

Silence and Memory: 'They are Waiting for Us to Die'

BASED ON MY field research in Timor-Leste, I develop two arguments in this book. First, when transitional justice is mechanically applied without consideration of the barriers found not only in the laws and policies of implementation but also those that emerge at the community and family level, there is a higher threshold for women to access these justice processes. Second, the transitional justice literature pays insufficient attention to the welfare structures that are produced after a conflict, and this relationship between the violations and economic justice has major consequences in times of peace. The mechanisms of transitional justice may perpetuate the silence and exacerbate the invisibility of and discrimination against women, both immediately after the conflict and in the long-term. The intertwining of memory and silence with invisibility and discrimination that I will show is embedded in the transitional justice mechanisms is the focus of this chapter.

This chapter shows, first, how the silence and discrimination against women that frame the whole process of transitional justice are connected to their subsequent lack of recognition in the public space. Second, it focuses on the narratives of women who have been silenced as against the dominant narratives of the state that have surged after the conflict. I then reflect on some of the main human rights issues for Timorese women today and I illustrate how their violations are framed within a continuum from conflict to peace. Silence may therefore have an effect on women's lack of participation and recognition after a conflict. I end by examining what women want from transitional justice.

I. WOMEN'S SILENCE AND LACK OF RECOGNITION AFTER A CONFLICT

Violence against women has been defined as

> any act of gender-based violence that results in, or is likely to result in, physical, sexual or psychological harm or suffering to women, including threats of such acts, coercion or arbitrary deprivations of liberty, whether occurring in public or private life.[1]

[1] Declaration on the Elimination of Violence against Women (DEVAW), Article 1.

Although we may have an automatic mental association, violence inflicted on women is only a part of their experience in conflict and/or large-scale human rights violations. Enloe (2014) has shown, for instance, how the participation of women in a conflict is multidimensional because they can participate with their bodies and labour.

Highlighting their multiple roles, Kumar (2012: 79) argues that women are survivors: not only do they suffer from the crimes that are committed against them, but they also may participate in the conduct of the mass crimes, struggle to keep themselves and their families alive in the middle of economic and physical collapse and contribute to the recovery and reconstruction of affected societies. When exploring women's participation in the TRC of South Africa, Ross (2003: 164–65) also reflects on women's participation as multiple forms of resistance, including individual acts of caring, but these stories may remain 'unacknowledged, underexplored, and in danger of slipping from the historical record'. Noticing these tensions between voice and silence, Ross (2003: 164–65) concludes that they are 'the products of social processes that give different weight to particular forms of experience and subjectivity'. Like her, I am also interested in exploring how the complexity of women's experiences in conflict may be silenced by the mechanisms put in place to provide justice.

The silence concerning the crimes against women through post-conflict justice is not new. During the Second World War, the Japanese enslaved over 100,000 women as part of a horrendous military tactic (Sellers 2011: 117). The practice allegedly boosted the health of the troops by supplying recreational sex, it avoided sexual diseases that could have lowered the fighting capacity of the soldiers, it decreased espionage and leaks and it prevented soldiers from raping other girls and women (Sellers 2011: 117). These women, who were known as 'comfort women' by the Japanese, were sexual slaves recruited through various means, including deception, coercion, and brute force (Chinkin and Kaldor 2013: 174).[2] They were enslaved by Japan in all of the territories it invaded, including Timor-Leste. When the Japanese army retreated, the women and girls were left behind with a common belief that they were prostitutes who voluntarily offered their services (Sellers 2011: 117–18).

In contrast to the prosecution of crimes against male slaves, the crimes against sex slaves were not taken into account by the prosecution at the Tokyo Trial (Sellers 2011: 118–20). Reflecting on what she calls 'fractured legal clarifications', Sellers (2011: 115–16) points out that enslavement has become a crime mostly associated with men, while sexual slavery is identified as feminine as if one were of graver nature than the other, and as if women, because they are women, could not be enslaved. Sellers (2011: 116) argues that this failure to

[2] '"Comfort Women" is the Japanese Imperial government's euphemism for the women and children they trafficked as sex slaves between 1932 and 1945, until the end of World War II' ('Comfort Women' Justice Coalition).

redress the crimes committed against sex slaves during the Second World War, 'exerted a prejudicial influence upon precepts of wartime female slavery and the understanding of enslavement'. The fractured legal clarifications were then extended to the jurisdictions and case law of the ICTY and the SCSL: while the convictions for enslavement at the ICTY partially corrected the impunity related to the slavery of 'comfort women', certain cases at the SCSL failed to charge as the crime of enslavement 'abductions, rapes, forced conjugal relations, domestic tasks and other duties imposed on females by male soldiers' (Sellers 2011: 116). Sellers' concern thus is that while wartime sexually-abused female slaves are deprived of the fuller designation as 'subjects of enslavement', the perception of enslavement that is adopted is that it is non-sexual, labour-intensive and restricted to prisoners of war or civilian internees (Sellers 2011: 117, 120).[3] Similarly, as MacKinnon (2017: 13) reflects on the role of law, 'women's sexuality is at the core of the way we are socially defined and therefore denigrated as women and because sexuality has been largely ignored as a factor in women's inequality to men'.

Dogopol also makes a connection between past and future. She argues that in the same way as crimes committed against the 'comfort women' were known to the Allies and were not given the appropriate treatment it deserved at the Tokyo Trial because of 'discretionary' decisions, there is still today a lack of sufficient attention to crimes committed against women and other groups by those in power (Dogopol 2011: 248, 260). Based on her analysis of cases at the ICTY and ICC, Dogopol (2011: 245–46) calls for a sense of ethical obligation in the decision-making of prosecutors and those investigating the commission of war crimes and crimes against humanity, to give a gender approach to their work. In practice, this means that 'prosecutors explain the operation of the criminal justice system to the public and make transparent their process of decision-making to victims of crime' (Dogopol 2011: 247). Ašimović Akyol (2019) also observes how in Bosnia after the Dayton peace agreement, while 'different narratives of the past dictate today's realities', many rape survivors are still fighting with authorities to get a victim of war status, have little legal protection and are dealing with stigmas in their communities. Women are therefore still excluded. In this regard, the case of Timor-Leste is emblematic. Sexual slavery has been committed against several generations of Timorese women, who repeatedly found themselves in a situation of abandonment. As I will show, the cycle of silence against their voices continues.

[3] Civil society and feminist academics organised a symbolic trial called Women's International Tribunal on Japanese Military Sexual Slavery, held in 2000 in Tokyo. The objective was to gather testimony from victims and make a judgment on Japanese military sexual slavery from the perspective of international law and gender justice. The judges found the Japanese State and the Emperor Hirohito guilty of war crimes and crimes against humanity and asked the government for an apology and to provide compensation to the surviving victims. It made visible the violations that had been ignored or erased from history (*cf* Chinkin 2001).

Thinking about women's silence, I found Arendt's concept of space of appearance illuminating. Arendt makes a connection between the *polis*, the organisation of the people where acting (action) and speaking (speech) arises, and a concept that she calls space of appearance, 'the space where I appear to others as others appear to me, where men exist not merely like other living or inanimate things but make their appearance explicitly' (Arendt 1998: 198–99; 2016: 285). If citizenship of a nation-state is, for Arendt, how people secure their rights and a space of appearance, Timorese women, whose narratives are silenced, may be deprived of their full citizenship in the new post-conflict state. As a result, the lack of recognition in the space of appearance leads to the deprivation of their human rights (Arendt 2017: 387–88).[4] This also connects to Arendt's concept of power, defined as the ability of a group to act in concert (Arendt 1972: 143). As she further writes, power is 'where words are not used to veil intentions but to disclose realities, and deeds are not used to violate and destroy but to establish relations and create new realities' (Arendt 1998: 200). If women are silenced through transitional justice mechanisms, their power in the space of appearance of the political community is thus dismissed. This lack of power is what kills political communities (Arendt 1998: 200).

Women's experiences in Timor-Leste raise then the issue of the tensions between voices and silences that surged during the implementation of transitional justice and beyond. As Granville (2012: 373) asserts, 'transitional justice needs to critically interrogate the relationship between memory construction and state- and nation-building goals that may not be directly linked to the aims of transitional justice'. Without addressing the situation that women endured, the state contributes to further women's silence and stigmatisation. When referring to violence against women and silence, Solnit writes that it

> is often against our voices and our stories. It is a refusal of our voices, and of what a voice means: the right to self-determination, to participation, to consent or dissent, to live and participate, to interpret and narrate (Solnit 2017: 19).

The CEDAW Committee in its GR 30 (2013: para 78) has also stated that 'passive acquiescence of past violence reinforces the culture of silence and stigmatization' and unless we understand this, it will be difficult to ensure equality for women after a conflict. I want to go, however, beyond the legal definition of violence, to explore the many ways in which Timorese women were involved in the resistance and affected by the conflict.

Because of its impact on history, it is necessary to think about 'the "reconciliation with reality," the catharsis, which according to Aristotle, was the essence of tragedy, and, according to Hegel was the ultimate purpose of history, came about through the tears of remembrance' (Arendt 2006a: 45). While reflecting on the objectivity of history, Arendt (2006: 49) argues than non-discrimination

[4] While Hegel focuses clearly on the idea of struggle for recognition, for Arendt, although implicit, is central for her concept on rights.

is 'much easier to achieve than noninterference' since discrimination was a social matter rather than a political one. I differ with Arendt over this issue. The experience of Timorese women in transitional justice demonstrates that both discrimination and public and private interference go hand-in-hand, contributing to women's lack of recognition in the public space. What are thus the narratives that have been shaped in Timor-Leste connected to transitional justice? As I will show in the following section, the narratives of some women may have been dominated, or even silenced, by those in a powerful position.

II. ON WOMEN'S SILENCE IN TIMOR-LESTE

Different reports have highlighted how human rights violations against women during the Indonesian occupation were widespread and systematic. My interviews in the different municipalities also confirm that the violence and coercive control that some of these women experienced were not so uncommon in the whole of Timor-Leste. Among all the violations against them that were mentioned, I noticed that in contrast to other conflict situations, where the recognition of women as 'forced wives' has been accepted (Coulter 2009: 130), in Timor-Leste the women who participated in the interviews did not name the crimes that they suffered. Although there may be cases where women wished of their own free will to be with Indonesians, it would be an absurdity to deny the extent, for instance, of forced marriage and sexual slavery in Timor-Leste. Women who went through the experience of 'temporary' forced marriage and sexual slavery introduced themselves to me as the women of Indonesians, asked for an apology – for having been related to them – and added that thanks to their sacrifice, members of their families and communities were still alive.

A woman in Aileu who was also subjected to sexual slavery told me the following story:

> They 'threatened' me in my house, from 1982 until they left in 1999 … My family were high authorities during Portuguese times, but when the Indonesians started 'threatening me', they felt ashamed … They were coming to my house 'kalan kalan' (every night) … I got five children from the Indonesians. If I wanted to get married, people insulted me – to many Timorese I became an Indonesian mistress.

She decided then not to marry afterwards and to raise her children alone. She continued, 'if you married a Timorese after being a mistress, you will be treated badly … I am sorry we became the mistresses of those troops.'[5] This woman did not know about the CAVR, nor did she receive any assistance.

Because these arguments were repeated to me across the different Timorese municipalities, I will proceed to reflect on them. Those coerced into forced marriage who lived as wives of Indonesians were forced to fulfil male sexual

[5] Interview with Participant 12, Aileu, Aileu, Timor-Leste, 20 January 2017.

needs and do what are conceived to be womanly activities. As often happens during armed conflicts, some of these women who were subjected to forced marriage told me that they did so to be protected from being raped by groups of men. But let me be clear: the 'temporary' marriage of many of these women was forced, as it lacked their free consent as well as negotiation with their families according to customary practices.[6] Moreover, many of them were children and according to international law most child marriages may be considered forced marriages.[7] Women also explained that their 'marriage' did not mean that they stopped suffering from violence since their husbands would beat them. Those who were exposed to sexual slavery were gang-raped on a daily basis by the Indonesian military for a large number of years and they endured horrendous violence. Stories of sexual slavery were repeated by several of the women who participated in the interviews, for instance, in Baucau. They explained how the main hotel in the village, called 'Posada', served as a military centre during the Indonesian occupation and how they were picked up at night from their houses to be taken to a specific floor in this military base to be raped and tortured. They went through these experiences every day for years. These women could not leave the village because of fear, suffered sexual violence until 1999 and as result had several children by different soldiers.

Some of the interviewed women mentioned how despite what the community might think, their movements were indeed restricted and they needed to be available at any time for the Indonesians. I heard several stories of how the Indonesians used to hold parties and forced Timorese women to join them. 'Women were ordered to dance', they said.[8] Although some Timorese villagers may have thought they were having fun, we have seen similar episodes of sexual violence through macabre dancing in other situations of large-scale violence, causing a humiliating and painful effect on women's dignity. This has happened in Argentina, where there were cases of women who while being detained in torture centres, were taken out dancing (Lewin 2014). This also occurred in the *Kunarac* case in the former Yugoslavia, in which the ICTY identified rape as a form of torture and in which for the first time an international tribunal convicted a defendant of sexual slavery, women were forced to dance.[9] Dancing, cooking, and sexual abuse are about ownership, controlling someone's movement, psychology and physical environment, coercion and exclusivity. Deprivation of liberty and the coercion that they described is related to a right of ownership, features that are linked to sexual slavery.

[6] See International Protocol on the Documentation and Investigation of Sexual Violence in Conflict (2014: 86).

[7] 'Early marriage, or child marriage, has come to be recognized as purported marriage involving children under 18 years, although there are exceptions' (International Commission of Jurists 2016: 205).

[8] Interviews with Participants in Lalerik Mutin, Viqueque, Timor-Leste, 3–4 February 2017.

[9] ICTY, *Prosecutor v Dragoljub Kunarac, Radomir Kovac and Zoran Vukovic* (*Kunarac* case), paras 772–774.

Women who suffered forced marriage and sexual slavery also narrated the pressure that they received from local authorities, and even their families, to do so. The pressure on the girls and women to accept their fate came with threats about the killing of members of their families and community. Beatriz, in Lalerik Mutin, who became a leader in her village, said that she underwent social pressure to marry three times with Indonesians. As a result, she had two children, one of them with a disability.[10] Mário Carrascalão, a former governor of Timor-Leste during the Indonesian occupation, also said in a national public hearing that in some cases, women were offered to the Indonesians by their own family to receive a benefit (Post-CAVR 2008: 47). In Mauchiga, a woman said that after her husband was killed by the Indonesians, her husband's family, including her mother-in-law, asked her to go and live with Indonesians. A man then began coming to her house to rape her. Her in-laws were quiet. She became pregnant and lived under threat. When she then gave birth, the family-in-law did not want to take care of her and denied her food because she had a child from another man.[11] Carrascalão also added that low-ranking officers also tried to progress their careers by making Timorese women available to those officers of higher rank (Post-CAVR 2008: 47).

But these women may be recounting what was already known after the end of the conflict, although nobody seems to have listened. Already in 2003, there were accounts of a logic of sacrificing an individual for the protection of the group and that communities treated women as scapegoats and pressured them to accept violations (Harris Rimmer 2010: 295).[12] This, however, may not be new for Timorese women. Timorese women who participated in the Women's International War Crimes Tribunal on Japan's Military Sexual Slavery, held in Tokyo in 2000, revealed that Portuguese officials colluded in recruiting Timorese women, in order to save European women from rape (Cristalis and Scott 2005: 14). Men interceding to offer women to men is not unique to Timor-Leste. In Cambodia, a number of witnesses also described how team leaders, military leaders and village chiefs abused their positions by forcing women into prostitution for their subordinates (TPO 2015: 15).

In this regard, women mentioned that some village chiefs helped the Indonesian soldiers by showing them the houses where women lived to convince the girls to have sexual relations under coercive circumstances. Again, in Lalerik Mutin, it was the village chief who acted as an intermediary for the Indonesians by pressuring several girls to engage in sexual relations with the soldiers every night. There were five women in this group in Lalerik Mutin with the same memories: when they were girls, they had to come in the evenings to the office of the village chief, and from there, they were picked up by the Indonesian soldiers,

[10] Interviews with Participant 13, Lalerik Mutin, Viqueque, Timor-Leste, 03 February 2017.

[11] Interview with Participant 68, Mauchiga, Ainaru, Timor-Leste, 11 November 2016.

[12] Harris Rimmer cites Karen Campbell-Nelson, 'East Timor must tell of atrocities by Indonesians', The Jakarta Post, 9-10 June 2003.

taken to the military base, raped, and then brought back to the office of the village chief at 5 am.[13]

One of them was a woman who was 12 years old at that time and who said that she was violated 'kalan kalan', meaning every night.[14] Another woman in Lalerik Mutin, who suffered from SGBV, said that she is convinced that the village chief gave her name to the Indonesians. 'He was surely scared', she said.[15] She was only a teenager and she was also discriminated against by the community, which afterwards called her, and the others who experienced the same ordeal, the 'mistress of the *bapas*', among other pejorative names. The point that I want to make is that Timorese local authorities played a fundamental role in facilitating the commission of crimes against young girls and women. I heard similar testimonies in different villages, and this seems to have happened throughout Timor-Leste.

The connection between the actions of the resistance and the Indonesians' reprisals against women was also apparent on numerous occasions. The women in Baucau described how when the resistance movement attacked the Indonesians, the latter were crueler to them at night because their friends had been killed in combat. Several of the women said that the Indonesians put plastic bags on their heads so they could not see the men's faces and that after being raped every night, they had permission to take a shower before being allowed to return to their house. Naked in the bathroom, the women hugged each other while crying after the Indonesians took revenge against them. It was punitive rape under coercive circumstances.

The phenomenon of violations of women as reprisals because of the actions of the resistance is also illustrated by the example of the 1982 attack organised by Falintil forces in Dare, Ainaro. This led to reprisals by the Indonesians in several villages, including Mauchiga. Under suspicion of having cooperated with the resistance, women and children became political prisoners for several years. Torture, rape, sexual slavery and forced displacement were among the many crimes committed against its residents. There was then a ceasefire, which would end in 1983, when the resistance organised an attack. Again, in retaliation, the Indonesians massacred at least 200 villagers in Kraras, Viqueque (Leach 2017: 82). After the attack, women and children were relocated by the Indonesians to another village called Viqueque Villa, and from there they were sent to a village called Lalerik Mutin. This is why this village is commonly known as the 'Widows' Village'.[16] The critical point is that there may be silence about the connections between the actions of the armed resistance and women's suffering.

[13] Interviews with Participants in Lalerik Mutin, Viqueque, Timor-Leste, 03-04 February 2017.
[14] Interviews with Participant 25, Lalerik Mutin, Viqueque, Timor-Leste, 03 February 2017.
[15] Interview with Participant 24, Lalerik Mutin, Viqueque, Timor-Leste, 03 February 2017.
[16] This village was already mentioned in the report of the SR on Violence against Women in early 1999 (UN 1999a).

I interviewed around 20 women in this village, and almost all of them narrated stories of SGBV, including of being forced to get 'temporarily married to Indonesians' – which in reality covered sexual slavery. A woman who was 12 years old at that time said that after Kraras, people were relocated to Vicare. Several girls were separated from their families and were brought to live with the Secretary of the Village. He then started bringing the '*bapas*' to rape the girls every night for four months, until they were relocated to Lalerik Mutin. Another woman, for instance, said that a village chief told her that because she was from Kraras, she had to marry an Indonesian. If not they were going to kill all her family. She said to him, 'I don't want to and I don't care', but he told her, 'There are other daughters of village chiefs who are marrying Indonesians, why don't you do that?'.[17] She ended up 'marrying' the commander of Viqueque for one year and there was the same modus operandi: every night she had to go to the office of the village chief, from where she was taken at 8 pm to the commander's office, raped, and brought back to the office of the village chief at 5 am – always through the back door. She endured this for a year, until the real wife of the commander came from Indonesia, and he left her. She was 15 years old. The women in Lalerik Mutin even said that there was a time during which the village chief told the girls to remain permanently at his house. This situation lasted from 1983 to 1993.

When I asked the women their opinions about the role of some specific village chiefs, I was surprised that the women could rationalise and accept the chiefs' decision-making with the excuse that they did so in order to protect their own safety. We may therefore have community leaders, who were part of the resistance while also collaborating with the Indonesians, and who may later have had a fundamental role in the local implementation of the CAVR. This made me think about how 'Eichmann in Jerusalem' became controversial because of Arendt's comments about the responsibility of the Jewish Councils in the facilitation of the commission of crimes against the Jews (Arendt 2006b: 125, 214).[18] Pushing for this idea of avoiding 'black and white' thinking, Arendt (2006b: 230) also writes about Anton Schmidt, an Austrian Nazi who was executed for saving Jews during the Holocaust. There is a similar example in Timor-Leste. At the highest point of the violence in 1999, militias started recruiting youths, but many of these young boys decided to escape to the mountains and to fight with the resistance, rather than committing atrocities. Arendt's point was that in the most atrocious circumstances, amid the evil of humanity, there are always people who will stop and make a reflective judgment (Arendt, 2006b: 49; 1971). Arendt focuses on who one is in a particular

[17] Interview with Participant 24, Lalerik Mutin, Viqueque, Timor-Leste, 03 February 2017.

[18] The Jewish Councils were intermediary bodies used by the Nazi administration to enforce their orders and regulations to Jewish communities, particularly within the ghettos. They remain controversial until today since they had to comply with Nazi demands, including the preparation of lists containing names of Jews for deportation (Holocaust Encyclopedia 2019).

situation, and by remembering the rabbinical saying, 'Let them kill you, but don't cross the line,' she follows Socrates, who claims that 'it is better to suffer wrong than to do wrong' (Arendt, 2006b: 119; 2006a: 239). Thinking thus is our essence as human beings.

Why did the violence against women last for the totality of the Indonesian occupation? Besides the role of the village chiefs, some of the women who were subjected to daily sexual violence said that the battalions kept their names on a list, to ensure that these women were also 'available' for the new arrivals. When asked if the Indonesian commanders knew about their rapes, some of them replied that it was impossible that groups of girls were taken every night to military bases for around 15 years without the commanders being aware, or without them knowing about the lists of women that were kept in the military bases. Moreover, some of them indicated that commanders also participated in the rapes. One woman in Aileu said that she was taken once to the commander of the battalion but that when the latter looked at her, he laughed and said 'this is a kid, not a woman.'[19] Another military man of lower rank then said 'this is for me to play with.' She was raped and ended up having four children by the Indonesian army. But sexual violence against women did not only occur in military facilities – this could happen in police stations and in other public places under Indonesian control, such as schools. The women in Mauchiga, for instance, mentioned that after the attack of the resistance in 1982, not only were they tortured and raped at the Dare sub-command post, but they were also raped when they were temporarily relocated to the Dare Primary School. 'The excuse for the sexual violence in Dare was always interrogation', a woman said.[20] Women narrated terror scenes when they were separated from their own family and neighbours as the Indonesian military came at night and picked up the young girls in order to rape them.

The fact that women present themselves as the 'wives' of Indonesians, followed by an apology, suggests there is denial, a lack of recognition, that they were victims of horrendous crimes. Indeed, while these women paid with their bodies to avoid killings and revenge, they were at the same time stigmatised and discriminated against by their communities and even their own families. An expression that was repeated by the women interviewed was '*ema ko'alia*' meaning that people were gossiping about them. Wandita, Campbell-Nelson and Pereira (2006: 292) argue that 'community misperceptions of non-consensual sexual relations lead to the view of women victims of sexual violence as immoral "fallen women"'. These women were exposed and pressured to be victims of forced marriage and sexual slavery to save their families and communities, and they were repaid with stigmatisation and blame. Many of them were in fact just girls when, under coercive circumstances, they

[19] Interview with Participant 48, Aileu, Timor-Leste, 20 January 2017.
[20] Interview with Participant 18, Mauchiga, Ainaru, Timor-Leste, 11 November 2016.

were forced to engage in sexual relations with Indonesians and their collaborators. Martin and SáCouto also make an observation about the blame women tend to take. More specifically, they pointed out that only after the *Sepur Zarco* case – the first time a Guatemalan court convicted former military members for acts of sexual violence committed during the civil war – was there a shift in the blame from women to the perpetrators, helping the women 'to heal from the stigma and isolation they experienced and to regain their dignity within their community' (Martin and SáCouto 2020: 256).[21] Without justice and recognition of past harms, we continue seeing the tensions between voices and judgement, resulting in an ambiguous acceptance/denial that in reality these crimes were committed against women. Moreover, in Timor-Leste there is a denial of the fact that women being sexual slaves means that they were slaves and that consent has no validity when we talk about enslavement. This echoes Ross (2003: 64–71) when she explains how South African women were taunted by the authorities about ideologies of womanhood and were constantly called 'whores' because of their actions, making them think that their political choices were aberrant, affecting their sense of security in their identities. This shows how 'physical violence, gesture and language can work to unmake the self through instituting radical doubt' (Ross, 2003: 71). Violence against women can have so many layers, going to the deepest level of one's self identity.

There is a crucial dichotomy between the attribution of a passive and active agency for women that results in a lose–lose situation for them. The coercive circumstances in which the violations were committed combine women's lack of agency with a self-perception of having an active role with their bodies to save their beloved ones and contribute to independence. In other words, women thought they were active by paying with their bodies, but in reality, they did not have real power over their decisions. They were adolescents and under pressure from members of their families and their wider community. They had a passive agency because of the coercive circumstances. For the politicians, usually male, it is the contrary. Some influential male politicians I interviewed stated that these women were active agents in becoming mistresses to the Indonesians, but they also saw those women as passive since they did not actively contribute to the resistance as other women did, and therefore they did not deserve the support of the new state; for example, they could not apply for reparations as victims of the conflict. Using this logic, women's failure to resist led to their further denigration. This is the narrative that became common in times of peace, leading to the denial of women's agency and role. As a result, there was neither follow-up to the situation of these women, nor did they receive any support for the children who were the result of the sexual violence. Instead of

[21] In Court, women covered their faces so as to protect their identity to ensure their safety and prevent discrimination against them. After they won the case, they eventually removed their mantas from their faces (Gilmore, Guillerot and Sandoval 2020: 46). For an account of the trial see J-M Burt (2019).

recognising the totality of the harms they suffered (*cf* Denov and Drumbl, 2020: 368), women, living in poverty, felt they were rewarded with discrimination and abandonment. They may have become bothersome, of no interest. The state acts as if they were already in limbo, dead. As one woman in Dili said, 'They are waiting for us to die'.[22]

This section ends by highlighting the extent of silence about reproductive rights violations. A large number of women had children born out of rape. A case of a woman in Viqueque who was gang-raped by the Indonesians was illustrative of this fact. She was alone because her husband was in the mountains with the resistance. This woman told me that she had several children with her husband. When I asked if she got pregnant from the Indonesians, she said yes, but that that specific child had died.[23] I also interviewed five women who went through forced pregnancy, forced contraception and forced abortion. Women who suffered sexual violence mentioned how they were forced to have an abortion and given medicines to avoid them getting pregnant, including injections and herbal remedies. A woman from Los Palos, who was raped over several years, told me how that she was forced to have four abortions and take substances to avoid becoming pregnant. After independence, the woman insisted that her main frustration was that after taking unknown substances over such a long time, in addition to having lost so many years of her life and already being old, she was not going to be able to conceive a child. She was thus concerned about her loss of reproductive capacity resulting from torture and sexual violence, which can be considered a differentiated impact of these violations. 'I asked God', she said, and he gave her the gift she desired.[24] She became a mother. Because transitional justice was blind to violations of a reproductive nature, she had to rely on divine justice.

I could not stop wondering where these men were getting these contraceptives until I found that Indonesia had implemented a National Programme of Family Planning (KB) on its territory. Because of the conflict in Timor-Leste and the rejection of the programme by the local women, for a variety of reasons including distrust and religion, the Indonesian state involved the military in its promotion at the village level and it was in particular mandatory for those women whose Timorese husbands were public servants (Post-CAVR 2008: 33, 50). As a result, the programme was developed directly by the commander, with contraceptives sent by the central government, and women who did not give genuine consent, could be required to take them for as much as 15 years without pause (Post-CAVR 2008: 50). It has been reported that up to 62 per cent of family planning used was injectable, a long-lasting contraceptive called *Depo-Provera* (Cristalis and Scott 2005: 38).[25] Women were

[22] Interview with Participant 34, Dili, Timor-Leste, 27 February 2017.
[23] Interview with Participant 30, Viqueque, Timor-Leste, 03 February 2017.
[24] Interview with Participant 55, Los Palos, Lautém, Timor-Leste, 12 January 2017.
[25] In Apartheid South Africa, according to some estimates 80% of black women in rural areas were also given *Depo-Provera* as a form of contraception despite studies showing its connection to a health risk (Cock 1991: 36).

told that the injections were a type of vaccine, and the general atmosphere of distrust and lack of transparency deterred women from attending clinics (Cristalis and Scott 2005: 38). They may have had good reasons. Cristalis and Scott (2005: 38) argue that many Timorese women may have been forcibly sterilised in the 1980s.

In 2018, an exhibition in Baucau recalled the family planning programme that was implemented in Timor-Leste by the Indonesian authorities. The programme had the support of the World Bank and the Ford Foundation and it included '(a) distributing contraceptive pills at random, without instruction on their use; (b) injecting people, without any explanation regarding the purpose of such injections; (c) sterilising people without their prior consent, or knowledge'.[26] Timor-Leste being so small, there may be strong grounds to believe that the contraceptives provided during this family planning programme, supported by international organisations, may have been used to facilitate and exacerbate the sexual violence against women during the Indonesian occupation. This leads us to think about the complicity of international humanitarian aid actors in the commission of crimes.[27] Jackson (2019) recognises the moral dilemmas these actors face on the ground but in contrast to prosecutorial discretion – which in practice means that their complicity has not been explored by international criminal tribunals – he proposes 'a defence of necessity'. In other words, international humanitarian actors should justify why specific measures needed to be implemented.

Finally, silence can also be a personal decision. A woman in Claco who was forced into sexual slavery said: 'I knew many women who suffered from sexual violence during the war, but they don't want to talk because they are ashamed to tell their story. Some of them say what happened happened'.[28] In this regard, Parpart and Parashar argue that

> silence can be a coping mechanism, a choice, an action that can help deal with toxic and often dangerous situations … an essential survival strategy, a comfort and a crucial mechanism for dealing with hostile and often dangerous environments. (Parpart and Parashar 2019: 5)

It took many decades, for instance, to hear the personal narratives of the Holocaust survivors (Coulter, 2009: 23). In *Eichmann in Jerusalem*, Arendt (2006b: 8) describes how during the 1961 trial of Eichmann, the courtroom was filled with survivors, who 'knew by heart all there was to know' and 'listened in public to stories they would hardly have been able to endure in private …'. This was 15 years after the end of the war. Similarly in Cambodia, after decades of silence, a growing number of survivors are now challenging the stigma around

[26] This information was extracted from an exhibition at Baucau Convention Center called 'A Nossa Vitoria e apenas questão de tempo', August 2018. Source cited: Cover of the Second Pastoral Letter issued by Dom Ximenes Belo on Family Planning, 3 March 1985.

[27] MacKinnon (2017: 175) mentions that sex trafficking in India increased by 300% when Bill Gates spent thirty million on providing condoms in the sub-continent.

[28] Interview with Participant 20, Claco, Manufahi, Timor-Leste, 17 January 2017.

sexual violence by speaking out about their experiences of forced marriage, rape and sexual abuse under the Khmer Rouge and revealing the hidden dimensions of their suffering, which continues to have an impact on Cambodian society (WSD Handa Center for Human Rights and International Justice, 2017). As Arendt (2006a: 183) argues, people may have human shields that can take many years to fall away. But if the trials concerning the violations committed during the Second World War are considered to be the modern genesis of transitional justice, why is it then that today we create justice processes in which people who do not talk immediately about their violations are considered to be outside the system? Where is the understanding of silence as a way of expression? Is this the consequence of the widespread mechanisation of transitional justice? Silence as a personal choice may also be ignored by transitional justice mechanisms.

This leads us to think that although experiences can be drowned and erased by dominant single narratives, public perceptions can also change through the years. Curiously, by calling for the recovery and reclamation of the 'revolutionary spirit', Arendt places a lot of emphasis on storytelling, and the judgment of the spectator, so we keep alive 'the lost treasure', that truth that is always in danger of being lost through forgetfulness (Bernstein, 1986: 125, 127). This is why in this section I focus on women's silence. The question is still why numerous women who went through horrendous experiences did not participate in the transitional justice mechanisms that were available to them.

III. ON MEMORY: HYPER-MASCULINISATION OF SOCIETY AND NATIONAL IDENTITY

If some experiences of Timorese women have been silenced, what is in the memory of the country today? Gluck (2007) defines three types of memory in relation to a conflict: the first one, official memory, in which the governments have a role in defining history; a second one, vernacular memory, which is often constituted by collective accounts of the past, and which includes media representations of history; and a third, individual memory, which is based on a personal definition of particular events and how these shape one's identity. According to Gluck, these types of memory intersect with each other. In Timor-Leste, the official memory seems to drown out women's individual memories, while the vernacular memory may be moulded by business elites (eg the broadcasting industry) who are connected to the government and political leaders. Consequently, the official memory, together with the vernacular memory, may thus shape the national identity. And this is important because, as Granville (2012: 375, 383) puts it while studying Russia in the reconstruction of its post-Soviet identity, 'the outcomes of these strategies often depend on what is remembered and how'.

Reflecting how conflicts over contributions to the achievement of independence underpinned the 2006 violence, Leach (2017: 3) claims that the nation-building process in Timor-Leste has been complicated by the focus on the valorisation of the different actors in the independence struggle. However, Cunha (2017: 46) rightly argues that 'contemporary Timorese nationalist discourse is embedded in a profoundly patriarchal vision of virile heroes and warriors'. Cunha (2017: 46) further states that

> women are obfuscated and remain subaltern through a lack of official recognition of their stories of participation in the armed and clandestine resistance struggle. Instead, women have been conferred the status of victim due to their suffering during the war, which results in a loss of agency.

Rothschild (2017: 452) also argues that 'Timor's leaders have promoted a heroic narrative of the past not only to legitimise the state, to gain political support and to "buy the peace," but also to displace an alternative human rights narrative of the past'. Indeed, after the end of the conflict, no one spoke of the single mothers of the 'enemy' children but only of widows and orphans of the resistance (Corcoran-Nantes 2011: 85). Timorese women's experiences of abuse have therefore been considered shameful and hidden (Niner 2011: 49).

Why is it that women's stories were not part of the official narrative used constantly by the male Timorese leadership, in which independence was reached thanks to the bravery and sacrifice of male resistance fighters? Elites need to legitimise themselves. In 2006, for instance, Xanana Gusmão mentioned in a speech that the Timorese living in the eastern part of the country fought more than those on the western side (UN 2006: 20–21). I heard many times how this speech played a role in the violence which erupted in 2006 and in the sudden perceptions of differences between the population of the western and eastern sides of the tiny island. In 2017, 18 years after the end of the conflict, a new alliance of political parties, called Alliance of Change for Progress (AMP), was formed.[29] This alliance was composed of the National Congress for Reconstruction of Timor (CNRT), led by Xanana Gusmão, the People Liberation Party (PLP), led by Taur Matan Ruak, former Falintil commander, and the Party of the Enhancement of Timorese National Unity (KHUNTO), a new political party that counts on great support from youth involved in martial arts groups (Aspinall et al 2018: 161–62). During their political campaign for the parliamentary elections of 2018, they advanced the idea that Timorese independence was reached thanks to the actions of the armed front, downplaying the role of the other fronts.

Ricoeur (2004) refers to three abuses of memory: thwarted or blocked memory, which happens when the state and those in power block certain ways

[29] The alliance would prove to be short – it ceased in January 2020 after failing to pass the annual budget.

of thinking about history; manipulated memory, where events in the past are twisted to serve a particular narrative in the present; and enforced memory, which translates as not only the imposition of a certain understanding of the past, but also the imposition of moral obligations on people because of history. Lemarchand (2008) claims that in the case of Rwanda, the fact that the government tried to blur the lines of division between Hutus and Tutsis and to forget those Hutus who tried to save Tutsis, as well as those violations committed by the Rwandan Patriotic Front (RPF), illustrates the three types of abuses of memory described by Ricoeur.[30]

> This sharing of responsibility is what Rwanda's official ideologues refuse to acknowledge. Instead, every effort is made to manipulate memory, so as to exonerate the ruling elites of all responsibility in the circumstances that led to the abyss (Lemarchand 2008: 70).

Reflecting on the processes of uncovering truth after conflict, Clark (2008: 204) also claims that while some historians and political leaders may use the evidence gathered to serve wider social or political purposes, such as reinterpreting historical events or teaching the population moral lessons, this phenomenon can be abused, 'when elites manipulate evidence to serve self-interested, even corrupt purposes, such as purging history of their own crimes'. In Nepal, both the state and the Maoists committed crimes, including SGBV, during the conflict; however, these crimes were later ignored by the ruling elite in Kathmandu (Human Rights Watch 2014).

The government of Timor-Leste may also be committing all three types of abuses of memory. The CTF between Indonesia and Timor-Leste, for example, compiled information concerning the crimes committed not only by the Indonesians but also by the Timorese resistance.[31] According to a trusted source, the files containing the information concerning crimes committed by the resistance which were located at the Timorese Consulate in Bali, Indonesia, were made to disappear under Xanana's orders.[32] Bali was indeed the city where the CTF report was signed by the representatives of both countries (CTF 2008: xi).

[30] While some scholars argue that gacaca has been a state tool to collectivise the guilt of the Hutu, Clark (2010: 250) claims the contrary: because sentences have been lenient and the government has taught many genocide suspects that previous manipulative elites were primarily responsible for the genocide, this has fuelled many suspects' lack of remorse for their crimes and has proven unsatisfactory for many genocide survivors.

[31] A UN report about the 1999 escalation of violence in Timor-Leste also mentions that 'acts of violence and intimidation by pro-independence groups were also reported in the same period. The Minister of Defence of Indonesia is reported to have stated that until the signing of the ceasefire agreement on 21 April, pro-independence groups had committed 30 violent acts, including 14 armed terrorist attacks, the burning of a village, 2 violent demonstrations, 6 armed attacks against pro-integration groups, 2 armed attacks against the security apparatus, 3 murders and 2 acts of torture against members of pro-integration groups' (UN 1999b: para 27).

[32] According to the UN Impunity Principles (2005), Principle 14 states that 'technical measures and penalties should be applied to prevent any removal, destruction, concealment or falsification of archives, especially for the purpose of ensuring the impunity of perpetrators of violations of human rights and/or humanitarian law'.

The leaders of the resistance are today the leaders of Timor-Leste, and apart from reinforcing the heroes' narratives, it may also be convenient to minimise any possibility of criminal responsibility after the conflict. This may also partially explain why the government's focus has been on the narrative of forgetting the past and portraying itself, together with the Indonesian government, as a model of reconciliation. It may also explain why the government stopped engaging with transitional justice mechanisms years after independence.

The issue at stake is that within this narrative, owing to all these political manoeuvres, no position is left for women's individual memory. I am referring not only to those women who were in the resistance, mainly the clandestine front, but also to those who participated with their bodies and suffered gross human rights violations. Indeed, if official commemoration ceremonies, museums and memorials, monuments in public spaces, archives and databases are part of memory, in Timor-Leste when people talk about the resistance and its heroes, the public imagery is of a military man with a gun. Hence, the typical memorials built around the country are for military men (*cf* UN 2020: para 112–13). If the construction of these monuments represents a new era, in the case of Timor-Leste it still seems to be entrenched within the armed front composed mainly of men.

Based on her fieldwork about how violence affects everyday life in India, Das (2007: 121) recounts the inability of women 'to find a way of telling their story as part of the story of the nation'. I observed the same in Timor-Leste. The narrative of the history of the country is still founded on patriarchal values that largely ignore women's roles and contributions during the Indonesian occupation. It is true that the Museum of the Resistance has a very small section on women and that there was an exhibition about women in 2017, but their recognition I believe is insufficient. Women's stories still show feelings of pain, humility, anger and resentment and their inability to find a way to express their narratives made me think about the fallacy of regarding them as full members of a community. As Arendt (2006a: 147) argues about the concept of freedom, 'without a politically guaranteed public realm, freedom lacks the worldly space to make its appearance'. In other words, if the end of politics is freedom, Timorese women may have been left in a limbo in the narrative that is shaping the identity of the new state.

There is also an issue concerning the silencing of women and its impact on the '*gerasaun foun*' (new generation). I noticed that although my research assistant and my Timorese housemate were both highly educated and intellectually curious – a young new generation working on women's issues in Timor-Leste – they were neither exposed to, nor knew of, particular historical events such as attacks by the resistance and subsequent reprisals against civilians, and even less of women's stories. My observation was confirmed by Pereira's remark about how young Timorese have a weak grasp of the history of the conflict (Pereira 2017: 123). In a country where the young generation comprises around 70 per cent of the total population, it is worrisome that young Timorese may be unaware of former events that are central to Timor-Leste's history and their socio-political implications. But why are they so unaware? There are still challenges within the education system: there are no Timorese history school materials and no university teaches history. Post-conflict Timorese youth thus cannot rely on their current educational system to obtain a critical account of historical events; on the contrary, they are forced to rely on what the leaders of the state say. In practice this means that there is a risk that future history books will only tell one side of the story: that of those in power which narrates the male sacrifice and bravery in their successful military campaigns.

This reminds me of Haugbolle (2005: 194), who, when talking about the Lebanese young generations that were 'too young to remember or who emigrated and came back only after the war', mentions how their amnesia is a 'reaction to an amnesiac society, which does not let them know the war and has little to offer in terms of visions for the future'. Timorese youth may thus be passively impeded from acquiring a critical approach to history in regard to the effects of the Indonesian occupation on the civilian population, as well as the impact of the attacks committed by the resistance. This is problematic because 'freedom of opinion is a farce unless factual information is guaranteed' (Arendt 2006a: 234). Events and facts that affected women disproportionately may be passively forbidden.

Two further points are worth highlighting. First, it is not surprising that in a country where heroes are those who directly participated in a conflict and where combatant males are exalted in a militarised society, young unemployed males join martial arts groups (Fundasaun Mahein 2019).[33] These secret groups, which allegedly were originated in Indonesia to deal with a growing young, rebellious population, are in part responsible for violence in Timor-Leste today (Rahmani 2020; Fundasaun Mahein 2019).[34] To control them, there was even a proposal by the political party PLP of making military service compulsory for young males.[35] This supposedly progressive party ignored the fact that the leadership and society are already hyper-militarised and that teaching military tactics may worsen the rampant domestic violence in the country. Questioning the gender dynamics of the Apartheid regime in South Africa during its process of militarisation in the eighties, Cock (1991: 233) also stated that

> we have to dismantle the ideology of militarism – the notion that violence is a legitimate solution to conflict … to loosen the connection between militarism and

[33] Based on a labour force study from 2015, 'estimates that each year over 30,000 Timorese will reach working age but only 4,000 new formal sector jobs are being created' (Taur Matan Ruak 2020: 16).

[34] Rahmani (2020) explains that through these groups, Indonesia tried (a) to instill discipline in young people and inculcate them with patriotic feelings toward Indonesia, so (b) they could serve as pro-Indonesian militias carrying out punitive attacks or informing on Timorese independence supporters.

[35] According to Enloe (2004: 219), militarism is an ideology whose core beliefs are '(a) that armed force is the ultimate resolver of tensions; (b) that human nature is prone to conflict; (c) that having enemies is a natural condition; (d) that hierarchical relations produce effective action; (e) that a state without a military is naive, scarcely modern, and barely legitimate; (f) that in times of crisis those who are feminine need armed protection; and (g) that in times of crisis any man who refuses to engage in armed violent action is jeopardizing his own status as a manly man'.

> masculinity; to eradicate the notion that aggression and violence are acceptable forms of manly behaviour.

She further observed how 'military training involves a kind of social programming that teaches unquestioning obedience. In war men become sheep, not wolves. They follow and obey' (Cock 1991: 91).

This takes me to my second point. Since it is only recently that those highly educated Timorese youths have been entering politics, it is important that young generations embark on policy making with the ability to think critically about past events. Haugbolle (2005: 194) argues that the young Lebanese feel they are in a waiting position, referring to old generations in power, and I think this may be equally applicable to Timorese youth. It is important that the young Timorese should be aware of what Arendt calls factual truth – the truth that we cannot change – because a failure to remember is a failure to understand (Arendt 2016: 219; 2006a: 227, 259). The social and political are inter-related and, in a post-conflict situation, we may not see through this.

In the memory and forgetting debate, another question arises: how much memory is necessary for a society to move on? Forgetting is not the same as oblivion.

> Forgetting can sometimes be the only way to overcome divisions, for example, in post-conflict contexts. But oblivion can also stem from the sheer irrelevance of the past, and events that used to be part of the collective memory can disappear (perhaps to reappear later) (Haugbolle 2005: 197).

Forgetting means therefore to acknowledge the past. Arendt (2006a: 5, 10) also contrasts oblivion with the failure of memory, because for her, not only the future but also the past is a force. How is this relevant to the case of Timorese women? If Timor-Leste is a new state governed by former members of its resistance, we need to be aware not only that conflicts and wars are gendered and dominated by discourses of masculinity, but also that patriarchy surfaces within nationalist movements (Enloe 2014). As Balibar (1991: 102) puts it, 'nationalism has a secret affinity with sexism'. Hence, if women's access to justice is to be guaranteed, we need to understand 'how patriarchy, militarism and nationalism ... interact to produce gendered identities and experiences that are inimical to women in conflicts and transitions' (Reilly 2009: 97). The dominant narrative of the new state along with its memorials around the territory promote a hyper-masculine warrior identity by seeing the veterans as the heroes of the past while silencing their crimes and ignoring women's contributions to independence and their particular sufferings in the conflict. Transitional justice can therefore be used as a tool to promote specific narratives, while hiding others.

The danger is that specific narratives by those in power can delete factual truths, deform reality and be used to rewrite history. A woman from Aileu wisely said, 'We wait for too long until we forget that we are waiting, we just wait and wait until we forget.'[36] Within this logic, this may explain why the Timorese

[36] Interview with Participant 51, Aileu, Aileu, Timor-Leste, 20 January 2017.

national police continued to interpret the Law on Freedom of Assembly and Demonstration as requiring the organisers of a demonstration to obtain a permit, while banning a number of peaceful gatherings – not surprisingly those linked to demands for accountability for past crimes as well as those linked to corruption of public officials (OHCHR 2016b: para 49).[37] Arendt, in this regard, is disturbed by the fact that even in fully democratic conditions, because of the self-assurance and arrogance of those in power, the more people they have convinced, the more likely it is that they will end by conceiving their own misrepresentations and opinions as facts (Arendt 2006a: 251; 1972: 34–39). What was originally a hypothesis will turn into a fact and it will then be more difficult to convince people in the future of factual realities (Arendt 2006a: 87–88). In other words, history can be changed by men's actions. Consequently, 'the chances of factual truth surviving the onslaught of power are very slim indeed; it is always in danger of being maneuvered out of the world not only for a time but, potentially, forever' (Arendt 2006a: 227). This is important because 'truth that can be relied on disappears entirely from public life, and with it the chief stabilizing factor in the ever-changing affairs of men' (Arendt 1972: 7). No wonder that history has been written by men.

But women are still resisting through story-telling. Loney (2014: 65) claims that Timorese women use their memories to assert a space for themselves within a masculine narrative that emphasises the role of the guerrilla fighters and in which women are largely absent. Reflecting on memory, Arendt (2016: 222) also argues that 'experiences and even the stories which grow out of what men do and endure, of happenings and events, sink back into the futility inherent in the living deed unless they are talked about over and over again'. She continues,

> what saves the affairs of mortal men from their inherent futility is nothing but this incessant talk about them, which in its turn remains futile unless certain concepts, certain guideposts for future remembrance, and even for sheer reference, arise out of it (Arendt 2016: 222).

This is why, with Coulter (2009: 23), I prefer to exchange nationalistic celebrations of national heroes for women's personal stories. For me this means the applicability of intersectionality on memory, since 'placing those who currently are marginalized in the center is the most effective way to resist efforts to compartmentalize experiences and undermine potential collective action' (Crenshaw 1989: 167). It is thus the silencing that led to women's invisibility and discrimination against them: the lack of participation and recognition of women during

[37] *cf* Timorese Law No 1/2006. On 5 October 2021, the National Parliament passed an amendment to Law No. 5/2016 on the Establishment of Procedures for Pardons and Commutation of Sentences. JSMP (2021) shows its disappointment that with this amendment the President can exercise his competence to make it possible for crimes of corruption and other serious crimes to be pardoned and for sentences to be commuted.

transitional justice mechanisms. This not only has an impact on what is collectively remembered about women's experiences and roles in Timor-Leste today, but it also perpetuates women's violations after the conflict finishes.

IV. THE CONTINUUM OF VIOLATIONS AGAINST WOMEN

Transitional justice may set the basis for the new beginning of the state. Arendt builds on St. Augustine's idea of new beginning, to reflect on how nativity represents a new beginning in the world: the rupture of the past to initiate a new political beginning where plurality arises and everyone treats each other as equals (Arendt 2017: 629; 1998: 9). However, the new beginning of the state can also go wrong. Arendt highlights the danger that politicians by using manipulation, rather than persuasion, may destroy public freedom. Her concept of public freedom is based on 'a genuine recognition of plurality – where variable opinions, judgments, and persuasions are manifest – a politics which excludes any violence and coercion' (Bernstein 1986: 119). If that plurality is at risk, cycles of violence may break out again. When there is then a new opportunity for restructuring the post-conflict state, we may start seeing how public and private dynamics interfere in the new ladders of power, which lead to the perpetuation of the position of women as second-class citizens. If women are silenced during the transitional justice process, crimes committed against them, particularly those of a sexual nature, may therefore remain taboo, invisible, and even worse, be normalised, once the conflict is over. Because there is a lack of attention to continuums of violence, which reinforces inequalities (Ní Aoláin and Valji 2019: 57), this section explores therefore the continuum of women's violations from conflict to times of 'peace', whatever peace means.

As established by the CEDAW Committee, gender-based violence against women manifests itself in a continuum of multiple, interrelated and recurring forms, and in a range of settings (GR 35 2017: para 6). In this regard, several scholars have studied how violence against women in conflict, including sexual violence, is a reflection of patterns that occur in peacetime and how there is a continuum of that violence from conflict to peace (*cf* Cockburn 2004). Chinkin and Kaldor (2013: 180), for instance, observe that a lack of recognition of women and the impunity for the perpetrators leads to the normalisation of violence in times of peace, as shown for instance, by the high incidence of domestic violence. Others have focused on what happens when combatants return to their homes and the continuum of the violence moves to the private sphere. MacKinnon (2006: 185) claims that:

> when the army comes back, it visits on the women at home the escalated level of assault the men were taught and practiced on women in the war zone. The United States knows this well from the war in Vietnam. Men's domestic violence against women escalated – including their skill at inflicting torture without leaving visible marks.

Similarly, CEDAW GR 30 (2013: 34) on women in conflict states that 'conflicts exacerbate existing gender inequalities, placing women at a heightened risk of various forms of gender-based violence by both State and non-State actors'. Connecting discrimination and violence against women in a continuum, the Committee (GR 30 2013: 74) further states that:

> All barriers faced by women in accessing justice before the national courts prior to the conflict, such as legal, procedural, institutional, social and practical, and entrenched gender discrimination are exacerbated during conflict, persist during the post-conflict period and operate alongside the breakdown of the police and judicial structures to deny or hinder their access to justice.

This happens:

> when States have neglected to take measures during peacetime, to: a) overcome power imbalances and inequalities based on gender roles and discrimination against women and girls; b) ensure a conducive environment where women and girls have access and non-discriminatory exercise of their human rights, including in relation to employment, education, health (e.g. sexual and reproductive health and rights), access to land and natural resources, freedom of expression, association and assembly, and can freely develop their personal abilities, pursue their professional careers and make choices without the limitations set by stereotypes, rigid gender roles and prejudices; c) ensure accountability for violations of women's human rights, including GBV (OHCHR 2018: 39).

In her report on the DRC, the Special Rapporteur on Violence against Women also observes that the scale and the brutality of sexual violence and the fact that civilians are increasingly among the perpetrators of rape indicates a normalisation of the war-related violence (UN 2008a: 106). She cautions that by addressing sexual violence associated with war in isolation, the gender-based discrimination and violence that women encounter in times of 'peace' will be neglected and the war on women reinforced (UN 2008a: 106).[38] In this respect, while international law does not provide a definition of peace, Galtung (1969) argues that negative peace is the absence of armed conflict, while positive peace is about the absence of structural violence (social injustice). Peace therefore is not only a matter of reduction of violence but also about equality, development and the egalitarian distribution of power and resources (Galtung 1969: 183). If women in Timor-Leste suffer from personal and structural violence, they may not be experiencing either negative or positive peace but rather still living in violence (Harris Rimmer 2010). As a result, old and new generations of Timorese women still suffer from different intersectional forms of discrimination, while the state encourages a system that promotes their dependency and marginalisation, failing therefore to comply with guarantees of non-repetition.

[38] The Special Rapporteur also calls for the need of altering gender relations and supporting women's empowerment; if not, high levels of rape will persist (UN 2008a: 101).

When we explore Timorese domestic law, under the UN Administration, the constitution of Timor-Leste, adopted in 2002, guarantees equal rights between men and women. More specifically, Article 6 raises as one of the main objectives of the state (j) 'to promote an effective equality of opportunities between women and men', while Article 17 states that 'women and men have the same rights and duties in all areas of political, economic, social, cultural and family life.' Article 63 is about participation by citizens in political life and it reads (1) 'direct and active participation by men and women in political life constitutes a requirement of, and a fundamental instrument for, the democratic system.' The highest court in Timor-Leste had also recognised the principle of equality and social justice, framed within a protection of economic and social rights and the equality of opportunities (Oliveira, Gomes and dos Santos 2015: 416–17). Except for the Optional Protocol to CAT, the International Convention for the Protection of All Persons from Enforced Disappearance (ICPPED) and the Convention on the Rights of Persons with Disabilities (CRPD),[39] the rest of international human rights treaties, including CEDAW, were ratified by Timor-Leste after independence, between 2003 and 2004.

Although the formal acceptance of these treaties was an important step, there is still a gap between the current status and achieving equality and non-discrimination against women. In this regard, Timor-Leste has been criticised for not having a definition of discrimination against women either in its constitution or in its ordinary legislation because of a decision not to adopt a specific gender equality law (OHCHR 2016a: para 9). While doctrinal lawyers may also feel they accomplished their task once the laws are adopted, the focus on the drafting of the law rather than on the disparities in practice, may contribute to the cycle of violence against women. But even if specific laws that prohibit discrimination against women have not been drafted, there is broad agreement that the principle of non-discrimination has become a *jus cogens* provision, meaning an interpretive norm of international human rights law that does not allow for any provision to the contrary.

Because the situation of Timorese women is far from ideal, the state has failed in its three general obligations to eliminate all forms of discrimination against women: to eliminate direct and indirect discrimination, to improve the de facto position of women in society and to eliminate wrongful forms of gender stereotyping (CEDAW GR 25 2004, para 6-7). The CEDAW Committee in its concluding observations has indeed recommended Timor-Leste 'establish clear procedures for filing complaints about discrimination against women, ensure that effective remedies are available to women whose rights have been violated and impose adequate sanctions for such violations' (CEDAW 2015: para 11(a); GR 33 2015). Moreover, there is still rampant violence against women, including domestic violence and sexual violence, early pregnancy and maternal mortality. Women face greater difficulties in accessing justice, education and land and experience limited participation in political and public life. Timorese women

[39] At the time of the publication of this book (2022), Timor-Leste is in the process of ratifying the CRPD.

may further be excluded from the economic and social benefits designed by the state after the conflict (CEDAW 2015: para 32).

More specifically, violence against women, including domestic violence, remains widespread after the end of the conflict in Timor-Leste (CEDAW 2015: para 16). Already the Chega! report noted that male survivors of detention and torture had fallen into a pattern of violent behaviour (CAVR 2005: 2585). In a study, three in five women aged 15 to 49 (59 per cent) had experienced physical and/or sexual violence by a male partner at least once in their lifetime while 14 per cent of girls and women had been raped by someone other than their partner (The Asia Foundation 2016: 49, 63). A law that criminalises domestic violence was approved in 2010; however, women are still in a vulnerable position owing to issues such as economic dependence, accessibility and delays in the formal judicial system, referral of the cases to the informal justice system, social pressure, a culture of silence, fear of stigmatisation or re-victimisation and the general lack of awareness among women and men (CEDAW 2015: para 16; UNDP 2011).[40] As a consequence, there are very low reporting and conviction rates for cases of domestic and sexual violence against women as well as limited medical, psychological and legal assistance available to them (CEDAW 2015: para 16).

To rebuild the legal infrastructure, the UNTAET initially intended to establish two sets of courts: eight district courts in the different municipalities and a court of appeal.[41] However, they only managed to establish four formal courts in the country – in Dili, Baucau, Suai and Oescussi – the same courts that exist today. As a result, most of the cases go through the traditional customary system, which does not always make decisions that support women (CEDAW 2015: para 10). In the remote village of Claco, in Manufahi, I met Cesaltina Toreção. Cesaltina came to share with me the story of her mother who was sexually assaulted during the Indonesian occupation. Cesaltina was at the market one day, when she was informed by a neighbour that she was not the daughter of her father but of an Indonesian. When Cesaltina finished telling the story of her mother, she asked immediately for help to resolve her current situation. She said that she had five children but because of the physical and psychological violence inflicted by her husband, she had decided to separate from him. They went through the traditional system and it was decided that the 'maternal line' should be cut out from the children's lineage. 'At least if they could allow me to see them', she said.[42] Not only did the traditional system not take into account the violence committed against her, but following their customary practices, in case of a divorce the custody of the children remained within the father's lineage. This illustrates the continuum of the violence and discrimination against different generations of women in the same family.

[40] CEDAW has stated that under no circumstance should cases of violence against women, including domestic violence, be referred to any alternative dispute resolution procedure, eg mediation and conciliation (GR 33 2015: paras 56, 58(c); GR 35 2017: para 45).

[41] UNTAET Regulation 2000/11.

[42] Interview with Participant 17, Claco, Manufahi, Timor-Leste, 17 January 2017.

While travelling in the municipalities, I was also warned about the continuation of cases of sexual violence, particularly cases of sexual abuse against children, including incest, and how their disclosure was taboo in the communities. This is in line with the concerns of the Committee on the Rights of the Child (CRC) about the widespread sexual abuse of children in Timor-Leste, including incest (2015: para 36; *cf* US Department of State 2021). Few cases of violence and even fewer cases of sexual abuse against children go to court because the law places primary responsibility on parents to initiate proceedings in cases of sexual abuse for a child under 15 years of age, practically trapping the child when the alleged offender is a parent (OHCHR 2016b: para 30). Moreover, during my interviews I heard about cases of marital rape, including from a well-educated woman in Dili whose father was a local leader who was himself a victim of enforced disappearance in 1999. The government is nevertheless reluctant to criminalise incest as well as marital rape as specific offences in the Criminal Code (CAT 2017: para 32; CEDAW 2015: para 16). In other words, we are talking about widespread sexual violence in conflict continuing on to widespread sexual abuse in times of 'peace'.

The new generation of Timorese girls and women – at all levels of society – are also being affected disproportionately by early pregnancy and their lack of access to reproductive rights and education. The teenage pregnancy rate is 24 per cent and nearly one in four girls and young women have had a child before the age of 20 (Plan International 2017). Among the group aged 15–19 years, 50 per cent already have more than one child (Plan International 2017). Moreover,

> the risks of health complications related to teenage pregnancy are extremely high, and maternal mortality rates in 15–19 years old are 1,037 per 100,000 live births, meaning they are twice as likely to die as older women (Plan International 2017).

This contributes not only to a high rate of child marriage in the country – 19 per cent of young women between 20–24 years old have married before 18 – but also to girls dropping out of school (UNFPA 2017: 4; US Department of State 2021). This is not only due to their new personal situation but also to the fact that girls who get pregnant may not be accepted by their schools to resume their studies. In addition to early pregnancy, gender-based violence and the lack of adequate sanitation and sanitary supplies for those who reach puberty are causing the rate of school drop-out among girls to remain very high at almost 50 per cent between the primary and secondary levels, especially in rural areas (CEDAW 2015: para 26). The lower level of education, cultural norms and stereotypes put women in a disadvantaged position when pursuing job opportunities in Timor-Leste (US Department of State 2018: 21).[43] Moreover, although there are allegations that discrimination against women is common throughout the

[43] See CRC GC 20 (2016: paras 26–27) and CEDAW GR 36 (2017) on the right of girls and women to education.

government, cases go unaddressed, while the rights at work of pregnant women are not protected (US Department of State 2021).

In a society where there is a hyper-masculinisation as well as very conservative Catholic views – 98 per cent of the population is Catholic – it is still taboo to speak about contraceptive methods. In 2017, for instance, the then Minister of Health made a decision not to promote in its HIV/AIDS campaign the 'C method' (use of condoms) to the general public – with the exception of those considered to be 'at risk' such as gays and prostitutes (and even for them, condoms were limited to existing stocks).[44] The same former minister also presented as a family planning proposal the 'Billings method', a natural technique that encourages women to identify their fertility patterns by examining the appearance of vaginal discharge as the leading form of contraception, while access to other forms of contraception would be granted only to those who were married (Plan International 2017). Although her proposal was rejected by civil society, in practice not only do women get denied access to condoms or a reproductive health adviser to explain contraceptive choices to them when they go to a rural clinic, but there are also instances where women are asked where their husbands are before they are provided with help.[45] With the exception of situations in which it is necessary to protect the life of the mother, abortion is a criminal offence in all other cases, including those in which a pregnancy could result in a woman experiencing severe pain and suffering, such as those related to rape, incest or severe fetal impairment (CAT 2017: para 34).[46] Timorese women's access to reproductive rights is therefore denied according to the stereotype that they are incapable of making healthcare decisions in their own interests. This shows more deeply not only women's subordination in their families and societies, but also the denial of their intellectual capacities and moral agency and the effects of their lack of recognition in their access to the distribution of health services (Cook and Cusack 2010: 12, 59).[47]

The Timorese women who suffered sexual violence committed during the Indonesian rule also 'continue to experience social stigma and ostracism, resulting in feelings of shame, and have limited access to medical, psychological, reproductive and mental health services or treatment' (CEDAW 2015: para 18). Women who participated in the interviews described, for instance,

[44] 'Unavailability of goods and services due to ideologically based policies or practices ... must not be a barrier to accessing services' (CESCR GC 22: para 14).

[45] CEDAW requires that states should report on the measures to eliminate barriers that women face to healthcare, including 'requirements or conditions that prejudice women's access, such as high fees for health-care services, the requirement for preliminary authorization by spouse, parent or hospital authorities, distance from health facilities and the absence of convenient and affordable public transport' (GR 24 1999: para 21). See also CESCR GC 22 on the right to sexual and reproductive health (2016).

[46] 'criminalisation of abortion, denial or delay of safe abortion and post-abortion care ... are forms of gender-based violence that, depending on the circumstances, may amount to torture or cruel, inhuman or degrading treatment' (CEDAW GR 35 2017: para 18).

[47] *Melleh v Ireland*, CCPR Com No 2324/2013; *LC v Peru*, CEDAW, Com No 22/2009.

how members of their communities could mistreat them today. A woman in Claco recounted how some men invaded her land and, when she protested, they told her to 'shut up' because she had been a 'mistress of the *bapas*'.[48] Men therefore can take advantage of women's former violations and deepen women's stigmatisation for their own benefit. Access to land is of utmost importance to ensure economic and social rights.[49] As Banda (2012: 374–75) observes, the lack of rights to land makes women extremely vulnerable to poverty and eviction and negatively affects their economic options and food security.

In Timor-Leste, a new law that regulates land manifests 'equality between women and men' and prohibits 'any discrimination in respect to ownership, acquisition, management, administration, enjoyment, transfer and disposition'.[50] However, in practice rural women have 'limited access to decision-making processes concerning the use of land' and traditional inheritance systems continue to exclude women from land ownership (US Department of State 2021; OHCHR 2016a: 37, 88).[51] When husbands die, women have no right to land. Moreover, according to Cummins, while in patrilineal areas land passes to the sons because women are expected to get married and leave the family, in matrilineal areas men generally make decisions concerning lands that should pass to daughters (UN Women 2018: 23). In a country where the total population is nearly 70 per cent rural, women's limited access to land affects their economic independence with regard to men. This is complicated by the fact that Timorese women's economic empowerment has not been sufficiently mainstreamed within the state's overall poverty reduction and development strategies and women's access to credit, including microcredit, remains insufficient (CEDAW 2015: para 32(c)). Women's economic dependence on men refuels domestic violence.

As for their political participation, the assignation of quotas for women in parliament has been viewed as a top-down measure to eliminate discrimination against women in political and public life (Wittkopp 2012: 208, 215; CEDAW Art 7; CEDAW GR 23 1997).[52] Following the elections held in May 2018, 33.8 per cent of the Timorese parliament was composed of women, ie 22 out of 65 Members of Parliament (MPs), which made it the 34th country in the world in terms of the presence of women in parliament (IPU 2019). Although this was the result of a law that requires at least one-third of candidates on party lists to be women (CEDAW 2015: para 4), encouraging women's political participation has not been sufficient, since Timorese men still dominate the public sphere. On the other hand, women's representation in government decision-making

[48] Interview with Participant 14, Claco, Manufahi, Timor-Leste, 17 January 2017.
[49] *cf* Almeida (2021).
[50] Law on Lands No 13/2017.
[51] Article 14 of CEDAW and its GR 34 on the rights of rural women.
[52] See CEDAW GR 25 and GR 30 and UNSCR 1325 (WPS Agenda).

positions remains low at 20 per cent, and the proportion of female village chiefs is also extremely low at two per cent (CEDAW 2015: para 23).[53] The fact that women are elected also does not mean that they themselves embrace the equality agenda, but even if they do, this can be drowned out by the decisions of the male party leaders. To reach the full and equal political and public participation of women, substantive and transformative equality have been proposed as ways to break down the barriers to decision-making positions. As Wittkopp (2012: 198, 212) suggests, substantive equality requires that women be given the same possibility to influence the decision-making process and therefore the outcomes in state laws and policies, while transformative equality requires that women's inequality be addressed in access to education and resources and that violence against women be eliminated, all of which impede women's access to political posts.

Following sexual violence and torture, psychological damage and moral injury against Timorese women, there was no emotional support provided to the victims. Women in some cases live close to the men who committed the violations. In a recent study, experiences of intimate partner violence were also found to be significantly associated with negative mental health consequences for women (The Asia Foundation 2016: 97). Data from the Ministry of Health also indicates a rise in the number of cases of mental illness identified from 2,109 between 2004 and 2007 to 3,743 in 2009 (Kakuma et al. 2015: 43). Linking different forms of violence, including GBV, to mental health, the Special Rapporteur on the right to health has stated that good mental health 'requires the creation of enabling environments that value both social connection and respect through non-violent and healthy relationships at the individual and societal levels throughout life' (UN 2019b: paras 87, 89). In contrast, the lack of recognition of the victims by the state may contribute to the continuum of the trauma of the population.

In this respect, I recognise that Christianity and traditional healing practices have played a fundamental role in the treatment of trauma in Timor-Leste today (Barnes et al 2019). Reflecting on the meaning of gender from an African feminist perspective, Banda (2016: 60) argues that 'the impact of colonialism and the spread of foreign religions had all played an important part in forcing an evolution in gender relations'. While both law and religion have their own limits, she sees substantial changes that human rights and religion have brought within African societies as opportunities for positive transformative change (Banda 2016: 60). However, if Timorese politicians and society apply radical interpretations of both Catholicism and customary practices, we may be witnessing the worst of the embrace between the two worlds for women. The relationship of the Timorese with the Catholic Church and traditional

[53] Banda (2012: 373) explains how the CEDAW Committee while interpreting Article 14 (rights of rural women) has emphasised 'the need for States parties to address women's under-representation in community organisations and has called for women's equal representation on villagers' committees'.

practices may indeed be in a process of reinforcement after the end of the conflict. Although Timor-Leste is a secular state, Catholicism became a proxy expression of national identity against Indonesia and has been valorised by the state for its participation in the process of national liberation (Leach 2017: 88, 137). Leach (2021), however, also observes that politicians may have a political interest in recruiting support within the powerful Catholic Church.[54] Hicks (2007: 14), on the other hand, refers to a resurgence of traditions after independence, because under the Indonesian occupation sacred houses, artifacts and other concrete representations of traditional culture were destroyed and people did not have access to them because of displacement and Indonesian centralisation. Trindade and Castro (2007) have also focused on the resurgence of East Timorese culture and traditions and they call for these to be included in peace processes and as tools to strengthen national unity.

The issue is that customary traditions may reinforce traditional hierarchies and discriminatory practices, including the failure to recognise marital rape, domestic violence and shared custody rights of children. Moreover, 'the hierarchy of the Church continues to wield "active" power through its political interventions, particularly in the area of sexual and reproductive health' (Richards 2017: 171). In this connection, Charlesworth (2014) invites us to reflect on who is speaking for culture, religion and tradition and who are the beneficiaries of discriminatory practices. Those who advocate 'traditional' roles for women today incompatible with ideas of gender equity are indeed attempting to enforce a subordinate role for women to ensure their own privileges (Niner 2011: 42). This idea reverts to Galtung (1969: 179), who affirmed that 'when the structure is threatened, those who benefit from structural violence, above all those who are at the top, will try to preserve the status quo so well geared to protect their interests'.

Furthermore, sometimes 'traditions' appear or claim to be old but are often quite recent in origin and sometimes invented (Hobsbawm 1983: 1). Hobsbawm (1983: 1) uses the term 'invented tradition' to define a 'set of practices, normally governed by overtly or tacitly accepted rules and of a ritual or symbolic nature, which seek to inculcate certain values and norms of behaviour by repetition, which automatically implies continuity with the past'. Invented traditions, he continues, 'are responses to novel situations which take the form of reference to old situations, or which establish their own past by quasi-obligatory repetition' (Hobsbawm 1983: 2). Why are these 'invented traditions' important? Because they are highly relevant to the recent historical innovation of the 'nation' and its associated phenomena: 'nationalism, the nation-state, national symbols, histories and the rest' (Hobsbawm 1983: 13).

While Catholicism may be an expression of nationalism as a reaction to Indonesia, the revitalisation of customary beliefs and practices may also be

[54] Controversially, in 2021 Xanana publicly supported Richard Daschbach, a former priest who was defrocked by the Pope due to long-standing cases of sexual abuse against girls (Leach 2021).

an expression against the UN administration and the continuous presence of international actors. We have seen in other cases a revalorisation of traditions after a conflict or the end of colonial periods. Reflecting on the legacy of colonialism in Africa and the subsequent period of nationalism, Mamdani (2001a) suggests that custom was enforced, chiefs were sanctified, while women were silenced, with a view of custom that cannot be changed but that in reality reinforces a domestic authoritarianism as an authentic tradition. Similarly, Banda (2005: 19) claims that after the independence of African countries there was a romanticised notion of restoring 'customary law' and 'African culture' to their former glory. However, women were not served by the version of customary law that took form after colonialism: instead of being a dynamic and flexible version of the custom of pre-colonial years, it was the 'court/state/man manufactured hand-me-down of the colonial era' (Banda 2005: 19–23). When we look at the history of Timor-Leste, the territory was organised into several traditional kingdoms before the Portuguese arrival. The different '*liurai*' (local kings) had more power than village chiefs, but the Portuguese relied on the latter to serve their own interests (Leach 2017: 227). If we wear post-colonial lenses, the narrative being imposed on the country should also recognise the stories of Timorese queens during the Portuguese colony and how after the 1890s, indigenous political authority became a male affair (Hägerdal and Krammen 2017: 18–19).

In a country where the construction of national identity is ongoing, I was struck by how men from different strata in society relate to women. I hear that a common practice by some '*ema boot*', meaning top and powerful people, who are mainly politicians, is to have several women. Indeed, they marry one woman and have other mistresses, some of them living in Bali, and the men cover their expenses. The mistresses/concubines are called '*feto kiik*' (small woman), '*feen ki'ik*' (little wife) or '*cama rua*' (second bed). In a conversation with a current minister, he showed his concern that this practice could have an effect on corruption among politicians since they become financially responsible for several homes. I was also struck by the widespread sexual harassment by males in the streets of Dili. When I arrived in Dili, I was advised that women could not go running because (a) men could masturbate in front of them, or (b) men could come and grab women's intimate parts. At first, I suspected that this was an exaggeration by foreigners, until I started hearing episodes that happened to close friends. It then happened to me at 3 pm on a weekday next to the National Parliament in central Dili. When I reported my incident to the policemen, my case was disregarded by the police because I did not know the perpetrator and they could not send the case to the prosecutor's office.

We may be observing a correlation between the hyper-masculinisation and militarisation of society on the one hand, and women's violations and current status on the other. Coulter (2009: 133–34) argues that war rape was 'part of a culture among the combatants that had resonance within the larger Sierra Leonean society, a setting in which masculinity, to some extent, was defined through multiple sexual relationships', while Utas (2005: 418) mentions that during the war in Liberia, rape was related to 'a celebration of a hyper-masculine warrior identity'. In the case of harassment by males, while some people may think that this is an amusement for young boys and therefore not of great importance, this personal experience made me reflect on three issues concerning women's access to transitional justice. First, telling an intimate story that concerns a feeling of shame several times and seeing that those responsible for enforcing the law do not take the incident seriously may be very frustrating, if not, re-traumatising. Second, despite all the international investment and work on gender mainstreaming with the police, this small incident shows how officers may still err in legal procedures concerning the admissibility of cases of a gender nature (*cf* UNDP 2013). Third, it is also of concern how this normalisation of violence causes women, both foreigners and Timorese, to restrict their freedom of movement because of fear, and that top politicians do not strongly take a stand against it. The next section is about what kind of justice women want after experiencing a conflict and their views on the issues that they struggled to resolve and for which they wished to receive support.

V. WHAT WOMEN WANT

After my interviews in several of the municipalities of Timor-Leste, I realised that what women were offered by the domestic application of transitional justice was very different from the women's definitions and notions of justice. When I asked women how they envisage justice, rather than talking about prosecutions or truth commissions, they had a tendency to focus on economic and social rights and on the recognition of their experiences. Some women considered that perpetrators should be brought to justice, but women mentioned more uniformly that they see justice as education for them and their children, housing, having a job and learning a skill, access to and protection of their lands, and even birth certificates. They not only connected justice with development, but also made a connection between what happened to them and their current situation 20 years approximately after the end of the conflict. Women also look for a space, for an acknowledgement of their violations and their roles during the Indonesian occupation.

More specifically, women said that they would like to have access to education and/or receive capacity-building so they could learn a skill, an activity. They dream about work opportunities to become self-sufficient and sustain their lives. They also mentioned frequently having a kiosk, which highlights the importance of this occupation in the community, a way of generating an income but that also allows access to independence and information. We have seen some intent from the international community to support skills training and income-generation programmes for women. For instance, in other post-conflict situations, women were taught hairdressing and soap making, but there is a limit to the feasible number of hairdressers or soap makers in a village, particularly when there is not much local demand. Coulter (2009: 188, 206) argues that in the case of Sierra Leone, only a few types of skills training were offered to the women, for them to become gara tie-dyers (traditional textiles), tailors, hairdressers and soap makers, which were not only skills that offered little economic gain, but also activities that could not all be absorbed by the local small economy. I agree with Coulter (2009: 192, 206) when she says that while projects and training can make women more self-confident and cope better with society, we cannot rely on skills that radically exceed demand and on projects that are not economically viable.

Solutions may depend on the immediate flux of money from donors, who may be more interested in a quick fix and indicators that look good, rather than in long-term sustainability. The fallacy behind that approach is that 'how indicators are named and who decides what they represent are fundamental to the way an indicator produces knowledge' (Merry 2011: S84). Merry (2011: S83) notes that the use of indicators for good governance produces an 'objective knowledge' that requires technical expertise to measure and count people, but that does not take into account political debate, context or history. Moreover, in times where everything is measurable and indicators have become the basis for calculating efficiency, the risk is that indicators become easy to manipulate and inflate by employees who need to justify their positions.[55] This has an impact in a post-conflict situation.

In Timor-Leste after the conflict, the creation of women's cooperatives and income-generation activities were supported. In fact, the majority of the women I talked to in the different villages were part of the cooperatives that ACbit still supports today. They knitted together while waiting to talk to me and also showed me proudly the products that they make together – the traditional woolen garments called *tais*. However, I noticed that there was no commercial demand for their products. This may not be new and the Nove-Nove is an example. This is a women's group composed mainly of widows and named after the date they lost their husbands in the ninth month of 1999 (AJAR 2015: 235). The Nove-Nove received international support from the UK's Department for International Development (DFID) to form a cooperative in the market of Maliana, Bobonaro, together with the provision of three tractors to help with farming and training in skills such as sewing (Hunt 2017: 70). An evaluation in 2002 found that some of the activities envisaged were not successful given that funds were provided without sufficient preparation to the mostly illiterate women with no experience of running an organisation or project, and as a result the 'relatively self-sufficient women quickly became dependent on aid funds' (Hunt 2017: 70). Wandita, Campbell-Nelson and Pereira (2006: 297) also argued in 2006 that these widows' groups 'were hampered by continuing

[55] *cf* the 'false positives' scandal in Colombia, where the military executed thousands of innocent civilians in the mid-2000s to inflate the body count of 'guerrilla members killed in battle'.

problems related to the basic running of the organisation, lack of resources and internal conflicts'. Once international support goes away, their activities become unsustainable.

But better to have a room of one's own. Many women who managed to obtain the veterans' pension explained to me their decision not to marry because they wanted to have power of decision over their own income. The issue is how to support the cooperatives and activities in a sustainable way so that there is a real feeling of empowerment rather than an artificial one. Finally, they may not be financially successful, but I found their cooperatives empowering in other ways. Not only do they give them a clear sense of camaraderie, belonging and support, but they also are a source of information about public policies, about the state and their rights.[56] They work as a network where women can share and make visible their experiences and demands. I see these groups as a tool of consciousness and solidarity that makes women aware of their rights and makes them act in concert to face their invisibility and silence so they can demand recognition.

Two connected points require some elaboration. First, while we focus on the past and overlook sexual violence, we may lose the point that is the most important for my respondents, what allows them to be empowered and to transform their lives. Perhaps, instead of activities where they visit the places where the violations happened and bring back traumatic events over and over again, which are connected to the western idea that talking is healing, it is better, as the women requested, to learn a skill, an activity that is sustainable. As Clark (2008: 200) argues, 'trauma may also stem from material deprivation resulting from conflict'. Second, studies have shown that the best way to deal with mental health issues is to have something to do, to have a sense of purpose, a future orientation (DeLargy 2013: 67).[57] The connection between women contributing to their own development and the development of the nation leads us to think about the imbalance between the lawyers' focus on prosecutions and public policy makers' focus on development, and about how the latter should also be part of justice for victims.

Some of the women also mentioned how after the sexual violence, they had intimate health problems. They also referred to the use of contraceptive methods which they feared would prevent them from conceiving after the conflict. This made me think how we have cases of sexual slavery, forced marriage, rape (including gang rape) where women did not receive any appropriate healthcare. Women may end with sexual diseases, problems with pregnancy, infertility, vaginal problems, incontinence and other serious reproductive injuries that resulted from sexual violence, forced and irregular contraception and/or unsafe abortions. These violations are not always visible and may have

[56] Article 14 of CEDAW and its GR 34 (2016) recognise the importance of cooperatives for the protection of women's rights.

[57] DeLargy (2013) cites Hobfoll et al (2007).

effects in the long-term. It is thus of great concern that after a conflict, widespread medical intervention, particularly focusing on gynaecological and reproductive health is not provided. The absence of these programmes reinforces the denial of women's sexual agency. This is about thinking of the impact of sexual violence on health and framing justice through rehabilitation, medical and psychological care as well as social services.

While one of the main wishes of the women is to have a house, there is a link to their lack of recognition. The state provides funds to NGOs to build houses for people in vulnerability. The issue at stake is that the state may be hiding behind these NGOs in order to remain silent about who these people are, many of them women victims and thus rights-holders. The right to housing should be framed within a public policy that encompasses the official recognition by the state of the situation of many of these women. This takes me to my next point. Although some feminists reject the idea of connecting women and children because it ostensibly reinforces the stereotype of women as mothers and carers only, the reality is that after a conflict we are in the presence of women who are left alone in charge of several children born of rape and in a situation of abandonment. Timorese women mentioned their personal struggle of being responsible for their children with few resources and their desire to give them an education.[58] Some of their children also have disabilities. By leaving these women alone, the state and international community render meaningless the best interests of the child, the guiding principle enshrined in Article 3 of the CRC and in the laws of many domestic jurisdictions. We have seen similar cases of child abandonment in other conflicts.

In the case of Nepal, there was a lack of acknowledgement and support for children born from SGBV (What Works 2018: 58). Neither has the UN carried out any follow-up on the children fathered by their own peacekeeping forces, including after the scandals of sexual violence, for instance in Haiti. But also, children born out of sexual violence are a symbol of the violence and discrimination against women and how this may have an effect on them in the long-term. For instance, it is only recently, more than 25 years after the genocide in Rwanda, that we are talking about the intergenerational discrimination against the children of those Hutus who were *génocidaires* and of those who were born of sexual violence (Torgovnik 2019). Not only should children born of rape be recognised as autonomous victims (UN 2020: para 28), but by not recognising the complexity of the situation of these women and their children, the state may reinforce the discrimination against them.

This takes me to what seems to be a more practical point but which in reality has to do with a fundamental human right, the right to an identity and nationality. Women who had children by the Indonesians mentioned their struggle to obtain birth certificates for their children. The birth certificates used to be

[58] *cf* ACERWC, *Michelo Hunsungule and Others (on behalf of children in Northern Uganda) v Uganda*, Decision, Communication No 1/2005, 15–19 April 2013, para 71.

controlled by the Catholic Church, so a requirement was to have the name of the father.[59] Since many of these women were gang-raped during the course of several years, they did not know the name of the fathers of their children. Some of them spent years trying to regularise the situation of their children, travelling from one village to another one, looking for someone to help them resolve a fundamental right which is the right to have an identity.[60] The CRC Committee found that those Timorese children who are not in possession of a baptism certificate face discrimination in their access to education and other services.[61] We are talking about women as second-class citizens producing stateless children and the perpetuation of the cycle of violence, intersectional forms of discrimination and social exclusion.

Corcoran-Nantes (2011: 85) found that people wanted to 'move on' with their lives and that for practical reasons both in the present and the future, they would abandon any recognition of 'unusual times'. With very few exceptions, women told me the contrary. Women wanted their experiences during the years of the Indonesian occupation to be recognised: the violations they endured and their work as part of the resistance. The women are labelled as wives of the traitors and together with their children have been rewarded with discrimination and social stigma. Many of the women who suffered sexual violence experienced rejection: they were later abandoned by their husbands and lost their support networks. There was also total impunity for the perpetrators and no public awareness of what their victims went through. A woman narrated the process of de-humanisation she experienced when she said that she could not forget that when she got pregnant by the Indonesians, people in her village, instead of using the words '*isin rua*' for pregnant woman, called her '*kabuk todan*', which means heavily pregnant in the case of animals. Her house was also called 'sacred house', mocking the number of Indonesian men going inside of it.[62]

We may also see two processes to which women have been exposed, which may have excluded them and made them more outspoken. First, the male-centred pensions of veterans and memorials and monuments have perhaps encouraged Timorese women to speak up, given that the unequal tangible effects in society have become increasingly relevant. Second, victims of the violence of

[59] As part of Fretilin's secular policies in the 2000s, the government replaced baptismal records with civil registrations; however, this was perceived as a clash between the church and the state (Leach 2017: 159).

[60] Articles 2, 3 and 7 of the CRC establish the responsibility of the state for the protection of the right to have an identity. See also CRC GC 14 (2013) on the right of the child to have his or her best interests taken as a primary consideration (art 3, para 1), para 26; ACERWC, *Michelo Hunsungule and Others (on behalf of children in Northern Uganda) v Uganda*, Decision, Communication No 1/2005, 15–19 April 2013, para 81(3).

[61] When examining the situation of Timor-Leste, the CRC Committee (2015: para 24) showed its concern that 'certain groups of children, especially children of returnees, children who are not in possession of a baptism certificate, children born out of wedlock, children conceived from sexual relations among family members, and children with disabilities, face de facto discrimination, most importantly with regard to access to education and other services'.

[62] Interview with Participant 50, Baucau, Timor-Leste, 13 January 2017.

2006 also received reparations, which may have an effect on making the victims of the 1975–99 conflict more eager to advocate for their access to reparations (ICTJ 2010: 17). In this respect, I found that women want to find their space of visibility, a recognition of their experiences in the society of the new state.[63] In Manufahi, a woman said that the Indonesians threatened to kill her family and she was forced to marry an Indonesian. After some time, he left her. She was then sexually assaulted by other Indonesians and she bore two children. She told the story that in one occasion there were 20 women in a room and the Indonesians were calling one by one, name by name. She had been forced into sexual slavery for the military in Claco. She was living with sister and brother, and she could be picked up at any time, day and night. She was only 15 years old. She decided to tell her story because there was no justice. She said: 'the community said that I was a mistress, a whore, and I felt ashamed'. She did not know about CAVR and she first told her story to ACbit in 2016. She submitted the paperwork for the veterans' pension in 2009 because she wanted the state to recognise her suffering, but she never received an answer. She had worked for the OPMT from 1975 to 1999.[64]

So much academic and UN training made me very cautious about everything that is related to victims of sexual violence. Sometimes, I even received well-intentioned recommendations to hide the identities of the victims as much as possible, and I wonder to what extent we contribute to making such individuals invisible. The first time I met a group of women victims was in Gleno during a commemoration for the death of Ana Lemos, a case to which I will refer later.[65] What I observed there was a group of women sharing the same red T-shirts with a human rights slogan. They were united and posing proudly in group pictures. Should they avoid being recognised and hide themselves? Reflecting on shame, Solnit (2017: 92) remarks how traditionally the names of rape victims were not reported by the media, allegedly to protect them, and how 'this tradition had the additional effect of insisting on the notion that they have been shamed, keeping them invisible, isolated, and silent'. During the activities in Aileo, we also asked a woman if we could take a portrait of her. I felt uncomfortable asking, until I saw that the woman not only posed with a lot of confidence, but also amazed me by opening her blouse to show a hidden T-shirt with the face of her disappeared son. She had come prepared with that T-shirt, had it hidden during the interview and did not show it until the

[63] States have an obligation 'to address prevailing gender relations and the persistence of gender-based stereotypes that affect women not only through individual acts by individuals but also in law, and legal and societal structures and institutions' (CEDAW GR 25 2004: para 7). See CEDAW Art 5(a) and Holtmaat (2013: 96, 111) on transformative equality and structural discrimination.

[64] Interview with Participant 20, Claco, Manufahi, Timor-Leste, 17 January 2017.

[65] Ana Lemos's family participated in several of the mechanisms of transitional justice (the Special Panels in Timor-Leste, but also the Indonesian Ad Hoc Human Rights Court for East Timor, and both the CAVR and the CTF). However, those who committed the crime remained at large in Gleno and Indonesia and the family only received compensation from the UN after a difficult process.

moment of the photo. These women are looking for recognition. Narratives can change. The enslaved women in South Korea passed from being discriminated against to being seen today as national heroes.[66] It is just a matter of time before these Timorese women are also seen as heroes. The question is how soon a new reality can be created.

VI. CONCLUSIONS

Transitional justice with its apparent neutrality, is male-dominated, and it may become a tool for silencing women and promoting the dominant narratives of those in power. Timor-Leste's post-conflict society is deeply patriarchal and hyper-militarised, a system that is also supported by people who are invested in applying very conservative versions of religion and customary practices. As a result, today in Timor-Leste, militarisation is everywhere and all the time: the usual male veterans are in the memorials, commemorations, radio and television. The issue is that a militarised dominant narrative does not allow for critical reflection on the different ways in which women participated and experienced the conflict according to their gender: not only did they suffer from specific violations but they also participated in different ways in the resistance. Many of the women suffered gross violations of human rights, including sexual slavery and forced marriage, and the social stigma and cycle of discrimination continue against them and their own children. There are also no discussions about the role – if not complicity – of local authorities, communities and even family members in the violations committed against women, some of whom would later have a role in the local implementation of transitional justice mechanisms. The state may do so to avoid responsibilities, but this may also be connected to national identity construction. Indeed, when we talk about the past, we are shaping not only history but also the identity of a nation. The interviews with women highlight the different layers of classes that are being formed after a conflict and how difficult it is for them to fit into them. Since this affects structures that specifically favour some, women may become 'bothersome', which may help to explain the lack of political will by the government to recognise women's agency during the conflict. As a result of dominant narratives and the silence of others, women are still apologising for having been connected to Indonesians, while in reality they were victims. The silence furthers women's invisibility and discrimination, perpetuating their situation of disempowerment in the long-term.

But silences can also be active until they break. Women's individual memories and personal stories are also part of the history of a nation; it is just that they need a space where they can fit and be recognised. History can be rewritten

[66] In January 2021, a South Korean court demanded that Japan accept legal responsibility for the systematic sexual enslavement against these women (UN 2021b: para 21).

but if those individual narratives are not rescued, there is the risk of losing them forever, and with that the plurality that is essential in the public space. To be aware of factual realities is important in understanding women's current situation and so that the same mistakes are not repeated by a society. Recognising what happened and women's wishes for justice will ensure plurality and equality in the new beginning of the state. In this regard, the imposition of international justice, from a liberal point of view, is not necessarily the best for women, or for what they want and need. I have shown not only how transitional justice can be dominated by lawyers and be very legalistic, but at a more theoretical level, how we are also in the presence of western-based neo-liberal accounts of human rights that impose what they think is right for others, a justice conception that ignores intersectionality and excludes development. How does society decide what post-conflict justice should be about? Transitional justice does not necessarily match what people want when it ignores the specificities of the perceptions of justice of those who are most affected: to understand women's relation to conflict and peace is to understand women's conception of justice in the form of economic and social rights. I agree with MacKinnon, for instance, when she argues that 'economic and social rights make access to rights of citizenship meaningful' (2006: 137). In this regard, after the end of a conflict, women want to improve their living conditions and cover their basic needs for themselves and their children. People's needs and desires should be a priority. Moreover, SGBV is not only about the prosecution of rape but also about the relationship between the subordination of women and how their increased vulnerability to violence continues in times of peace. The pain of the women may have been aggravated by their limited, if not complete lack of, participation in the different transitional justice mechanisms that were presented to them. This is the focus of the following chapters.

A group of women in Gleno, Ermera, wearing T-shirts which said, 'I am a survivor, a change leader' in a Mass of remembrance to honour Ana Lemos – a Timorese leader who had been tortured and killed in 1999. © Noemí Pérez Vásquez.

Women in Aileu. The second woman from left to right had come prepared with a T-shirt showing the face of her disappeared son, had it hidden during the interview and did not show it until the moment of the photo. © Carlos Oviedo.

4

Women and Prosecution: 'We Captured the Dogs But Not the Owners of the Dogs'

THIS CHAPTER FOCUSES on women's participation in the prosecutions that were carried out in Timor-Leste after the conflict. More specifically, I start by providing the context of the creation of the Serious Crimes Unit (SCU) and the Special Panels for Serious Crimes. I then discuss the legislation that was drafted and the accounts of SGBV crimes against women that reached the Serious Crimes Process. I proceed to discuss the public and private: from the investigations and the proceedings, including the strategy of the prosecution, the evidence collection and the legal reasonings, to the private dynamics, including a culture of silence and fear of participating in something unknown. I show how issues with the drafting, interpretation and application of UNTAET's regulations concerning the temporal mandate (*ratione temporis*) (ie the time period covered); the subject matter mandate (*ratione materiae*) (ie the issues covered); the territorial/geographic mandate (*ratione loci*) (ie the territory and country/ies covered); and actors mandate (*ratione personae*) interfered in the prosecution of cases concerning women's violations. The chapter ends with some reflections concerning the convictions and sentencing and explores their follow-up. It concludes that although prosecutions are at the core of transitional justice, in the case of Timor-Leste, crimes against women, including those of SGBV, were under-reported, if not invisible. In order to provide a feminist legal historical analysis of the transcripts and their content, I not only take into account all the interviews with women but also with those who participated as judges and investigators in the judicial process. I am also grounding my research in the archival work carried out during six-months at the District Court of Dili, where the court records of the Special Panels are located.

I. PROSECUTIONS IN TIMOR-LESTE

After the end of the conflict, although various UN experts recommended the establishment of an international tribunal, the Security Council had a more ambiguous position (AJAR 2015: 163). On one hand, it recommended judicial action and the establishment of an international tribunal, and on the other, it did not seem ready to establish a tribunal similar to the one for the former Yugoslavia or to go against the will of the leadership of Indonesia and Timor-Leste (de Araújo e Corte-Real, Cabasset and Durand 2014). Walsh (2011: 179) argues that an international tribunal, such as the one in Nuremberg, was not possible to implement in Timor-Leste because the state's right of self-determination was the outcome of political compromise, not a defeat of Indonesia. There was indeed international goodwill towards the reforms led by President Abdurrahman Wahid, including his commitment to establish an Indonesian Ad Hoc Human Rights Court for East Timor with jurisdiction over crimes against humanity and genocide (AJAR 2015: 163). Moreover, after the ICTR and ICTY's experiences, there were hesitations over the benefits of international tribunals, partly because of the high costs incurred by international courts compared to the low number of prosecutions, but also because of the low participation of locals.

UNTAET therefore established in 2000 the Serious Crimes Process, composed of a hybrid tribunal called the Special Panels and the SCU. These bodies had jurisdiction to investigate and try those responsible for 'serious crimes', including genocide, war crimes, and crimes against humanity committed at any time (during and prior to 1999) as well as murder, sexual offences, and torture, committed between 1 January 1999 and 25 October 1999 (ICTJ 2010: 7).[1] The Special Panels were composed of a mix of East Timorese and international judges, prosecutors and investigators. UNTAET regulations also called for two Special Panels to function as part of the Dili District Court, and one at the Dili Court of Appeals, each comprising two international judges and one Timorese judge (Katzenstein 2003: 251).[2] The SCU, within the general prosecution branch, ran from 2000 to 2005 and was responsible for the investigation and prosecution of the crimes. The first regulations issued by UNTAET established that public officials were to observe international human rights law (Sannerholm 2012: 231).

The Serious Crimes Process in Timor-Leste, however, was plagued by a broad range of problems. Progress in the investigations was slow and judges had no prior experience in international criminal law (Martin and Mayer-Rieckh 2005: 138–39). The system was criticised for being complex and expensive, with three judges serving on one panel, and for imposing standards that were too high in the transitional period (Sannerholm 2012: 165–66). Hirst argues that the SCU lacked a coherent prosecutorial strategy; that the Special Panels lacked basic facilities such as translation and transcription; that its jurisprudence was weak and in some cases flawed; that there was a lack of adequate defence representation; and that there was a weak outreach to the community, including victims

[1] UNTAET Regulation 2000/15, on the Establishment of Panels with Exclusive Jurisdiction over Serious Criminal Offences (6 June 2000), ss 1, 2, 4; UNTAET Regulation 2000/11; UNTAET Regulation 2001/25, s 9.

[2] Katzenstein (2003) cites Linton (2001).

and witnesses (ICTJ 2008: 7–8). Already in 2003, there were reports of insufficient funding[3] and because there was no support staff – including legal clerks, secretaries and transcribers – judges were expected to do their own research, writing, and editing; because of the heavy load on a small number of interpreters (into four languages) there were limitations to the access to translations and questions about their quality, impeding the filing of appeals and forcing many hearings to be postponed; and there were allegations that there were not even official transcripts of some cases (Katzenstein 2003: 259–61). Because of the particular history of Timor-Leste and the hybrid nature of the Serious Crimes Process, there was also a clash of cultures within the UN, marked by the division between the Portuguese and the Anglo-Saxons (Da Silva 2012: 37). Moreover, although Portugal and Indonesia were civil law countries, both civil law and common law were applicable, adding a major complexity and cultural tension, which the UN tried to alleviate with a quick one-week course for the judges on common law in Darwin, Australia.

Nevertheless, the main frustration with the Serious Crimes Process would be that the vast majority of those indicted, including all the most senior suspects of the 1999 violence, such as the former Indonesian Minister of Defence General Wiranto, were still in Indonesia.[4] Although Indonesia had signed a Memorandum of Understanding to extradite criminals, it never extradited anyone.[5] Burgess (2005: 141) argues that those most responsible remained beyond effective prosecution because of

> the combined effect of the evacuation of Indonesian military and Timorese militias from East Timor in September 1999, the resistance by Members of the Security Council to an international tribunal, the problems with the ad hoc tribunal in Jakarta and the national limits of the jurisdiction of the Serious Crimes Unit.

The mandate of the SCU was to complete all of its investigations by 30 November 2004 with the final case heard by the Special Panels in May 2005, when the Security Council discontinued its work, reflecting a lack of political will within the Timorese government and the UN (ICTJ 2008: 7–8).

Indonesia created an Ad Hoc Human Rights Court for East Timor, with jurisdiction over crimes against humanity and genocide to try those responsible for the 1999 violence. The widespread perception, however, was that their trials were a farce and that the role of this court was insignificant (AJAR 2015: 163). However, the information concerning the data of the trials is not consistent among the examined sources. A first source indicates that the Indonesian proceedings finished in August 2003, with the acquittal of 11 members of the security forces and four other individuals who were sentenced to short prison terms and remained free pending appeal (*The Washington Post* 2003).

[3] Their total budget for the period 2003–2005 was approximately US$5m per year, which was only a small percentage of the budget of UNTAET (and later UNMISET) and also relatively small in comparison with the budget of the ICTR and ICTY (Ostowar 2020: 103–4).

[4] Wiranto was charged for crimes against humanity.

[5] A memorandum of understanding.

The International Center for Transitional Justice (ICTJ) (2010: 7) suggests that out of the 17 Indonesian military, police, civil servants and a Timorese militia leader who were tried by the Indonesian Ad Hoc Human Rights Court, all were acquitted either immediately or upon appeal. Harris Rimmer (2010: 234) mentions that, of the 18 defendants, only six were found guilty of crimes against humanity, all with sentences of imprisonment below the specified minimum legal limit for these crimes.

The exception was for Eurico Guterres, a Timorese militia leader behind the 1999 Liquiçá Church Massacre (Harris Rimmer 2010: 234). However, following the appeal process, those convicted were acquitted and Eurico Guterres became one of only two people whose trial ended in a conviction (Harris Rimmer 2010: 234).[6] After beginning his 10-year sentence in 2006, this was overturned by the Supreme Court and Guterres was also released in 2008.[7] Sexual offences were not brought to trial at all and the court environment was distressing to all but military participants (Harris Rimmer 2010: 243–49). For instance, I heard several times from UN employees in Dili the story of how a mother was questioned for five hours and asked if her daughter had wanted to be raped.[8] In the end, those accused were mid-level officers and militia leaders who were eventually acquitted, and therefore the ones who were most responsible remained free, while those who were tried in Timor-Leste were mostly low-level perpetrators (AJAR 2015: 163). To describe the Serious Crimes Process, a savvy rural woman said to me, 'we captured the dogs but not the owners of the dogs.'[9]

II. THE LEGISLATION

The Security Council Resolution 1272 that established UNTAET gave the Special Representative of the Secretary-General the capacity 'to enact new laws and regulations and to amend, suspend or repeal existing ones.'[10] The investigation and prosecution of 'serious crimes' were supposed to involve cases of genocide, war crimes, crimes against humanity, murder, sexual offences and torture.[11] With some exceptions, UNTAET regulations adopted the wording of the ICC when it refers to genocide, crimes against humanity and war crimes (Katzenstein 2003: 251).[12] More specifically, genocide could include killing members of the national, ethnical, racial or religious group; causing serious bodily or mental harm to members of the group; deliberately inflicting on the

[6] Abilio Soares was also sentenced to 3 years' imprisonment, less than the minimum sentence of 10 years. See: www.internationalcrimesdatabase.org/Case/41/Soares-(Abilio).

[7] Lestari (2021).

[8] See also Harris Rimmer (2010: 249–50).

[9] Interview with Participant 73, Maliana, Bobonaro, Timor-Leste, 24 January 2017.

[10] UNSCR 1272 (25 October 1999) (S/RES/1272), para 6.

[11] UNTAET Regulation 2000/15.

[12] Katzenstein (2003) cites Linton (2001).

group conditions of life calculated to bring about its physical destruction in whole or in part; imposing measures intended to prevent births within the group; and forcibly transferring children of the group to another group.[13] As for war crimes, UNTAET regulations cite grave breaches of the Geneva Conventions, so crimes could include murder; torture; willfully causing great suffering, or serious injury to body or health; unlawful deportation or transfer or unlawful confinement. They also mention the laws and customs of war, including: intentionally directing attacks against the civilian population as such or against individual civilians not taking direct part in hostilities; committing outrages upon personal dignity, in particular humiliating and degrading treatment; committing rape, sexual slavery, enforced prostitution, forced pregnancy, enforced sterilisation, or any other form of sexual violence also constituting a grave breach of the Geneva Conventions; intentionally using starvation of civilians as a method of warfare; among others. In case of a Non-International Armed Conflict, this includes violence to life and person, in particular murder of all kinds, mutilation, cruel treatment and torture; committing outrages upon personal dignity, in particular humiliating and degrading treatment; intentionally directing attacks against the civilian population as such or against individual civilians not taking direct part in hostilities; committing rape, sexual slavery, enforced prostitution, forced pregnancy, enforced sterilisation, and any other form of sexual violence also constituting a serious violation of common Article 3 of the Geneva Conventions.[14]

Crimes against humanity could include murder, enslavement, forcible transfer of population, imprisonment or other severe deprivation of physical liberty, torture, enforced disappearance, and other inhumane acts.[15] Crimes of sexual violence within crimes against humanity, could involve rape, sexual slavery, enforced prostitution, forced pregnancy, enforced sterilisation, or any other form of sexual violence of comparable gravity.[16] Torture, on the other hand, was defined as

> any act by which severe pain or suffering, whether physical or mental, is intentionally inflicted on a person for such purposes as obtaining from him/her or a third person information or a confession, punishing him/her for an act he/she or a third person has committed or is suspected of having committed, or humiliating, intimidating or coercing him/her or a third person, or for any reason based on discrimination of any kind.[17]

When it comes to the offences of murder and sexual violence, according to UNTAET regulations, they could be outside the framework of genocide, crimes against humanity, war crimes and torture so they could be considered to be

[13] UNTAET Regulation 2000/15, s 4.
[14] UNTAET Regulation 2000/15, s 6.1(c).
[15] UNTAET Regulation 2000/15, s 5.1.
[16] UNTAET Regulation 2000/15, s 5.1.
[17] UNTAET Regulation 2000/15, s 7.1.

ordinary crimes according to the Indonesian penal code. The Special Panels and the SCU were therefore granted jurisdiction over crimes under both international and national law, and they enjoyed primacy over the ordinary national courts for offences within their exclusive jurisdiction (Dicker and Keppler 2004; Nouwen 2006: 197; ICTJ 2006b: 23). UNTAET Regulation 2000/15 also refers to universal jurisdiction of the Special Panels over genocide, war crimes, crimes against humanity, murder, sexual offences and torture.[18] When referring to its temporal jurisdiction, UNTAET regulations mention that it covers murder, sexual violence and torture as long as committed between 1 January 1999 and 25 October 1999.[19] This means that there was no limitation of the temporal jurisdiction over genocide, war crimes and crimes against humanity. It also means that individual cases of sexual violence that were committed before 1 January 1999 were assumed per se to be ordinary crimes, if not found to be within the scope of crimes against humanity.

UNTAET decided to regulate the prospective law of Timor-Leste from 25 October 1999 onwards, while it decided not to determine what the law of Timor-Leste had been prior to October 1999, considering it to be a political issue to be decided by the Timorese authorities (Ronen 2012: 298). Indeed, the first UNTAET regulation provides that 'until replaced by UNTAET regulations or subsequent legislation of democratically established institutions of East Timor, the laws applied in east Timor prior to 25 October 1999, shall apply in East Timor'.[20] The question then was which laws to apply as subsidiary – those from the Portuguese times or the Indonesian ones? Since there was no reference to the source or content of those existing laws and regulations either in the resolution or in the debates preceding its adoption, UNTAET would decide to apply Indonesian law as the subsidiary law in Timor-Leste unless and until UNTAET or Timorese legislation existed or unless Indonesian law contradicted international human rights standards (Cristalis and Scott 2005: 100; Ronen 2012: 295–96). Consequently, the legal jurisdiction for the crimes committed pre-October 1999, provided that 'the courts in East Timor shall apply the law of East Timor as promulgated by Section 3 of UNTAET Regulation No. 1999/1.'[21] Again, without determining the territorial law of East Timor, UNTAET, vaguely, provided that crimes committed pre-October 1999 would be judged according to the law as referred to in Regulation 1999/1, which meant de facto application of Indonesian law (Ronen 2012: 298–99). The decision to use Indonesian law was in order to avoid a legal vacuum and provide continuity in the initial phase of the transitional administration, to avoid the practical difficulties of reverting to Portuguese law or introducing a new legal code and to avoid a situation in which the few local Timorese lawyers, who had

[18] UNTAET Regulation 2000/15, s 1.3.

[19] UNTAET Regulation 2000/15, s 2.3; UNTAET Regulation 2000/11, s 10.1(d), (e).

[20] UNTAET Regulation 1999/1, s 3.

[21] UNTAET Regulation 2000/11, s 5.1; UNTAET Regulation 2000/15, ss 3.1 and 4. These regulations were later replaced by Regulation 2001/25, which reproduces the jurisdiction provisions, s 5.1.

been mostly trained in Indonesia, were excluded from the new legal system (Ronen 2012: 295–96; Bull 2008; 194).[22]

The issue would, though, be taken some years later to the Court of Appeal, which still functions as the Supreme Court. On 17 July 2003, the Court of Appeal re-examined the case of Armando dos Santos, a member of a Pro-Indonesian militia group who had been indicted for murder and other inhumane acts as crimes against humanity committed in April 1999 and convicted in September 2002, under Indonesian law, of murder, and sentenced to 20 years' imprisonment (Ronen 2012: 299).[23] At that moment, there was a disagreement within the Special Panels: while one Panel wanted to apply Portuguese law, the other wished to apply Indonesian law (Da Silva 2012: 258).[24] When the prosecution appealed the decision, submitting that dos Santos should have been convicted of crimes against humanity rather than murder, the Court of Appeal concluded that Regulation 1999/1 referred to Portuguese law and the majority proceeded to declare dos Santos guilty of crimes against humanity under Portuguese law (Ronen 2012: 229–300; Da Silva 2012: 258).[25] There was the argument that the crime was committed during the Indonesian period, which was never recognised as legitimate under international law (Da Silva 2012: 258). Ronen (2012: 229–302) argues that by favouring Portuguese law, the Court was not only breaking with the Indonesian system, but it was also manifesting a desire of some of its members to promote the Portuguese culture over the Indonesian. Moreover, the Court needed to consider the few Timorese justice officers as against all Portuguese-speaking legal advisers who were in the country to help with the rebuilding of the judiciary (Da Silva 2012: 258–59).

The decision was controversial for the Timorese leadership and the UN legal advisers. The Prosecutor-General then filed an application with the Court arguing that the erroneous rulings of the Court of Appeal would render illegal the decisions of the courts in all the criminal cases heard in the preceding years (Ronen 2012: 300). Unable to reach a decision about the legality of the Indonesian occupation, the Special Panels and the Dili District Court continued to interpret Regulation 1999/1 as referring to Indonesian law (Ronen 2012: 301). The issue was later resolved when the National Parliament passed a law in October 2003 in which it revoked the use of Portuguese legislation

[22] This is still an issue of great concern in Timor-Leste. While in several universities, aspiring lawyers continue to study the laws in Bahasa Indonesia, today these are mainly drafted in Portuguese and some translated into Tetum, ie many law graduates are unable to read the laws (Portuguese is spoken by approximately only 10 per cent of the population). There are allegations that this incongruency is motivated by universities owners' pursuit of financial gains.

[23] Public *Prosecutor v Armando dos Santos* (Case No 16/PID.C.G./2001/PD.DIL).

[24] Da Silva recounts how one Special Panel, composed of three judges from Germany, Burundi and Timor-Leste, declared that they had decided not to apply Portuguese law, but Indonesian law as a subsidiary law in their judgments and that their working language was English. A second Special Panel, composed of three judges from Brazil, Italy and Timor-Leste adopted Portuguese law as subsidiary law and Portuguese as their working language (Da Silva 2012: 258).

[25] Ronen (2012: 304) considers that the conviction of dos Santos on the basis of Portuguese law amounted to retroactive penalisation, violating the principle of *nullum crimen sine lege*.

and confirmed that Indonesian law continued to apply in Timor-Leste, unless revoked or replaced by subsequent laws; that Indonesian law was the subsidiary law under both Regulation 1999/1 and the Constitution; and that it was made to be applicable retroactively to East Timor's day of independence, 20 May 2002 (Da Silva 2012: 258–59; Article 19 2005: 20; Ronen 2012: 301–2).[26]

Moreover, although crimes committed against women could fall under any of the serious crimes defined in the UNTAET regulations, there are several issues that may have affected women's participation and recognition in the prosecution process. Separating sexual offences from genocide, crimes against humanity and war crimes facilitated a presumption that they were ordinary and not within the logic of sexual violence in conflict, reducing the visibility of cases concerning women. For instance, sexual violence against Timorese women was committed in a widespread and systematic way, which satisfies the legal elements of crimes against humanity. But also, the interviewed women referred to reprisals taken by the Indonesians against their villages, inhabited mainly by women and children, which could be classified as war crimes. Genocide, on the other hand, has been considered by international tribunals to have a very restrictive application. However, the UN Special Rapporteur on extrajudicial, summary or arbitrary executions stated in the 1999 report on the situation of Timor-Leste 'that political protesters and members of ethnic minorities had been deliberately targeted and subjected to ill-treatment in detention, which at times had led to their death' (UN 1999a: 23). By ethnic minorities, he seems to refer to the Timorese people and by the use of 'deliberately targeted' seems to refer to intent.

The use of a gender focus may make it easier to see the scope of the commission of the crime of genocide. In *Kadić v Karadžić*, a US Federal court for the first time established the legal recognition of rape as an act of genocide (MacKinnon 2017: 152). When a woman of a community is destroyed, the community is destroyed: 'their communities scattered, their families devastated if they remain at all, their capacity for intimate connections damaged or destroyed, what they survived is … precisely an attempt to destroy peoples as such' (MacKinnon 2017: 155). When Jackson (2015) reflects on Apartheid South Africa's chemical and biological weapons programme – implicated in kidnappings, poisonings and murders – he observes that very little attention was paid to its anti-fertility research component. Based on testimony from the TRC, he argues that there was a reasonable basis to believe that the international crime of conspiracy to commit genocide was committed: secretively, anti-fertility drugs were administered to black South Africans with the intention of curtailing birth rates. He continues, 'the imposition of a fertility vaccine of this kind, without consent, clearly constitutes an act of genocide under Article 2(d) of the Genocide Convention' (Jackson 2015: 943). Imposing measures intended to

[26] Law No 10/2003 on the Interpretation of Article 1 of Law 2/2002 of 7 August on the Sources of Law. In the Constitution of Timor-Leste, s 165, adopted in March 2002, the Parliament states that the applicable laws in Timor-Leste were the ones 'in force' de facto.

prevent births within a group with the intention to destroy it is one of the acts that defines the crime of genocide.[27]

Looking at the violations of reproductive rights, particularly of forced sterilisation, there could be grounds for considering a hidden intent to slowly destroy the Timorese population. The 'intent' to destroy the Timorese was also raised by a former health worker of the Indonesian family planning programme, at the National Public Hearing of the CAVR that focused on violations against women (Post-CAVR 2008: 50). He said 'in my opinion, the programme KB was a political strategy used indirectly by the Indonesian government to bring more Indonesians. This programme aimed at the indirect killing of the indigenous population of Timor-Leste' (Post-CAVR 2008: 50). Harris Rimmer (2010: 286) also points out that the CAVR process was the only transitional justice mechanism to mention forced maternity. However, she claims that not only should this crime have been seen as a violation in its own right, with the women as individual victims, but also it should have been regarded as a violation with wider, genocidal aspects (Harris Rimmer 2010: 286). In addition to subjecting women to measures intended to prevent births, the Indonesians also displaced people from their villages – sending those from the mountains to dry areas where they struggled to survive – children were forcibly taken to Indonesia, and cultural Timorese traditions such as *Uma Lulik* (sacred totem houses) were forbidden.[28] As I will show, the classification of killings as crimes of a much graver nature could also have rendered invisible other passive means of destruction, to which women may be more exposed.

Some of the women interviewed were sexually assaulted in custody and this may have amounted to torture. The point is that by separating off sexual violence as an ordinary crime, the Serious Crimes Process missed the opportunity to frame the commission of these crimes according to grave breaches of international law. Second, by overly focusing on rape, the Special Panels failed to reflect the variety of SGBV crimes committed against women during the totality of the conflict, including sexual slavery and forced marriage. Third, although the Serious Crimes Process focused de facto on the crimes committed during the 1999 violence, according to their regulations, there was no limitation of the temporal jurisdiction over genocide, war crimes and crimes against humanity. As showed by the interviews with women, the violence against them could be inflicted at any time over a long period, so the Special Panels failed to

[27] The *Akayesu* case was also the first judgment by an international court for the crime of genocide. ICTR, *Prosecutor v Jean-Paul Akayesu* Case no ICTR-96-4-T, Judgment, 2 September 1998. Jackson (2015: 943) notes that although 'there is yet to be an international criminal prosecution for genocide on the basis of imposing measures intended to prevent births', in the *Eichmann* case of 1961 (District Court of Jerusalem), among several other crimes, Eichmann was also convicted of crimes against the Jewish People on the basis that he took measures calculated to prevent births among Jews.

[28] I am aware that at the suggestion of Raphael Lemkin, the drafters of the 1948 Genocide Convention considered the use of the term 'cultural genocide' but later dropped it from their consideration.

see the continuum of SGBV during the 24 years of the conflict. In this regard, Katzenstein (2003: 274) argues that although the Special Panels had jurisdiction to deal with crimes against humanity committed at any point, the investigations were hindered by the UN/USA relations, as international complicity would have surfaced if the trials had gone into too much depth.

Finally, it is paradoxical that despite the regulations concerning serious offences and the focus of resources on trials with the highest standards and support from international expertise, Indonesian laws, which were the laws studied by the Timorese, would be determinant in the chain of justice in the Serious Crimes Process. Indonesian law did not escape criticism. Based on her visit in 1998, the UN SR on violence against women had pointed out that in the Indonesian Penal Code, introduced by the Dutch, the rape law only referred to sexual intercourse and not to any other form of sexual violence; it required corroboration, including the testimony of two witnesses; and although the woman did not have to prove absence of consent as in common law jurisdictions, the evidentiary procedure was still weighted against her (UN 1999b: para 53). She also remarked on how women's groups have pointed out that the judiciary has been extremely lenient to convicted rapists, sentencing them to imprisonment for between a mere three months and one year (UN 1999b: para 52).

III. ACCOUNTS OF CRIMES COMMITTED AGAINST WOMEN

There are discrepancies among the different sources regarding the number of people indicted and convicted. Laakso (2007: 141) notes that, according to the Office of the Deputy Prosecutor-General for Serious Crimes, by February 2005, out of the 392 suspects that were indicted, 303 were presumed to be outside of Timor-Leste, including 37 Indonesian military commanders and officers of the Indonesian National Army (TNI), 4 Indonesian chiefs of police, 60 Timorese TNI military officers and soldiers, 1 former governor and 5 former district administrators.[29] The Commission for Truth and Friendship (CTF 2008: 125) report mentions that from 2000 to 2005 the Special Panels completed 55 trials. Peake (2013) refers to 403 people who were indicted. An Asian NGO with expertise on this topic mentions that the SCU led to 95 indictments involving more than 360 persons (AJAR 2015: 163). On the other hand, the ICTJ records that the SCU indicted 391 persons, but while one report mentions 84 convictions, another one mentions 81 convictions (ICTJ 2008: 7–8; 2010: 7). In the Dili District Court, where the cases are located, I was informed that out of a total of 440 people who entered into the process of the Special Panels after 2005, there were 89 convictions, 339 people awaiting trial, most of whom are likely to be in Indonesia, and 12 discontinued cases. I believe that this confusion stems from some misunderstanding between the total number of *indictments* as against

[29] Laakso cites the Office of the Deputy Prosecutor-General for Serious Crimes (2005).

the total number of *people indicted*, but I am appalled by the fact that despite it being such a recent conflict and justice process, there are already so many discrepancies in the data.

I also asked at the Dili District Court for the data and statistics concerning women, including SGBV. The statistics in the Excel spreadsheet provided were so limited that it was not possible to extract this information. Based on the information provided by local NGOs, out of the 95 people who were indicted, there were only 8 involved in SGBV crimes, 6 of them being rape as a crime against humanity (AJAR 2015: 163). As for the convictions, only one accused was convicted of rape as an ordinary crime and another for rape as a crime against humanity, meaning that out of all the sexual violence that Timorese women experienced, only two cases in the whole country managed to received prosecutorial 'justice' (Cambodia Defenders Project 2012: 20; AJAR 2015: 163). Sexual slavery, forced marriage and other types of gender-based crimes were never charged by the SCU, neither were any of the crimes, including of SGBV nature, committed before 1999 (AJAR 2015: 163).

In any case, the first conviction for rape by the Special Panels was in September 2002, with the case of Francisco Soares, a former militia commander, accused of raping a woman after taking her from an Indonesian military base in Becora in September 1999 (Cristalis and Scott 2005: 96–97). The panel found Soares guilty under section 285 of the Indonesian Penal Code, which stated that: 'whosoever uses force or the threat of force to coerce a woman who is not his wife to have sexual relations with him is liable to imprisonment of 12 years' (JSMP 2002a). The panel found that the fact that he had a wife and children should not be considered a mitigating circumstance in sentencing (JSMP 2002a). Nevertheless, the fact that Soares knew the victim had a boyfriend was considered to be an aggravating circumstance (JSMP 2002a) – as if she were someone else's property and her honour was attached to a man. Soares was sentenced to the maximum penalty of 12 years and served four years of imprisonment (Cristalis and Scott 2005: 96–97).

The Lolotoe case was the first and only one to include rape as a crime against humanity alongside charges against superiors based on the actions of their subordinates. The original indictment filed by the Deputy General Prosecutor on 6 June 2001 charged five individuals with crimes against humanity, and the trial began on 8 February 2002. The militia commanders José Cardoso Ferreira (alias Mouzinho), Joao Franca da Silva (alias Joni Franca) and former village chief Sabino Gouveia Leite were indicted jointly on 27 counts of crimes against humanity, including counts of murder, rape, torture, imprisonment/severe deprivation of physical liberty and persecution, committed as part of a deadly terror campaign in 1999 in Lolotoe, Bobonaro, near the border with West Timor (JSMP 2003; Cristalis and Scott 2005: 97). Among the many victims in this case, three young women were kept in a house for several weeks, with the complicity of the village chief and under the suspicion that they had had relationships with Falintil fighters and had been providing food to them. The three women were raped repeatedly from May to July 1999 (Cristalis and Scott 2005: 97).

The women were later taken by three of the men accused on the original indictment to Atambua, West Timor, where they were forced, under coercive circumstances, to have sexual relations. To avoid pregnancy, the men also injected substances into the buttocks of two of the women. The accused men admitted having had sexual relationships with the women but claimed that the women had consented. On 5 April 2003, Mouzinho was sentenced to 12 years' imprisonment after being found guilty of crimes against humanity including murder, rape, torture, imprisonment/severe deprivation of physical liberty and inhumane treatment (JSMP 2003; Cristalis and Scott 2005: 97). This means that the rape of the three Lolotoe women occurred as part of a widespread or systematic attack against the civilian population in Lolotoe, Bobonaro.

The other two accused persons – 2nd Lieutenant Bambang Indra, an Indonesian military commander in Lolotoe, who committed sexual violence against a second woman, and Francisco Noronha, an intelligence officer for the Indonesian military – remained at large in Indonesia (JSMP 2003). According to the criminal procedure being used, the law did not permit a hearing without the presence of the accused in court so the public prosecutor asked for the severance of the case for the two aforementioned accused. After the beginning of the trial, Joni Franca and Sabino Leite then pleaded guilty and their cases were severed. This meant that individual judgments were rendered in each of these cases after hearings in which the prosecution introduced evidence to satisfy the Court that the guilty plea was in fact supported by evidentiary facts.[30]

On 29 October 2002, Joni Franca agreed to plead guilty to crimes against humanity, including imprisonment/severe deprivation of physical liberty and torture (JSMP 2003). In other words, he admitted having committed torture against other people but not the sexual violence against the third woman. The rape committed against her was thus not included in his plea and this agreement was accepted by the prosecution. He was sentenced to five years' imprisonment. On 20 November 2002, Sabino Gouveia Leite pleaded guilty to crimes against humanity, including imprisonment/severe deprivation of physical liberty and inhumane acts (JSMP 2003). Leite was sentenced to three years' imprisonment and was released in December 2002 after serving two-thirds of the sentence (JSMP 2003). Mouzinho was the third and final defendant, among those accused who were present in Timor-Leste, to be convicted of rape as a crime against humanity in the Lolotoe case. Although he personally raped two of the women, Harris Rimmer (2010: 172) considered it unfair that he was convicted of the rape of three victims as part of a common enterprise. The fact that of the other two accused who committed the rape, one remained in Indonesia and the other did not include that crime in his plea is an illustration of the lack of accountability for SGBV crimes against women.

In practice, genocide and war crimes were not charged before the Special Panels so all the charges involved either crimes against humanity or under domestic law. According to Reiger and Wierda, the reasons may lie in the

[30] As required by UNTAET Regulation 2000/30, s 29a.

fact that prosecutors preferred to charge the crimes of 1999 as a widespread campaign against a civilian population than as crimes in the context of an armed conflict (ICTJ 2006b: 23). This would also be clearly seen in the Lolotoe case. The Trial Chamber did not consider that the evidence showed systematic rape as a 'weapon of war' but did consider that sexual assault was employed as a means of expelling the local civilian population through the use of terror. There was a disagreement, though, and this came from the female Timorese judge, Maria Natércia Gusmão Pereira, who initially thought that the sexual violence was indeed inflicted as a weapon of war.[31] As was even claimed by the CTF (2008: 132), it was established beyond reasonable doubt that there was a systematic attack against the civilian population in the Lolotoe sub-district, that the attacks were part of an orchestrated campaign of violence and that this included intimidation and threats to life, unlawful confinement, rape, torture, assaults, murders, and forced displacement, carried out by members of the militias, the military, and police, with the acquiescence and participation of civil authorities. In the case of Lolotoe, Sabino Leite provided information to the militia about the three women and this led to their detention in an operation jointly conducted by the militia and the military, armed with automatic weapons (CTF 2008: 130). This shows that women relatives of independence supporters were a particular target and how, through the existence of lists of names and the targeting of specific individuals, there was a level of organisation rather than mere random violence (CTF 2008: 133). CTF accounts support the reasoning of the Timorese female judge that rape was indeed used as a weapon of war. However, Maria Natércia would then follow the reasoning of her male international colleagues that sexual assault was employed as a means of expelling the local civilian population through the use of terror rather than as a weapon of war. This leads us to reflect on what domestic judges are expected to learn from international judges.

When it comes to the sexual violence, the case focused on these three women when they were taken to Atambua, West Timor and on the crime of rape. During the trial of the Lolotoe case, there was no reference to forced contraception, which was a missed opportunity to reflect on the use of contraceptives by the Indonesian military and militias as part of the commission of SGBV crimes against women.[32] The Court records also mentioned that the three women, together with a fourth one, were first deprived of their liberty and placed at the house of Sabino Leite's family, where they were forced to

[31] Interview with Participant 108, 15 March 2016.

[32] In 2019, the Colombian Constitutional Court issued a landmark decision recognising that women and girls who were subjected to forced contraception and forced abortion by their own armed groups should be recognised as 'victims of armed conflict' (De Vos 2020). De Vos (2020) argues that because this decision is one of the very few in the world to specifically recognise reproductive violence as a form of harm committed against women and girls in times of conflict, it sets an important legal precedent in recognising a form of gender-based violence that has long remained invisible.

cook for them and the militias. There are accounts that in that house there was sexual violence committed against them, including rape, and it is argued that the fact that they were forced to work in those conditions amounted to sexual slavery (Cristalis and Scott 2005: 97).[33] The CTF (2008: 130) only mentions that during the entire time of their detention 'they were guarded and lived under the threat of death if they did not obey'. The case at the Special Panel does not go into detail on what happened to the women in that house, neither were these experiences taken into account in framing the charges. The fourth woman was a witness in the case so she was not considered a victim and her name was provided. Adding to the confusion of the facts about the women's experiences, one of the transcripts reads that when the Defence questioned Victim B concerning her different statements, she responded that she told investigators that the accused had raped her. She explained that 'she narrated her story to the investigator through an interpreter and that when the statement was read back to her it was in English.'[34]

Furthermore, in the *Lolotoe* case, while the crimes committed against these three women were dealt with as a group, the other victims in the same case, particularly concerning murder, were dealt with in a more individual way and the prosecution relied on such a large number of witnesses that the evidence became repetitive. There is an issue of balance but then the question is how to limit the number of witnesses in this kind of situation. The Lolotoe trial was the second major crimes against humanity case to be tried by the Special Panels after the case of Los Palos, in which Jony Marques and nine other defendants were convicted of crimes against humanity for the killings of nine people, including several Catholic priests and nuns who were travelling by car to Baucau and a teenage boy who witnessed the incident (UN 1999a: 30). Although the trials of the Special Panels began in January 2001, by December 2001, two years after UNTAET's establishment, only the case of Los Palos had been completed (Bull 2008: 234). With the conviction of Mouzinho in April 2003, only 13 persons had been convicted of crimes against humanity (JSMP 2003). We need to remember that the SCU ended its investigations in 2004 so by 2003 the Special Panels could have speeded up the process in order to balance due process with the necessity to continue with other cases. This may explain the CTF's opinion that the *Los Palos* and the *Lolotoe* cases were the two most important ones since on the one hand, the prosecution seek to establish the general context in which crimes against humanity took place and on the other hand, the Court tried to summarise and analyse the prosecution and defence positions and to consider all their witnesses, whereas the cases that followed were, according to the CTF, mostly based on reports (CTF 2008 125–26).

[33] Special Panels for Serious Crimes, Case number 04/2001, *The Prosecutor v Jose Cardoso and 4 Others* also known as the *Lolotoe case*, para 105; para 120.

[34] Case number 04/2001, also known as the *Lolotoe* case. Testimony of the witness Victim B, para 297.

While international criminal tribunals may have an over-focus on women's experiences of conflict in cases of sexual violence, the example of the Special Panels in Timor-Leste demonstrates that even these crimes remained largely invisible. The question that follows is why there was such invisibility if, before the Special Panels started, there were already reports that SGBV against Timorese women was widespread and systematic. In a joint mission of UN Special Rapporteurs to Timor-Leste in November 1999, the SR on extrajudicial and summary executions, the SR on torture and the SR on violence against women condemned the widespread, systematic and gross violations of human rights and international humanitarian law committed in Timor-Leste (UN 1999a: 7). In their report, they further stated that 'there have been continuing allegations of extrajudicial killings, torture, disappearances and acts of sexual violence attributed to members of the Indonesian National Army (TNI) and pro-Government militias and paramilitary groups' (UN 1999a: 16).

The SR on violence against women observed that even before the 1999 violence, women were particularly vulnerable to gender-specific human rights violations, including rape and sexual harassment, committed by the Indonesian armed forces (UN 1999a: 46). She highlighted that before May 1998 rape was used as an instrument of torture and intimidation by certain elements of the Indonesian military, particularly against relatives of political opponents as a form of revenge or to force their relatives out of hiding (UN 1999a: 46). She also found evidence of widespread violence against women during her visit in 1999 and provided the testimonies of several women (UN 1999a: 48–56). She raised cases of torture and sexual slavery and how sexual violence was used as a strategy of intimidation, particularly against female family members whose husbands had left the village during the period from January to July 1999 (UN 1999a: 52). She stated that

> it is clear that the highest level of the military command in East Timor knew, or had reason to know, that there was widespread violence against women in East Timor. There were cases of sexual slavery, sexual violence as a means of intimidation and sexual violence as a result of the climate of impunity created by the security forces operating in the island (UN 1999a: 48, 62).

On 22 September 1999, the Indonesian National Human Rights Commission (Komnas HAM) established the Commission for Human Rights Violations in East Timor (KPP-HAM), whose mandate was to gather facts and information concerning violations of human rights that occurred in East Timor from January to October 1999.[35] The KPP-HAM (2000) also released a report stating that they had found evidence that strongly indicated:

> a planned, systematic, wide-scale and gross violation of human rights, mass murders, torture and ill-treatment, disappearances, violence against women and children

[35] The Commission of Inquiry for Human Rights Violations in East Timor (KPP-HAM) was supposed to determine if there was enough evidence to suggest that gross human rights violations had occurred and, if so, make recommendations as to who should be subject to further investigation

(including rape and sexual slavery), forced evacuation, property destruction and implementation of a scorched-earth campaign, all of which constitute crimes against humanity.

The report mentioned that women and girls were molested by both the militia and the authorities in both East Timor and in the refugee camps in West Timor and that the crimes against them included torture, forced sex with underage girls, sex slavery and rape (KPP-HAM 2000). The report mentioned cases of women and girls from Ainaro and Liquiçá who were abducted, gang-raped and made sexual slaves by the militias for several weeks (KPP-HAM 2000). Moreover, the report stated that rape could take the forms of (a) a perpetrator and one woman, (b) more than one perpetrator and one woman, (c) gang-rape of a number of women in one location, and (d) use of a certain location for repeated acts of rape (KPP-HAM 2000). Rape and sexual enslavement occurred in civilian homes, military headquarters and refugee camps both before and after the popular consultation (KPP-HAM 2000). The report ends by claiming that the crimes against humanity were part of a systematic programme that resulted from extensive planning, in which militias, the Indonesian military, civil authorities and the police had a role (KPP-HAM 2000). Thirty-two officials and militia leaders were also named as responsible for the commission of crimes against humanity (Burgess 2004: 136). The CAVR (2005: 302–3), which was functioning in parallel with the Serious Crimes Process, also extensively collected the widespread and systematic violations against women from 1975 to 1999 and it particularly made explicit that sexual violence and sexual slavery were widespread in 1999.

Therefore, there was already information at the time about the scale and magnitude of SGBV against women in Timor-Leste. The Special Rapporteurs made, for instance, a reference in their report to the massacre of Suai. Backed by the Indonesian military and the police, the militia surrounded the church grounds and opened fire indiscriminately on the two churches where civilians had sheltered on 6 September 1999 (UN 1999a: 33). There were up to 200 people killed, including three priests, and their bodies were allegedly taken away on army trucks (UN 1999a: 35; Human Rights Watch 2004). The SR commented that 'two women gave eyewitness testimony describing how women had been killed after having been raped by Indonesian police and militia' (UN 1999a: 35). The KPP-HAM (2000) report also mentions that 'rape took place at the district military command of Covalima on September 6, after several women were taken there following the Suai church massacre. Laksaur militia members tried to rape them'. The KPP-HAM (2000) mentions the case of Alola, a third level junior

and prosecution by the Office of the Attorney General. The KPP-HAM (2020) investigation and report explicitly considered the role and responsibility of the TNI, the Indonesian military. It was not supposed to conduct an investigation to establish individual criminal responsibility. Their report was, however, submitted to the Indonesian National Human Rights Commission and then to the Indonesian Attorney General for the purpose of investigation and prosecution in an Indonesian Human Rights Court. The CTF (2008) would later discredit the KPP-HAM for relying on allegedly flawed evidence.

high school student from Suai who, together with other women, was taken on 5 September 1999 to West Timor and forced to become a sexual slave.

The CTF (2008: 190–91) also collected information of SGBV committed against women and girls in Suai:

> many witnesses offered detailed testimony of specific instances where military or police personnel did not make due efforts to intervene during an attack. For example, in the case of gender-based violence, one of the victims named Esmeralda dos Santos stated that at the time, she and her three friends named victim A, victim B, and victim C, were raped for one week by the militia at SMP 2 high school in Suai. The rape was committed in front of many people, by armed perpetrators while TNI and Police were acting as 'guards' to the group of refugees.

The CAVR (2005: 302–3) also documented that after the massacre at the church in Suai on 6 September, many women taken to the nearby school and repeatedly raped before being forced over the border, where many were held in sexual slavery. Although the case of the massacre of Suai entered into the Serious Crimes Process, there was only one indictment of several militia members for rape as a crime against humanity committed against one individual, and since the militias were in Indonesia, there was eventually no conviction for crimes of SGBV nature (CAVR 2005: 2982).[36]

Most of the cases of violations against women I interviewed occurred before 1999, while six cases concerning women occurred or continued to occur until the 1999 escalation of violence. However, not all of the six cases of human rights violations in 1999 were considered for prosecution at the Special Panels for Serious Crimes, including the case of a woman, 12 years old at the time, who was gang-raped twice by a group of 10 militiamen in Ermera. Moreover, it is noticeable that out of the 77 women interviewed, only seven had interacted with the Special Panels for Serious Crimes and of these seven participants, only one case was specifically concerned with women's violations. In other words, out of the 77 women in our sample, there was only one case that managed to pass through the prosecutorial system. This was the case of Ana Lemos, a UNAMET local staff and prominent CNRT member, to which I will refer later.[37]

The fact that there were only two convictions of rape and also the fact that there was an insignificant number of indictments for sexual violence illustrate the invisibility of the grave crimes committed against women because of their gender. Furthermore, the focus specifically on rape meant that cases of sexual slavery, forced marriage, and other violations, such as those of a reproductive nature and forced nudity, were neglected. In the *Lolotoe* case, for instance, although the women were forced to be subjected to injections to avoid pregnancy, there was no reference to these violations of reproductive rights in the indictment or during the hearings. One of the transcripts mentions that after receiving an injection, one of the victims felt dizzy and became unconscious,

[36] Case number 09/2003, also known as the Maternus Bere case or Suai Church massacre case.

[37] Ana Lemos was in The Ermera indictment facts, case 12/2004 (still pending).

before being raped.[38] These facts were treated as collateral damage and without importance. Following the jurisprudence of other international tribunals, such as the ICC and the SCSL, those crimes could have been treated as 'other inhumane acts.' This is where the public and private dichotomy become a central issue in transitional justice. Charlesworth, Chinkin, and Wright (1991) have famously argued that by failing to understand the interconnection of the public and the private and the interplay of their power dynamics, international law not only generated but also prolonged women's subordination and exclusion from spaces of power. This chapter turns now to the criminal investigations to make sense of why there was such a low participation by women and why there was such a lack of recognition of the crimes committed against them.

IV. THE PUBLIC: THE INVESTIGATIONS

I have already shown that when the Special Panels started, there were numerous accounts of the widespread and systematic SGBV against women, not only during the years of the conflict, but also during the 1999 escalation of violence. Moreover, although there was an over-focus on sexual violence in the international criminal law system at that time, these discussions were limited to the Special Panels. The Brazilian judge of the Special Panels told me, for instance, that they did not receive very many cases concerning women.[39] My conversation with her made me understand how difficult it was to bring justice in a country destroyed by war, but it also left me curious. I then decided to follow the chain of justice.

After a conflict, the Special Panels face a large number of grave and serious violations of human rights, a large number of perpetrators, limited personnel and financial resources, and a pressure to deliver justice within a short timeframe. With the establishment of the SCU in 2000, the international General Prosecutor identified 10 priority cases, involving 202 accused, 183 of whom were still at large, to focus on those cases involving murder (there were approximately 1400 murder investigations) (ICTJ 2006b: 19).[40] The selection was based on the following criteria: the number and type of victims, the seriousness of the crimes and their political significance, and the availability of evidence (ICTJ 2006b: 19). Besides the crimes committed in Lolotoe and Los Palos, this would respond to

[38] Case number 04/2001, also known as the *Lolotoe* case, testimony of witness B, para 90.

[39] Interview with Participant 92, 15 November 2016.

[40] These were: the Liquiça Church massacre (6 April 1999); the murders at the house of Manuel Carrascalão (17 April 1999); the Kailako killings (April 1999) and Maliana Police Station killings (2–8 September 1999); the Lospalos case (21 April–25 September 1999), the Lolotoe case (2 May–16 September 1999); the Suai Church massacre (6 September 1999); the attack on Bishop Belo's compound and the Dili Diocese (6 September 1999); the Passabe and Makaleb massacres (September–October 1999); cases of deportations, persecution, killing of UNAMET staff and atrocities carried out by TNI Battalion 745 (April-September 1999); and sexual violence cases carried out in various districts (March-September 1999) (UNTAET 2001).

the massacres such as the ones in Liquiçá, Suai and Maliana – because they were considered to be graver. The issue is that women suffered SGBV crimes *in addition* to suffering the violations experienced by men, such as murder, torture, and forced displacement (CAVR 2005: 2675). The women interviewed explained that men and women experienced the conflict in different ways. By prioritising murder, men could have become the predominant victims covered by the cases, while crimes of SGBV could have been left out. This is why women's participation at the Special Panels was mostly as witnesses about militia members who committed murder (AJAR 2015: 165). The questions are, then: who defines the gravity and the hierarchies of crimes, how are they defined, and who are understood to be victims? These seem to be arbitrary and subjective decisions and because they are so blurred, may fail to meet the expectations of victims.

Remarkably, in addition to the focus on murder, most of the people indicted in the early stages were treated as individual criminal cases with indictments including only ordinary domestic law charges of murder, rather than, for instance, crimes against humanity (ICTJ 2006b: 18–19). The early SCU investigations were then criticised for having a narrow, case-based approach and failing to focus on the systematic nature of the violations that had occurred during 1999 as well as on the role played by the Indonesian military apparatus (ICTJ 2006b: 18–19; CTF 2008: 92). If the intention of the Special Panels was to follow the legislation of the Rome Statute and the experiences of the ICTY and ICTR, this may have become irrelevant on the ground. This recalls Palmer's assertion about the ICTR that 'the Tribunal's increasingly clear focus on its contribution to international criminal case law, rather than the broader objectives articulated in its initial mandate, shows the dynamic nature of transitional justice' (Palmer 2015: 62). On top of that, by 2003, the Deputy Prosecutor of the SCU noted that a lack of resources, combined with an approaching deadline for ending investigations, eliminated the possibility that all cases could be investigated and prosecuted (Katzenstein 2003: 259–60). Mandates and legislation are important but so are the personal decisions concerning the priorities of public institutions.

The collection of evidence by the investigators was also a determining factor in the invisibility of cases against women. At a dinner in Dili, I met a former international police investigator of the SCU, who explained to me his experience concerning the selection of cases for the prosecution. There were only two investigators for each of the large 13 municipalities and they had to travel there to carry out the investigations. This was in tune with Katzenstein's assertion that 'the number of investigators ranged from two to ten' (2003: 259). The investigator also explained that they acted on reports from the villagers, mainly reports of mass graves, and they visited the places to find out and corroborate the details where the alleged killings and massacres had happened. Not only did the prosecutor prioritise the hierarchy of the crimes, but by only having two people on the ground for each municipality, it was difficult to investigate properly crimes of other natures.

Furthermore, there were allegations of problems with the internal dynamics. There were allegations that some investigators were reluctant to leave the comparative comfort of Dili to go to any of the 13 municipalities to interview witnesses and at one point, prosecutors and investigators clashed over who was in charge of deciding which cases should take priority (Steele 2002: 81). At one point, owing to internal tensions and discrepancies with the head investigator, his position was terminated, which made the SCU operate without a head investigator (Katzenstein 2003: 276). This led to prosecutors, many of whom lacked experience conducting investigations, assuming charge of investigators (Katzenstein 2003: 276). All of this was aggravated first by the fact that incriminatory evidence was deliberately destroyed by the militias – from the destruction of documents to the hiding of corpses – but also by the loss of evidence since 2003, allegedly as a result of the UN's disorderliness (KPP-HAM 2000; Katzenstein 2003: 262). Justice was therefore being shaped *ab initio*.

To complicate matters further, women's access to justice may be affected by a patriarchal UN. In 1999, the SR on violence against women manifested her concern that the Australian-led International Force East Timor (INTERFET), at the beginning of its mandate, did not include any expertise in cases of sexual violence, nor 'a special unit or specially trained investigators who may be able to identify, report and investigate cases of violence against women' (UN 1999a: para 58). A lack of a gender approach in the investigations meant that cases could go unnoticed. In Ermera Vila, I met Ligia, a local female leader who is coordinator of the women's group and has tried to run for election as village chief. Ligia explained to me that in the crisis of 1999, a commander had come to her house and offered her uncle US$1000 so he could take her to Indonesia. The uncle accepted, 'because he was scared', she said. She then escaped and married her cousin to avoid suffering from sexual violence. Another woman, nevertheless, was raped by the same commander, she said. Ligia also said that when the Special Panels came to her village, they were not talking to the victims of sexual violence. This happened despite the fact that in Ermera Vila and Gleno, from April to September 1999, there were at least 50 women raped. The Indonesians were coming to their houses, and if the parents were present, they had to accept, out of fear; if not they were killed. There were also many single women around because their families were in the mountains. Women of all ages and physical appearance were targeted. Women were sexually abused even next to the police station. The sexual violence continued even after the elections in September, and up to November.[41]

Moreover, the UN SR also called in 1999 for medical professionals, in particular those qualified to conduct medical examinations of possible victims of rape and sexual abuse (UN 1999b: para 74(3)). Several reports written after 1999 mentioned the participation of forensic experts in analysing corpses, but there is more vagueness in the literature concerning forensic experts and medical

[41] Interview with Participant 44, Emera Vila, Ermera, Timor-Leste, 8 November 2016.

professionals in dealing with cases of sexual violence (UN 1999a: para 40). There were also issues with the statements. In the *Lolotoe* case, one of the women who suffered sexual violence was questioned about the differences between her statement to an investigator at the Maliana Police Station and her testimony in court. She testified in court that sexual intercourse took place between her and Francisco Noronha, between her and Mouzinho and between her and Bambang on several occasions. When she was pressured on the issue, she replied in court, 'I told them, but they didn't write it down'.[42] There was therefore a gender imbalance in the investigation teams, a lack of consistent attention to sexual crimes during the investigation phase, and a lack of appropriately trained investigators, which has constrained the prosecution of rape and sexual crimes in the aftermath of conflict (Walsh 2013: 65).[43] This all means that SGBV crimes against women could have gone unnoticed from the very beginning.

Although sexual offences were listed as serious crimes, UNTAET was also later criticised for having lacked a clear gender strategy, gender expertise, and collaborative links with civil society women's groups (Cambodia Defenders Project 2012: 20). A lack of experts and training on gender may have had implications for evidentiary practices and legal advice and therefore an impact on the prosecutions of crimes committed against women. In my interviews in Dili, local NGOs not only referred to the poor collaboration of the SCU with them, but also to how in the beginning the latter did not know how to collect the data. By 2001, Fokupers, a local non-governmental organisation that works on women's issues, documented 182 cases of gender-specific violations committed in 1999 (CAVR 2005: 2666). ACbit's director described how local NGOs were the bridge with the victims and gave information to the SCU until they found out that the SCU were contacting the victims without letting them know.

Fokupers would later criticise the role of the UN in providing justice to victims of SGBV because these crimes were not seen as a priority; survivors found it difficult to speak with UN investigators, who were mainly male civilian police; there was a lack of female interpreters; and more generally there was a lack of interest in working with national women's NGOs (Cristalis and Scott 2005: 93). This may explain why there was a point at which 'the (female) deputy prosecutor for serious crimes claimed that no further cases could be brought to court, as women victims declined to come forward' (Wandita Campbell-Nelson and Pereira 2006: 316). Therefore, although local women's groups had presented their data on SGBV crimes to international investigators from the beginning, mismanagement in the early phases of investigations, the fact that no specific measures existed to ensure that SGBV was investigated, and that there was a delay in the establishment of a sex crime team, all had an effect on the prosecution of cases concerning women (Wandita, Campbell-Nelson and Pereira 2006: 315–16).

[42] Case number 04/2001, also known as the *Lolotoe* case. Testimony of the witness Victim B.

[43] The CEDAW Committee suggests to 'use gender-sensitive practices (e.g., use of female police officers) in the investigation of violations during and after conflict to ensure that violations by State and non-State actors are identified and addressed' (GR 30 2013: para 17(d)).

The lack of gender sensitivity shown by the justice provided by the UN has not been unique to the Timor-Leste case. In the final report of the Kosovo Human Rights Advisory Panel, a quasi-judicial body whose mandate was to evaluate the United Nations Mission in Kosovo's (UNMIK) actions against international human rights instruments, the Panel found that in the *Kostić* case, concerning abductions taken place during an armed assault by the Kosovo Liberation Army (KLA) on the villages of Opterusa and Retimlje, UNMIK did not exercise due diligence in the investigation of violence against women (Nowicki, Chinkin and Tulkens 2017: para 49; HRAP 2016: para 85).[44] Moreover, the Panel found that the failure by UNMIK to conduct gender-sensitive investigations might have contributed to the general lack of documentation of conflict-related sexual violence in Kosovo, which hampered victims' access to justice and reparations (Nowicki, Chinkin and Tulkens 2017: para 49). As we can see, structures are not neutral entities, they are composed of, directed and shaped by individuals, and exploring their identities is an important component in women's law research (Bentzon et al 1998: 114). From the beginning, the investigations of SGBV against women were weak and transitional justice processes may have contributed to the silencing of the crimes committed against them. Now, I turn to the proceedings.

V. THE PUBLIC: THE PROCEEDINGS

There may have been issues concerning the misapplication of laws during the proceedings. In the *Los Palos* case, in which charges of crimes against humanity were adjudicated, the judges, for instance, discussed the existence of a state of 'armed conflict' which is a requirement for war crimes but not for crimes against humanity (Katzenstein 2003: 266).[45] I also saw the separation of rape from torture, not only in the prosecutions, but also in other mechanisms of transitional justice implemented in Timor-Leste. As international law has demonstrated, it is not the case that men are tortured, and women are raped, but also that sexual violence can be inflicted as part of torture. If rape indeed is perpetrated with the intent of punishing and intimidating the victim, then it falls under torture. By neglecting this connection, we may add a layer of difficulty for women's access to justice by the competent tribunal, including a proper judicial investigation.[46]

[44] *Bogoljub Kostić and Others v UNMIK*, case 111/09 and others, Kosovo Human Rights Advisory Panel, opinion of 23 October 2015. The group abducted was composed mainly of women, and in the Panel's view, 'investigation of any situation when women are deprived of liberty by a party to the armed conflict must take into account the potential possibility of sexual and gender-based violence against them' (HRAP 2016: paras 85–86).

[45] Katzenstein cites the *Judicial System Monitoring Programme* (JSMP Case Report), *The General Prosecutor v Joni Marques and 9 Others* (*The Los Palos Case*) (2002), at 29–30.

[46] In 1996 the Inter-American Commission on Human Rights (IACHR) addressed for the first time the concept of sexual violence as torture, and access to justice for victims in the individual case system (IACHR 2015b, para 25). On addressing the rape in the case of Raquel Martín de Mejía in Peru, the IACHR (2015b: paras 25–27) determined in its decision the elements set forth

There were numerous accounts of women held in official custody and sexually assaulted in order to obtain from them information or as a punishment for their relations with members of Falintil. The failure to see the connection between sexual assault and torture may constitute a barrier for women's access to veterans' pensions. Cases of SGBV were restricted to charges of rape, but in reality, some of them could have fallen into the category of torture or sexual slavery. The denial of the true nature of the crimes committed against Timorese women has an impact on women's invisibility in terms of their political agency. The further denial of the extent of sexual slavery in the country may also amount to a moral debt. The women who were taken to West Timor were not only sexually assaulted but also forced to carry out activities such as cooking and cleaning, and this may fall more under the category of sexual slavery.

In the *Leonardus Kasa* case, a member of the Laksaur militia from Cova Lima district was indicted in December 2000 with one charge of rape of a woman in West Timor in September 1999 (Harris Rimmer 2010: 154–58). The judges of the Special Panels would declare that because the case was charged as a crime of rape in violation of section 9 of UNTAET Regulation 2000/15 and Article 285 of the Indonesian Penal Code, they did not have universal jurisdiction with regard to 'ordinary' sexual offences committed in 1999 and that there was a dissonance between the context of the offence and the charges (Harris Rimmer 2010: 154–58). More specifically, the Special Panels considered that they had universal jurisdiction over genocide, war crimes, crimes against humanity and torture, but not over individual cases of murder and sexual offences such as this (Harris Rimmer 2010: 160). The case should have been charged as rape in the context of a crime against humanity instead of a charge of rape under domestic law (Harris Rimmer 2010: 160). According to Harris Rimmer (2010: 161–62), not only did the prosecutor err in charging this crime as an ordinary offence rather than as a crime against humanity, a war crime or an act of torture, but also the Special Panels erred by not seeing that universal jurisdiction deals with a crime of a gross human rights violation and that does not depend on a link with the territory where the crime took place, the offender or the victim.[47]

Then there were the 'classic elements' of consent and corroboration, which in cases of sexual violence, have usually been used to discredit women. In general, a survivor's credibility is usually challenged upon cross-examination 'in an attempt to discredit his/her testimony' (International Protocol on the

in the Inter-American Convention to Prevent and Punish Torture to prove the existence of torture: (1) 'an intentional act through which physical and mental pain and suffering is inflicted on a person'; (2) 'committed with a purpose', and (3) 'by a public official or by a private person acting at the instigation of the former'. The IACHR (2015b: paras 25–27) has also taken into account the physical and psychological suffering caused by rape and the possibility of the victim suffering 'ostracism' when a woman reports these acts.

[47] Facing this common reality in which states do not assume responsibility for crimes of SGBV, the Great Lakes Pact – Protocol on the Prevention and Suppression of Sexual Violence against Women and Children, adopted 30 November 2006, affirms that crimes of sexual violence in the Great Lakes Region of Africa shall not be subject to statutory limitations (Article 6(6)).

Documentation and Investigation of Sexual Violence in Conflict 2014: 135). However, in the context in which international crimes are committed (eg mass violence, duress, detention, threats and coercion), because a genuine consent is impossible, consent is therefore obviated (International Protocol on the Documentation and Investigation of Sexual Violence in Conflict 2014: 135). This has been largely discussed by other tribunals.

In the *Akayesu* case, where the defendant was found individually criminally responsible for crimes against humanity for sexual violence, the Chamber considered that 'coercive circumstances need not be evidenced by a show of physical force' but 'can be inherent in circumstances like armed conflict or military presence of threatening forces on an ethnic basis'.[48] There is no need, then, for the prosecution to show evidence of physical force when we talk about coercion and it is the accused who must substantiate that the evidence of consent is credible. In the *Kunarac* case which concerned the proof that rape occurred 'without the consent of the victim', the Appeals Chamber emphasised that, in the types of prosecution being brought before the Tribunal, the prosecution's burden of proving coercive circumstances will generally not be difficult to discharge (Brammertz and Jarvis 2010: 107). In other words, the act of force – if the women actively resisted – is not a necessary element of the crime, but only the victim's lack of genuine consent.[49] The focus thus shifted in the 2000s from force/coercion to absence of consent through coercive circumstances, such as detention and factors of violence, and today, under international criminal law, 'once the background circumstances which would establish the existence of genocide, crimes against humanity or war crimes have been met, there is almost a presumption of non-consent on the part of the victim' (Hayes 2016: 375).[50]

Corroboration is also not a legal requirement in crimes of sexual violence under principles of international criminal procedure, so in the absence of witnesses, documents, medical reports, photos, or any other evidence, 'a survivor's own testimony can be sufficient evidence of the commission of a crime of sexual violence' (International Protocol on the Documentation and Investigation of Sexual Violence in Conflict 2014: 135).[51] In other words, while

[48] *Prosecutor v Akayesu*, Case No ICTR-96-4-T, Judgment, paras 688, 692–97 (2 September 1998).

[49] ICTY, *Kunarac* Appeal Judgment, paras 128–30. This reasoning was followed by the jurisprudence of the ECtHR in *MC v Bulgaria* (Application no 39272/98), 4 December 2003, [2003] ECHR 651.

[50] Rule 70 of the Rules of Procedure and Evidence of the ICC states that in cases of sexual violence: (a) consent cannot be inferred by reason of any words or conduct of a victim where force, threat of force, coercion or taking advantage of a coercive environment undermined the victim's ability to give voluntary and genuine consent; (b) consent cannot be inferred by reason of any words or conduct of a victim where the victim is incapable of giving genuine consent; (c) consent cannot be inferred by reason of the silence of, or lack of resistance by, a victim to the alleged sexual violence; (d) credibility, character or predisposition to sexual availability of a victim or witness cannot be inferred by reason of the sexual nature of the prior or subsequent conduct of a victim or witness' (ICC 2002).

[51] Rule 63 of the Rules of Procedure and Evidence at the ICC (2002).

the presence of corroboration can strengthen a case, its absence does not mean that the evidence on which to base charges or indeed a conviction will be insufficient (International Protocol on the Documentation and Investigation of Sexual Violence in Conflict 2014: 135). Based on ICTY and ICTR procedures, a UNTAET Regulation states that 'cases of sexual assault require no corroboration, limits the use of consent as a defence by the suspect, and bars admittance of the victim's prior sexual conduct as evidence' (AJAR 2015: 367, fn 100).[52] In the *Lolotoe* case concerning three women who were raped, the defence used nevertheless the argument of consent.[53] The issue is that there is a tendency to see sexual violence as opportunistic, based on the spasmodic desire of the male perpetrator, and therefore disregarded. Moreover, questions such as the following ones were posed to the victims: 'Did you ever tell Rosalino that you don't want to sleep with him?', 'Did he say anything?', 'What did Rosalino do with his gun while he raped you?' and 'While Rosalino raped you, did you scream or try to fight him?'[54] This shows how because of stereotyping, 'judges, prosecutors and law enforcement officials misinterpret or misapply laws, adopting rigid standards about what they consider to be appropriate behaviour for women and penalising those who do not conform to those stereotypes' (CEDAW GR 33 2015: para 26).

The judicial system thus can contribute to the stereotyping of women by creating narratives of women as men's sexual property and of a male sexuality that enables sexual exploitation of women through sexual assault and violence, which not only minimises women's agency and their right to bodily integrity, but also denies their dignity as a human being (Cook and Cusack 2010: 27; CEDAW GR 19 1992: para 11). In this regard, the CEDAW Committee has held that there should be no assumption in law or practice that a woman gives her consent where she does not physically resist unwanted sexual conduct.[55] Moreover, 'there is an acknowledgement that it would be absurd to put questions about consent to a survivor of crimes committed during the context of international crimes', and that 'the potential harm that a suggestion of consent could cause to a survivor far outweighs any evidentiary benefit of posing the

[52] UNTAET Regulation 2000/30 on Transitional Rules of Criminal Procedures, Section 34.3. Rule 96 of the Rules of Procedure and Evidence of the ICTR and ICTY provides that in cases of sexual assault: '(i) the victim's testimony does not need to be corroborated; (ii) consent is not permitted as a defence if the victim: (a) was subjected to or threatened with or has had reasons to fear violence, duress, detention or psychological oppression, or (b) reasonably believed that if the victim did not submit, another might be so subjected, threatened or put in fear; (iii) before evidence of the victim's consent is admitted, the accused must satisfy the Trial Chamber in camera that the evidence is relevant and credible; and (iv) the victim's prior sexual conduct shall not be admitted in evidence or as defence.' See ICTY IT/32/rev. 49 (22 May 2013) and ICTR ITR/3/Rev.1 (29 June 1995).

[53] Case number 04/2001, also known as the *Lolotoe* case.

[54] Case number 8/2002, *The Prosecutor v Gonsalves et al*, also known as the *Atabae* case. Paulo Gonsalves was a militia man, and according to one of the testimonies, was also a village chief.

[55] *Vertido v Philippines*, Communication No 18/2008, CEDAW/C/46/D/18/2008, 16 July 2010, United Nations.

question' (International Protocol on the Documentation and Investigation of Sexual Violence in Conflict 2014: 135).

The use of consent as a defence argument in cases of sexual violence perpetuates a message of sexism and loss of dignity. MacKinnon (2017: 289), for instance, believes that 'consent is a pathetic standard of equal sex for a free people' and proposes a redefinition of rape that excludes this concept.[56] More specifically, she claims that consent definitions put the victim on trial:

> it makes the case be about what she was thinking, or what he thought she was thinking, rather than about what he did. It makes rape occur in someone's mind, not by his body on her body (MacKinnon 2017: 286).

According to MacKinnon (2017: 287), consent as a concept was originated in Western law, as the basis for legitimising the obligation to obey the laws of the state (the doming power) by its subordinates (the governed). The idea thus that a woman consents because she is there and does not leave leads to the belief that silence in sex – as in governing – is consent, not dissent (MacKinnon 2017: 287). When it comes to the definition of rape, MacKinnon (2017: 289) supports the one used by the ICTR in *Akayesu*, in which rape is defined as a 'physical invasion of a sexual nature committed on a person under circumstances which are coercive'. Non-consent is seen as redundant and because of its absence, coercion – which can be physical as well as circumstantial – is present, ie the definition is on the force side but is not limited to physical force (MacKinnon 2017: 289).[57]

In any case, in the *Lolotoe* case, the Panel considered 'as persuasive the absence of consent as the central element of the definition of the crime of rape' and said that it was not necessary to demonstrate the use of force or that the perpetrator physically overpowered the victim because the context of the rape, a sufficiently coercive or threatening situation, would render the act non-consensual.[58] Sexual violence is per se about an imbalance and abuse of power. The women who suffered the sexual violence in the *Lolotoe* case were indeed incapable of providing genuine consent in a coercive environment. Moreover, a constant cross-examination of women who have suffered SGBV can also lead to deep emotional and psychological distress. Charlesworth and Chinkin (2000: 328) write that:

> the right to a fair trial is typically interpreted as a right of an accused to procedural safeguards to prevent an unjust conviction. It must be balanced against the right of

[56] Although the ECtHR in *MC v Bulgaria* and the CEDAW Committee in *Vertido v Philippines* have said that consent is the core of an equality approach, MacKinnon argues that this endorses 'the active/passive model of sex and social conditioning to trauma and the acquiescence that goes with it' (MacKinnon 2017: 288–89).

[57] MacKinnon (2017: 289) goes further by arguing that, while in international criminal law circumstances concerning war, genocide and crimes of humanity make concern invalid, in peacetime domestic settings those circumstances should include psychological, economic, and hierarchical forms of coercion. As such, 'coercion, defined to include all forms of inequality including gender, not lack of consent, is thus the essence of gender crime, including rape' (MacKinnon 2017: 319).

[58] Case number 04/2001, also known as the *Lolotoe* case.

> victims of crime to be able to recount their experiences without intimidation. Giving priority to the right to a fair trial over other rights in the context of sexual violence illustrates the claim that human rights law has been predicated upon concerns of men and that it fails to take account of the life experiences of women.

The women in the *Lolotoe* case went through several interviews and corroborations, describing their distressing violations over several years without any psycho-social support. In the beginning the women gave detailed information. At one point in the process, the defence also argued that the women should not be called victims but witnesses, since the crimes against them were not proven and the presumption of innocence had to be applied.[59] In other words, to be called a victim, they suggested, a person must have been murdered or show some visible harm. This could be perceived as the justice system questioning the honesty of the women who suffered sexual violence: they were supposed to pass from being victims to being witnesses.[60]

In addition to slowing down the process, the constant repetition of such an intimidating crime over many years in a formal and distant structure that projected distrust towards them must have been a great emotional burden on these women. The transcript from one of the last interviews describes how one of the victims was not comfortable anymore and how, at one point, she decided to remain silent and to stop the interview. When asked if she wanted to continue with the statement? She replied:

> I spoke already about these things. I told this already to Fokupers and the police. I really do not feel comfortable to repeat everything again. I would prefer to finish the statement now. It is not easy for me to talk about these things and as I said I was already questioned about that.[61]

Another woman also said: 'I do not want to give a statement about anything. I am tired of giving statements. My case was not followed up by the court and I was questioned that often already. I do not want to state anything more.'[62]

Reflecting on the power of criminal trials to achieve closure for the victims, Cameron (2008: 57) argues that although it is necessary to allow the questioning of witnesses to ensure a fair trial, a tough cross-examination may likely reopen terrible wounds. Nesiah (2011: 145) also argues that judicial processes are often alienating for victims and in some cases may even disempower them. Law therefore may not only deny women's equal access to justice by excluding

[59] Case number 04/2001, also known as the *Lolotoe* case, para 32.

[60] The defence of one of the accused argued that none of the victims participating in the case, including the three women who were raped, could be called victims in the proceedings, since the commission of the violations was not proven. The defence proposed to use the term 'witness' instead. The Judges ordered the use of the term victims for the three women. The defence then went to the Court Judge Administrator, accusing the judges on the Panel of bias towards the prosecution. After suspending the normal procedure and spending time in new deliberations, the decision of the Court Judge Administrator supported the decision of the judges of the Special Panels. The proceedings then re-started.

[61] Case number 04/2001, also known as the *Lolotoe* case.

[62] Case number 04/2001, also known as the *Lolotoe* case.

harms that happen particularly to women from the legal definition of harm, but also 'collaborates by depriving women of credibility through the institutionalized belief that we are likely to lie about sexual assault and by legally defining sexual assault from the point of view of the perpetrator' (MacKinnon, 2017: 29). MacKinnon (2017: 14) cautions that

> many women who have gone through rape trials see the trial as an extension of the rape. The burdens of proof, the legal assumptions, the disbelief they encounter, mean that their sexuality can be violated without consequences to the violator.

Victims, particularly women, may face constant interruption during their testimony, be asked inappropriate questions – even in cases of sexual violence, or simply be forced to remain silent about a certain crime and be asked to elaborate on another one, as happened in the ICC. In Timor-Leste, there was also criticism of how victims and witnesses were treated during hearings and how this treatment could have deepened their trauma and led to their re-victimisation. The women who were raped and who participated in the *Lolotoe* case became progressively tired, angry and distrustful of the trial, showing how understandable it is that women could become hostile and reluctant to testify. Moreover, we can imagine what they could have felt when, after giving their testimonies over several years about something so intimate, they were later informed that only Mouzinho was convicted, since of the other two, one was in Indonesia and the other was convicted of other crimes. To come back to the impact of adopting a definition of gravity, I also noticed that in the *Lolotoe* case, while the three women are constantly mentioned as a group, victims A, B and C, there was a more individualised attention to the other violations, mainly murder, and I observed how this would also be reflected in the large number of witnesses for the latter.

A 'goldmine' was the word used by a former UN employee who participated in UNTAET to describe the court records of ordinary crimes.[63] The Special Panel of the District Court of Dili that dealt with ordinary crimes was established before the Special Panels for Serious Crimes, so cases of rape that occurred in 1999 could have ended by being treated as ordinary domestic crimes. This is important because there is also a different definition of consent in cases under international criminal law as opposed to cases under domestic Timorese law. While a lack of consent is not an element in a crime of sexual violence as a crime under international law, in domestic contexts, survivors of crimes of SGBV are often obliged to demonstrate to the court that they did not consent to the sexual act (International Protocol on the Documentation and Investigation of Sexual Violence in Conflict 2014: 135).[64] The Indonesian domestic penal law

[63] Interview with Participant 108, 15 March 2016.

[64] Reflecting on the participation and recognition of women throughout the Dayton Peace Agreement concerning Bosnia and Herzegovina, Chinkin and Paradine (2001: 125) argue that rape was under-reported and convictions were hard to establish 'because of the requirement in domestic law that the prosecution prove lack of consent and because in many instances of prejudices about women's sexual availability and unreliability'.

was harmful in this respect. Since 1998, the SR on violence against women had manifested her concern about the legal requirement that the testimony of victims of rape must be corroborated, provided for by Article 185(2) of the Indonesian Code of Criminal Procedure: 'The testimony of one witness is not sufficient to prove that a defendant is guilty of the act of which he is charged' (UN 1999b: para 38). This meant that 'the necessity of corroboration puts the burden of proof on the victim and ultimately ensures that the victim is the one being subject to trial' (UN 1999b: para 38). She also noticed that punishment for rape under the Penal Code 'is lenient compared to other jurisdictions and any reform of the law should increase the punishment for rapists and other perpetrators of violence against women' (UN 1999b: para 39). Thus, the Indonesian legislation added a further barrier for women victims of rape in 1999 to access justice.

To make the situation more complicated, after independence the justice system did not develop as quickly as expected: as early as 2004 there was a caseload of over 1000 new matters of 'less serious crimes' to be decided by the Dili District Court (Burgess 2004: 154). It then became obvious that not only were the courts unable to deal with the huge number of past cases, but also those close to the border of jurisdiction as a 'serious criminal offence' would not be addressed either (Burgess 2004: 154). In addition, beyond the three Timorese judges involved in hearing serious crimes cases either at trials or appellate hearings, there was virtually no social or professional interaction between the international and national judges in the courts of ordinary jurisdiction, and national judges were left to deal with these crimes on their own (ICTJ 2006b: 12–16). Because of this lack of interaction, there was not any follow up or monitoring. We simply do not know what happened in those trials.

Judicial vagueness and gaps that result in the invisibility of SGBV cases may be a common feature in post-conflict justice processes. In Rwanda, for instance, the perception by ICTR investigators that rape was a lesser crime and not worthy of investigating led to few rape cases being prosecuted (Graybill 2012: 211–14).[65] In the ground-breaking case of *Akayesu*, it was as a result of an *amicus* brief prepared by domestic human rights organisations that the prosecutor amended the initial indictment of genocide to include rape as a crime against humanity and a war crime (Graybill 2012: 211–14). After the verdict, however, prosecutors were reluctant to bring indictments for crimes of sexual violence, and as a consequence, 'at the tenth anniversary of the genocide, only 30 per cent of cases tried included rape charges, and only 10 per cent of those defendants were found guilty for their role in widespread sexual violence' (Graybill 2012: 211–14). On the other hand, not only did the Rwandan domestic courts prioritise murder, but also although defendants may have included those who committed acts of rape and sexual torture, few if any of the dossiers included these charges (Graybill 2012: 212–13).

[65] Under pressure from international women's groups, in July 1996, a sexual assault committee was created within the tribunal to address problems related to the investigation of gender crimes (Graybill 2012: 211–14).

Graybill (2012: 213) suggests that this was due to the fact that the law did not expressly define the legal elements of either crime, such as force or coercion, making court verdicts inconsistent, law enforcement confused and SGBV against women ignored. The then deputy minister of justice in Rwanda, Gerald Gahima, recognised that 'rape has not been receiving the attention it deserves. The main focus has been on the killings and not as many women were killed' (Graybill 2012: 213). Although rape could not be prosecuted initially in gacaca, a change in the law in 2008 allowed cases of rape to come under this jurisdiction, which meant that if a suspect's confession and apology were accepted at a gacaca panel, he or she could receive a reduced sentence, as was the case with other crimes prosecuted by gacaca (Graybill 2012: 213–14). Some women's groups felt this change minimised the seriousness of rape and believed the sentences were too lenient (Graybill 2012: 213). The example of legal pluralism in Rwanda shows that Timor-Leste is not the only case where the justice that is provided after a conflict presents additional barriers to the prosecution of cases of SGBV against women.

Finally, this revives interrogations of 'justice' and the catalysing effect of judicial international interventions. What are the ways in which the international community can support a state emerging from the debris of conflict more effectively? If there is a focus on prosecutions, then these initiatives should also be adapted to local needs. Palmer found in her work that Rwandan courts trying genocide suspects appeared more interested in developing judicial capacity than in implementing international due process standards, particularly because of the huge backlog of cases that Rwandan courts were facing (Palmer 2012: 153). Weill and Jovanović (2012: 241) also pointed out how the Serbian War Crimes Chamber and Prosecutor were apparently keener on learning practical skills, including evidence gathering, rather than on applying international law properly. After interviewing key people who participated in the Special Panels and after the six months that I spent at the Dili District Court, I reached similar conclusions. It should not be about focusing on the best legal standards, but about guaranteeing that no rights are violated. Today the justice system is swamped by an overload of cases and this obviously has an effect on women's access to justice. I now revert to private elements intervening in the justice process.

VI. THE PRIVATE INTERFERENCE

Not only do the relevant laws, procedures and public agents have an impact on the investigation and prosecution of cases concerning women and their subsequent invisibility, but private dynamics also matter. Indeed, in every society, there exist 'elaborate and complex, and sometimes competing, rules which govern people's actions and behavior' (WLSA 1999: 4). On the one hand, there are policy makers, who imagine themselves innocent of political commitment and identity, with their policy initiatives presented as best practices (Kennedy 2004: 130), while on the other hand, there are institutional rules that shape both the preferences and behaviour of political actors and political outcomes (Chappell 2016: 10). The apparent neutrality of the UN Special Panels and SCU had in reality not only many different layers of substantive and procedural issues that affected women's participation and recognition, but their role was also shaped by community structures and individual local agency. In this regard, Ross argues that while researchers attributed women's silence to a 'general stigma' that associates rape as a private act, in the context of political violence or detention, rape may be deliberately public. What is at stake is not the privacy of the act but how society acknowledges it as a form of violence and makes provision for its recognition as injury (Ross 2003: 23).[66]

The UNTAET policeman I met in Dili also told me that when he and his colleague were arriving in the municipalities to carry out the investigations, people in the communities showed them the locations of mass graves. We need to think who these people were and how, within the same villages, others may be more affected by economic and social barriers, such as poverty and lack of education. Having just two investigators for each municipality meant that they were geographically and financially inaccessible to the majority. There may be a culture of silence that impeded the reporting of cases regarding sexual violence. I heard from several of the interviewees that Timor-Leste in general has a deep culture of silence, particularly in cases of violence against women. In several testimonies at the Special Panels for Serious Crimes, my attention was drawn to one of the cases in which a woman described how after a militia man raped her in 1999, her family in the house acted as if nothing had happened: 'Of course they heard it but they would never talk to me about it.'[67] Another woman said that her family told her that it was better to forget: 'Let it be, he is a married man, you are a married woman, he raped you, it doesn't matter, just pray to God'.[68] Another woman also said 'I never spoke to anyone else other than my parents about being raped'.[69] These examples show how women and their own family could have decided to hide violations of a sexual nature, for reasons of shame and stigma, from other family members and more generally from the wider community.

As Chinkin and Paradine (2001: 125) argue, rape in the context of armed conflict is seen as a 'crime against honor – a woman's or her family's public reputation – rather than as a crime of violence or as an instrument of war'. Honour has been attached to women, which in practice has meant that if women are dishonoured the family is also dishonoured. The silence of the family could have pressured women to keep quiet. This has been the assumption even according to the international law that regulates the protection of civilians in conflict.[70]

[66] Ross (2003) cites Goldblatt (1997).

[67] Case number 8/2002, *Gonsalves et al*, also known as the *Atabae* case.

[68] Case number 8/2002, *Gonsalves et al*, also known as the *Atabae* case.

[69] Case number 8/2002, *Gonsalves et al*, also known as the *Atabae* case.

[70] Again, in International Humanitarian Law (IHL), rape is described as an attack on honour, a form of indecent assault and as an outrage upon personal dignity (Evans 2012: 120).

The reflection of the connection between rape and honour is important, particularly in a culture such as the Timorese, where the value of women is related to their fertility. According to their customs, marriage is not only between two people, but between two families, and while the male brings – especially economic – security and protection, the woman brings her reproductive capacity. This is part of a custom called *Barlake* and, with the exchange of goods, it also involves economic resources from the family of the male towards the family of the wife.[71] It could have been that women and family members were making rational choices concerning the gains and costs of denouncing SGBV crimes against women. But the connection between rape and honour can also be de facto related to the honour of men – not those who are related to the victim as in the Geneva Conventions, but the perpetrator. In the *Lolotoe* case, Joni Franca preferred to accept that he committed several of the crimes with which he was charged, including torture, but rape was not part of his guilty plea.

There is a historical factor which I also find important. Already in 1999, the UN SR on violence against women highlighted that given 'the long-standing impunity enjoyed by the military with regard to crimes of sexual violence in East Timor, there was no possibility of victims reporting the incidents or attempting to seek justice' (UN 1999a: 56). Families and communities were exposed to crimes of SGBV during 24 years of conflict and assumed that these types of crimes were not taken to formal justice. The role of the investigators could further be affected by the unpopularity of the former Indonesian justice system, which was 'seen as corrupt and nepotistic, mixed with fear of torture' (Hohe 2003: 348). Indeed, the culture of silence was not new during the times of the Serious Crimes Process. The UN SR on violence against women had noted before how, although women were particularly vulnerable to SGBV violence, rape often went unreported because of fear of retaliation by the Indonesian army (UN 1999a: para 46). The system may have contributed to the enforcement of that culture of silence. Moreover, there could be community pressures on women to resolve their cases within community processes (What Works 2018: 36).[72]

In addition, this is a system that they would know better and was more accessible. Hohe (2003: 353) claims that after seeing that the establishment of an official judiciary was taking so long, villagers started to revert to local justice. She further described how in the early days of the violence, when people could not deal with their cases at the local traditional level, they turned for 'official' support towards the National Council of Timorese Resistance (CNRT)

[71] Wandita, Campbell-Nelson and Pereira (2006: 289) claim that a *Barlake* means that in a marriage 'a women simply moves from her father's domain of power, influence and control into the domain of her husband and his family', carried out within a process that excludes women from access to basic economic, social, and political rights. In addition to linking the practice of *Barlake* to domestic violence, according to the US Department of State (2021), 'some communities also continued the practice of forcing a widow either to marry one of her husband's family members or, if she and her husband did not have children together, to leave her husband's home.'

[72] The authors cite Ganguly (2014).

(Hohe 2003: 352). The CNRT had been established in 1998 as an umbrella organisation for all the resistance parties that were opposing the Indonesian occupation, so it is understandable that the population saw them as the legitimate power succeeding the Indonesian exodus (Hohe 2003: 352).[73] With a wide presence in the country, CNRT then assumed a quasi-legislative and judicial position in which they dealt with a large range of cases, and only if they could not handle them would they be taken to the UN Civilian Police (CIVPOL) (Hohe 2003: 352). However, even more intriguing is that, already in 2003, Hohe (2003: 352) mentions that 'the only crime for which the police would be addressed in the first instance was in the case of murder'. In other words, cases of SGBV seem to have been left in a limbo, jumping from one system to the other one. This all shows how the interaction of international and local public and private forces conflate together to silence SGBV against women.

People's unfamiliarity with and lack of confidence in the Special Panels could have also contributed to the low reporting of cases concerning women. In fact, the women interviewed described how they avoided participating in the formal justice of the Special Panels. One woman in Liquiçá said, for instance, 'women prefer not to share their stories because we were afraid to be called to the tribunal'.[74] Another woman in Lalerik Mutin said that she avoided participating in a formal court because of fear. She said, 'what if they prove me wrong'.[75] She thought that it was too intimidating to participate in a trial and have some lawyers asking her questions and contradicting what she experienced. Because of how the system works, she had a point. This is probably what was going to happen to her. This also reminded me of the story of a friend, a lawyer working at the criminal trials in Cambodia, and how when they were putting questions to a fisherman about what he was doing on a specific day during the Khmer Rouge regime, the man was confused and intimidated: ordinarily one cannot enumerate what one does every day.

VII. SENTENCES, WOMEN AND THE FOLLOW-UP

When it comes to the sentences and penalties, UNTAET Regulation 2000/15 provided for imprisonment not exceeding 25 years.[76] However, rather than

[73] Not to be confused with Xanana's present day CNRT (National Congress for Timorese Reconstruction) political party.

[74] Interview with Participant 60, Liquiçá, Liquiçá, Timor-Leste, 25 January 2017.

[75] Interview with Participant 59, Lalerik Mutin, Viqueque, Timor-Leste, 03 February 2017.

[76] As a matter of comparison, Harhoff (2008: 134–35) interprets the practice regarding prison sentences in the ICTY as: '(1) From 3 to 6–8 years of imprisonment: covers single or small scale criminal conduct in which genocide is not included (i.e. violations of the laws and customs of war and GC war crimes, and crimes against humanity), and where (a) the number of victims as well as (b) the temporal and territorial scope of the crimes is limited and where (c) the perpetrator has not acted with any degree of cruelty towards his victims; (2) from 8 to 20–22 years of imprisonment: crimes would ordinarily still not include genocide, but offences featuring a higher number of victims,

simply reflecting on the sole transplantation of laws and institutions, it may be more interesting to reflect on the local adjustments and resistance that will resurface in the transitional justice process (Sannerholm 2012: 239). For instance, in determining the terms of imprisonment for genocide, crimes against humanity, war crimes and torture, it established that the panel could follow the general practice regarding prison sentences in the Timorese courts as well as under international tribunals. This meant that for crimes of murder and sexual offences, the penalties would follow the Timorese Penal Code, which meant the Indonesian Penal Code.[77] The Special Panels tried to take into account the aggravating and mitigating circumstances as well as the conjunction of acts and the gravity of the crimes. According to Article 64 of the Indonesian Penal Code (KUHP), only one of the most severe penal provisions should be imposed.[78] If there were cases in which an accused, for instance, was charged with crimes of imprisonment, torture and inhumane acts, the convicted person was going to be jailed for only for one of those crimes. Moreover, according to the jurisprudence of the Court, a single judge, namely the presiding judge of the Panel or the individual judge who pronounced the sentence, also had the competence to decide on the supervision and execution of a prison sentence, including the ordering of his/her conditional release.[79] It is not about keeping men locked up with high sentences, but about finding the logic that after spending years on trial for crimes against humanity, convicts are sentenced according to domestic law and a single judge could offer conditional release.

Although after the end of the conflict the congress of the former CNRT initially recommended an international tribunal to bring Indonesian generals to trial, feelings of disenchantment and injustice started to surface when the UN justice was not only incapable of bringing those who were most responsible for serious abuses from Indonesia, but also those who were prosecuted were only middle- and lower-ranking Timorese (Leach 2017: 125).[80] Based on the UNTAET regulations, once the work of the Special Panels was concluded, the cases were transferred in 2005 to the caseload of ordinary crimes (Katzenstein 2003: 271–72). When this happened, because of the focus on good relations with Indonesia, the Timorese government embarked on a narrative of reconciliation and granted presidential pardons to those who had been convicted,

some extended temporal or territorial scope and involvement of brutality, cruelty or recklessness; (3) from 22 to about 35 years of imprisonment: may include genocide and will be relevant to offences committed against a large number of victims over an extended period of time in a wider geographical and with a high degree of brutality, cruelty or recklessness; most convicted persons fall into levels 2 and 3; and (4) from about 35 years to life imprisonment and covers all criminal conduct for which the gravity exceeds the third level.'

[77] UNTAET Regulation 2000/15. Timor-Leste would approve its own Penal Code in 2009.

[78] Art 64(1) of KUHP further states that 'in case of difference, the most severe penal provision shall be imposed.'

[79] UNTAET Regulation 2000/30, section 48.1. See also *Prosecutor v. Joni Marques and 9 others*, Case no 9/2000, SPSC, Decision on the application for conditional release of Alarico Fernandes, 17 April 2002.

[80] Leach (2017) cites Outcomes of the CNRT National Congress (21–30 August 2000).

even for crimes against humanity. Mouzinho, for instance, the only person to have been convicted of rape as a crime against humanity in 2003, was granted a presidential pardon in 2008 (AJAR 2015: 247). Eventually, in Timor-Leste, presidential pardons were granted to everyone, including to those who committed crimes against humanity. According to a UN employee interviewed in 2017, to her knowledge there was only one person detained.[81] She wondered why, giving the impression that the person must be so low profile that he could have been forgotten among all those pardons.

The pardons granted by the Timorese government would also reveal and produce some tensions. There were issues of local resistance to the Special Panels. When the prosecutors of the SCU issued indictments for crimes against humanity to seven top Indonesian officers, including General Wiranto, Xanana expressed dismay at the move, saying that close ties with Indonesia were of the utmost importance and that reconciliation and truth seeking were themselves forms of justice (*The Washington Post* 2003; Leach 2017: 125).[82] Therefore it was not a surprise that the Timorese government did not continue the work of the Special Panels once the mandate of the latter ended. Vinjamuri (2017: 120) uses the term 'backlash' as 'a behavioral response to the application or clear anticipation of a specific policy or institutional practice that is perceived to be in opposition to the interests or values of a particular actor or set of actors'. Experiences of other criminal tribunals have also shown this tension. As may have happened in the Serious Crimes Process, inside the International Criminal Tribunal for Rwanda (ICTR) in 2008, for instance, 'participants were conscious of the political difficulties raised by the requirements of state cooperation' (Palmer 2015: 72). Other scholars go further, arguing that in the case of transitional justice, the success that international actors can have on this type of justice depends after all on the cooperation of national governments (Nouwen and Werner 2011).

When the Timorese leadership started offering pardons, they also received international and local condemnation. According to the ICTJ (2010: 4), the offering of pardons meant that most perpetrators responsible for serious crimes escaped justice or served relatively short periods of imprisonment. Something similar was experienced in Rwanda. Given that in over 15 years the ICTR managed to process a little less than 100 cases, Rwandan authorities and observers of the process estimated that it was going to take more than a century to try some 135,000 detainees (estimated by 1999) to deal with all genocide suspects, including those that were still at large (Ndahinda and Muleefu 2012: 153–54). By 1999, the Rwandan government conceived as undesirable that there were tens of thousands of genocide suspects in jail without the possibility of trying them in a short time and that their continued detention amounted to a violation of the presumption of innocence (Ndahinda and Muleefu 2012: 155). In a pragmatic

[81] Interview with Participant 82, Dili, Timor-Leste, 09 November 2017.

[82] Hirst argues that it was this indictment against Wiranto that led leaders to publicly distance themselves from the process (ICTJ 2008: 11).

decision, the government decided to free them provisionally and deal with them in both domestic courts and the gacaca community-led process. Gacaca, which derived from a traditional method of conflict resolution that excluded professional lawyers and judges, was criticised for being an 'illegitimate' form of justice for punishing genocide perpetrators, that did not follow due process and that violated individual rights (Clark 2010: 3, 83).

The focus on formal prosecutions with the highest standards as well as the refusal to use other alternative methods to deal with past abuses may reflect an international imposition. As argued by Nino concerning the dilemmas faced by Argentina's successor democratic government, sometimes this 'duty' to punish above all else must cede to alternatives that are not ideal but necessary in a particular context and time (Nino 1991).[83] Scholars have also challenged the widespread assumption that trials deter future crimes and produce long-term stability, and that amnesties foster impunity and ultimately undermine peace (Clark 2018: 187–229). In fact, insisting on the illegality of amnesties may reduce national options for addressing large-scale conflict, as seen with the role of the ICC in Northern Uganda (Clark 2018: 187–229).

Reflecting on the establishment of the Special Panels by a UNTAET regulation, Hohe (2003: 338) argues that there was a contradiction between a lack of resources and a will to establish a 'perfect' Western justice system. However, as Sikkink (2017: 179) argues, 'human rights activists might work less on constantly pressing to raise the standard of accountability and more on making sure that existing standards of accountability are not flouted'. While tribunals of international criminal law typically focus on *best* standards, the priority should be that *minimum* standards are accomplished. This could accelerate the pace of these processes, include more cases beyond murder and be more instructive for local justice staff. Moreover, international donors, rather than focusing on the application of international law, should accept that the local justice agents and institutions in a post-conflict society may be more interested in receiving international funding and infrastructure support, particularly where all infrastructure has been destroyed and there are not enough local trained personnel for the administration of justice (Kristjánsdóttir, Nollkaemper and Ryngaert 2012: 324). These societies may indeed be primarily interested in 'effective, output-oriented,

[83] The international discourse of human rights can also show signs of malleability through time and among actors. Although used in particular in the initial transitional justice processes of South America and South Africa, amnesty laws were increasingly considered unacceptable according to the international human rights discourse. Clark (2018: 187–229) observes that while the UN increasingly holds that international law prohibits the use of amnesties for gross violations and insists on prosecutions within peace negotiations, the ICC also briefs international mediators about the illegality of using amnesties for suspects of these crimes during peace talks. This was a substantial shift at the ICC, given than during the Rome conference in 1998 many delegates expressed sympathy for the amnesty model promoted at that time by the South African TRC. Clark (2018: 187–229) suggests that because amnesties for serious crimes are neither clearly prohibited by international criminal law, nor mentioned in the Rome Statute, the international legal basis for the rejection of amnesties is weaker than many advocates have proposed.

quantitative justice that provides a measure of accountability, rather than qualitative, input-oriented justice based on international due process standards' (Kristjánsdóttir, Nollkaemper and Ryngaert 2012: 324). The issue must be that 'those who develop humanitarian policies often see themselves giving advice rather than making policy, formulating proposals which others – the real rulers – will need to implement' (Kennedy 2004: xvii). We are therefore in a situation in which international resources are directed towards costly prosecutorial procedures, while local people and leaders' concerns may be more related to covering their immediate basic needs.

Crucially, the pardons provided by the Timorese elites, the '*ema boot*', seemed to be the beginning of patterns of political interference in the domestic judiciary. After the grave and serious crimes committed in 1999 were transferred to the ordinary criminal justice system, UNTAET regulations established the presence of judges with a specific rank to deal with crimes against humanity and other past gross human rights violations. Because of the lack of local judges with this rank, there were international judges and prosecutors who remained in the country and continued to deal with some cases. However, in 2014 the government took the decision to expel international judges, prosecutors and other judicial actors who were fulfilling functions in the judicial system. This resulted in impeding the investigation, prosecution and punishment of grave and serious crimes, and raised concerns about judicial independence in the country (CAT 2017: para 8). The CAT Committee (2017: para 8) remarked that Timor-Leste stopped providing 'any information on the status of the 396 completed investigation files reportedly handed over by the SCU to the General Prosecutor of Timor-Leste in June 2013'. There was not only active executive interference in the decision to leave cases related to the Special Panels aside, but presidential pardons were even being granted in a wide variety of cases, including an incest case. Later, although a law would be adopted to limit the grant of presidential pardons and protect the independence of the judiciary, it is interesting to see that the rejection of an international prosecutorial system prompted judicial interference by local elites. Calling the UN agenda of state-building a 'mission impossible', Bull (2008: 9–14) argues that UN transitional administrations have failed not only to create an enabling 'space' in which internal processes of change could occur but also to deal with the legacies of the past and establish effective state justice institutions after their interventions.

It is not surprising then that the cases of the Special Panels are today gathering dust – no one refers to them in public discourse – that the state has not invested in controlling their data and statistics, and even less in having a gender approach, and that there are allegations that some files have disappeared.[84] This says a lot about the role of justice and its connection with memory, silence

[84] The CAT Committee has recommended that Timor-Leste consider including the database on victims, alleged perpetrators and witnesses compiled by the SCU and given to the government in 2013 in a publicly accessible national archive (2017: para 9(d)).

and the production of history in the country. Arendt and other scholars have argued that the role of the court is only to look at the evidence in the proceeding and to prove the culpability of the accused, rather than look at more systemic issues. More specifically, Arendt criticised how the prosecution in the *Eichmann* case posed questions on antisemitism as a whole rather than focusing on what he specifically did, and how there were testimonies after testimonies having nothing to do with Eichmann. The issue is that by focusing on isolated events, we may have failed to frame the large scale and gravity of the crimes, and this is critical for history production. Palmer (2015: 65–66) recounts how although the creation of a historical record was not explicitly included in the ICTR's mandate in 1994, there were divergences of opinion between those who supported the role of the tribunal to contribute to history-making, and those who believed that its role was more limited to accountability. Schabas (2008: 221) showed more optimism by crediting the ICTR with clarifying the historical truth of the genocide in Rwanda.

Besides having a role in conducting prosecutions, criminal tribunals can also contribute to the general history of a country. The cases at the Special Panels offered detailed contextual information to facilitate the decisions of the judges. Their records are such a rich historical source, particularly when there is a lack of history textbooks, as is often the case in many of the countries in the South, and particularly when a new state has come out of a war. The testimonies of victims and official documents of the Special Panels are so illustrative and detailed that it is difficult to compare them with any historical book. I also see another risk of leaving everything behind. The CTF recognised that the SCU archives contain the largest amount of evidence concerning the 1999 violence in Timor-Leste, including all the information of the indictments of high-ranking Indonesian military officers (CTF 2008: 258, 263). If Timor-Leste would like to keep the option of following the Argentinian path of delayed prosecutions or other alternatives for the future, it will be wise to maintain these records available and well-preserved. However, although these records are of immeasurable value to history and the possibility of future trials, unfortunately it is important to be aware that they do not sufficiently reflect women's narratives and experiences.

I now want to revert to the treatment received by the women interviewed. One woman in Ermera Vila said that she gave her testimony about the murder of her foster sister to the Special Panels, only to find out later that her testimony was also used without her knowledge by the CAVR and by the victim's biological brother to obtain compensation. There were also stories of rural women, for instance, who were brought for the first time to Dili and who were left alone in hotels in order to participate in the process. But also, as Komakech (2012: 127–28) argues, the law of retributive justice favours a modernist epistemology, which is impersonal and centred on impersonal principles, transcending custom and history. Several of the women I interviewed whose husbands and male relatives were killed in Maliana in September 1999, participated in the Special Panels. They complained about the lack of information given to victims and their relatives as well as the absence of follow-up concerning the cases in which they participated, to the point that some of them said that they heard about the convictions on the radio years after they had participated (*cf* Bianchini and Rubert 2020: 439). Other women also mentioned how they did not know what had happened to the cases at the Special Panels and whether criminals were still in prison. Women also described their anguish at the human remains of their relatives being sent to Dili for further investigation, not knowing when they were going to be able to recover them. According to Timorese traditional rituals, it is imperative that the bones of a person can rest in peace so that the deceased will not bring negative consequences for the family. Families believe they can be cursed if they do not carry out the proper rituals. Women therefore did their utmost to recover the bones as soon as possible.[85]

Of the three women who suffered the sexual violence in the *Lolotoe* case, two have already died (AJAR 2015: 247). It is easy to imagine what the women felt about telling their stories in a difficult justice process, expecting they were going to obtain justice from the '*malae*' (foreigners), and that not only did the UN justice process not address sufficiently the violations that they endured, but their new state was also granting pardons to those who were convicted and encouraging what had happened to be forgotten. MacKinnon argues that women who have been through the experience of sexual violence should raise their voice, while Solnit (2017: 92) claims that 'shame has silenced people, isolated them, and let the crimes continue'. I agree with them that cases of SGBV are conceived as shameful crimes, but I also see a difference between an independent domestic judicial system, and one such as the Special Panels dealing with mass crimes after a conflict and exposed to so much political interference. Victims, who were later called A, B and C, were extremely brave to talk about their cases, but they were also exposed to a great deal of distress and did not see any results. I praise their courage in raising their cases for the general benefit of their society, but I am less optimistic about the personal costs they incurred throughout the justice process. It must have been hard to go through a time-consuming process characterised by so little trust, without seeing justice for the gross crimes that were committed against them.

I also noticed that cases related to sexual violence are surrounded by a significant amount of cross-information. To secure the anonymity of witnesses, the Istanbul Convention requires that states ensure 'that measures may be adopted to protect the privacy and the image of the victim.'[86] The CEDAW Committee in its General Recommendation 30 (2013: para 81(f)) has also asked states to adopt the 'appropriate mechanisms to facilitate and encourage women's full collaboration

[85] *cf* CESCR GC 21 (2009) on the right of everyone to take part in cultural life (art 151(a)).

[86] Council of Europe Convention on preventing and combating violence against women and domestic violence (2011), Article 56(1)(f).

and involvement in transitional justice mechanisms including by ensuring that their identity is protected during public hearings and their testimonies are taken by female professionals'. Consequently, the three women during the *Lolotoe* case were identified as Victim A, B, and C throughout the proceedings, while their names were widely available in the CTF and local NGOs reports. The issue is that as Ross (2003: 63) argues in the case of South Africa, although rape is common, the need for anonymity, or at least concealment of some victims, suggests that 'neither the threat of violence nor the stigma attached to rape has abated'. Women should have the freedom to decide how they want to deal with the confidentiality of their own cases.

Finally, many of the women interviewed expressed their disapproval of militias who had been convicted being pardoned. For instance, when I asked a woman in Mauchiga who had suffered from sexual violence by the Indonesian military as a teenager about justice, she said that 'they need to punish the people that raped, "*maubere*" (the people) are to be blamed, but also the government leaders.'[87] Reflecting on the reconciliation embraced by the Timorese government, Peake (2013: 120) writes that 'friendships, family ties, and allegiances were stronger than any indictment could be'. To think that the dominant narrative of the government is the truth annihilates any possibility of plurality and individual dissent. Plurality is the condition *per quam* of all political life, because 'we are all the same, that is, human, in such a way that nobody is ever the same as anyone else who ever lived, lives, or will live' (Arendt 1998: 7–8). One day when I was in the tribunal doing research, an old man suddenly appeared in our office. The man was covered in dust, evidently very poor and had come from Kailaco, a faraway village in Bobonaro. The old man did not speak Tetum, so we had to wait until a Timorese working at the court who spoke the old man's dialect could be found to translate. The old man then explained that he had travelled to the Dili District Court to see if the person who had killed his son had been convicted. He gave the name of his son but they could not find him in the system. The old man had made his trip in vain. I found it so heartbreaking that after 18 years, he was still looking for an answer.

VIII. CONCLUSIONS

The Serious Crimes Process was inhibited by public-private interference in taking serious account of women's violations. Biases in the legislation, the investigations and the proceedings led the cases concerning women to be invisible among the convictions of the Serious Crimes Process, and sexual offences may have fallen into a limbo, as if these crimes were committed in a no man's land. For instance, the prioritisation by the prosecution of cases concerning murder and massacres would lead the investigators to pose questions that did not necessarily cover

[87] Interview with Participant 19, Mauchiga, Ainaro, Timor-Leste, 10 November 2016.

women's experiences. Moreover, although there was widespread and systematic violence against Timorese women, the violations they were subjected to, particularly those of an SGBV nature, seem to have bounced around not only between the different mechanisms of transitional justice, but also within them.

Although there was no temporal limitation on the jurisdiction to explore genocide, war crimes, and crimes against humanity, the Special Panels and SCU in practice focused only on the crimes committed in 1999, failing to see how systematic and widespread were the violations committed against women during the totality of the Indonesian occupation. The Serious Crimes Process also dealt with crimes of murder and sexual offences as ordinary crimes, but by doing so, they were considered to be ordinary and isolated events, failing to frame the large scale and gravity of the crimes and their nexus to the conflict and mass atrocities. Then, because the priority was murder cases, SGBV violations were not taken into account as being part of international criminal law, so they were transferred to the domestic system as if they were isolated crimes. But in the messiness of a country that came out of war, because of the lack of capacity of local institutions, they could have ended up being dealt with by different community structures. In addition, when the local level is examined, neither the UN local police nor the local customary system was in charge of dealing with cases of SGBV. It is possible then that these crimes fell into the domain of local structures of the CNRT, which despite enjoying the confidence of locals, was also not the proper institution to deal with them. In summary, although none of these entities had the jurisdiction or capacity to deal with them, there may have been cases concerning SGBV as crimes against humanity that could have been dealt with directly by the ordinary courts, by the CNRT or even by the traditional system. Moreover, stereotyping and the idea that these crimes were less grave could also have affected local actors.

The limited conversations also seem to have focused on rape, while other crimes, including sexual slavery, forced marriage and those of a reproductive nature, did not receive any attention, despite the fact that they may have amounted to crimes against humanity, war crimes and/or even genocide. It is difficult to know what happened but what is certain is that in practice it seemed as if no one was in charge of dealing properly with SGBV cases. There was a failure to investigate and prosecute SGBV from its inception. But private dynamics also mattered. Personal, family and community interactions – where there are considerations of stigma and gain – may also lead to silences and the subsequent under-reporting of crimes committed against women. Altogether, all these public and private dynamics may have contributed to the downplaying of the violations suffered by women not only during the 1999 escalation of violence but throughout the Indonesian occupation. As a result, out of all the SGBV violations suffered by Timorese women, there was only one conviction for rape as a crime against humanity and another conviction for rape as an ordinary crime.

Moreover, not only was there a pronounced lack of accountability and justice for crimes against women, but the UN-led prosecutions also existed along with gender discrimination and exclusion against them, violating therefore the principle of equality. SGBV crimes were arbitrarily assumed to be crimes of lesser gravity. If the rationale of criminal tribunals is to deter crimes from happening in the future, this was a missed opportunity to reflect on the crimes committed against women, including those of a SGBV nature, and to leave a legacy for ordinary local courts that reflects the importance of dealing with these crimes. This confirms that despite the vast literature, advocacy and innumerable debates concerning sexual violence in international criminal law, international and hybrid courts have a tendency to have a poor record of SGBV prosecutions. The lack of value of the international discourse may also be present in the power imbalance within hybrid tribunals, which are meant to be sustained by a cooperation among equals. In practice, the internationals perceive themselves as bringing the best standards and there may still be practices imposed on the locals which do not necessary lead to the best results. The best example is the female Timorese judge being right about considering that sexual violence was a weapon of war, in contrast to her male international counterparts. This was a particular opportunity to raise the importance of addressing the crimes committed against women, particularly of SGBV. The paradox is even more evident when the Indonesian legislation, which the Timorese may have a better knowledge of than foreigners, would be determinant in the flow of the justice process. There were cultural issues that were not taken into consideration by the logic of the Serious Crimes Process. Gradually, the Special Panels realised their incapacity to bring back from Indonesia the main perpetrators of the crimes committed in 1999 and in the end focused on the convictions of smaller 'Timorese fish'. When the mandate of the Special Panels ended, the cases, many of which included grave breaches of human rights, were subsequently left with the prosecutor's office. The Timorese leadership would distance themselves from the convictions already issued and the government would eventually grant presidential pardons to those convicted.

Those three women who were chosen in the *Lolotoe* case progressively manifested their frustration about participating in a process that required them to repeat the same painful information over and over. Of the three perpetrators who were indicted for the commission of crimes of SGBV as crimes against humanity, only one was convicted. He would later receive a pardon from the Timorese government. The next chapter focuses on women's access to truth commissions.

One case file of the Special Panels for Serious Crimes among several that I reviewed at the Dili District Court. © Noemí Pérez Vásquez.

In Ermera, women who had been victims of human rights violations during the Indonesian occupation pose together for a group. © Noemí Pérez Vásquez.

5

Women, Truth and Reconciliation: 'Here Comes the Victim'

THIS CHAPTER DEALS with women's access to the truth commissions and with how a number of structural and institutional factors constrained their participation and recognition. I start by describing the design and implementation of the Commission for Reception, Truth, and Reconciliation – known by its Portuguese acronym of CAVR – and then explore its focus on and interaction with women. Although my primary focus is the CAVR, because I also interviewed women who participated at the Commission for Truth and Friendship (CTF) between Indonesia and Timor-Leste, I also examine its relevance for cases concerning Timorese women. Based on my fieldwork, I then explore women's participation, reconciliation, healing and recognition. More specifically, I have a deeper look at women's participation in these commissions, and I show how most of the interviewed women surprisingly did not know of or did not participate in the CAVR. I later reflect on the reconciliation concepts employed both by the CAVR and by the government, arising out of political forces and the role of the CTF itself. There are currently several concepts of reconciliation co-existing in parallel within the political discourse. I then elaborate on truth and women's healing after their participation in these commissions and I end the chapter with a section on women's recognition through this restorative process and the political follow-up.

I. THE CAVR

Although established under the UN administration, the CAVR was a national initiative to establish the truth regarding past human rights violations during the 24 years of the Indonesian occupation of Timor-Leste. It was established under a UN Regulation in July 2001, following a unanimous request by the Timorese resistance, which was at that time under Xanana's leadership, and it enjoyed the support of both the community and the historic political parties such as Fretilin and UDT (Walsh 2017: 66).[1] Although the CAVR was mandated to operate for two-and-a-half years, in practice the CAVR started in 2002 and functioned for four years until the end of 2005, after presenting the Chega!

[1] UNTAET Regulation 2001/10.

report to the president of Timor-Leste on 31 October 2005 (Walsh 2011: 207–8).[2] The CAVR was led by seven Timorese Commissioners, who themselves selected regional commissioners, and unlike the Special Panels, it was composed of a high number of locals and a small number of international advisers (Hohe 2003: 351). More specifically, the CAVR was mandated to pursue the following tasks: (1) truth seeking, by documenting human rights violations committed on all sides between April 1974 and October 1999, (2) facilitation of reconciliation between perpetrators of less serious crimes and their victims and communities through a community-based reconciliation process, (3) reception and victims support which aimed at increasing the recognition and respect of victims, restore their dignity and rehabilitation, (4) reporting on its work, findings and recommendations, and (5) organising its archives and records for future reference (CAVR 2005: 34–48; Walsh, 2011: 207–8). In addition to truth and reconciliation, following the model of the South African TRC, the Timorese added the term '*acolhimento*' ('reception/welcoming/acceptance') to highlight that it was victim-focused (Walsh 2017: 66).[3] Accordingly, the six main divisions of the commission were: truth seeking; community reconciliation; reception and victim support; community outreach and public information; administration; and finance (Wandita, Campbell-Nelson and Pereira 2006: 294–95). The reception and victim support division was in charge of looking after the victims' needs and of developing and administering an urgent reparations programme (Wandita, Campbell-Nelson and Pereira 2006: 288).

How did the CAVR work in practice? At the CAVR, there were local initiatives and national public hearings. At the community level, there were individual statements, local public hearings for revealing the truth or promoting community reconciliation, healing workshops, and other events and discussions. According to Walsh (2017: 67), the truth-seeking process of the CAVR gave 'thousands of ordinary Timorese in all parts of the country a chance to share their experience, to be listened to and honoured, and to have their stories recorded in the CAVR's archives'. The local public hearings were supposed to have been carried out in the '*sucos*' (villages) of all the municipalities in Timor-Leste. According to the CAVR, they organised 52 local public victims' hearings, 217 public hearings for 1,404 perpetrators, collected 7,669 individual statements on violations from victims and witnesses, conducted more than 1,000 interviews, held six three-day healing workshops for victims and gave out reparations to a small number of victims with 'urgent needs' (CAVR 2005: 1179, 2528; Post-CAVR 2008: 5; Rothschild 2017: 447). There were also eight national public hearings, which focused on major themes and which were organised in Dili and broadcast on television and radio (Burgess 2004: 156). Burgess (2004: 156) describes one of them:

> In an unprecedented event, in December 2003, all major national leaders, including the President, Prime Minister, President of the Parliament, Chief of the armed forces,

[2] Chega means in Portuguese 'enough, stop, no more.'

[3] Walsh (2017: 66) emphasises that although the CAVR was influenced by the South African TRC, it was not a foreign import or clone.

> heads of all major political parties, and a number of serving Ministers gave public evidence of the events of the civil war, in which they had participated. The event included significant public evidence given by these leaders of the roles which they played in the conflict, acceptance of responsibility, apologies to victims, and previously unreconciled leaders hugged and wept together on national television.

The Chega! report, which was composed of four volumes and 2,500 pages, was published in 2005 and received high praise for its historical overview of the conflict: it concluded that crimes against humanity and war crimes had been committed in Timor-Leste during the 24-year period (Walsh 2011: 227). The report also provided a list of exhaustive recommendations on a large range of issues concerning the role of a state, including public policies on health and education, the provision of reparations and the creation of an institute of memory as a follow-up institution, recommended to help to deal with the past. The report, nevertheless, would not be supported by Xanana Gusmão, the Timorese President at the time, who criticised it for its 'grandiose idealism' (Kent 2008: 11). As a result, after its publication, there was no follow-up on its recommendations until 2016.

II. FOCUS OF THE CAVR ON WOMEN

Of the seven national commissioners at the CAVR, two were women, allegedly strong proponents of women's rights (Wandita, Campbell-Nelson and Pereira 2006: 294). The commission aimed at achieving a gender balance in the composition of the commission staff at the municipality, regional, and national levels, and was endowed with a training unit at the national office, which was in charge of conducting internal training including on gender issues (Wandita, Campbell-Nelson and Pereira 2006: 294–95). As explained above, there were eight major thematic national public hearings organised in Dili, and one of them, held in April 2003, focused on women and conflict (Post-CAVR 2008). The CAVR was praised for taking a 'combination approach', in which there was not only the incorporation of SGBV into its mandate, but also a multifaceted understanding of women's experience of human rights abuse (ICTJ 2006a: 5). The Chega! report would end with a chapter that focuses on the specificities of women's experiences during the Indonesian occupation and how it affected their rights. The drafting of this chapter was the result of a six-month research project on women and conflict, conducted, in cooperation with two local women's NGOs, by a team of five women who interviewed nearly 200 women throughout Timor-Leste (Wandita, Campbell-Nelson and Pereira 2006: 295).[4] Moreover, the CAVR also received 260 statements regarding women's violations as part of a

[4] Fokupers and Etwave were the two women's NGOs that were involved in the design and delivery of the CAVR's collective reparations programme (Wandita, Campbell-Nelson and Pereira, 2006: 296).

submission from Fokupers, a women's NGO (CAVR 2005: 1917).[5] The CAVR's research project on women and conflict found clear evidence of:

> the widespread and systematic nature in which members of the Indonesian security forces openly engaged in rape, sexual torture, sexual slavery and other forms of sexual violence throughout the entire period of the invasion and occupation ... [T]here was a widely accepted practice for members of the security forces to rape and sexually torture women while on official duty, in military installations and other official buildings. These practices were covered by almost total impunity (AJAR 2015: 164).

The CAVR found that SGBV against women was committed as crimes against humanity, and made specific recommendations to eliminate these crimes and to assist the victims (AJAR 2015: 164). Regarding women's participation, the CAVR documented 853 counts of sexual violence (rape, sexual slavery, forced marriage, forced or coerced contraception and abortion, and other forms of sexual violence) from 1974 to 1999, and out of the 853 counts 769 were related to women (CAVR 2005: 108–9, 526).

> The most frequently reported form of sexual violence was rape at 46.1% (393 out of 853 cases), followed by an aggregate of other forms of sexual violence at 27.1% (231 out of 853), and sexual slavery at 26.8% (229 out of 853) (Wandita, Campbell-Nelson and Pereira 2006: 291).

However, due to under-reporting, the CAVR (2005: 2040) suspected that the total number was likely to be several times higher, 'in the thousands, rather than hundreds'. Similarly, of all reported incidents of sexual violence, 16.7 per cent (142 out of 853) occurred during the violence surrounding the referendum in 1999 and, out of all these, there were only 47 cases of rape reported, 81 per cent (38 cases) of which occurred in western districts of Timor-Leste or in West Timor (CAVR 2005: 1954; Wandita, Campbell-Nelson and Pereira 2006: 291). Although this meant that women in the western districts, which experienced more violence during the post-ballot period, reported a higher incidence of sexual violence, the number of cases reported may be very low and not reflect the real scale of the violations. This may be because, of the 7,669 individual statements of victims and witnesses collected during the 18 months of operations of the CAVR, only 21.4 per cent of them were from women, meaning that out of the whole Timorese population only 1,642 women gave statements (CAVR 2005: 1917). In fact, while Robins indicates that the 7,669 individual statements represented only two per cent of the population, Hayner has only one per cent, both percentages in either case extremely low (Robins 2012: 97; Hayner 2010: 40).

Concerns about the participation of the population are further increased by the fact that out of all these 7,669 statements, while the majority of men

[5] According to Wandita, Campbell-Nelson and Pereira (2006: 296), Fokupers submitted to the CAVR its database of approximately 300 interviews with women victims and witnesses of human rights violations, which had predominantly taken place in 1999.

and women deponents reported violations experienced by others, only about one-third of the deponents reported violations against themselves (Wandita, Campbell-Nelson and Pereira 2006: 291). Moreover, 3,482 men as against 1,384 women were involved in village-level discussions on human rights violations across 284 villages in more than 60 sub-districts, and specific sessions for women were conducted in just 22 of these villages (CAVR 2005: 1917). Wandita, Campbell-Nelson and Pereira present similar numbers. They argue that, although one in five community discussions per sub-district was targeted exclusively at women, only 24 of 297 community discussions documented were women-only meetings, an imbalance that the CAVR district teams viewed as problematic (Wandita, Campbell-Nelson and Pereira 2006: 295). Only 14 women were selected to participate in the national public hearing on women and conflict, while a total of 18 women gave testimonies in other thematic public hearings (CAVR 2005: 1917).[6]

This data highlights that the proportion of women participating in the different schemes of the CAVR was particularly low compared to that of men. This stemmed from several reasons: district teams struggled to engage rural women in the CAVR activities; there was community resistance to women's participation in public activities; reliance by CAVR staff on other deponents' statements to identify victims; men were the heads of households; and even simply personal hesitations for women to come forward (Wandita, Campbell-Nelson and Pereira 2006: 296). Walsh (2011: 179–80) also argues that while the Serious Crimes Unit (SCU) and Special Panels for Serious Crimes dealt with serious crimes, defined as war crimes, crimes against humanity, killing and sexual offences, the CAVR was mandated to address less serious crimes, such as arson, looting, intimidation and killing of livestock. But since I have shown that cases of SGBV may have become invisible to the Special Panels, by following this logic we see then a loophole in how the justice being provided dealt with SGBV crimes suffered by women.

Moreover, although Timorese women's reproductive rights were also particularly targeted, very few cases were reported. The CAVR gathered documentation of only 11 cases concerning reproductive rights: six cases of women who were coerced into using birth control, three cases where pregnant women were tortured and subsequently miscarried, and two cases where perpetrators of sexual slavery forced women to have an abortion (Wandita, Campbell-Nelson and Pereira 2006: 291–92). Wandita, Campbell-Nelson and Pereira (2006: 291–92) claim that 'the CAVR was unable to substantiate allegations of forced sterilization'. They believe that the small number of reported cases of reproductive rights violations may be explained by the fact that relatively few Timorese women were successfully forced to accept birth control measures and that deponents were unaware that reproductive violations were human rights violations

[6] Wandita, Campbell-Nelson and Pereira (2006: 295) mention that 13 women were invited, selected through a process that sought balanced representation in several ways.

(Wandita, Campbell-Nelson and Pereira 2006: 291–92). Based on the data collected during the fieldwork, I argue that cases concerning reproductive rights were under-reported at the CAVR.

III. THE CTF AND ITS FOCUS ON WOMEN

In December 2004 the presidents of Indonesia and Timor-Leste agreed to create a Truth and Friendship Commission (CTF) to 'establish the conclusive truth' regarding the events of 1999 in Timor-Leste. Although the CTF was supposed to be a bilateral body composed of respected nationals from both countries, it was mainly operated and controlled by Indonesia (Walsh 2017: 70). At the time, many commentators concluded that its function was to grant amnesties, which was within its terms of reference, and therefore to override the CAVR, whose mandate was finishing in 2005 so it ended up being boycotted by the UN, Indonesian and Timorese NGOs and the victims themselves (Walsh 2017: 70; CTF 2008: 15).

However, when the CTF report was released, it accepted that (1) gross human rights violations had occurred in East Timor in 1999, and that these violations included murder, rape and other forms of sexual violence, torture, illegal detention, and forcible transfer and deportation carried out against the civilian population, and that (2) institutions were responsible for these acts (CTF 2008: xiii–xiv, 305). The CTF report also did not recommend anyone for prosecution or amnesty; neither did it name or clear the names of any individuals responsible for the violence, but it did recognise that the Indonesian military and its militias were principally responsible for the crimes (CTF 2008: xix, 297; Walsh 2017: 70). More specifically, although the militias were the primary perpetrators of the crimes, the CTF (2008: 291) mentions patterns of co-perpetration and support in the structural interconnections between the TNI and militia and other paramilitary groups that had developed over time and that local TNI facilities were used for illegal detentions, where severe forms of mistreatment of civilians, including torture and sexual violence took place. Accordingly, the CTF (2008: 293) concluded to have identified institutional responsibility of pro-autonomy militias and pro-independence groups, but because of the achievement of Timorese independence and the fact that these groups no longer exist, the report added that 'a conclusion about their institutional responsibility would have only a symbolic value'. In other words, the CTF first blamed institutions without naming individual perpetrators, and second, it declared the (by then) extinct militias as the main perpetrators.

Although the CTF did not explicitly grant amnesties, it represented the end of the conversation about what happened between the two countries and it was hard for the international community to go against their bilateral agreement. It can thus be argued that there was a de facto amnesty. Moreover, although the CTF's mission was to conduct research into the historical background, political dynamics, and institutional structures that shaped events before and during 1999, Hirst argues that the CTF did not prioritise the interests and participation of victims (ICTJ 2008: 1; CTF 2008: ix, 8). For instance, at their public hearings they heard evidence from only 14 victims or direct witness from the Timorese community (ICTJ 2008: 28). She further expresses her concern not only that witnesses were produced by a party centrally implicated by the evidence, but also that the victims and witnesses were identified and brought to Jakarta by Indonesian military staff (ICTJ 2008: 27). Indeed, some of the UN and former CAVR staff interviewed described how victims and witnesses were terrified when they were taken to Indonesia to participate in the CTF. Similarly to the CAVR, the CTF (2008: xxi) also recommended an official acknowledgment through expressions of regret and apology for the suffering caused by the violence in 1999. The official apology never arrived (*Al Jazeera* 2008).[7]

Although the CTF was heavily criticised, there are some features that can be rescued. The CTF (2008: x, 8) report and records serve as a common historical source for the two nations regarding the violence committed in 1999, particularly concerning information on specific crimes, as well as on the crimes committed by the Timorese resistance. For instance, in a section on sexual violence, the CTF (2008: 119) mentions that the prosecution of sexual violence was not a priority for the SCU and that murder was prioritised above all other offences. However, it claims that the SCU investigative files contain considerable evidence of the perpetration of sexual violence by the militias and several cases allegedly committed by pro-independence supporters (CTF 2008: 119). The cases of SGBV that occurred in Suai during the 1999 violence are illustrative. The report states that after the attack at the church in Suai, women were separated from the general population and taken to certain detention centres, including the Suai Kodim, a school building and a camp at Betun, West Timor (CTF 2008: 119). Many of these women reported sexual assaults that occurred in these places and believed that they were targeted because of the perception that all of the individuals seeking refuge in the church were independence supporters (CTF 2008: 119). Women described their experiences of being raped during detention by the militia, police and Indonesian military (CTF 2008: 119–20). A woman stated in her testimony that

> militia came to us in the middle of the night and withdrew the blankets from our faces and looked at us. If they liked a woman they just pulled her away into another room … I told the policeman that I was three months pregnant. He didn't care … we were taken at the same time and raped in different rooms (CTF 2008: 120).

Another woman described how after being forced into a camp in Betun, 'women were raped night after night by the militiamen, usually at the same time each night' (CTF 2008: 120). The CTF (2008: 121) accepts that sexual violence targeted pro-independence supporters to punish families or

[7] In contrast to what the film 'Sergio' wanted to make its audience believe.

individuals that were perceived as pro-independence and to intimidate and terrorise the population. The CTF report claims that when the SCU was conducting its investigation of the murders that occurred during the attack on the church at Suai, although it became apparent that a significant amount of sexual violence had occurred in the aftermath of the attack, there was no serious attempt to conduct an overall investigation of them (2008: 119). It also mentions that owing to the lack of investigations arising from the SCU's failure to attach sufficient priority to sexual violence cases, evidence is far from complete (CTF 2008: 121).

From a historical point of view, the CTF also gathered invaluable documents: these are the records of the violations committed by the resistance collected by the Indonesian government, unique in the narrative of the conflict, since Indonesia collaborated neither with the SCU nor with the CAVR. The report concluded, for instance, that although the evidence clearly proved that pro-autonomy militias were the primary direct perpetrators of gross human rights violations in 1999, pro-independence Timorese groups were also responsible for gross human rights violations in the form of illegal detentions that targeted civilians who were perceived as pro-autonomy supporters and that these could amount to crimes against humanity (CTF 2008: xiv, 248, 291). However other sections indicate that the resistance's violations did not amount to crimes against humanity, showing inconsistencies in the report (CTF 2008: xiv, 248, 291). The CTF also comments on extrajudicial killings and destruction of property committed by various pro-independence groups, which clearly did not amount to crimes against humanity (CTF 2008: 237–48). It also offers information on SGBV committed by the resistance. I found it illuminating that in one account of sexual slavery committed by a Falintil commander, the CTF (2008: 250) mentions that although Falintil investigated the incident, the case was not fully or adequately pursued and, even worse, that the senior leadership in Falintil may have issued instructions not to discuss the case further.[8] This throws into doubt the internal procedures of the resistance concerning the way they deal with SGBV crimes committed against women.

Finally, the CTF report also recommended identifying the whereabouts of the estimated 4,500 children from Timor-Leste who were forcibly taken to Indonesia during the occupation, and although civil society has taking the lead in reuniting them with their Timorese families, the recognition of this ongoing violation and the need for cooperation between the two countries was an important feature of the report (CAT 2017: 10; CTF 2008: xx).

[8] Out of the total reported counts of sexual violations, they documented that 93.3% (796/853) were attributed to Indonesian security forces and auxiliaries, 2.5% to Fretilin (21/853), 1.2% to Falintil (10/853), 0.6% to UDT forces (5/853), 0.1% to Apodeti forces (1/853) and 0.9% to others (8/853) (CAVR 2005: 1914). The Chega! Report also mentions that Fretilin and UDT were also responsible for atrocities committed during the civil war and it estimates that East Timorese were the perpetrators of between 1,500 and 3,000 deaths (CAVR 2005: part 186).

IV. WOMEN'S PARTICIPATION

Out of the 77 women interviewed, only 19 confirmed that they knew of or had participated in the sessions organised by the CAVR. In other words, an overwhelming majority of women reported that not only did they not participate, but that they had never heard of the CAVR. The majority of them only revealed their experiences in 2012, as also happened in the case of the women who suffered from sexual slavery during many years at the Pousada Hotel in Baucau. Reflecting on how the processes of truth commissions are delineated by local elites and supported by the international community, Robins (2012: 86) argues that the CAVR process itself was not well-known to victims and that their needs should have been given priority in the transition. My own findings also reveal not only a low level of participation of women at the CAVR, nor even much knowledge of it, but also discrepancies concerning the scale of the violations that they suffered.

The explanation may be partially found in the selection process. Teresinha, the coordinator of the women's cooperative in Maliana, said that 'the CAVR did not get everyone's story; they were only after general data.'[9] In Lalerik Mutin, it was also explained to me that there were local hearings in the communities together with national public hearings in Dili. As a result, most of the interviewed women did not participate because 'representative cases' were chosen in the communities. At the national public hearings on women and conflict, the 14 women invited to speak were selected 'through a process that sought balanced representation in several ways' (Wandita, Campbell-Nelson and Pereira 2006: 295). Moreover, at the local level, a community leader in Viqueque explained that the CAVR did not conduct mass interviews because the conflict was too recent and because people outside the villages could not come. Instead, the CAVR relied on the village chiefs to identify specific cases. Because village chiefs facilitate the connection between central government and local communities, they would indeed have had an important role in the implementation of the CAVR. The issue is that, as explained by Manuela Leong Pereira and the women in Lalerik Mutin, village chiefs were also complicit in the commission of the violations against women. I heard several times how they had been key in providing the names and showing the houses where the women lived to the '*bapas*' (Indonesians), therefore facilitating the sexual violence committed against them. The same is shown by the close cooperation between the Indonesian military, the militia and the village chief in the Lolotoe case, in which, according to the CTF (2008: 131), all of them cooperated in a long series of crimes committed over a substantial period of time against both pro-independence supporters and their families, particularly the women. In the case of Lolotoe, the village chief was prosecuted, but this does not mean that there were no other people who played a role in the commission of crimes

[9] Interview with Participant 73, Maliana, Bobonaro, Timor-Leste, 24 January 2017.

against women and who may have been employed in the transitional justice mechanisms.

My point is that during conflict there may be people who are both good and evil and who may have an interest in deepening the layers of discrimination against women once the justice mechanisms begin. I doubt that village chiefs would promote the participation of women who suffered SGBV in cases in which they could be implicated, which makes us reflect upon who the speakers in community-based processes really are. This is relevant to the answer of a woman in Maliana who, when I asked about her participation at the CAVR meetings, said that she was not important and that usually only '*ema boot*', meaning the important people, were invited to those meetings.[10]

But the excessive focus on killings may have permeated the selection process of the CAVR. For instance, it struck me that while I collected information on five cases concerning reproductive rights, including forced contraception, forced pregnancy and forced abortion, the Chega! report only mentions having collected 11 cases during the whole of its mandate. When Nesiah et al claim that SGBV was explicitly taken into account by the CAVR and that these topics were identified as critical avenues of investigation, she gives the example of how when they organised a household-mortality survey, the CAVR included at least one woman in each research team who conducted a separate interview with at least one adult woman in every household (ICTJ 2006a: 19). That household-mortality survey could have made other types of violations invisible.

In Baucau I met Maria de Fatima, who said that after independence she received a visit from two people. She was not sure if they were part of the Special Panels for Serious Crimes or CAVR but said that she was only asked if she had family members who had been killed. She answered that question, but she did not talk about her experience of daily sexual violence for almost 20 years. When asked why, she said: 'because I had not been asked'. She told her story for the first time in 2012 after hearing the director of ACbit asking if there were women present in the church who experienced sexual violence in the Pousada Hotel of Baucau during the Indonesian occupation. 'I raised my hand', she said. The same woman has now become a local leader within the women's group supported by ACbit and she currently supports herself and her four children, born of the rapes she endured, through the selling of the typical Timorese breakfast, fried plantains. In the main room of her house, there are photos of her family and the director of ACbit, which reveals her deep gratitude to the director of the NGO. Through this organisation, not only did she hear for the first time that what happened to her was not her fault, but this single mother also received help to build her house. She felt recognised by them.[11]

In contrast, when I asked those who had access to and participated in the CAVR local activities why they did so, I realised how many victims may have

[10] Interview with Participant 2, Maliana, Bobonaro, Timor-Leste, 24 January 2017.
[11] Interview with Participant 56, Baucau, Timor-Leste, 13 January 2017.

taken part for reasons other than an interest in knowing the truth and/or reconciliation. Indeed, some women who participated in the local public hearings explained that they participated 'just in case something was given'. Because of this 'something', women explained that it was better to go so they could have information regarding any financial assistance and/or aid from the state. In this connection, many of those who talked about their violations manifested their disappointment that no help was provided. On many occasions, I heard the expression 'there was no result'. Ligia, from Ermera Vila, for instance, said that she thought if she could tell her story at the CAVR something could have happened, but nothing did. She felt better, though, after sharing her story at CAVR, but there was no result. She wanted to receive skills training. The CAVR started a project but then it was stopped. 'Better not to promise anything', she said. Only 12 people were chosen to talk at the CAVR hearings. Today, many women do not want to talk for shame, while other women want to talk but they are threatened by their partners with divorce if they do so. But 'if there are no results, better to stay quiet', Ligia said.[12]

People may feel compelled to testify for reasons beyond truth and reconciliation but people in villages would also go and watch. It is inevitable that there will be expectations from a system that comes from outside their communities and which invites them to tell their stories. We can imagine what it is like to live in a village that suffered and witnessed gross human rights violations for 24 years and then suddenly to see, after the end of the conflict, white Land Cruisers and black Land Rovers all over the country. On the other hand, fewer than five out of all the interviewed women mentioned a moral obligation, saying that they participated because at that moment 'it seemed to be the right thing to do' and even less convincingly because 'it was the thing everyone was doing'.

At the same time, according to the community leader in Lalerik Mutin, many women who were raped decided to remain silent. Some of those few women who participated in the CAVR local discussions also confessed to having remained silent because they were afraid to participate, while others thought that other people's violations were of a graver nature (*cf* UN 2020: para 21). When I interviewed the women in Maliana, most of them described their husbands' and male relatives' experiences. This interlinkage between men and women's violations was also noted by Ross in her account of women's participation at the TRC in South Africa. Ross (2003: 5) observed how women were 'speaking mainly of men's suffering' and how they 'addressed their own experiences of harm and activities of resistance to the Apartheid State only indirectly'. I also found some other similarities with Ross (2003: 126) when she describes how some women felt their pain to be limited in comparison with that suffered by others, while for some other women, their experiences of torture and loss were not widely known and they feared being labelled. Goldblatt (2006: 55) also observed how at the South African TRC, 'women tended to downplay or omit their own harsh

[12] Interview with Participant 44, Emera Vila, Ermera, Timor-Leste, 8 November 2016.

treatment at the hands of the authorities when talking of their relatives' and how the TRC tried in some instances to encourage women to talk about their own suffering – some of them were indeed victims since they were detained, beaten, and so on.

Goldblatt (2006: 57) further mentions an urban bias in the work of the TRC and how because its offices were located in urban centres, rural women had less opportunity to contribute to this process. After interviewing women who lived in remotely located houses, my impression is that the same could have occurred in the CAVR process. I understand that sessions were organised by villages, but this also made me reflect on how those who live in more isolated locations may also become invisible to the system. But local meetings may also be full of power dynamics. Some Timorese women attended such meetings and just observed. Some indicated that it was out of simple curiosity, but others may have been intimidated by the system. As Palmer (2015: 142, 167) also noticed at the gacaca court in Rwanda, there were people who were silent because they did not know how to present themselves or answer the questions posed to them. These processes therefore can be very intimidating and affect women's participation, particularly that of those coming from the lowest levels of society. A woman who was subjected to sexual violence and whom I met in Mauchiga said that the CAVR came to her village for four days but that she participated only once at their hearings. She said that questions were generic and not everyone talked, some people remained silent. In fact, she did not talk because she was afraid.[13]

But silence can also be a legitimate way to participate and this may be in tension with the programmatic agenda of a truth commission. People who participate in truth commissions are not only required to talk about very intimidating traumatic experiences, but they also need to do so within a short timeframe, as if they don't, they may be left out. Ross (2003: 125) recounts how the methodological failure of the TRC in South Africa was related to problems of sample and time-scale: the biases resulting first from relying on individuals who self-identified themselves as victims compared to the many South Africans who experienced human rights violations and who did not come to the commission – for instance, many women and girls who chose not to testify about violations they themselves had experienced – and secondly from the pressure of time which denied the importance of establishing relationships to reveal stories of violence and pain. People may feel obliged by circumstances to participate and therefore they may end up in a passive role. I see then an imbalance of power between a truth commission and people's agency. There should be, in contrast, an ethical responsibility to recognise that silence is a legitimate response to pain and is an act of conscious agency (Ross 2003: 50; Coulter 2009: 17–18). In that regard, Ross (2003: 164–65) suggests the need for a new language of social suffering,

[13] Interview with Participant 23, Mauchiga, Ainaru, Timor-Leste, 10 November 2016.

'one that permits the expression of the full range of experience, admits the integrity of silence, recognises the fragmented and unfinished nature of social recovery, and does not presume closure'.

I conceive truth commissions as the Arendtian public space in which everyone can hear each other's opinion, particularly the opinion of victims. In contrast to the protagonist's role that perpetrators have at trials, truth commissions should therefore offer a platform of participation to both the survivors and the perpetrators, without implying immediate consequences to either. Although Arendt was not concerned with equality in these public spaces, she did clarify that equality is a feature of plurality, and 'if men were not equal, they could neither understand each other and those who came before them nor plan for the future and foresee the needs of those who will come after them' (1998: 175). The issue is then how to ensure that everyone is allowed to share their stories and to participate on an equal basis, without discrimination and whenever they feel they are ready.

The point that I want to make is that women's mere presence does not necessarily mean they agree with the goals of truth and reconciliation. In this world of indicators, we may consider the presence of people as a success, but in reality, it is possible that they do not understand what the implications of their presence are or that they are only there as observers and actively silent. One woman in Maliana mentioned how after participating in the local gatherings of the CAVR, she was brought to Dili to participate in one of the public hearings of the CTF between Indonesia and Timor-Leste. The woman said that she was brought as part of the audience, as an observer. She saw Xanana and the Indonesian leadership talking. When it was finished, she was taken to the CAVR to hear about forgiveness and reconciliation. Then she was brought back to her village. The woman seemed not to understand her presence in Dili and said that she did not agree with what she was hearing in the commissions. I was also told by Aliança Golçalves in Ermera Vila that the testimony that she gave to the Special Panels was used for the CAVR. When I asked her how she found out about this, she said that it was because she was the witness of the killing of her foster sister and the information she gave was later taken by other family members to the CAVR.

This killing was the case of Ana Lemos, who worked with UNAMET in Emera and who was an outspoken supporter of independence. After the referendum, Ana Lemos was tortured, including through sexual violence, kidnapped and killed by the militia and the Indonesian military. Ana's foster sister recounted how her family could see Ana and hear her being attacked in the garden of their neighbours. Although she did not participate in the CAVR, Aliança Golçalves was one of the few women who were taken to Indonesia to present their testimony at the CTF. This all raises doubt not only about women's access to these commissions in general, but also about their effective participation in this kind of initiative. Moreover, this raises concerns about the extent to which these truth commissions were locally owned and understood by the communities, and the extent to which they managed to ensure a genuine reconciliation between the victims and their perpetrators.

V. DIFFERENT RECONCILIATION DISCOURSES

As described above, one of the goals of the CAVR was to contribute to rebuilding broken communal relationships. As part of its programmatic agenda, perpetrators of non-serious crimes would be eligible for a Community Reconciliation Process (CRP). The hearings for reconciliation to address less serious crimes adapted the customary practice of '*nahe biti boot*' to settle disputes, where discussions and negotiations take place: people sat and shared a big woven mat, dressed traditionally, and a ritual elder opened the meeting by addressing the forefathers (Hohe 2003: 351; Walsh 2017: 67). The perpetrators had to admit the crime and ask for forgiveness in front of a local panel, chaired by a Regional Commissioner and composed of three to five leaders, including a local catechist from the Catholic Church, a traditional spiritual leader and elders, including two women (Burgess 2004: 150; Hohe 2003: 351). Everyone was allowed to speak after the hearing, and subject to the community's approval to accept the return of the perpetrator: the panel had to decide on the appropriate penalty, such as an apology and/or community work (Hohe 2003: 351). The CAVR organised reconciliation ceremonies across Timor-Leste for 1,400 individual cases of low-level perpetrators of the 1999 violence, mostly young men recruited by the militias, and the families and communities they had offended (Walsh 2017: 67; CAVR 2005: 2482). It was estimated that, from a total population of fewer than one million people, by 2004 30,000 and 40,000 community members had attended and participated in a CRP procedure (Burgess 2004: 153). According to Walsh (2017: 67), the CAVR was proud of its innovative community reconciliation process and victims participated actively in hundreds of community reconciliation ceremonies.

Participation in these reconciliation ceremonies was voluntary and they offered perpetrators acceptance back into their communities and immunity from future prosecution (Walsh 2017: 67). Before being declared eligible to participate at the CRP, perpetrators had to pass through a scrutinising process to ensure they had not committed serious crimes. We should recall that the CAVR was established to work in parallel with the Special Panels for Serious Crimes and the institutions were intended to cooperate with each other: on the one hand, the CAVR had authority to refer cases to the prosecutor as a result of its truth seeking function; on the other hand, the CAVR was obliged to refer statements from deponents who came forward to participate in the community reconciliation process to the Office of the General Prosecutor, who, having exclusive jurisdiction over serious crimes, would decide whether to transfer a case to court or to allow the local reconciliation hearing to proceed if the perpetrator was not implicated in serious crimes (Hohe 2003: 351; Wandita, Campbell-Nelson and Pereira 2006: 288).

Unlike the South African TRC, the CAVR did not offer amnesty for serious crimes in return for full disclosure (Walsh 2011: 177). This distinction would, though, be less clear in practice. Burgess (2004: 154) states that although in the beginning 'under no circumstances' could serious criminal offences, in particular murder, torture and sexual offences, be dealt with in a CRP, this was later amended to 'in principle'.[14] This allowed the prosecutor to decide not to exercise jurisdiction over situations that might technically have constituted serious criminal offences (Burgess 2004: 154). Thus, when the Office of the General Prosecutor returned the matter to the CAVR for hearing, it indicated that a decision was made not to exercise jurisdiction, while avoiding indicating that it was not a serious crime (Burgess 2004: 154). Because it was obvious that owing to the overload of cases, not only could the Dili District Court not deal with all the 'less serious crimes', but could also not deal with 'serious criminal offences', any incentive to prosecute from potential participants in the CRP was removed (Burgess 2004: 154).

The concept of reconciliation would start to become more blurred over the years. Already in 2005, Indonesia and Timor-Leste had created the CTF and although it was established to investigate the events of 1999, the CTF was more focused on regional diplomacy than justice (Leach 2017: 162). In parallel, the Timorese president started granting pardons to people convicted of serious crimes by the Special Panels, based on the opinion that justice, conceived mainly as accountability, might work against ensuring an internal reconciliation between those who supported the idea of 'autonomy' of Timor-Leste as part of Indonesia and those who fought for independence. Those in power, the '*ema boot*', indeed actively started to encourage a narrative about forgetting the past, and argued that their country should focus on the future by establishing friendly relations with Indonesia. They visualised an external reconciliation with Indonesia, a country with which they would maintain undeniably strong cultural links and which was to be their most important economic partner.[15]

With all these elements, the government of Timor-Leste today promotes itself as an example of international reconciliation, sending copies of the Chega! report, which contains 2,500 pages in four volumes, to foreign governments and politicians for them to see the success of the Timorese model – an example of good truth and reconciliation practice. However, with the exception of 18 interviewed women, none of the other women knew of the existence of this report and none of the interviewees had read it. When I asked people from the government and NGOs if they had read the report, their answers were also negative. Note the full report is available in English, Portuguese and Indonesian, but not in Tetum.[16] To further complicate matters, the Chega! concept of reconciliation is different from the one that is being used by the government. While reconciliation

[14] UNTAET Regulation 2001/10.

[15] Clark (2010: 172, 176, 215) claims that, given that poverty and economic hardship were the main problems of Rwanda, over time the government also employed a rhetoric that the country must move 'beyond' genocide to pursue other national objectives, particularly economic development.

[16] *cf* http://chegabaita.org/wp-content/uploads/2020/01/Chega-for-Peace-3-1.pdf.

for the CAVR was supposed to be only for perpetrators of lesser crimes, the government is talking about reconciliation for those who committed grave violations of international human rights law and serious violations of international humanitarian law. Today we thus have a country where two colliding concepts of reconciliation co-exist, a double discourse in which – depending on whether the actors are politicians or working with human rights – different meanings of reconciliation are being used.

Aboueldahab (2017: 3) has noted the same distorted applicability of transitional justice vocabulary, when she argues that transitional justice has been used to block criminal accountability for past atrocities committed by political leaders in the Arab region. In Timor-Leste, there have been changes in the narratives concerning reconciliation and an adaptability of transitional justice vocabulary to accommodate the interests of the elites. From the original meaning given by the CAVR that excluded cases concerning serious offences, the government now uses 'reconciliation' as synonymous with impunity for the offenders. Therefore a key transitional justice concept that has approval within the international human rights discourse is being used without giving much detail of the controversies that it entails. In practice, the government is sharing the Chega! report with third parties, neglecting the fact that the CAVR made recommendations for future prosecutions of past atrocities.

This has an impact on the post-colonial identity of the new nation. Leach (2017: 211) notes, for instance, how Timorese government policy reflects 'a mix of commemorating nationalist history, but within a particular framework of reconciliation which prioritised development and veterans over justice for civilian victims'. By exploring the relationship between Mandela and FW de Klerk, du Toit (2018: 8) argues that in the case of South Africa, reconciliation did not mean forgetting past abuses committed under Apartheid, but rather the realisation of their interdependence led to reconciliation. In the case of Timor-Leste, economic dependency on Indonesia, and not interdependence, is what may have led Timorese leaders to talk about a type of reconciliation that involves the consignment of crimes to oblivion at the expense of values of rights and justice (*cf* Ostowar 2020: 107; Strating 2019: 274).[17] This point of view is not necessarily shared by the women interviewed.

Indeed, when asked about the reconciliation impact of the CAVR sessions, the interviewed women said that they participated more for reasons of curiosity than for reconciliation with those who inflicted the violations on their communities. One woman from Lolotoe said that her family prohibited her from attending a CRP meeting but she decided to go, not because she was supporting the reconciliation of her community with a militia man in particular, but because she was curious. She wanted to see what those meetings were

[17] Strating (2019: 272) observes that the most significant bilateral relationships for guaranteeing Timor-Leste's sovereign independence are today Australia and Indonesia. There are estimates that 856 Indonesian companies operate in Timor-Leste today (De Sousa 2021).

like. Another woman in Mauchiga said that she participated in a CRP meeting with a former militiaman, but that she stayed quiet and that she did not understand the process. The majority of women also said they were opposed to the reconciliation promoted by the national politicians and that those who committed the crimes should be brought to justice. Moreover, some of them strongly resented the perpetrators of crimes and were keen to point out that their own participation in the CAVR did not necessarily mean they were prepared to reconcile. I found these answers illuminating in the deconstruction of the idea of the success of truth and reconciliation sessions. Is the number of people that attend the best way to measure success? Or the feelings of satisfaction of the victims after being heard? Or do we measure success according to the depth of the truths revealed and the extent to which they lead to reconciliation? In the case of South Africa, Hayner (2010: 3) mentions how despite the efforts of the TRC, people still demanded justice and punishment for their perpetrators, and where justice was not possible, the minimal requirement for forgiveness was to be told the full, honest, and unvarnished truth. But in Timor-Leste, there was no justice, but also no truth. As Maria Inmaculada cleverly expressed, 'Reconciliation should come together with justice … until now, we don't know why the Indonesians did all that punishment.'[18]

In this regard, a particular violation mentioned by the women was the disappearances of their loved ones. Many Timorese families never recovered the bodies of their relatives. Moreover, according to the UN, 4,534 children were estimated to have been displaced to Indonesia during the chaos of the integration programme (Vice 2017). Since the end of the conflict, civil society organisations from Indonesia and Timor-Leste, together with the national human rights institutions from both countries, have been working to find the stolen children, only managing to identify about 40 of them, mostly males (AJAR 2015: 136). Although Arendt (1998: 240–41) recognises that 'the act of forgiving can never be predicted', forgiving is a reaction that frees from consequences both the one who forgives and the one who is forgiven. In other words, for Arendt 'forgiveness is the key to action and freedom'. However, there are crimes, extreme evil, that cannot be forgotten or forgiven, and which are beyond human love and solidarity (Arendt 1998: 241; 2017: 602; 2007: 471). The search for truth allows us to understand. This is why the right to the truth is contemplated in the convention on enforced disappearance and it has been widely recognised by regional human rights courts.[19] But what can Timorese people expect when even the body of

[18] Interview with Participant 33, Dili, Timor-Leste, 27 February 2017.

[19] *cf* IACtHR, *Zambrano Vélez et al v Ecuador* (Merits, Reparations and Costs). Judgment 4 July 2007; IACtHR, *Gudiel Álvarez (Diario Militar) v Guatemala* (Merits, Reparations and Costs). Judgment 20 November 2012; ECtHR, *El-Masri v The Former Yugoslav Republic of Macedonia*, 13 December 2012; African Commission on Human and Peoples' Rights (ACHPR), Resolution 111 (XXXXII) 07 'Resolution on the Right to a Remedy and Reparation for Women and Girls Victims of Sexual Violence', 28 November 2007. The UN Impunity Principles also recognise the right to the truth and the role of truth commissions in fulfilling this right (UN ECOSOC 2005).

Nicolau Lobato, the first Prime Minister of Timor-Leste, was never found after being shot by the Indonesians in 1978? The Indonesians have never revealed what they did with the body of the Timorese hero (Magalhães 2016). Timorese people were required to forgive and forget.

Clark (2008: 194) defines reconciliation as 'both a process and an endpoint, requiring individuals and groups to interact and cooperate in often difficult circumstances, to discover solutions to their problems and thus to build stronger future relationships'. In Timor-Leste, however, the gaps between public discourse and personal experiences may fuel intergenerational resentment. In the different municipalities, some of these women mentioned how militias benefited from the Indonesian system. When the conflict finished the women hoped that those who opposed the Indonesians and who were seemingly alienated in their own country would receive attention from the government. In contrast the women said that the Timorese politicians had made a pact with the former militias, employing them in the government so that the latter are now in power as well. Many women victims also expressed resentment that sons of the militiamen currently occupy positions in the government while their children, many of whom supported the resistance, are struggling in their daily lives. Some of the women believed that they suffered a great deal and because everything was forgotten, the children of militias were in a better socio-economic position than their own children. In other words, the children of militias have therefore jobs and better living conditions, reflecting a general disparity between militias and pro-independence supporters. Burgess (2004: 152) described something similar in 2004 when he referred to feelings of discontent related to victims continuing to be in situations of poverty, exacerbated in some cases by the fact that perpetrators may be economically better off. Hidden feelings of resentment and anger, if manipulated by politicians, may be a factor in revenge and political instability in the future. Reflecting on the Hutu and Tutsi and the genocide in Rwanda, Mamdani (2001b: 321) argues, for instance, that 'since the colonial period, the cycle of violence has been fed by a victim psychology on both sides'. He cautions that latent feelings of victimhood, trauma and resentment may produce subsequent feelings of victimhood in future generations, planting the 'seeds' of further violence (Mamdani 2001b). This returns us to the question of how to measure the success of truth and reconciliation commissions in general.

Victims may also respond differently to their sufferings: those who prefer to forget or even repudiate their past and those who sincerely prefer to forgive. In the case of Ana Lemos, for instance, although other members of her family, including mother, brother, and male children work to keep her memory and the cause of the victims alive, her daughter, Fidelita, told me that she would prefer to leave everything behind and continue with her life. This connects to Hayner's remark that, while some victims want to forget, other victims want to remember and tell their stories so they can begin to recover (Hayner 2010: 2). There is no right or wrong approach but what I find alarming is the imposition of narratives and silences by the state and the role played in this imposition by transitional justice mechanisms. While Bennett (2012: 19) argues that in endogenous legal cultures of Africa, people are inclined to restore relationships rather than to punish or use force, I felt that the same reductive narrative is being imposed by political leaders in Timor-Leste.[20] This is an assumption that kills the idea of plurality and individuality. In the case of Rwanda, Clark (2010: 47) argues that while legal critics are misguided in dismissing gacaca as an illegitimate system, the Rwandan government wrongly romanticises gacaca as a form of justice automatically acceptable to all Rwandans. He further criticises an official view that sees reconciliation as a short-term process that occurs during gacaca hearings, equating reconciliation with restoring a sense of unity that the government believes is latent within Rwandan communities (Clark, 2010: 339). Reflecting on the Timorese top-down imposition of a concept of reconciliation that amounts to impunity, I found the story of Maternus Bere emblematic.

Bere was a former militia commander who participated in the Suai Massacre and who was indicted by the SCU on several charges, including the abduction of Alola dos Santos, but who was not prosecuted because he remained at large in Indonesia. When he entered Timor-Leste in 2009, the police arrested him and transferred him to Dili. When I was in Dili, a former MP told me how a heated debate had taken place in the Parliament between those who wanted Bere to be prosecuted and those who wanted to release him. He further told me how members of parliament cried out of frustration when they found out that the government had ordered his release to the Indonesian Ambassador to Timor-Leste. Xanana and Ramos-Horta, respectively Prime Minister and President of Timor-Leste at the time, ordered Bere's release despite the fact that only a judge could order the release of an indicted criminal from prison (La'o Hamutuk 2010). This made me think of Arendt's scepticism of the parvenus, who after obtaining power and influence, 'feel humiliated in sharing their fate' and insist on forgetting, while, she continues, there are others, the unpopulars, who insist on telling the truth (Arendt 2007: 274). By leaving aside the work of the Special Panels, CAVR, CTF and everything related to post-conflict justice, the Timorese leadership may assume that they are working on reconciliation, but instead what is left behind is oblivion. A conclusive and fixed truth is rather scary, since it may be more connected to deception. Politicians may show us the story they want to hear and create the narrative that they wish to be the one that defines the nation. People start believing their story through self-deception and the danger is that this may lead to totalitarian tendencies arising in the state (Arendt 1972: 6–7). In December 2020 and August 2021, the government of Indonesia awarded medals and National Defence Patriot certificates to 11,485 former 'East Timor fighters', including a 'First Class Service Star' to the militia

[20] Clarke (2009: 126) mentions that forgiveness and reconciliation are central to the Acholi beliefs in Northern Uganda; rather than revenge, justice is instead a means of restoring social relations.

deputy commander Eurico Guterres, responsible for the 1999 Liquiçá Church Massacre (Carrascalão 2021).[21]

VI. WOMEN'S HEALING AND THE UNDERSTANDING OF TRUTH

The idea of healing by participating in the activities of truth commissions has been central within transitional justice. Healing refers to 'individuals' regaining a sense of inner wholeness; that is, healing of their own identity, as captured in the phrase 'to find oneself again' (Clark 2010: 42). At the CAVR, for instance, not only did victims have a 'right to justice and the truth', but 'justice, truth and mutual understanding' were 'essential for the healing' of victims (Rothschild 2017: 448). Linked in this way, truth-telling with healing, the CAVR asserted that 'statement-taking was the first step in the healing process the Commission was promoting' and that its public hearings were 'valuable occasions for … healing' (Rothschild 2017: 448). In addition, the CAVR organised more local private hearings, focused on victims' healing and linked to the Commission's programme on counselling, referrals and reparations for the most vulnerable (Walsh 2011: 279). These were composed of six three-day 'healing workshops', including one focusing on women and in which professional mental health workers participated (CAVR 2005: 2527–28).[22] Only 156 victims participated in these six 'healing workshops', of which 82 were women (CAVR 2005: 2528). This not only reveals that it was a short-term project that focused on a small number of people, but it may also suggest a greater emphasis on the production of reports, indicators and checklists, rather than on the genuine healing of the people.

The issue of whether truth commissions are therapeutic is a contested point. Coulter (2009: 169) states that in the case of Sierra Leone, the idea of publicly sharing a story of personal experience of violence and trauma in the TRC or the Special Court was presented as a way of reconciling the nation with its violent past, but 'whether it helped individual women to come to terms with and move on from their personal experiences of violence in the same way is questionable'.[23] In fact, she observed how women and girls in the communities, instead of supporting the therapeutic talking as a way of dealing with trauma, believed that abducted women and female ex-combatants would be best served by forgetting the whole episode, without ever talking about pain, violence and suffering (Coulter 2009: 174). Alleging that 'revealing is healing', the South African TRC was also depicted in the popular imagination as

[21] The Indonesian Defense Minister Prabowo Subianto is himself a former platoon commander who participated in the Seroja (Lotus) Operation, which marked the military invasion of East Timor in 1975. *cf.* Carrascalão (2021) and CNN (2020).

[22] Wandita, Campbell-Nelson and Pereira (2006: 296–302) note that Fokupers staff members with experience in psychosocial and group counselling joined with CAVR staff to conduct healing workshops.

[23] Coulter cites Shaw (2005).

a healing intervention, in which commissioners treated victims as wounded bodies and the truth-telling as the opening and cleansing of unhealed wounds (Ross 2003: 12).[24] Ross (2003: 2) further comments that 'notwithstanding the rhetoric about healing that accompanied the Commission's work, and historians' claims of recording's emancipatory effects, people do not necessarily want their activities and experiences to be widely known'.

With Robins (2012: 84), I am also critical of this Western perception according to which, by talking about traumatic experiences in a group, a victim will feel better and heal. Bistoen (2016: 3) also blames the West for the assumption that wounds do not heal with the passing of time but need to be addressed in their own right. This is even more perverse if there is no follow-up, since victims may be left with a stigma. As the Special Rapporteur on the right to health has stated, harmful stereotypes (including gender stereotypes) and stigmatisation in the family and community may dismantle the supportive and inclusive environments that are required for the good mental health and well-being of everyone (UN 2019b: para 37). Similarly, Mannell et al (2018: 92) claim that 'the focus of the biomedical approach on trauma as a pathology of the individual does not acknowledge the patriarchal structures and gender inequities that perpetuate both GBV and women's suffering'. In Mauchiga, a woman said that in the CAVR hearings 'we needed to talk, but I did not like to bring all these memories back' and after participating, 'there was nothing, no solution … Today, higher people do not recognise us as victims.'[25]

In the 2000s, Timorese leaders stopped cooperating with the Special Panels and failed to embrace the Chega! report when both finished their mandate in 2005 (Kent 2008: 11). Xanana, the President at the time, stated that the recommendations of the CAVR, which included calls for punitive justice and reparations, could be used to 'manipulate our people's state of mind' (Kent 2008: 11). It is not surprising then that after people participated in these mechanisms, there was no follow-up by the government. This had an impact at the state and community levels. The information from the statements of the CAVR was supposed to be entered into a Human Rights Violations Database and converted into statistical and demographic data on violations (Rothschild 2017: 447). However, not only were the Special Panels' archives left out, but I was also informed that the records and database of the CAVR were in a precarious state and that information may have been lost. I was also appalled by the lack of state support to the Max Stahl Audiovisual Archive Center (CAMS), an incredible historical jewel which contains a great political and cultural audiovisual legacy of Timor-Leste. Furthermore, other recommendations of the Chega! report about using its findings in the education sector were not

[24] Meffert et al claim that 'there is little to no evidence on the specific impact of providing legal testimony'. Based on other studies, they observe that 'the assumed "therapeutic value" of human rights processing may be "more wishful thinking than fact"' (2016: 3).

[25] Interview with Participant 15, Mauchiga, Ainaru, Timor-Leste, 11 November 2016.

implemented either. Why is this important? Because we may forget the importance of the local understanding of what the truth is: 'people's understandings of what occurred during periods of mass violence' (Clark 2008: 203).[26]

In Baucau, when I carried out the interviews, the women who suffered from sexual slavery told me that after the referendum, the Indonesians took them by plane from Baucau to Indonesia. When I asked them why they were specifically transported in a plane, which I considered to be a luxury, the women did not know why. My first wrong assumption was that these women were taken in planes because they were sexual slaves of the Indonesian military. Only afterwards, when going through the records of the Special Panels, did I understand how the Indonesians and the militias forced the displacement of the Timorese people using planes, boats and trucks after the referendum in order to make the international community believe that Timorese people were against the pro-independence results. This is the kind of information to which people should have access so they can also understand their participation in history and put their experience in context. Ross (2003: 102) argues that 'scholars should seek signs of recuperation not solely in the integrated psyche but also in the extent to which there is acknowledgement of individual harm within communities of affect'. Women's experiences were not unique, but they were part of a policy.

To make matter worse, because there was no regular follow-up provided to the participants of the CAVR and communities, several women said that after participating at the CAVR they 'received nothing'. People come, victims talk in the sessions, statements are taken, and then the people leave. By revealing details about crimes in small communities where gossip is part of daily life, we may contribute to women's further discrimination and stigmatisation. A woman in Mauchiga told me, for instance, that after taking refuge in a school, at night Indonesian soldiers took her away along with other girls to commit sexual violence against them. The family and community witnessed when they were taken away. She then participated in the CAVR session in case some help was provided. In the hearing, she said that she was raped, without giving too many details. As a result, the whole village got to know her experience. She told me how she decided never to get married, that this has been haunting her all her life and that until today she is sad because as a rape victim, she cannot take communion at Church. When she walks around people say 'here comes the victim'.[27]

Another woman in Mauchiga said that while being displaced and located at the school in Dare for a year, the Indonesian military came to look for her and other young girls at night. They committed sexual violence against her. Due to the 'threats' she was suffering from, her grandmother offered her aunt to the Indonesians and Hansips, so that they would leave her grandchild alone.

[26] Principle 14 of the UN Impunity Principles (2005) states that 'the right to know implies that archives must be preserved'.

[27] Interview with Participant 19, Mauchiga, Ainaro, Timor-Leste, 10 November 2016.

Her aunt was separated and taken away to live with one of them – that did not work out either because that particular man continued being violent and committing rapes. This woman said she participated at the CAVR hearings but 'there was no result'. She said 'I am always referred to as 'victim, victim' but there is no help'.[28] I also heard cases of women feeling depressed after telling their stories. A woman in Los Palos said, for instance, that she felt manipulated by the CAVR, that after participating in their sessions there were no results, and that she felt depressed because she could not look at her husband because of shame. She added 'I know two other women who died of shame.'[29] There was thus a further re-victimisation against those women who participated in the CAVR sessions, particularly those who suffered SGBV: wounds were open, known by their communities and left up in the air. There was no reciprocity for their participation.

This idea of healing through truth-telling within a specific format and time-frame may also be problematic. Not only can truth commissions become silencing mechanisms because they limit participation and time, and select certain violations and experiences without considering others, but they also promote the idea of healing a nation through an official single collective memory about what happened, implying that 'truth' is somehow something constant and unchanging, and not a contested process and something that is not always desired (Coulter 2009: 169).[30] Walsh (2017: 68) notices there is a growing tendency, including at the highest levels of Timorese society, to rebrand the Chega! report as history and to promote it as an educational resource in itself for its information value. However, he argues, by doing so, this distorts the CAVR's raison d'être (Walsh 2017: 68). But objectives can evolve. In Rwanda, for instance, although the gacaca courts were established through an Organic Law with objectives oriented toward punitive sanctions, their mandate was progressively extended to include a focus on truth-telling, reconciliation and reintegration of prisoners (Palmer 2015: 119). However, among all of these, 'truth' was later identified as the principal contribution by the authorities and participants, leading even the personnel inside gacaca to view their central contribution as obtaining a better local understanding of the conflict (Palmer 2015: 10, 132, 142). I do think that truth commissions' reports make an important contribution to the history of a country but they should not be considered the only sources since personal stories will continue to emerge.

VII. WOMEN'S RECOGNITION AND POLITICAL FOLLOW-UP

The CAVR would define victims as persons who have 'suffered harm … as a result of acts or omissions over which the Commission has jurisdiction to

[28] Interview with Participant 67, Mauchiga, Ainaru, Timor-Leste, 11 November 2016.
[29] Interview with Participant 9, Los Palos, Lautém, Timor-Leste, 12 January 2017.
[30] Coulter (2009) cites Shaw (2005).

consider,' but it further specified that victims were 'primarily civilians or non-combatants' who were 'not directly involved in the armed struggle' (CAVR 2005: 2495; Rothschild 2017: 447). Keeping in mind that under international humanitarian law, during war, armed combatants are legitimate targets, Rothschild argues that while technically the CAVR's definition of victim excluded most members of Falintil, informally the CAVR extended victimhood to all Timorese – as shown, for instance, when it proclaimed that 'we are all victims' – and noted that 'on some levels, all East Timorese people and the society as a whole were victims of the political conflicts of 1974–99' (Rothschild 2017: 447; CAVR 2005: 2512, 2612). Ultimately, Rothschild (2017: 452) argues that the two categories of victim and veteran are not mutually exclusive, because although the CAVR defines victims as primarily civilians or non-combatants (excluding members of Falintil), it included civilians who were part of the clandestine front. Women ended though being denied access to reparations (as victims) and being excluded from the veterans' pensions as members mainly of the clandestine front, but I will expand on this point later.

I want to highlight the difference between the perception and treatment of a man who says he has been tortured because of his bravery and support for the resistance, as some politicians told me proudly that they had been, and the social consequences for women who were subjected to SGBV. Without any follow-up mechanism and recognition from the state, transitional justice may be contributing more to the problem rather than to the solution by leaving women labelled as 'victims'. This further marginalises women and perpetuates their disempowerment. While victims are usually conceived to be those individuals whose rights have been abused or violated, in most conflict analysis women may be equated to victims (Coulter 2009: 149). Chinkin and Kaldor (2013: 168) argue that 'the terms "protected" and "victim" used to describe women imply weakness and subordination, which, in turn, perpetuate women's lack of empowerment in peacetime situations and mask the reality of women's experience of violence and insecurity'. Sometimes because 'victims' are seen as implying passivity and acceptance of the violation, the term 'survivor' is used as a way of reflecting the agency, resilience and courage of women and girls subjected to violence (International Commission of Jurists 2016: 3–4; OHCHR 2011b: 5). In recent years, after I had finished my field research in Timor-Leste, and following the example of other nations like Rwanda, Timorese women who suffered SGBV during the Indonesian times started being called survivors by civil society.[31]

I also observed that besides the feminisation of the word 'victim' in Timor-Leste, those particular women who suffered SGBV may be associated with those supporting Indonesian perpetrators and therefore who did not obtain the veterans' pensions. As a result, while the veterans may be considered heroes, the victims have suffered stigma and feelings of shame. Rothschild (2017: 461) argues that if the CAVR had more clearly highlighted the variety of

[31] *cf* ACbit (2019: 4).

ways in which Timorese victims not only suffered violence but also worked to resist it, this could potentially have prevented the emergence of a victim–veteran binary narrative. More specifically, she argues that victims' testimonies included stories of agency and resistance but these were subsumed within the CAVR's overwhelming framework of violations and suffering (Rothschild 2017: 461). Something similar took place at the TRC in South Africa. Ross (2003: 75–76) describes how the activities of the TRC promoted a victim and passive agency of women, foreclosing on investigation of power and resistance, and undervaluing women's activities in resistance. In Timor-Leste I observed this idea of the passivity of 'victims' during the conflict; this has resulted in entitlement deprivations. Women's further marginalisation after the end of the conflict helps to explain why so many of them introduced themselves with an apology for having suffered SGBV.

This takes me to my next point. Resentment may not only be against the militias and their children but, as I also perceived, there may be feelings of anger against those who managed to receive the pension and live a more comfortable life. Many women interviewed started revealing what happened to them in 2012 through the outreach activities of ACbit. Although ACbit has provided a space for them to express their experiences, I believe that the fact that others have been chosen by the state as the recipients of help may partially explain why so many women are talking about what happened to them in recent years. Faced with the impossibility of receiving any significant support from the state, women therefore may be making a connection between their human rights violations and the veterans' pensions. We have seen similar examples in other post-conflict situations. Coulter (2009: 177) described how in war-torn Sierra Leone, in order for women to be accepted into one of the vocational programmes implemented by NGOs, because these organisations also tried to deal with psychosocial needs, the telling of your 'war story' was often mandatory. To put it simply, 'families had to negotiate between their wishes for the total obliteration of shameful war-time experiences on the one hand, and the material gain these narratives could produce through access to skills training programs on the other' (Coulter 2009: 177). It requires courage to talk in the public space. This reminds me how Arendt's concept of speech is not only about revealing your own pain but should be connected with persuasion to act. By revealing what happened to them, women want to be heard and recognised as legitimate subjects to claim and receive reparations.

Finally, in 2010, there was a draft law in the Timor-Leste parliament for the establishment of an 'Institute of Memory' but because of the lack of political will, it was never approved (Walsh 2017: 71). In 2016, more than 10 years after the Chega! report, the Prime Minister, Araújo, authorised the creation of a working group to review the status of the CAVR recommendations in order to analyse which of them had been implemented throughout the years by the Timorese state in an independent way (Walsh 2017: 71). The working group was composed of people who had experienced working in the CAVR as well as members of civil society and the government, and they were allowed to look at all the recommendations, with only two exceptions, namely accountability and reparations. In July 2017, the government created the Chega! National Centre (CNC) as an institute of memory to facilitate the implementation of recommendations made by the CAVR in 2005 and CTF in 2008 respectively, including continuing the documentation of Timorese resistance to Indonesian occupation and ensuring that the most vulnerable survivors of past human rights violations would be cared for (Amnesty International 2018; Walsh 2017: 76).[32] The centre replaced a Post-CAVR Technical Secretariat and is based at a former colonial prison and former Indonesian centre of detention and torture in Dili (Walsh 2017: 76). While the main planned activities of the CNC included memorialisation, education, solidarity with victims of past human rights violations, and outreach, it was no surprise that the CNC did not have a mandate to address the CAVR's recommendations on justice and reparations for victims of serious human rights violations (Amnesty International 2018). At the time of my interview with the Director of the CNC in 2017, the institute was still establishing its plan, starting to organise women's events, and among many concerns, anticipating the re-organisation and recovery of its archives and records. By 2021, CNC began establishing its official national archives, although the Director recognised that in order to develop Timor-Leste's National Archives, there were still some difficulties, mainly the absence of a decree-law to protect the archives and the lack of infrastructure and human resources.[33] Their mission, though, is complicated by a dependency on the state's political and financial support, framed by the will and interests of key Timorese politicians. If such institutions are not autonomous and independent, they risk becoming an instrument of specific narratives.

VIII. CONCLUSIONS

To what extent did women have access to their local truth commission? Did they understand the point of their participation? Did participating have positive results for them? Women's participation was limited in the sessions organised by the CAVR. Women who suffered from sexual slavery and/or forced marriage, were, in some cases, pressured at that time by their communities and family members, including the village chiefs. Because the latter would later have a role in the selection of 'representative cases', there could have been biases in the selection of cases to avoid inconvenient truths being revealed. Intersectional forms of discrimination also interfere in the selection process and may limit the participation of those considered less important in a community. Another

[32] The Chega! National Centre was established through Decree Law No 48/2016.
[33] *cf* Martins (2021).

challenge for truth commissions is related to the space and timeframe limitations, which force women to talk within a specific format. Truth commissions should be instead about offering them the opportunity to relate their experiences whenever they are ready, without pressure. In a post-conflict situation, local meetings of a truth commission organised by people who are external to the communities may attract massive participation, but as the interviews showed, this does not necessarily mean that people understand and share the same objectives as the organisers. Moreover, if there is no follow-up after these sessions, or if there is no recognition of women, particularly those who suffered SGBV, truth and reconciliation commissions may, by encouraging their participation and revealing these crimes in their communities, expose them to further discrimination.

After the end of the conflict in Timor-Leste, reconciliation seems to mean not only the reconciliation between Timorese people, ie between those who supported the integration with Indonesia and those who supported independence, but also seems to involve the reconciliation between two states. The great majority of women interviewed were keen to point out that their participation in the CRP sessions did not necessarily mean that they were prepared to reconcile, and a few stated that they preferred to leave everything in the past. Going beyond the topic of national and international reconciliation, different meanings of reconciliation have been used in parallel throughout the years. While for the CAVR, it concerned lesser crimes, apology and acceptance by the community, for the government, it has been all about amnesty and oblivion for certain more serious crimes and people. In this regard, in the case of Timor-Leste, the dichotomy between justice on the one hand, and reconciliation and peace on the other, still seems to be very controversial. By using a loose concept of reconciliation, the government may ignore local feelings of resentment not only against the perpetrators of crimes and former militias and their children, but also against those who managed to receive veterans' pensions. It takes time to lower one's shield. However, the fact that those recognised as veterans by the state are the main recipients of support may encourage women to talk more openly about their experiences and violations during the conflict. Women may be looking for recognition in the public space, and so far the only such space available to them seems to be the one offered by civil society and, more recently, the new institute of memory. The next chapter focuses on women's access to reparations.

An interview in Viqueque. © Carlos Oviedo.

Depending on women's local cooperatives, they preferred to be interviewed alone or in front of the others because 'they all had experienced the same'. Here with a group of women in Baucau. © ACbit.

6

Women's Access to Reparations: 'Men Were the Most Affected'

THIS CHAPTER DEALS with the different frameworks of reparations that appeared after the conflict and how the interplay between the public and private spheres hindered the access of women to this right. From the point of view of the participation and recognition of the victims, the chapter focuses on the different reparations alternatives that were seemingly available for them after the conflict. The chapter starts by providing a contextual analysis of the complexities of reparations. It then explores the reparations considered and/or granted by all the usual transitional justice mechanisms, trials and truth commissions. More specifically, I first examine the reparations granted by the UN through the Special Panels for Serious Crimes and then those which were granted to the families of the UNTAET who were killed because of their UN work. Then I explore the extent to which women had access to reparations through the CAVR and the CTF. I also examine the Timorese state, including the drafting of a law on reparations for victims and I end with a section that discusses the way forward. The chapter ends by concluding that both the Timorese state and the UN were reluctant to provide reparations for victims and that in those limited cases where such reparations were granted, women faced higher thresholds to access them and suffered from different intersectional forms of discrimination.

I. THE COMPLEXITY OF REPARATIONS

Victims are persons who may have suffered individually or collectively, and in addition to the persons who suffered the direct harm, the concept can also be extended to family members or dependants. More specifically, the UN soft-law Basic Principles on the Right to Reparation for Victims define victims as:

> persons who individually or collectively suffered harm, including physical or mental injury, emotional suffering, economic loss or substantial impairment of their fundamental rights, through acts or omissions that constitute gross violations of international human rights law, or serious violations of international humanitarian law. Where appropriate, and in accordance with domestic law, the term "victim" also includes the immediate family or dependants of the direct victim and persons who have suffered harm in intervening to assist victims in distress or to prevent victimisation. A person

> shall be considered a victim regardless of whether the perpetrator of the violation is identified, apprehended, prosecuted, or convicted and regardless of the familial relationship between the perpetrator and the victim (The Basic Principles 2005: para 8).[1]

Reparations are mainly about assuming that harm has been done and/or a loss has unjustifiably occurred (Rubio-Marín 2009: 89). The Basic Principles affirm in their preamble that violations of a grave nature constitute an affront to human dignity and that 'reparation should be proportional to the gravity of the violations and the harm suffered' (The Basic Principles 2005: preamble and Article 15; Lawry-White 2015: 151). Despite having been neglected in the past, reparations for victims have been progressively recognised in international human rights law, including in the soft legal sources created by UN treaty bodies and are now widely accepted by states (OHCHR 2005: 5).[2]

For instance, the main core international human rights instruments reflect this. The Human Rights Committee (HRC) has stated in its General Comment 31 (2004: para 16) that Article 2(3) of the ICCPR concerning the obligation of states to provide an effective remedy requires reparations be made to individuals whose rights have been violated.[3] The HRC has further stated in its GC 31 (2004: para 16) that in addition to appropriate compensation referred to in Articles 9(5) and 14(6), reparation can involve restitution, rehabilitation and measures of satisfaction, such as public apologies and public memorials, guarantees of non-repetition and changes in relevant laws and practices, as well as bringing to justice the perpetrators of human rights violations. The CAT uses the term 'redress' in its Article 14 and its committee elaborates on the five forms of reparation: restitution, compensation, rehabilitation, satisfaction and guarantees of non-repetition (GC 3 2012: para 6); whereas the CEDAW Committee has stated that Article 2(b), which concerns adopting legislation prohibiting discrimination and promoting equality of women and men, provides:

> appropriate remedies for women who are subjected to discrimination contrary to the Convention. This obligation requires that States parties provide reparation to women whose rights under the Convention have been violated... Such remedies should include different forms of reparation, such as monetary compensation, restitution,

[1] The UN Basic Principles do not entail new international or domestic legal obligations but rather identify mechanisms, modalities, procedures, and methods for existing legal obligations (Rubio-Marín 2009: 68).

[2] It was only after World War II that victims of human rights violations had a right to pursue their claims for redress and reparation before national justice mechanisms and, eventually, international institutions, and that remedies progressively developed in international human rights law as a requirement to obtain justice (van Boven 2009: 21).

[3] Although sometimes reparations and the right to remedy are used interchangeably, they do not necessarily mean the same. According to the International Commission of Jurists, 'the right to a remedy guarantees, first of all, the right to vindicate one's rights before an independent and impartial body, with a view to obtaining recognition of the violation; cessation of the violation, if it is on-going; and adequate reparation. The right to a remedy is also linked in several ways to the right to reparation: an independent assessment constitutes the first step in obtaining reparation and indeed the term remedy is sometimes understood as comprising reparation, for example by the Human Rights Committee' (2018: 52).

> rehabilitation and reinstatement; measures of satisfaction, such as public apologies, public memorials and guarantees of non-repetition; changes in relevant laws and practices; and bringing to justice the perpetrators of violations of human rights of women (GR 28 2010: para 32).

The CEDAW Committee has further recommended in its GR 33 (2015: para 19(b)) that remedies should be adequate, effective, timely, holistic and proportional to the gravity of the harm suffered. Furthermore, the committee recommends that remedies for civil damages and criminal sanctions should not be mutually exclusive and that states should create specific funds to ensure that women receive adequate reparation in situations where the individuals or entities responsible for violating their human rights are unable or unwilling to provide such reparation (GR 33 2015: para 19(b)). The UN Basic Principles and other soft-law documents such as the International Law Commission's Articles on the Responsibility of States for Internationally Wrongful Acts (ILC Articles) (2001) have also confirmed that remedies include restitution, compensation, rehabilitation, satisfaction, and guarantees of non-repetition as forms of reparation for victims of gross violations of international human rights law or serious violations of international humanitarian law.

I will now explore these forms of reparations before dealing with the Timorese experience. Restitution aims to restore the victim to their original situation as it was before the gross violations of international human rights law or serious violations of international humanitarian law occurred and it may include, for instance, restoration of liberty; enjoyment of human rights; identity, family life and citizenship; return to one's place of residence; restoration of employment and return of property (The Basic Principles 2005: para 19). Compensation is more a matter of economic measures –proportional to the damage and gravity of violations – resulting from violations, such as: physical or mental harm; lost opportunities, including employment, education and social benefits; material damages and loss of earnings; moral damage; costs required for legal or expert assistance, medical, psychological and social services (The Basic Principles 2005: para 20). Rehabilitation is about legal and social services, such as medical and psychological care, meaningful employment, education, skills training, and other initiatives, such as microcredit (The Basic Principles 2005: para 21; Rubio-Marín 2009: 109–13; CEDAW GR 33 2015: para 19).

Satisfaction, on the other hand, is about due recognition of victims through symbolic forms of redress, such as the disclosure of the truth to the extent that such disclosure does not cause further harm or threaten the safety and interests of the victim; recognition and effective measures aimed at the cessation of wrongdoings and violations; the search for the whereabouts of the disappeared, for the identities of the children abducted, and for the bodies of those killed; an official declaration or a judicial decision restoring the dignity, the reputation and the rights of the victim and of persons closely connected with the victim; public apology, including acknowledgement of the facts and acceptance of responsibility; commemorative events; inclusion of an accurate account of the violations in educational material at all levels, renaming of streets and public facilities, establishing a day of remembrance, building monuments, museums and memorials (The Basic Principles 2005: para 22; Rubio-Marín 2009: 114–16).

Finally, guarantees of non-repetition are about the implementation of reforms that seek to guarantee not only that victims will not be victimised again, but also that no new victims will be generated, such as: effective civilian control of military and security forces; strengthening the independence of the judiciary; reviewing and reforming laws contributing to or allowing the commission of violations (The Basic Principles 2005: para 23; Rubio-Marín 2009: 116–19). In this regard, the SR on violence against women has argued that non-recurrence involves a discussion about the underlying structural causes of the violence, their gendered manifestations and the broader institutional or legal reforms that might be called for to ensure non-repetition (IACHR 2015b: para 59).

Since Article 34 of the ILC Articles states that full reparation shall take the form of restitution, compensation and satisfaction 'either singly or in combination', this means that the forms of reparations are not alternatives to one another but complementary: in particular cases, reparation may only be achieved by the combination of different forms of reparation (International Commission of Jurists 2018: 24). The recognition, for instance, that is provided through satisfaction measures can also facilitate victims' psychological and social rehabilitation. Another example is the right to the truth. This right is confirmed by The Basic Principles and echoed by the Impunity Principles, which uphold victims' right to know the circumstances in which violations took place and state that its fulfilling is not only a form of satisfaction, but also a guarantee of non-repetition (The Basic Principles 2005; UN ECOSOC 2005; Lawry-White 2015: 150).

Moreover, since restitution is about returning to one's situation prior to violation or abuse, it cannot by itself be an adequate remedy for SGBV as it does not deal with the root causes of the violence and maintains discrimination (International Commission of Jurists 2016: 76).[4] This awareness has been translated into the concept of 'transformative reparation' which is so entrenched within feminist discourse and according to which special measures must be designed to remedy discrimination and to also act as guarantees of non-repetition (International Commission of Jurists 2016: 76). The SR on violence against women has also stated that reparations for women:

> should strive to have a transformative potential. This implies that reparations should aspire, to the extent possible, to subvert instead of reinforce pre-existing patterns of

[4] Lawry-White (2015: 148) argues that restitution may not be appropriate for victims of human rights or humanitarian law violations because in certain cases restitution may return or condemn a victim to a situation of marginalisation and poverty. Reading (2019: 235–60) contests what she believes is a limited understanding of restitution: based on what its original concept entailed, restitution is both a material and non-material process that operates across different domains and at various scales and local and international levels, eg the payment of money, the return of property, judicial processes, state apology, but also cultural, symbolic, and spiritual acts and stories.

> cross-cutting structural subordination, gender hierarchies, systemic marginalisation and structural inequalities that may be at the root cause of the violence that women experience before, during and after the conflict (UN 2010: para 85).

While Gilmore, Guillerot and Sandoval (2020: 16, 55) observe that there is no evidence that reparations can transform a society, they believe that gender-sensitive reparations can translate into opportunities and suggest as a guiding principle that decision makers consider the potential transformative effect of their benefits. As such, they conceive the transformation to have (a) an individual potential in which victims' self-esteem is raised while they advance their positions in the family and community because gender gaps are shortened, and (b) a structural potential in which gender structures are challenged and there is a better coordination with development and other social interventions (Gilmore, Guillerot and Sandoval 2020: 60). I agree with their cautious approach. Indeed, although reparations have widely been supported by those promoting the elevation of economic and social rights status to the level of civil and political rights, their provision and/or implementation are not exempt from challenges. As with the concept of gravity, by declaring that we may have direct and indirect victims, we may create an unexpected ranking effect, where some victims are deemed more important than others. Moreover, by extending the concept of victims within the concept of reparations, there are financial implications since implementation programmes are highly dependent on the availability of resources, which are usually limited in post-conflict societies. Because of the financial burden of providing reparations on an individual basis, collective reparations have acquired an important role, particularly within the Inter-American system of human rights, and have been applied with a great deal of creativity.[5] For instance, Waldorf (2019: 131–49) advocates for legal empowerment to be seen as a form of collective reparations, specifically legal rehabilitation for impoverished victims of mass atrocities. In this regard, Roht-Arriaza (2019: 105–30) considers that guarantees of non-repetition are collective measures that come close to the concept of transformative justice because they require a bottom-up analysis of root causes and prevention, including economic, social and cultural rights violations; a broadening of institutional reform and a forward-looking agenda; a focus on process and on how reforms take place.[6]

However, there are also challenges when reparations are framed within the collective. Collective rights may further undermine individual human rights because they depend on the hierarchies of the group, a fact which becomes evident when we ask who is authorised to represent the collectivity of victims

[5] Oette argues that in the case of the African Commission on Human and Peoples' Rights, a greater focus on collective violations has allowed claims on behalf of all victims, and in such cases reparation measures tend to be of a general and collective nature – their follow-up procedures are, though, often not very effective (2009: 223).

[6] Not only should guarantees of non-repetition do what is needed to make sure violations do not happen again, but also they should look to other potential victims of the same types of violations (Roht-Arriaza, 2019: 105–30).

(Oette 2009: 223). In this regard, Moyo (2012: 274) emphasises that 'feminists do not share the absolute positive attitude that post colonialists seem to have towards the collective, noting that groups can also be sites of abuse'. When we think about rehabilitation, a dilemma that also arises is that by placing too much emphasis on service packages as a form of reparation – as Rubio-Marín (2009: 110) argues – there is:

> the risk of blurring the conceptual distinction between services that people are entitled to *as citizens* and reparations for victims of violations of human rights *as victims*, thus ultimately diluting the recognition dimension of reparations programs by turning them into general development or assistance programs.

If reparations are about recognition, how can a distinction be made on the ground between those whose rights were violated and the others? In Peru, for instance, because of the tension caused by the fact that reparation measures were confused with development or poverty eradication programmes, NGOs spoke out against this approach, arguing that when there was no direct relation between violations and reparation measures, the reparative nature of the gesture disappears, perpetuating the invisibility of the most vulnerable groups of victims, including women (Guillerot 2006: 163). In other words, while reparations programmes target specifically victims, the aim of aid programmes is supposed to satisfy basic needs to which citizens have a right per se (UN 2021b: para 60). Reflecting on how the dispossessions in Apartheid South Africa were part of a larger strategy that dehumanised and infantilised blacks, Atuahene (2014: 12) makes a connection between 'dignity takings' and Apartheid, and the need for 'dignity restoration' which involves both acknowledgment of past harm and constructive efforts to compensate for economic suffering and disenfranchisement. Dignity restoration thus required the state to address the full extent of the harm caused by dignity takings, which included the deprivation of property, but also of human worth, agency and community, ie the loss of dignity for those considered sub persons (Atuahene 2014: 26, 108).[7] Like Atuahene, I also conceive the recognition of the agency of the victim and harm as a crucial element within reparations.

Nevertheless, despite the international legal discourse concerning reparations for victims, the case of Timor-Leste shows, firstly, how there may be a predominance of individual compensation over other forms of reparations and, secondly, how neither the state nor the UN seem to be ready to assume responsibility for the financial implications of their implementation – there may be political and financial interests. In this regard, Hopgood (2017: 297) claims that

[7] Dignity takings are 'when a state directly or indirectly destroys or confiscates property rights from owners or occupiers whom it deems to be sub persons without paying just compensation or without a legitimate public purpose' (Atuahene 2014: 3). While sub persons' physical bodies are visible, their dignity is invisible: they are thus denied recognition of their humanity or full mental capacity (Atuahene 2014: 31).

human rights norms are now contested concepts where 'the phrases "this is a human right" and "human rights give rise to the following binding obligations" are not just disagreements about how a concept is properly used but about what the concept entails in a more foundational sense'. The risk therefore is that we may have been pushing for an idea of human rights related to an entitlement to money and by doing so, we may have hindered women's access to other forms of reparations that may have even more importance for them in the long term.

II. REPARATIONS PROVIDED BY THE UN, INCLUDING THE SPECIAL PANELS

Already in 1999 there were discussions about reparations for victims in Timor-Leste. After her mission in 1998, for instance, the SR on violence against women expressed her concern about the children of Indonesian soldiers in Timor-Leste and how some of them were the result of rape and/or sexual slavery (UN 1999b: para 58). She noticed how some of the women and their children were having a very difficult time, not only because of poverty, but also because the sight of the children often reminds them of the rape, and how some of these children were either abandoned or treated badly, while the single mothers were suffering from stigma in their communities (UN 1999b: para 58). She then called on the Indonesian state to accept responsibility for assisting these women in the upbringing of these children, by providing compensation or housing and education (UN 1999b: para 58).

It was therefore no surprise that when UNTAET Regulation No 2000/15, established the Special Panels and the SCU, it contained a specific reference (section 25) to the creation of a Trust Fund for victims: 'a Trust Fund may be established by decision of the Transitional Administrator in consultation with the National Consultative Council for the benefit of victims of crimes within the jurisdiction of the panels, and of the families of such victims.'[8] Moreover, 'the panels may order money and other property collected through fines, forfeiture, foreign donors or other means to be transferred to the Trust Fund.'[9] The Trust Fund, however, was never established. Moreover, although the Indonesian Criminal Procedure Code in force at the time and used by the Serious Crimes trials provided that anyone who suffered loss as a result of a crime may request compensation from the court, the provision was also never used with regard to the Serious Crimes cases (ICTJ 2010: 7).[10] This means that while attention was focused on the accountability of perpetrators, reparations did not extend in practice to the victims who participated at the trials of serious crimes.

[8] UNTAET Regulation 2000/15, s 25.
[9] UNTAET Regulation 2000/15, s 25.
[10] Articles 98–101 of the Indonesian Criminal Procedure Code 8/1981.

The decision not to establish the Trust Fund may reflect the tensions concerning budget allowances at that time. Jarat Chopra (2000: 31), the former head of the Office of District Administration at UNTAET, stated that:

> UNTAET's implicit agenda bore the ominous hallmarks of a typical UN 'exit strategy' by avoiding committed engagement in problem-solving; holding a face-saving election after a reasonable period; and withdrawing without having built adequate local capacity. Overall, the fraught UN effort did not appear to justify an annual operating budget of $750m for salaries and logistics, nor did it appear to be a responsible means of disbursing the additional $500m committed by donors for East Timor's development.

To complicate matters further, Steele (2002: 83) argues that under the 'assessed budget' of roughly US$600m a year, the UNTAET mission was not permitted to finance health, education or other public services. While victims, therefore, were required to participate in the criminal procedures, not only was there no assistance provided to them, but there were also controversies around budget allocation destined to cover basic needs. This may deepen this idea of an 'international community' that is simply not available to back the human rights up when needed (Kennedy 2006: 108).

But the UN was also required to grant reparations for the killing of 14 Timorese local staff who were killed because of their work with UNAMET during the violence in September 1999. Out of the 14 UN Timorese employees, who were mainly hired to support the organisation of the referendum, there was only one woman among the victims. This is the case of Ana Lemos, which was also taken to the Special Panels for Serious Crimes and to the CTF between Indonesia and Timor-Leste. Before being killed and her body made to disappear, Ana Lemos was tortured and sexually assaulted in front of her family house, where her children, all minors at the time, were living, together with Ana's mother and a foster sister. Ana's foster sister narrated how they could hear her screaming outside of the house and could not do anything for her.

After the killing of Ana, her children were raised by the maternal family. Their uncle, a former commander with the Falintil, started working for the UN after the conflict. He submitted an application to obtain reparations from the UN, which was to consist mainly of monetary compensation. Curiously, out of all the cases of UN employees who were killed and whose families applied, the case of Ana Lemos was one of the very few rejected at first instance. According to Ana's brother, the UN alleged that she had only been working with the organisation for four days. As mentioned to me by a former UN employee, there were also allegations that rather than being killed because of her UN work, a condition that was necessary to provide the compensation, there were stories that ranged from her being killed because of her advocacy of independence, as many of her country people were, to her killing being connected to a husband who had allegedly been pro-Indonesia. The stories sounded like a denial of her political and professional agency as a UN employee and like typical male stereotyping of the romantic life of a woman. When I heard these stories, they reminded me, as Cook and Cusack (2010: 66) argue, how a gender stereotype has this dignity-diminishing effect when it treats women as second-class citizens by virtue of the fact that they are women, marginalising them further in their relationships and in society more generally. Rather than recognising the bravery and progressiveness of a woman at that time, we hear stories about her behaviour that diminish her dignity.

Ana Lemos's brother managed to appeal the case with the support of a UN international employee, working on human rights in Timor-Leste. They won the appeal and after the struggle, they managed to obtain compensation that was provided to Ana Lemos's three children. I have no doubt they managed to get this compensation because of the insistence, connections and cleverness of Ana's brother, who was working at the UN, and the good intentions of the UN international female staff. I only wonder to what extent, if these people had not supported the case – in other words, if Ana's family had been less well connected and badly informed and the UN international staff had not decided to confront the system in a way they believed to be right – they may have lost the case and thus been denied legitimate access to reparation. People in a more vulnerable position would have suffered an injustice from the system.

After the appeal, while Ana Lemos's children received only a lump sum, the children of other UN Timorese local male staff who were killed, received a monthly payment on condition that they continue their studies. Nobody could explain to me the difference in treatment. Surprisingly, there were also allegations of a UN policy that, in my opinion, would have a greater effect on women: the widows of those men who were killed could receive the monthly compensation for their children as long as they remain unmarried. The majority who received the compensation would be the spouses of men killed. As a result of this policy, women were impeded for practical reasons from conducting their lives as they wished. In this regard, I was informed by a former UN staff member involved in the process how the UN would every year send letters in English – a language the families did not understand – asking whether their circumstances (eg children studying and the spouse unmarried) were still the same. If they were not, the compensation was discontinued.

This would not be the first case of UN irregular compensatory practices. The Kosovo Human Rights Advisory Panel, in their evaluation of UNMIK concerning adequate compensation for moral damage suffered by complainants, noted that as underlined by the Special Representative of the Secretary-General, under Resolution 52/247 (1998), the UN is not permitted to pay compensation other than for material damage or physical harm (Nowicki, Chinkin and Tulkens 2017: 94). In other words, the UN does not pay compensation for moral damage. This is why in May 2015, 'the SRSG alerted the UNSC of the situation, advocating the establishment of a suitable mechanism to compensate for moral damages, as well as for further investigation by appropriate judicial authorities of inconclusive cases' (Nowicki, Chinkin and Tulkens 2017: 94). The panel, however, was never made aware of any results and because the complainants did not obtain redress, they have been victimised twice by UNMIK: 'by the original human rights violations committed against them and again by receiving no compensation through this process' (Nowicki, Chinkin and Tulkens 2017: 94). In the case of Ana Lemos, I also see issues of re-victimisation and moral damage. After a difficult process, Ana's children only managed to have access to the compensation seven years after the death of their mother. The UN mechanism put in place further seemed to ignore the socio-economic violations suffered by Ana's own children – what they endured while their mother was attacked. This means that there may not only be a higher threshold for women to access UN reparations for human rights violations, but also that the UN mechanism may not be the best example to follow, showing a lack of value attached to the international discourse on reparations. After the experience of Ana Lemos's family in accessing UN reparations, in August 2019 the UN in Timor-Leste announced that one of their meeting rooms would be named after her.

III. REPARATIONS PROVIDED BY THE TRUTH COMMISSIONS

Under the lead of the Working Group on Victim Support, the CAVR established an Urgent Reparations Programme for the most vulnerable, which accounted for approximately US$160,000, about three per cent of the CAVR's total three-year operational budget (CAVR 2005: 2615; Wandita, Campbell-Nelson and Pereira 2006: 304). More specifically, the programme consisted of five main forms of reparations: (1) monetary compensation to victims, which consisted mainly of one-off emergency grants of US$200; (2) referral of victims to services, such as urgent medical and psychological care; (3) healing workshops; (4) funds to local NGOs to provide services to persons identified through the programme, including equipment and training for people with disabilities; and (5) collective reparations in conjunction with three NGOs in a small number of communities, such as establishing survivors' self-help groups, commemoration of events, and the provision of tombstones for victims (CAVR 2005: 2538; Wandita, Campbell-Nelson and Pereira 2006: 302–5). Beneficiaries were victims identified from among those who gave statements to the CAVR and it was decided that the urgent reparations programme would be carried out as a 'silent programme' in order not to create a bias in the truth seeking process (Wandita, Campbell-Nelson and Pereira 2006: 301–4). This means, as confirmed during an interview with a former employee of this scheme, that not many victims knew about the programme.

The monetary compensation was financed by the Trust Fund for East Timor administered by the World Bank and most beneficiaries used it to meet medical costs, children's school fees, as start-up costs for income-generating activities, to repair their homes or to purchase food and other basic needs (CAVR 2005: 2541; Wandita, Campbell-Nelson and Pereira 2006: 304). However, out of all the people in Timor-Leste who suffered serious violations of human rights, only 712 people received the US$200 one-off grant, 516 were men and 196 were women, which meant that only 27 per cent of those who had access to it were women (CAVR 2005: 2539). Concerning the referrals of victims to medical and psychological care, the CAVR granted funds to support local health NGOs that provided direct assistance to 417 victims (Wandita, Campbell-Nelson and Pereira 2006: 305). More specifically, 322 men (77 per cent) and 95 women (23 per cent) received the assistance offered by local NGOs and church groups, such as medicines, referral to district hospitals, and basic counselling and support, including home visits (CAVR 2005: 2539). The number of participants was even lower for the healing workshops, since out of the 712 recipients of the US$200 grant, only a third of them, meaning 156 victims (82 women and 74 men) were invited for one of the six three-day workshops that were carried out (Hayner 2010: 41; CAVR, 2005: 2528). As for collective reparations, the local NGO HAK Association worked with victims groups in communities where there was a high degree of SGBV against women: in Klaras, Viqueque, they built a community education centre and in Mauchiga, Ainaro, they organised activities to plant vegetables, developed marketing networks for farmers and commemorated the mass violations that took place after the rebellion of 1982 (Wandita, Campbell-Nelson and Pereira 2006: 305–6).

This means that of all Timorese who suffered gross violations of international human rights law and serious violations of international humanitarian law over 25 years, only 196 women received the one-off grant of US$200, 82 of whom participated in the healing workshops, while 95 women received psycho-medical assistance. In a conversation with a UN international staff member, who worked with the provision of reparations both in Timor-Leste and Kosovo, I was concerned to hear that she considered the experience in Kosovo of dealing with a small number of victims better suited than the Timorese approach, since in the latter case there was an intent to create a very ambitious programme for a large number of victims that ended up not being implemented. Moreover, in the Timorese case not only was there a very low number of people who received urgent monetary compensation, but even among those who received it, there was a disproportionately low number of women who had access to this form of reparation, despite the widespread and systematic violations against them.

Wandita, Campbell-Nelson and Pereira (2006: 307) argue that the issue was that the percentage of women identified as beneficiaries of the urgent reparations scheme was dependent on the women's participation in the statement-taking process, the proportion of which we know was relatively low at 21.4 per cent (*cf* CAVR 2005: 54). Barriers that affect women's participation would thus later have an impact on their access to reparations from the inception of the programme. When I also asked the former employee of the urgent scheme why the disproportion between men and women was so significant, he said that that was because 'men were the most affected'. It was easier to go to the communities and see who, for instance, had been tortured and left with visible injuries. The problem is that women's experiences in conflict are very complex and their violations may not be visible. We can further think about intersectionality and the effect of having a programme that was carried out without publicity, if not secrecy, and how this may have privileged those better informed and with better connections. Moreover, there is the issue of familial interference. It was known that Timorese families often prohibited victims from speaking out about abuse as it would bring disgrace upon their family (Niner 2011: 49).[11] One woman in Liquiçá said, for instance, 'I know many in the community who were "punished" but they don't want to say it because it is a secret, they are ashamed'.[12] The former employee of the Urgent Reparations Programme also confirmed that they were aware that in many cases women did not want to reveal what had happened to them.

The reality is that women not only face additional issues that men do not, but they are also affected by gender-based barriers which may be ignored by truth commissions. Ross (2003: 12) argues that the South African TRC, for instance, by having this notion of equitable treatment for all, stripped away context and the effects of power, while those considered victims were those who were subjected to bodily injury crimes, ie limited to those having 'traces on the body'. Nesiah (2011: 143) is, though, concerned that bodily integrity injuries such as SGBV are the privileged frame narrative for women's subjectivity. I agree with her but the provision of reparations in several contexts shows that there is not only the limitation of women's subjectivity to SGBV, but that even those cases are downplayed. In Bosnia and Herzegovina, for instance, the CEDAW Committee expressed concern at the situation of victims of sexual violence of the 1992–95 armed conflict – most of whom were women, female heads of households and internally displaced persons – as they and their specific type of suffering were not sufficiently recognised in the respective legal frameworks for civilian war victims, limiting, if not impeding their access to health care related to their traumatic experiences and putting them at risk of eviction from their accommodations (CEDAW 2006: para 37).[13]

In Timor-Leste, although the Urgent Reparations Programme was supposed to include reparations for victims of sexual violence, in practice we see that

[11] Niner cites Pereira, R. (2004).

[12] Interview with Participant 60, Liquiçá, Liquiçá, Timor-Leste, 25 January 2017.

[13] In 2019, the CAT Committee mandated Bosnia and Herzegovina to provide compensation, a public apology and free medical and psychological assistance to a Bosnian Muslim woman who had been raped by a Bosnian Serb soldier in 1993. The Committee further asked the state to set up a war crimes reparations programme, including for sexual violence (Ašimović Akyol 2019). However, there is no political will to implement what the government has signed, including the National Action Plan of the UNSC Resolution 1325 (Ašimović Akyol 2019).

the continuing hierarchy of gravity affected women's access to reparations. And I am not only talking about rape not being taken into consideration as part of reparations schemes, but also about other violations of SGBV that are even more difficult to determine in the public space, such as violations of reproductive rights, forced marriage and forced domestic labour (Rubio-Marín 2006: 31). In the case of the urgent reparations provided by the CAVR, forced labour and forced use of contraception were not, for instance, included because the number of incidents documented by statement takers and research units was negligible (Wandita, Campbell-Nelson and Pereira 2006: 302–3).[14]

Something similar has happened in other contexts. A hierarchy of harms had an effect in Sierra Leone, where women who had been subjected to SGBV often experienced exclusionary outcomes compared to survivors of other forms of conflict-related violence, leaving a vast majority of those who had registered as sexual violence survivors without the reparations that they were entitled to (What Works 2018: 33). Guillerot (2006: 159–60) argues that in the case of the Peruvian TRC, violations were classified according to a scale in which death and disappearance were considered the most serious violations, as they affected the right to life; followed by disability, as it entailed a loss of the ability to generate income; and imprisonment, as it entailed the interruption of a life project; whereas rape ended up at the bottom of the scale because it was not considered to have any impact on such rights or abilities. As a result, many harms that affected mostly women were excluded from the list of crimes to be redressed, which made it impossible for some of the women who suffered them to qualify as direct victims and to access reparations, including in cases of rape (Guillerot 2006: 155–58). Moreover, the effects of violations on health, including reproductive health, such as unwanted pregnancies, sexually transmitted diseases or sterility, were not taken into account as aggravating elements, and neither were their potential consequences – such as rejection by husbands, impossibility of getting married and/or community stigmatisation – all of which make a means of livelihood impossible (Guillerot 2006: 159–60).

Women who suffered from violations may indeed be left not only with serious physical and psychological injuries, but also with stigma, shame and isolation from their families and communities, which may have repercussions in their later livelihoods (Hayes 2016: 370). Moreover, different hierarchies in society may have facilitated the participation of some specific victims, while making it more difficult for others. This is even more relevant in the delivery of collective reparations, where special mechanisms were recommended after the CAVR in order to listen to women victims within the 'collective' (Wandita, Campbell-Nelson and Pereira 2006: 317). For instance, I found it revealing that

[14] In its urgent reparations programme, the CAVR identified killings, disappearance, detention, torture and sexual violence as crimes to be addressed because of their severity and the longevity of their impact, while forced displacement and destruction of property were not included because of the large percentage of the population affected (Wandita, Campbell-Nelson and Pereira 2006: 302–3).

the CAVR would only later realise the importance of land rights for women victims, as shown by the example of the hundreds of women in Lalerik Mutin, who after being forcibly displaced by the Indonesian military to new lands, which they then cultivated for 20 years, faced uncertainty regarding their entitlement since it was traditionally owned by another clan under customary law (Wandita, Campbell-Nelson and Pereira 2006: 306).[15] The focus of truth commissions may therefore neglect issues that are of utmost importance for women, as has happened in other contexts.

In this regard, Ní Aoláin and Turner (2007) have highlighted how despite the fact that both the Chilean and Guatemalan truth commissions had broad mandates to effect social reconciliation and restitution, in practice they took a very narrow 'civil and political rights' approach, leaving aside other forms and locations of conflict-related harm to women, including domestic violence or conflict-induced impoverishment. Mamdani (2000: 180–82) has also raised how the South African TRC focused too much on the perpetrators rather than the beneficiaries of the structural violence and on the racial discrimination entrenched in Apartheid. He argues that the TRC forgot to make a connection between social and economic injustice and the denial of basic needs for the victims (Mamdani 2000: 180–82). This is linked to Ross's observation that because a large number of South African women, who might have been eligible to make statements, were not recorded as victims by the TRC, they were not eligible for individual reparation (2003: 163). Ross (2003: 163) argues that this limitation had implications for women, who per se represented the most unskilled members of society, suffered the highest rates of unemployment and lead the poorest households in South Africa.

We know that victims were encouraged to make recommendations for reparations after their statement and/or oral testimonies during hearings, while collective recommendations followed group discussions during healing workshops and community mapping exercises (Wandita, Campbell-Nelson and Pereira 2006: 302). However, although these recommendations were the basis for the reparations policy in the Chega! report, because of technical and language difficulties and lack of time and resources, the reparations unit of the CAVR did not complete a quantitative analysis of the hundreds of recommendations received (Wandita, Campbell-Nelson and Pereira 2006: 302). In this respect, I found difficult to assess the rest of the reparations provided, particularly because the CAVR did not conduct its final evaluation of community reparations before it was dismantled, adding this task to the 'to do list' in the next stage of its operations (Wandita, Campbell-Nelson and Pereira 2006: 306).

How then are we supposed to analyse a programme that may be replicated in other contexts? The issue is that gender mainstreaming within transitional justice may be seen as part of a checklist rather than a critique of the gender

[15] In contrast, when the IACHR (2015: para 73) reflects on reparations with a gender perspective in Colombia, it underscores the restitution of land for women victims of forced displacement.

status quo (Ní Aoláin, Haynes and Cahn 2011: 12–14). This makes me think about Tia Beatriz in Lalerik Mutin. Not only did she suffer horrendously from SGBV during the Indonesian occupation, but she was also left with children as a product of that violence and one of them, her daughter, was born with a disability. It is already hard to be young in a wheelchair, but more so in a remote village where roads are made of clay and one's movement is greatly restricted. And the state does not do anything for them as victims. In fact, Tia Beatriz said that after participating in a CAVR public hearing what she received was a machine to grind corn, but because she did not know how to use it, she gave it away. Until now I have been referring to urgent reparations that were provided during the CAVR process. I now turn to the reparations that were envisaged in the Chega! report.

IV. REPARATIONS ESTABLISHED IN THE CHEGA! REPORT

When the Chega! report was published, the CAVR suggested a large range of reparations for victims of human rights violations, disregarding their past political affiliations and including victims of violations committed by the armed resistance (Wandita, Campbell-Nelson and Pereira 2006: 308).[16] Avoiding individual financial assistance, the CAVR favoured collective and symbolic reparations which were mainly focused on rehabilitation and satisfaction of victims, including the delivery of social services and material assistance for the most vulnerable who continued to suffer the consequences of violations after the conflict: for example, victims of torture and/or sexual violence, people with mental and physical disabilities, widows and single mothers, children affected by the conflict, the poor, the sick, the illiterate or those living in isolation and communities who suffered large-scale and gross human rights violations (Walsh 2017: 68; Wandita, Campbell-Nelson and Pereira 2006: 308–10; ICTJ 2010: 6). As part of memorialisation, the CAVR also recommended commemoration ceremonies, dates, monuments and other initiatives to honour and remember victims of human rights violations, the development of educational materials on the Timorese historic struggle to uphold human rights, while, as measures of non-repetition, it recommended an education campaign to increase public awareness of the link between past abuses and current patterns of violence (CAVR 2005: 2621).

Because gender equality was one of the guiding principles within the CAVR, in its reparations programme there were calls for the protection of women's rights and the recognition of their role in the resistance; rehabilitation and

[16] In its recommendations for a national reparations programme, the CAVR defined victim as 'a person who, individually or as part of a collective, has suffered harm, including physical or mental injury, emotional suffering, economic loss or substantial impairment of his or her rights as a result of acts or omissions over which the commission has jurisdiction to consider and includes the relatives or dependents of persons who have individually suffered harm' (CAVR 2005: 2618).

compensation for victims of 1999; initiatives to eliminate violence against women; policies to promote gender equality in the police force, military, and all state institutions; and the addressing of prejudices against women victims of SGBV, including discriminatory practices by the church (Wandita, Campbell-Nelson and Pereira 2006: 316–17). The CAVR also recommended that 'at least 50% of resources in this program shall be earmarked for female beneficiaries' and it included benefits to '*inan mesak*' (mother alone, single mother), referring both to mothers who were not legally married when their partners were killed or disappeared and victims of sexual violence who had borne children out of rape, so as to ensure that children were not seen as victims of sexual abuse (CAVR 2005: 2616; Wandita, Campbell-Nelson and Pereira 2006: 309). More specifically, the CAVR recommended a scholarship programme for their children until they turned 18, as well as medical and social services, including skills training and microcredit for income-generating activities (CAVR 2005: 2620–21).[17]

How were they going to implement it? The CAVR, in addition to demanding a public apology from Indonesia, requested payments to a reparation fund established for victims, and urged Portugal, France, the US, and the UK to assist Timor-Leste in supporting victims' reparations, given their military assistance to Indonesia during the commission of atrocities (CAVR 2005: 2619–20). The recommendation was that the reparations programme should function initially for five years, allowing a two-year period to identify other potential beneficiaries (Wandita, Campbell-Nelson and Pereira 2006: 308–14; CAVR 2005: 2537, 2619). Although this was also supposed to be beneficial for those women who would reveal their experiences later, in practice many of the women interviewed revealed their experiences from 2012 with ACbit's activities. My concern is that not only may it be morally questionable to expect women to come forward and to reveal their violations because they will receive something in return, but also that while some will do so, it is reasonable to expect that some others may remain silent due to fear, stigmatisation and even because they lack the information and knowledge required to navigate the system. There are limitations and exclusions created by truth commissions, which may lead to long-term social consequences for specific individuals, particularly those in a situation of major vulnerability. In any case, the programme of reparations was never implemented.

We may think that this is a matter of financial resources particularly for the Timorese state, but because the recognition of women's contributions to the struggle has also been neglected and the government has focused on assisting the veterans, I argue that it is also matter of a lack of political will. The CTF recommendations would indeed suffer the same fate as the CAVR. Among its recommendations for reparations, although it excluded any reference to

[17] According to s 59(1) of the Timorese Constitution, the state only guarantees free primary education.

compensation, it included an apology from both the Timorese and Indonesian heads of state, acknowledging responsibility for past violence; healing programmes for survivors; investigation of the fate of disappeared persons and children separated from their parents during the conflict; and education and scholarship programmes for children who were victims of the violence (ICTJ 2010: 6). With the exception of a timid cooperation between Indonesia and Timor-Leste to look for the stolen children, the other reparation measures were never implemented.

Rothschild (2017: 444) claims that there is an emergence of a binary narrative, that has occurred as an unintentional result of the CAVR, that sets a feminisation of the category of victims in opposition to a state-constructed category of male veterans: by focusing on violations and victimhood, the CAVR constructed a category of victims perceived as lacking agency, in contrast with the category of agentive veterans.[18] As a result, because the victims are seen as non-agentive and non-resistant and the veterans are the celebrated figures in the current narrative of the past (a story of agentive heroic resistance to Indonesian rule), female victims are looked down upon by many Timorese, even by those who suffered violations themselves (Rothschild 2017: 443–44). This is why, she explains, despite the fact that the CAVR was large and well-funded and there was a high percentage of Timorese who suffered violations, Timor-Leste's victims' rights movement remained small, underfunded and unsuccessful in securing reparations (Rothschild 2017: 443–44). Based on my fieldwork, I agree with Rothschild's idea concerning a dialectical opposition between male veterans and female victims. Ross (2003: 132) also seems to raise the limitations entrenched within a truth commission when she says that:

> any understanding of violence and its effects is narrowed, women's experiences may be undervalued or unrecognised, and the possibility of expanding or legitimating the range of repertoires upon which people can draw in reconfiguring their lives may be missed.

Lawry-White (2015: 143–45) emphasises that the truth seeking activities of truth commissions have the potential to contribute to the reparations of victims: where the truth about violations suffered is officially endorsed and widely acknowledged and a space is open within the national discourse for victims to assert their rights, victims – who may have felt ignored – are empowered, their dignity is recognised and therefore the satisfactory and reparative effect of the historical record created by truth commissions is greater. The case of Timor-Leste shows that the reparatory effect of the truth seeking of truth commissions will depend on their follow-up and the reciprocity towards the victims who participated. Moreover, the focus on women's violations and victimhood by truth

[18] Rothschild (2017: 448–49) highlights how while the chapter on Timor's Resistance movement in the Chega! report is a mere 56 pages out of the 2,500-plus-page report, the main chapter on human rights violations is 1,421 pages long.

commissions as against narratives of resistance may generate unexpected consequences in a society in the long-term: these mechanisms may play a role in the accommodation between old and new power structures.

V. REPARATIONS PROVIDED BY THE TIMORESE STATE

Under the leadership of a female former MP Fernanda Borges, and with the support of the UN, a package of draft laws related to transitional justice was submitted to the National Parliament in July 2010. Following the recommendations of the Chega! report, one draft law focused on the creation of an Institute of Memory and another one on the creation of a national reparations programme. In my conversation with the former MP, she told me how in the beginning all the main political parties in the parliament supported the draft laws.[19] However, she soon realised that her project started being rejected by her male colleagues in parliament to the point that it was abandoned as 'waiting for approval'. It was allegedly too controversial, because it included the provision of reparations not only for veterans, but also for victims. More specifically, Borges said, there was an Article that covered both veterans and victims, but there were politicians who only wanted the inclusion of victims belonging to the political party of Fretilin, which would be discriminatory according to international human rights law. As a consequence of the opposition to the inclusion of *all* victims as beneficiaries, the Timorese Parliament did not approve either of the two draft laws. The draft law that was supposed to create the Institute of Memory was considered not to be controversial and was accepted by all parties, but because it was attached to the draft law on reparations for victims, it was also not approved until the former Prime Minister Rui Maria de Araújo took power in 2015 and brought it back to the table.

According to a well-known Fretilin leader, member of the Veterans' Commission and current MP, David Ximenes, victims should not receive reparations, because all Timorese in one way or another participated in the struggle.[20] In his opinion, if women supported the resistance, they could apply for the veterans' pensions through the OPMT, the women's branch of Fretilin. If women had supported the resistance, their names would be on the OPMT register. In contrast, if people could not fulfil the criteria to be veterans, it meant that they had supported the Indonesians, and for him, it was out of the question that these people should obtain support from the Timorese state. Ximenes's point of view dismisses violence against women, including sexual violence, as 'collateral damage'. Moreover, it ignores the fact that violence was committed against Timorese women as 'proxy violence' when the real target, ie male members of the armed resistance, could not be found and that attacks and violations against

[19] Interview in Dili, Timor-Leste, 6 November 2017.
[20] Interview in Dili, Timor-Leste, 6 September 2016.

the civilian population were committed as part of an organised plan (CAVR 2005: 1920, 2807). His view may also presuppose a denial of women's agency, neutrality and the fact that they can also participate in many ways during a conflict. Some of the women interviewed were, for instance, children and adolescents when they first suffered serious human rights violations, while others told me that they had not wanted to participate in or support either the resistance or the Indonesians. A woman from Mauchiga, when asked if she had participated in the conflict, replied 'I did not want to'. She was sexually assaulted when she was a teenager – including by a Commander – over several months. Along with other girls, she was also told by the village chief to get together with the Indonesians to save themselves. After her experience, this woman never participated in the conflict.[21] She did not control the circumstances that led to her victimisation.

In another interview, the former chair of the CAVR commission and currently MP for Fretilin, Aniceto Guterres, told me how before 1999, he was the only Timorese lawyer living in Timor-Leste and how he was trying to resolve cases of 'temporary' marriage, which 'was a common practice committed by the Indonesians'.[22] However, once he became an MP, he did not agree with the suggested law on reparations because the administering body would have been dependent on the Timorese state and not independent. His answer seemed to give undue weight to technical argument rather than focusing on the principle of state recognition of victims. But I was also told by Ximenes and Guterres that Indonesia and other countries, rather than the new Timorese state, should be responsible for and/or contribute to paying reparations, as happened when Germany paid reparations to the new state of Israel. They have a point, but the issue is that according to international human rights law, reparations are a state obligation. Moreover, it was not only the Indonesians who committed violations; so did the resistance and even actors who were in a greyer zone such as some village chiefs, who were the ultimate local representatives of the Timorese state.

It was, however, almost towards the end of my fieldwork in Timor-Leste and as I was becoming sharper in my interviews, that I started hearing whispers from important people that MPs may have realised that by approving a law that covered *all* victims – including those of crimes committed by the Timorese resistance – there might be consequences for the current leadership of the country. Individual rationality may lead some to ensure their own political survival as part of the 'good team'. This narrative may be entrenched in a construction of masculinity that enforces silences and consigns women's experiences to oblivion. This reminds us of Haugbolle's observations in Lebanon and how 'unconvicted war criminals walk the streets of Beirut as well as the corridors of the parliament.

[21] Interview with Participant 19, Mauchiga, Ainaro, Timor-Leste, 10 November 2016.
[22] Interview in Dili, Timor-Leste, 10 November 2017.

In this way the legal handling of crimes committed during the war has contributed to a culture of amnesia' (2005: 194). Elites may thus select the mechanisms of transitional justice that are more advantageous to them, while promoting the silence and oblivion of other issues. Reflecting on selectivity in the implementation of transitional justice in the Arab world, Aboueldahab (2017: 32) has also noted that the prosecutions in Egypt focused on corruption rather than human rights crimes, perhaps because the military and other state agencies worked to ensure that investigations and trials did not extend too far, so as not to harm their political interests and subject themselves to human rights prosecutions. Prosecutions instead served to scapegoat certain high-level individuals (Aboueldahab, 2017: 32). Similarly, Lixinski (2021: 10) has also emphasised the need to pay attention to cultural heritage and memorialisation after violence and the extent to which authorities co-opt these processes, including through the use of laws, to retell a history that favours them.

In Timor-Leste, the government, I argue, has been selective and vague with transitional justice vocabulary for its own benefit. While reconciliation has been used as a tool of foreign policy in the international sphere, internally the government avoids the use of the word 'victim' perhaps not because of active as opposed to passive connotations, but because it may be trying to avoid any financial responsibility towards them. For the same reasons, 'reparations' is a term not used today.[23] It is true that Wandita, Campbell-Nelson and Pereira (2006: 297) claimed in 2006 that the association of families of victims of 1999, predominantly led by males, mainly advocated justice, rather than other issues around victim rehabilitation and reparations. My findings more than 10 years later were different. Because victims were never truly assisted or recognised, today some of them are demanding more actively their access to reparations. I believe that the change derives from victims comparing their treatment with the veterans' treatment, which has been the focus of the government. Veterans enjoy not only pensions, but their roles are also exalted by the construction of militaristic and male-focused memorials. As Rothschild (2017: 451) argues, while the government has obstructed the draft law for a reparations programme for victims, 'Timor's state has not built any memorials specifically for victims, as it is currently doing for veterans in all 65 subdistricts. Nor has the state held any commemoration ceremonies explicitly for victims from the occupation'. This is also leading victims to make a connection between their violations and the veterans' pensions. I now revert to this story.

After the guerrilla offensive in the village of Klaras against the Indonesians in 1983, the Indonesians took revenge against the civilian population: they shot everyone in their path. One woman interviewed said that she and the women of her family were caught in the mountains after escaping the shootings.

[23] Note that while Germany has recently acknowledged committing genocide during its colonial occupation of Namibia and announced development aid worth more than €1.1bn, the aid package was called a 'gesture' rather than reparation (UN 2021b: paras 59, 61).

The Indonesians asked them who killed the Indonesian fighters, and they replied that they did not know. She was then taken to the local unit commander and raped over five months. The village chief then told her 'if you don't get married with them you will be violated until you die'. She then married an Indonesian for one year and later had an abortion. He left her. She submitted her papers for the veterans' pension in 2009 on the grounds of all the punishments she had received but said she had not received an answer.[24] These stories of violations and applications for veterans' pensions are replicated all over Timor-Leste. Again, as citizens, these women are looking for their recognition in the public space, however much the political and financial interests of those in power may impede their visibility. This takes me to my next point: an over-focus on compensation may have also contributed to the lack of recognition of women's experiences during the conflict.

The lack of approval of reparations for victims, mainly women, is associated with a political discourse of the elites that denies women's agency and equal status as citizens. Women, including the victims of SGBV, not only suffered from physical harm but also psychological trauma, and their violations may have long-term consequences for them. In the meantime, UN committees continue calling upon Timor-Leste to ensure the prompt redrafting of the draft law on reparations to provide redress for all victims of past human rights violations and to ensure that all victims of torture and ill-treatment, including sexual violence, obtain redress, including compensation and rehabilitation (CAT 2017, para 9(e)). Niner (2011: 49) also advocates recognition that women's abuse was a weapon of war and that as legitimate victims of war, they deserve acknowledgement and compensation, alongside other veterans. I agree with her that it is a matter of recognition, but I believe this idea of providing lump-sum payments and pensions as compensation is related to a neoliberal conception of human rights where individual rights have an association with money. There seems to be a misconception that reparations mean monetary compensations.

Rubio-Marín (2009: 103) argues that because material reparations are intended to help victims rebuild their lives, most reparations programmes have distributed lump-sum payments, pensions, or other forms of material compensation. Oette (2009: 233) also says that 'compensation remains the most common form of reparation awarded by human rights treaty bodies and courts in cases of mass violations'. In South Africa, for instance, a study looking at the impact of reparations on victims found that the government did little to help victims or to realise other forms of reparations beyond monetary payments, which meant that health, housing, educational and psychological assistance were neglected (Goldblatt 2006: 71). Atuahene also explains that while the Commission on the Restitution of Land Rights in South Africa was supposed to give people a choice between compensation, land or housing, it gave the majority of claimants

[24] Interview with Participant 10, Lalerik Mutin, Viqueque, Timor-Leste, 03 February 2017.

evicted from urban areas only the option of financial compensation because this was easier and quicker (2014: 105, 147, 157, 173). The issue is that there were differences of impact among the modes of restitution: land or housing were considered to have the greatest impact on people's wealth (Atuahene 2014: 173). For those who obtained compensation, there were a few respondents who received larger awards and who generally used the money for home improvements, which increased the value of their homes, while 70 per cent of urban claimants received small sums and generally used the money for daily survival or luxury items – the little money was split between the descendants and there was very little else they could do (Atuahene 2014: 156–57, 166).

When violations are widespread it is difficult to apply compensation on a case-by-case basis. The state cannot give money to everyone, particularly after coming out of a conflict. There are differences between the North and South that are not easily transferrable or sustainable, even more so in a post-conflict situation where there is a lack of all kind of resources. In the case of Timor-Leste, I argue that by having an over-focus on compensation in the form of lump-sum payments and pensions, women's access to other types of reparations may have been neglected. Atuahene argues that instead of a focus on reimbursement as a form of reparation, the focus should therefore be on dignity restoration: to rehabilitate the dispossessed and reintegrate them into society through an emphasis on a 'compensation that addresses both the economic harms and the dignity deprivations involved' (2014: 3–5).[25] The danger is thus that we may forget that the goal should neither be to take the case to a court, nor only to award compensation, but reparation is the recognition of the individuals themselves, acknowledging the harms they have suffered and their needs.

In Los Palos, a woman said that because her father had died during Portuguese times, she and her mother were in a vulnerable position, so the Indonesians had been sexually assaulting her since she was 15 years old and up until 1999. She became a sexual slave. She also said that in 2003, some people came to ask for a TV interview claiming that if she appears on TV, the government would help her. She accepted, but then she was criticised for it, felt more stigmatised; people called her a whore and she was even rejected by her son. When I asked her about justice, she said 'I want to have my worth again'.[26] Another woman in Mauchiga said that she liked to tell her story at the CAVR about the sexual violence she as a teenager, her three sisters and all the girls in her village suffered during the course of a month, so people could know what happened to them. However, she said that she did not see any results. She also said she wants those who committed crimes to be held accountable but that 'this depends on the government'.

[25] Atuahene (2014: 157, 163) concludes that the restitution (material) awards had a deep (intangible) meaning for the restoration of dignity: the receipt of a home or land symbolised the return of family pride and honour, while the financial awards were used to make home improvements and purchase tombstones, which became memorials to the loved ones who were forcibly removed.

[26] Interview with Participant 55, Los Palos, Lautém, Timor-Leste, 12 January 2017.

As a result of the sexual violence she endured, she suffered from health issues and is now seeking help to pay for the studies of her children and to build a house.[27]

Timor-Leste may have been implemented discrete policies that may be considered forms of reparations. However, there may be a fault line between post-conflict humanitarian policies and reparations that do not contribute to the recognition of harms. Let me refer to concrete cases. Although there is uncertainty regarding the extent to which women, including widows, were able to benefit, the Timorese government implemented a two-year programme called RESPECT to fund employment and livelihood activities such as labour-intensive infrastructure rehabilitation (roads, irrigation, markets, schools, re-forestation), vocational training, and support for agricultural and small-business endeavours (Wandita, Campbell-Nelson and Pereira 2006: 297). The government also supported the development of a memorial 'peace garden' where the remains of unidentified resistance fighters were buried (Wandita, Campbell-Nelson and Pereira 2006: 297). They were, though, not counted as forms of reparations either by local or international authorities at that time.

Moreover, as previously explained, after the post-referendum violence in 1999, international and local NGOs and some government agencies developed specific programmes for victims of human rights violations (Wandita, Campbell-Nelson and Pereira 2006: 288–89). Wandita, Campbell-Nelson and Pereira (2006: 297) observe that female victims groups, mainly composed of widows, such as the Nove-Nove in Maliana, were not organised around reparations, but with the intention 'to provide mutual support, address issues of economic survival, and continue the demand for justice and disclosure regarding the whereabouts of those who were disappeared'. Who decides that cooperatives that are formed to recognise harm and claim justice are not a form of satisfaction and rehabilitation? Moreover, the Timorese government today provides NGOs with funding that is used for the victims of the Indonesian occupation. ACbit, for instance, receives funds from the Ministry of Social Solidarity and the Fund for Civil Society Organisations of the Prime Minister's Office, and they have built houses for female victims (Pereira 2017: 121–22). I understand that the government needs support to provide social assistance to local communities, but the issue is that while women see an aid that comes from civil society, they do not see that the state recognises the harms they suffered and their long-term consequences.

Lawry-White (2015: 151) argues, for instance, that 'violations directed at a victim send an implicit message about a victim's value, dignity and place in the community' and that if ignored by the state, this further constrains the space in which they can enjoy their rights. How can women, then, come to terms with their sorrow and distress if the government is acting as if what happened to

[27] Interview with Participant 5, Mauchiga, Ainaru, Timor-Leste, 11 November 2016.

them was collateral damage; even worse, something that should be forgotten? The new institute of memory, the 'Centro Nacional Chega!' (Chega! National Centre – CNC), has as part of its mandate to assess what has been done under the Chega! recommendations. The CNC is therefore looking at all kind of policies except those concerning accountability and reparations – at least not explicitly. But the government forgets that humanitarian policies and reparations could co-exist based on the recognition of harm. It is, however, the fear of bearing responsibility for compensation that discourages the government from using the word 'reparations' and therefore the recognition of women's experiences.

Furthermore, as I heard several times from people in the government, including from MP David Ximenes that if a woman with a child needs help and cannot claim for a veterans' pension, she should go to the Ministry of Solidarity, where she can ask for a Bolsa da Mãe, a grant for mothers. This programme helps families in a situation of high vulnerability living below the poverty line on the condition that their children attend school and are immunised (OHCHR 2016b: para 53). However, not only may there be a lack of effective control of the programme to ensure that the requirements are fulfilled, but also this founding programme amounts basically to only US$4 per month (OHCHR 2016b: para 53). Why is this important? Because the minimum monthly amount that a veteran can receive is US$230 and the difference between who-gets-what has created a socio-economic imbalance within the local population, particularly in women's daily lives. This imbalance is absurd. CEDAW has recommended that Timor-Leste increase the investment from the national budget in the Bolsa da Mãe programme in order to redress its marginalisation and imbalance in comparison with the veterans' pension scheme, which is a male-focused programme and which receives the highest budgetary allocations (OHCHR 2016a: para 53; CEDAW 2015: 32(b)).

There may be, though, a general tendency for women to be excluded from reparations after a conflict, while they are told to apply for less convenient social programmes. Because a large number of women were not recorded as victims by the South African TRC and therefore not eligible for individual reparations, they ended being reliant on state assistance in the form of pensions and welfare grants (Ross 2003: 163). Atuahene (2014: 45, 72) also argues in the case of land restitution in South Africa, that not only 'for those who were excluded, instead of healing past wounds, the state may have inadvertently salted them', but also the poverty caused by an economic harm has an intergenerational impact. In Sierra Leone, although the TRC recognised children of victims of sexual violence as eligible beneficiaries of reparation programmes, in practice some of the victims of sexual violence had to approach the Ministry of Social Welfare, Gender, and Children's Affairs to seek meaningful assistance from the government for their children (King 2006: 258). Women from the worst affected regions in Sierra Leone were forced to migrate to other communities in search of a better livelihood through better services and infrastructure (King 2006: 269).

It is alarming that reparations policies remain so limited, if not discriminatory against women, and that in many states, the programmes have not even been implemented, remaining only on paper (cf Rubio-Marín 2006: 26-27). To sum up, the marginalisation of women's violations and experiences is not only a human rights matter, but it may be the result of power and economic competition as part of the re-accommodation of different social groups within a post-conflict state. In Aileu, one of the interviewees, who was first sexually assaulted at 14 years old, ended the conversation with the following reflection: 'you start thinking about what has been done to us and how the government does not help us.'[28]

VI. THE WAY FORWARD

A woman that I met, illiterate and today in her thirties, described how after being gang-raped over two days by the Indonesians, her vagina became purple and how she could not walk because of the pain. She was a child when that happened to her in 1999 and after that she felt depressed.[29] She did not know about the Special Panels for Serious Crimes or CAVR. She told her story first to ACbit in 2012 and now she is participating in her village women's group. When asked why she had decided to participate in this group, her answer was that she had three children by her first husband who later abandoned her. This woman found a new husband who himself had 10 children. Now she is raising 13 children in total, her husband is unemployed and they have no house. She is waiting to receive support to buy a new house and the women's group has been a source of information about possible aid programmes. This story reveals how sexual abuse and lack of post-conflict justice is entrenched in the continuum of the violations of economic and social rights.

Because there is a pronounced lack of commitment towards the provision of reparations after a conflict for redress of harm to victims, it seems that a change is needed. The conflict affected physical and mental health of Timorese women. Their violations also had an impact on their socio-economic well-being: many became mothers and female heads of households, and many of those who were sexually assaulted by the Indonesians and the militias were later rejected by their husbands and/or saw their chances of getting married being reduced. Although they are clearly currently in need of support, they have not been offered any consistent attention by the state. By denying reparations to female victims and relying on discreet ways to help them, including through limited welfare programmes, there is a tacit lack of recognition and denial of their violations. The state acts as if they were invisible and is if nothing had happened.

[28] Interview with Participant 40, Aileu, Aileu, Timor-Leste, 20 January 2017.

[29] *cf* ACERWC, *Michelo Hunsungule and Others (on behalf of children in Northern Uganda) v Uganda*, Decision, Communication No 1/2005, 15–19 April 2013, para 76.

Transitional justice, should, however, provide alternative and more effective ways of delivering justice according to women's perceptions: Timorese women see justice more as recognition and truth, to ensure their visibility in the space of appearance of the *polis* and the protection and enjoyment of their economic and social rights. This is similar to what was said to me by a woman in Mauchiga who suffered from sexual violence while being pregnant. Of her participation at the CAVR she said 'we told the story but for what? There were no changes at all.' Although she receives a monthly pension as a veteran, she said 'the veterans' pension does nothing to compensate for all the pain. The experiences of rape that we suffered are more than what we receive'.[30] Reparations should therefore not be limited to access to monetary compensation, which in practice is mostly denied anyway, but they should also be about rehabilitation, the symbolic, non-repetition and, I argue, should even be directed towards the collective and its intersections.

The reality is that despite the over-focus on compensation, when female victims are asked what material assistance they would like to have to better cope in the aftermath of violence, they often prioritise their basic needs and those of their family members. It is not surprising that women across the different municipalities of Timor-Leste associated justice mainly with economic and social rights: access to and enjoyment of education, for them and their children, health, housing, skills and employment, and even administrative procedures, such as birth certificates. These rights are not only about material gains, but also about social relationships. This means that in situations of scarce resources, placing the emphasis on rehabilitation services rather than payments may seem to be a better alternative, as it combines both development and reparations concerns (Rubio-Marín 2009: 109; 2006: 29).

Calling for international interventions to take local agendas more seriously, Firchow and MacGinty (2019: 261–80) observed that when 'ordinary' individuals in northern Uganda were asked questions about how they determined peace and safety in their communities they did not mention issues of civil and political justice, but instead they were often getting on with the task of reconciliation and development without very much external assistance in order to fulfill their basic needs. In this regard, Ní Aoláin, Haynes, and Cahn (2011: 257) use the concept of 'social services justice' as the link between immediate post-conflict humanitarian aid and longer-term development measures, and describe how it should 'become a critical aspect of any transitional justice and post-conflict reconstruction model, serving as a gender-central bridge between a recognition of the immediate needs of the population and long-term development'. They further argue that:

> Rights protection and service provision must not be viewed as exceptional or conditional on being a 'victim of a crime,' but as a part of the compact involved in the

[30] Interview with Participant 18, Mauchiga, Ainaru, Timor-Leste, 11 November 2016.

> ratification of treaties and of a broader set of obligations involved in post-conflict reconstruction for states and international institutions (Ní Aoláin, Haynes, and Cahn, 2011: 266).

Ní Aoláin, Haynes, and Cahn (2011: 266) see, therefore, an overlap between social services justice and an expanded concept of reparations and their connection to gender, in reparations programmes that include, for example, direct monetary transfers; social services such as scholarships for children of sexual violence victims, health clinics and vocational training; and microfinance projects that are linked to development. Reparations should thus encompass the secondary effects and differentiated impact of SGBV violations, eg forced pregnancy, sexually transmitted diseases, loss of reproductive capacity, unwanted motherhoods, the harms and longtime effects of conceiving children born out of rape (UN 2020: paras 32–34; Gilmore, Guillerot and Sandoval 2020: 55). Still worrisome is that children born out of rape are not recognised as autonomous victims, as well as the lack of attention given to access to medical aid and health assessment after a conflict (UN 2020: para 29(c)).[31] Because many forms of SGBV do not cause physical injuries, medical professionals should be trained to be aware of how women may present with psychological difficulties and how to ask women whether they have experienced violence without subjecting them to secondary victimisation (International Commission of Jurists 2016: 167).

I am also inclined to support the protection of economic and social rights through sustainable means as well as the idea that collective reparations can co-exist with development. Indeed, through income-generation opportunities and economic empowerment, reparations can also be a transformative process. In the case of Sierra Leone, Coulter (2009: 181) describes how her informants said that working kept them from being 'idle', that it was very important for them to be able to contribute to the household because this made them feel more respected and that having an income improved their relationships with their husbands. The issue again is how to define effective public policies that make these activities sustainable in the long-term. Bernstein (2009: 303) explores the possibility of giving victims compensation as shares in microfinance institutions rather than cash transfers, since it would encourage development in poor regions that are unable to dispense large compensation payments and would help women improve their status. According to her, in contrast to microcredit that is based on loans, microfinance gives beneficiaries new opportunities for savings and credit, without imposing any repayments, given that victims should not be responsible for paying for their own reparations (Bernstein 2009: 304). Microfinance would contribute thus to institution-building after a crisis and it would mean sustainable income-generating activities for the victims and welfare for mothers and their children (Bernstein 2009: 310, 322). I am attracted to Bernstein's ideas and I believe this is the path to follow, but it is important to see how they are applied and their impact in a social context.

[31] *cf* Dowds (2019) and Sánchez Parra (2018).

Although Goldblatt (2006: 74, 82) considers that neither the TRC process nor reparations had any significant impact on the unequal position of women in South African society, she rescues some positive measures related to guarantees of non-repetition and/or collective reparations for women: laws on prevention of domestic violence and rape; police and military sensitivity training; improved social services for women, including health and termination of pregnancy services; and measures to address women's poverty, land rights, and economic opportunities. Returning to Atuahene, she cautions that while the restitution programme in South Africa addressed the dignity harms in some cases and increased a few respondents' wealth, whites were still the main owners of land, meaning that the state missed an opportunity to address the still deeply unjust distribution of land or economic power in post-Apartheid South Africa (2014: 105, 157, 163).

The Inter-American system of human rights has also been more assertive concerning the provision of reparations in cases where there are large-scale violations and a lack of socio-economic resources. For instance, the Inter-American Court on Human Rights (IACtHR) is well-known for having taken a creative approach to collective reparations and for a focus on rehabilitation, satisfaction and guarantees of non-repetition, ranging from the provision of free medical and psychological services and access to clean water to the setting up of schools and medical dispensaries, the naming of streets, schools and plazas, and the setting up of memorials for victims (Evans 2012: 70–75; Cassel 2005: 96).[32] There is also the right to the truth and the need to understand the violations and their causes, including for cases of disappearances. In *Gelman v Uruguay*, for instance, the IACtHR ordered a factual investigation and immediate location of the remains of a disappeared victim as a form of reparation to the relatives who also became victims, ie the Court recognised their right to the truth (Lawry-White 2015: 150). In the context of violence against women during armed conflict, the case of *Dos Erres Massacre v Guatemala* has also been emblematic in the Americas.[33] In addition to holding the state internationally responsible for the lack of due diligence in the investigation, prosecution and punishment of the state agents responsible, the Court ordered the implementation of human rights training for different state authorities and the creation of a webpage to facilitate the search for children abducted and illegally detained during the internal armed conflict as measures to guarantee non-repetition (IACHR 2015b: para 72).

The Inter-American system has also embraced the concept of transformative reparations in cases of violence against women and gender-based discrimination. For instance, in the case of *González et al ('Cotton Field') v Mexico*, the

[32] *Plan de Sánchez Massacre v Guatemala*, IACtHR, Judgment, 29 April 2004, Series C, No 105; *Aloeboetoe et al v Suriname*, IACtHR, Judgment (Reparations), 10 September 1993, Series C, No 15.

[33] The case, which took place during the Guatemalan armed conflict between 1960 and 1996, involved the targeting of women with sexual violence and the massacre of 251 inhabitants of the community of Las Dos Erres from December 6 to 8, 1982 (IACHR 2015b: para 72).

Court highlighted the role played by gender stereotypes and historical discrimination in fuelling the problem of violence against women and underscored the need to go beyond mere restitution to design reparations that address the structural discrimination which promotes the repetition of violence against women (IACHR 2015b: para 59).[34] In the case of *Jessica Lenahan et al v United States*, the Inter-American Commission (IACHR) also recommended that the state investigate systemic failures of the police response, reform existing legislative measures to improve enforcement of restraining orders and adopt public policies and institutional programmes to remedy the stereotypes against domestic violence victims (IACHR 2015b: para 61). While in the case of *Paloma Angélica Escobar Ledezma et al v Mexico*, the IACHR called on the state to develop public education programmes to promote respect for women as equals and observance of their right not to be subjected to violence or discrimination; to incorporate a gender-perspective and harmonise forensic protocols with international standards in criminal investigations related to violence against women to prevent impunity; and to continue to adopt institutional programmes aimed at restructuring stereotypes concerning the role of women and promoting the eradication of discriminatory socio-cultural patterns (IACHR 2015b: para 62).[35] All these policy recommendations focus on the recognition of the agency of victims, on the promise that their violations will not be repeated and on the need to address discriminatory structures. These are examples of reparations that do not involve monthly monetary compensation and which a country with limited resources could implement. Timor-Leste needs to extend good reparation initiatives such as the naming of a school after Ana Lemos in Ermera Vila where young students learn about the former UN employee and the reasons why she was targeted.

Finally, Evans (2012: 100) argues that rather than an over-focus on individual responsibility, a connection of reparations to state responsibility may be a good idea so states become responsible for granting redress to victims of an armed conflict. The responsibility could also be extended to those states that participated in and/or facilitated the setting up of a system that caused so much damage to the population. In the case of Timor-Leste, this would comprise countries such as Indonesia and also others such as Australia and the USA, which, owing to strategic self-interest political motivations, supported the Indonesian occupation in

[34] *González et al ('Cotton Field') v Mexico*, IACtHR, Judgment of 16 November 2009 (Preliminary Objection, Merits, Reparations, and Costs), para 450; International Commission of Jurists (2016: 77).

[35] *Paloma Angélica Escobar Ledezma et al v Mexico*, Case 1175-03, Report No 32/06, Inter-American Commission on Human Rights. In the *Sepur Zarco* case, the court in Guatemala also supported the provision of transformative reparations which 'would transform the situation in which the victims [of SGBV] and their next of kin were at the time the crimes were committed and enable them and their community to significantly improve their lives' (Martin and SáCouto 2020: 260). However, four years after the verdict, 'only a couple of reparations have been implemented and the process to obtain legal land titles is at an impasse', causing disappointment among the women (Evrard, Mejía Bonifazi and Tine Destrooper 2021: 446).

Timor-Leste. The focus on the actions of the state may also perhaps serve to deter the commission of further crimes. In this sense, the case of Indonesia becomes emblematic not only because the post-Suharto governments have been reluctant to provide the truth about past gross human rights violations, including disappearances, but also because the military – including key commanders who should have been held accountable for the commission of crimes in Timor-Leste – kept an influential role in their democratic transition (*cf* Strating 2019: 282). Consequently, Indonesia may have shown little commitment over the years to stop the commission of crimes.[36] As such, we may think not only about the crimes committed in Timor-Leste, but also about the genocide of 1965 and the continuum of violations in Aceh and West Papua.

VII. CONCLUSIONS

As in Timor-Leste, but also as in other contexts, women's access to reparations was extremely limited, if not non-existent. There is a risk that reparations and their gender component may simply remain on a checklist without any effective implementation on the ground. While the UN, as part of its peace-building legacy, is promoting and recommending the enactment of laws that ensure reparations in post-conflict societies, the UN Special Panels never created a victims' fund, as mandated by UNTAET's internal regulation concerning compensation for victims in Timor-Leste. The case of Ana Lemos puts into question women's access to UN reparations and reveals the additional barriers that women may face. All this highlights the lack of value of the UN international discourse.

Furthermore, the recommendations of the Chega! report concerning reparations were never implemented, and the CAVR, during the years in which it operated, only managed to implement an urgent scheme which mainly consisted of a US$200 one-off grant. Women's access to this scheme was, however, also very limited: despite widespread and systematic violations committed against women, only 196 women in the whole of Timor-Leste managed to access it. The social and institutional behaviour of actors involved in the implementation of the programme may have prevented female victims from accessing the urgent scheme. But communities and families may also have been keen to keep silent about SGBV, making it more difficult for women to come forward. We see again the intersection of the public and private creating barriers for women in accessing, in this case, reparations.

The reparations programme was not implemented by the Timorese government. While the domestic draft law on the creation of a Timorese reparation

[36] After September 11 2001, Indonesia – the country with the largest Muslim population in the world – acquired a strategic political and economic significance in the region and in particular for the US (Ostowar 2020: 105).

programme was put on hold by the parliament, the government has instead focused its support on the provision of pensions for veterans. Those in power may have a political and financial interest in preserving the status quo: former members of the armed resistance and politicians may benefit from sidelining reparations for victims and exalting their own image as heroes, since this provides them with legitimacy and protects them from any prosecution for crimes committed during the conflict. However, by denying victims recognition, the state may discriminate against them even more, leading to the continuum of their victimisation. Policy makers and scholars working on transitional justice should thus contemplate those socio-economic structures that are heightened after a conflict, and which affect women's recognition and the guarantee of their equal rights as compared with men.

But I also argue that the over-focus on individual compensation, both by international and local actors, may have complicated women's access to reparations. The extension of the concept of victims and the over-focus on compensation have large financial implications for a state that is coming out of a conflict: there are a large number of victims whose rights have been violated but there are also priorities such as covering the basic needs of the population and the building up of institutions and services. Because the provision of reparations, and of compensation in particular, falls within domestic law and policy, it is dependent on the political will of the state. Moreover, states may also be unwilling to accept their obligation to allocate their limited resources to redress the violations committed by other actors, and be more concerned about policies that benefit the whole population and the stability of the new state. In practice, nobody seems to want to pay the bill for reparations, and as a result, redress for victims may tend to be greatly affected. This situation is leading Timorese women to become louder in their demands for reparations and even compare their violations and their current situation of impoverishment with those who managed to access the veterans' pensions. Rather than an over-focus on compensation, other types of reparations, such as rehabilitation, satisfaction and non-repetition, conceived within the collective and its intersections, may be more aligned to women's genuine desire for justice and could help to eliminate the fault-line between reparations and development. If not, the right of victims to obtain access to reparations may be a walk with a crown of thorns. Based on Timorese women's views of what post-conflict justice entails, the next chapter focuses on women's access to veterans' pensions.

The mother of Ana Lemos was a strong advocate for remembering what happened to her daughter. © Noemí Pérez Vásquez.

The local NGO ACbit has been working tirelessly for the recognition of the women whose rights were gravely violated before 1999. Photo taken during a local event in Ermera Vila, Ermera. © ACbit.

7

Women's Access to Post-conflict Benefits: 'Because I Did Not Hold a Gun'

Although veterans' pensions are not traditionally included as a mechanism of transitional justice, this issue was persistently raised by the interviewed women across the different municipalities in Timor-Leste. Consequently, because women associate post-conflict justice with their exclusion from the veterans' pensions and their current socio-economic situation, this chapter focuses on their access to this post-conflict benefit. Hence, I start in section I with an explanation of Disarmament, Demobilisation and Reintegration (DDR) programmes, which are the basis of the veterans' pensions that were implemented in Timor-Leste. Within this section, I explain how, as seen with other mechanisms of transitional justice, there has been a historical discrimination against women in their access to these programmes. In the next section, I focus on the Timorese veterans' pensions and I provide historical context and details of their design and implementation. Then I proceed to unpack all the barriers and layers of discrimination that resurface against women in the context of the veterans' pensions in Timor: from the legislation that established them to their implementation.

More specifically, I focus first on the legislation and policies and show how specific elements and clauses caused direct discrimination against women; namely, the division of labour, exclusive dedication, the requirement of having a witness, the exclusion of sexual violence itself and the exclusion of sexual violence as part of torture, the fact that it only included prolonged deprivation of liberty, and differences in treatment of women who remarry and of 'bush wives'. Second, I focus on the implementation of the veterans' pensions law and its programme. Women described experiences of mistreatment and rejection by local committees of veterans in charge of collecting the applications at the village level; of cases of corruption and of a practice called 'family system'; and of additional barriers concerning intersectionality for those who were illiterate, living in more isolated places, and who had more difficulty in accessing information. Third, I examine the private space and show how culture and family relationships also have an impact on the effective access of women to the veterans' pensions. In the final section, I show that the majority of Timorese women interviewed feel that there has been discrimination against them in their access to the veterans' pensions and how their invisibility and exclusion from this post-conflict economic compensation is entrenched in a logic of male militaristic patronage that has exacerbated women's lack of recognition as equal citizens in the new state. The chapter ends with some reflections concerning the limits of the discourse on rights.

I. DDR, VETERANS' PENSIONS AND THE EXCLUSION OF WOMEN

Since the late 1980s, the UN has increasingly been implementing Disarmament, Demobilisation and Reintegration programmes in countries that came out of conflict (UNDDR 2006: module 1.10, p 1). These programmes are defined as a:

> A process that contributes to security and stability in a post-conflict recovery context by removing weapons from the hands of combatants, taking the combatants out of military structures and helping them to integrate socially and economically into society by finding civilian livelihoods (UNDDR 2006: module 1.20, p 6).

The idea therefore is that former combatants give up their weapons and peacefully return to their families. However, because there is a presumption that after a conflict those demobilised may not be prepared to face the challenges of civilian life and may put at risk the recent political stability of a fragile situation, benefits are provided to facilitate their new life. Consequently, the demobilised are usually offered assistance and psycho-social support, commonly consisting of: (1) reinsertion, where severance payments seek to compensate for the loss of income received while in military service and usually calculated to cover basic needs for a limited period of time, commonly between 6 and 12 months; and (2) reintegration, for instance, through access to land, the provision of skills training, employment referral, or the implementation of micro-projects (World Bank 2004: 4). DDR programmes can vary in their implementation and accordingly there are cases where they can be achieved (i) through a combination of demobilisation and retirement (eg Chad); (ii) where combatants of both statutory and non-statutory forces are demobilised at the same time (eg El Salvador, Mozambique and Nicaragua); or (iii) where only combatants of non-statutory forces are demobilised after the conflict (eg Congo-Brazzaville, Guatemala and Sierra Leone) (World Bank 2004: 2).[1]

Although a demobilisation may refer to efforts to remove from service not only those who were in active service, but also those larger forces composed of non-professional combatants, complexities arise concerning who should be considered to be demobilised and therefore be provided with benefits. Budget restrictions on a new government usually lead to the reduction of the soon-to-be security forces, which means that some may be left out of the new state security

[1] Statutory forces are considered to be regular armed forces, while non-statutory forces may include liberation and guerrilla armies. In the case of Timor-Leste while the Indonesian was considered the statutory force, the Timorese resistance was the non-statutory force (World Bank 2004: 2).

apparatus, as in Cambodia, Rwanda, South Africa and Uganda (World Bank 2004: 2). Also, members of irregular forces, such as paramilitaries and those in underground political operatives, may often not be recognised as beneficiaries, creating some instability, as in Nicaragua, El Salvador, and Guatemala, where former paramilitaries also demanded their recognition and benefits (World Bank 2004: 2–3). The issue is that the law and DDR programmes may not reflect the messiness of war and may not embrace all of those who in one way or another participated in a conflict. This is where international law does not help. According to international humanitarian law (IHL), while members of state armed forces may comprise combatants and non-combatants, there is a recognition that in a NIAC, Additional Protocol II to the Geneva Conventions includes 'dissident armed forces and other organised armed groups' (ICRC 2005: 12). Although the practice is less clear regarding the situation of members of armed opposition groups, there is an assumption that combatants are those 'persons taking active/direct part in hostilities' (ICRC 2005: 12).[2] Who decides then what constitutes taking an active/direct part in hostilities? While those who carried weapons may secure their place in these post-conflict benefits systems, the different occupations and roles of women and girls during a conflict tend to be neglected by these programmes.

Women indeed are not just passive victims but many, voluntarily or forcibly through abduction or coercion, may become active participants in a conflict (Justino et al 2012: 90). There are those women combatants in regular armed forces and guerrilla groups, for example, in Zimbabwe, Sri Lanka, Eritrea, El Salvador, Northern Uganda and Colombia; those women members of clandestine groups carrying out a range of activities, including counterintelligence; but also those women who participate with their bodies, such as sex workers and slaves (Justino et al 2012: 89; Ní Aoláin, Haynes and Cahn 2011: 134).[3] Women can also be in the battlefields and their surroundings, including as cooks, cleaners, camp followers, girlfriends, and teen mothers (Vastapuu 2018: 11).[4] DDR programmes have, though, historically excluded women, denied their access to allowances and training resettlements, and ignored their subsequent needs (Ní Aoláin, Haynes and Cahn 2011: 136; CEDAW GR 30 2013: para 67).

For instance, in Sierra Leone, women ex-combatants faced difficulties in accessing benefits from the DDR programme since it favoured males: while an NGO report indicated that 12,000 women were involved in rebel groups during the conflict, only 506 went through the DDR process (King 2006: 261–62; Justino et al 2012: 90). Moreover, not only was the number of actual female fighters that entered the official DDR programme very low and did not accurately represent

[2] Definition of Combatants, customary IHL, Rule 3.

[3] Cock (1991: 184) argues, however, that 'the pattern of women's participation in both liberation and conventional wars seems to involve an exclusion from direct combat and from any exercise of power that would put them in positions of authority over men'.

[4] Vastapuu (2018: 54) compares the expression 'camp followers' to a housewife without a salary from her domestic duties.

the reality, but also those women who participated in the conflict with no weapons, such as labourers, 'wives', girlfriends, domestic workers and farmers, were not seen as a threat to the peace process or the cease-fire and therefore were largely ignored (Coulter 2009: 155–57, 179).

In Liberia, the reasons for the low participation of girls and women in the 'Disarmament' and 'Demobilisation' phases – also common around the world – were: (1) the unclear definition of 'combatants' (usually those who could present a weapon or ammunition); (2) communication and logistics, which give great power to male commanders to favour males in lists of combatants; (3) DDR officials' stereotypes about the roles of women and men, which marginalise females; and (4) long distances and deficient healthcare facilities – a challenge for women given their daily family responsibilities (Vastapuu 2018: 96).[5] According to Vastapuu (2018: 86), the 'Reintegration' phase was largely a failure. The overall culture within the UN was both highly masculine and militarised, and although gender was taken into account in the plans, these were never implemented (Vastapuu 2018: 111). Girls and women were further pushed back into their traditional societal statuses and the vocational training provided to them was highly gendered and had a long-term socio-economic impact: while they were being offered 'feminine' training (eg baking, hairdressing, soap-making, sewing), boys and men were trained in more valuable and marketable skills (eg masonry, plumbing, mechanics) (Vastapuu 2018: 112–13). If gender dynamics are neglected within DDR processes, girls and women veterans are typically left to fend for themselves (Vastapuu 2018: xvi).

The exclusion of women from DDR benefits may also be accompanied by a refusal to allow them to take part in the new state security apparatus, and as a result they may remain abandoned and without a comfortable place in society. In South Sudan, while women were instrumental during the north/south civil war in intelligence gathering and other so-called 'soft skills', there were not as many women active in the military (Maddox 2013: 83). In Burundi, the women's contingent of an armed group was excluded from the DDR process and those who were expecting to be integrated into the police force or the military also ended up being excluded (Mazurana and Cole 2013: 203). Moreover, DDR programmes may fail to acknowledge the particularities of women, including the fact that many female combatants suffer from SGBV, resulting in children born of rape, high levels of sexually transmitted diseases, and rejection or stigmatisation by families and other trauma (CEDAW GR 30 2013: 67). In the case of the DDR process in Colombia, Abdenur (2018) shows her concern about how female ex-combatants have been neglected, partly because of the broader gender stereotypes that present women narrowly as victims of conflict rather than tackling two contradictory dimensions of their experience: both victimhood and agency. Moreover, even if the demobilisation of women is taken into account, there may yet exist a tendency to apply stereotypical traditional notions of what

[5] Vastapuu cites Mazurana and Cole.

a woman should be, which do not necessarily match the expectations of former female combatants.

Stereotyping does indeed permeate these programmes. Accordingly, women's exclusion from post-conflict benefits may also be related to the imposition of male militaristic narratives and patronage systems which explain the disparities between these programmes and reparations for victims. In this regard, Coulter (2009: 15) claims that although there was ample evidence of the participation of women in armed combat in Sierra Leone, the popular notion of the soldier remained that of a male, highlighting the endurance of gendered ideas of war and peace. She further observes how structures of informal social networks and the patronage of big men limited women's leverage in a corrupt DDR programme, and how combatant men were not eager to share the material benefits of the programme (Coulter 2009: 159).

Showing women's exclusion from the political system in contrast to a new male political elite, Hale (2001: 361) poses an illuminating question about Eritrea:

> What does it mean for a party like the EPLF and its civilian counterpart to travel the route from liberation front – an organization devoted to empowering the disenfranchised groups (women, peasants, Muslims, workers) – to a government assigned to control and manage these very groups?[6]

She notes a change in agency, when she claims that 'while elites who entered the struggle as fighters returned as elites, peasants, with a few exceptions, returned as peasants' (Hale 2001: 361). Favali and Pateman (2003: 190) also observe how during the struggle for independence, the EPLF consistently spoke of women's rights: they constituted 40 per cent of the whole EPLF and almost a quarter of the frontline fighters. After the liberation, however, women's experiences have been affected by the tensions between tradition and modernity and just as the husbands' families could not accept those 'liberated wives', women became the most unequal members of an unequal society: having unequal rights in the allocation of land, their position in some rural areas not changing much for several hundred years, and having no economic power and a subordinate position in the private sphere (Favali and Pateman 2003: 11, 166, 190–91).

This takes me to my main argument. Women's exclusion from these post-conflict benefit programmes may not only be more common than expected, but because after a conflict resources are scarce, we may have new socio-political structures that arise and compete with each other. As part of this competition, former armed combatants position themselves as one of the main political forces in a country and as a result, as these programmes are framed within male and militaristic patronage systems, women's roles and experiences are depoliticised and subsequently not recognised. Therefore, those who manage to

[6] The Eritrean People's Liberation Front was an armed Marxist organisation that fought for the independence of Eritrea from Ethiopia. After independence, it transformed into the People's Front for Democracy and Justice (PFDJ), which serves as Eritrea's only legal political party.

access the veterans' pensions are part of an active political class, which not only influences the on-going narratives of history, but which may also enjoy specific benefits and privileges. In contrast, by denying access to post-conflict benefits to women, these programmes perpetuate socio-economic disparities. The political economy rationale behind them thus sustains an unequal treatment of specific citizens of the new state.

Finally, while there has been an extensive focus on the study and implementation of DDR programmes, less attention has been paid to the development of veterans' pensions. While in theory DDR programmes only address the short-term needs of demobilised combatants and may be considered urgent, veterans' pensions are a long-term entitlement of the retired military whose benefits are granted according to rank, years of service, and/or disability (World Bank 2004: 4, 7). Veterans' pensions are considered to be a domestic affair so international actors may move somewhere else with more urgent needs. However, I argue that veterans' pensions may have the greatest political and socio-economic impact in a post-conflict society in the long-term. Although they are not considered to mean the same, there has not been a clear separation between one and the other in the Timorese case. The system that supports the veterans, which may have begun as an assistance for the years of sacrifice and a help with reintegration into the new state, eventually became part of state welfare. The problem is that this post-conflict system is designed to set higher barriers and to discriminate against women.

II. THE VETERANS' PENSIONS IN TIMOR-LESTE

In Timor-Leste, the veterans' pensions programme is a subject that one hears about on a daily basis. During the Indonesian occupation, the resistance was organised on three fronts: the armed, the clandestine and the diplomatic. The armed front was located in the mountains, and according to a former employee of the Ministry of Solidarity, was divided into four regions, each and under the control of a commander with approximately 10,000 members. Because of its nature, the diplomatic front was smaller, and it benefited from the participation of activists such as José Ramos-Horta, Bella Galhos and Ines Almeida. People in the clandestine front lived in the villages acting as spies, carrying out counter-intelligence and supporting the armed resistance with their general subsistence. While the work of the three fronts was equally recognised in the preamble to the Timorese Constitution enacted in 2002, Article 11 entitled 'Valorisation of Resistance' anticipates the social benefits that were to be granted to the resistance, providing that the state

> acknowledges and values the historical resistance of the Maubere People against foreign domination ...,
>
> shall ensure special protection to the war-disabled, orphans and other dependents of those who dedicated their lives to the struggle for independence and national

> sovereignty, and shall protect all those who participated in the resistance against the foreign occupation …,

and shall render

> tribute to the national heroes.

Consequently, after the withdrawal of the Indonesian army, responsibility for the veterans fell on the president at the time, Xanana Gusmão, who had also been the former leader of the armed front. Several initiatives were taken to support the former members of the resistance. Firstly, all members of the Falintil were discharged and a new national defence force was established into which some, but not all, of its former members were recruited (World Bank 2004: 2). Xanana then commanded the four regional armed commanders to identify and register all the veterans at that time, to develop criteria for defining who could be considered a veteran, and to make recommendations on how to address concerns raised by the veterans (Silva 2015: 2). Between 2002 and 2004, three commissions were then established to identify and register the veterans of the resistance, and were more precisely mandated to document the Falintil and the clandestine command structures, to create a historical record and to verify the claims of individuals regarding their time spent in service (Silva 2015: 2; Rothschild 2017: 449).[7] In June 2005, a Secretary of State for Veterans and Former Combatants Affairs was also appointed within the Ministry of Social Solidarity with the objective of promoting valorisation policies and the recognition of the Timorese Resistance (Silva 2015: 2).[8]

In 2006, the Timorese parliament passed a law called the Statute of the National Liberation Combatants, also known as the Veterans' Law, which provides a legal definition of combatants, veterans and martyrs as well as their rights, duties and benefits.[9] Consequently, pensions and other benefits were granted to veterans and relatives of dead and disappeared persons in order to compensate for the economic difficulties caused by the time spent in the mountains and/or because of the effect of the absence of a family member, including supporting those who were left with the greatest needs, such as children and the elderly (ICTJ 2010: 8).[10] More specifically, the Statute entitled them to receive one of the following benefits: (1) a special retirement pension for surviving veterans with at least 15 years of full-time service, which meant not accumulated with study or paid labour activities or periods of imprisonment and exile, and determined by the leadership of the resistance; (2) a special subsistence pension

[7] The three commissions were: (1) Commission for Former Combatants' Affairs, meaning for those who fought before the Indonesian occupation from 20 August 1975 to 31 December 1978; (2) Commission for the Falintil Veterans' Affairs, from 1978 onwards; and (3) Commission for the Resistance Formal Structure Affairs, which basically concerned those from the clandestine front. According to Silva (2015: 2), there was also what is called a 'Supporting Base' composed of all the population that evacuated to the mountains when the Indonesians arrived in 1975.

[8] Decree Law 3/2005.

[9] Law 03/2006. This law was amended by the Laws 9/2009 and 2/2011.

[10] Decree Law 15/2008 on Pensions of the Combatants and Martyrs of the National Liberation.

for surviving combatants with at least 8 years of full-time participation in the resistance and for disabled former combatants; (3) a survival pension for the relatives of direct heirs of those who died in service (martyrs), in the following order of priority, depending on who was alive: widows, orphans, parents, and siblings; (4) or a lump sum, equivalent to an amount 12 times the minimum wage, for surviving combatants with 4 to 7 years' full-time participation in the resistance, and for indirect heirs of martyrs (Silva 2015).[11]

In summary, there was a special pension for those who worked for more than 15 years, a pension for those who worked between 8 and 14 years, a survival pension for the families of those killed and a lump sum for those who worked between 4 and 7 years. The amount of benefits was thus supposed to be calculated according to the total years of full-time service and the grade and position achieved as a member of one of the fronts of the resistance (ICTJ 2010: 8). After the law was enacted, the government organised the provision of veterans' pensions in two different stages: applicants were declared to be declarants in a first registration process, and they were granted a pension following a second application (Silva 2012: 5). Three registration campaigns took place from 2003 to 2005 as part of a first registration process that would end in 2007, when a Commission for Data Validation and Consolidation finished processing a total of 76,068 registrations (Silva 2015: 2).[12] Out of these 76,068 people who asked to be recognised as combatants or family of combatants, 10,482 were women, 14 per cent of the total.[13] Furthermore, the vast majority of women who received the pension obtained it as a survival pension, ie on behalf of a deceased male family member (Kent and Kinsella 2015a: 220; 2015b: 476).[14] This means that there is a very low number of women who received the veterans' pensions because of their own work.

When those selected started receiving their payments in 2008, there were allegations of community violence and people being killed as revenge for having obtained the pension. At that time, Timor-Leste was still showing signs of instability. Because of a large number of complainants alleged to have missed the first registration process, a second campaign of registration was carried out in May 2009 by the Ministry of Social Solidarity, with registration teams visiting all 65 sub-municipalities (Silva 2015: 2). However, because the registrations during this new campaign amounted to 124,003 applications, in contrast to the 76,068

[11] Decree Law 5/2012 and Law 9/2009. Silva (2015: 4) points out that following the approval of the Statute of National Liberation Combatants in 2006, the government approved the regulation for the pensions in the Decree Law 15/2008, amending this law five times, Decree Laws 25/2008, 35/2009, 25/2010, 42/2011 and 6/2012, this shows how sensitive and controversial the Pensions for Combatants and Martyrs of National Liberation has become.

[12] Silva cites World Bank (2008) and Database Reports (January and February 2015) of the National Directorate for Veterans Affairs of Timor-Leste (DNACLN, 2015).

[13] Based on information provided by the Ministry of Combatants Affairs on 5 September 2019.

[14] Kent and Kinsella cite the Secretary of State for the Issues of Ex-combatants of National Liberation.

applications of the first registration process, the government left this second process on hold (Silva 2015: 2).[15] The 124,003 applications represented almost double the number of people who were registered during the first campaign and the two campaigns together represented 200,071 applications, in a country whose population amounted to approximately 1,000,000 in 2008. The government may have realised the financial challenge of dealing with life-long pensions for so many people. Those registered during the first campaign already pose an enormous economic burden on the state. Silva (2015: 7) argues that because all the Timorese pensions are legally established as life-time benefits, which means that beneficiaries are entitled to receive the pension until their death, this represents a major commitment for the national budget.

As a comparison, in the Prime Minister's presentation of the 2021 State Budget Law Proposal, it was stated that the overall spending on social protection in the country is around US$166.7m – meaning eight per cent of the total state budget – of which US$93.6m goes to pension payments and healthcare for veterans, while only US$8.9m goes to improve the lives of vulnerable children under the Bolsa da Mãe (mother's allowance) programme. The amount that veterans receive is also high when compared with the budget of other key sectors, such as health (US$86m, ie four per cent of the total state budget – this is in COVID-19 times) and education (US$111.4m, ie five per cent of the total state budget).[16] To complicate the situation even further, there have been allegations that people who obtained the pensions may have falsified their documents and that there were some applicants and recipients who were too young to be veterans and to have fought with the resistance. I was told, for instance, by a former UN employee that in Oecussi, a former regional administrator highlighted such discrepancies. Why is it that the veterans' scheme absorbs so much of the national budget and that people try so hard to access it? The reason is that the pensions are very high: while monthly pensions are, for instance, between US$230 and US$575 and 'special people' can gain up to US$750, the minimum salary in the country is US$150, which very few people manage to obtain anyway.[17] The proportion of Timorese living in poverty is estimated at 41.8 per cent, with 30.3 per cent below the extreme poverty line of US$1.90 per day (World Bank 2019). Timor's payments to veterans are considered to be high in absolute terms and as a percentage of the budget and gross domestic product, also when compared with other post-conflict countries (Rothschild 2017: 449).

[15] Silva cites the DNACLN (2015).

[16] In the same speech, the government announced an increase of 45,134 beneficiaries under Bolsa da Mãe and around 23,000 more in the case of old combatants and their families. See Taur Matan Ruak (2020: 9).

[17] In 2008, the government approved a resolution that increased the value of the pension to $750 for fifteen prominent figures of the Timorese resistance or their heirs, including current Prime Minister Taur Matan Ruak, former President Francisco Guterres 'Lú-Olo' and former General Chief of Staff of the Armed Forces Lere Anan Timur (Lusa 2008; Silva 2015: 8).

Hence, whoever manages to have access to the pension becomes a privileged citizen in Timorese society.

Many of the women interviewed were outspoken about their past and some said that they were members of the resistance whose work had not been duly recognised. Others associated their participation in the conflict with their bodies and the harm they endured. There is no dichotomy between the two groups, and in many instances, a woman who identified herself as a member of the resistance could have suffered from a gross violation for being a woman. Accordingly, although in the Commission of Veterans I was told that the people who participate 'actively' in the resistance could apply for the veterans' pensions, out of the 77 women interviewed, whereas 43 submitted their applications, only 20 received a positive answer. Furthermore, out of these 20 women who have received recognition or continue to receive a pension, four are receiving pensions related to their connection to a man, usually a husband or brother, rather than because of their own work in the resistance. This means that out of the 77 women interviewed, only 16 have received recognition or a pension for their own work.

When I asked what kind of recognition they received, the women would answer quickly with the numbers '8–14', meaning they had managed to obtain the monthly desired life-long pension, or '4–7', meaning they obtained only a lump sum. While those who received the '8–14' pension were pleased, the ones who received the '4–7' lump sum complained, saying they deserve the pension instead. Indeed, the lump sum payments, which began in 2012, do not represent such a heavy burden on the state and were granted to those who applied in the first process (Silva 2012: 8). In addition to the pensions and lump sums, there were other forms of symbolic recognition granted, such as medals, the right to funeral honours and presidential decorations, while spouses and children also have the right, for example, to access state health care and education services free of charge and scholarships to assist with uniforms and books (Kent and Kinsella 2015a: 216). Some of the women interviewed said they had only received medals, but this was considered to be meaningless by some in comparison to the harms they had suffered and the difference between their current financial situation and that of those who managed to obtain a monthly pension. None of the women interviewed obtained one of the pensions granted to special people for over 15 years of work. There are 23 women who have applied for a pension and who are still waiting for a final decision from the government. This may indicate that they applied in the second registration process, the one that was put on hold.

Finally, women associate their roles and experiences with a lack of justice, including their exclusion from the veterans' pensions, and with how this has affected their socio-economic situation ever since. They understand how they were disadvantaged and/or neglected by the veterans' process and still refer to this feeling of powerlessness. Due to different barriers, there are higher thresholds for women to access this process, amounting to discrimination against them. This is the focus of my next section.

III. THE VETERANS' PENSION LAW AND DISCRIMINATION AGAINST WOMEN

The Timorese veterans' pensions law is discriminatory against women. It is biased, based on stereotypes and constructs women as inferior. Kent and Kinsella have already pointed out that the scheme's emphasis on rank and time served, including an 'exclusive dedication' requirement, has marginalised women's contributions and that provisions related to remarriage, second wives and vulnerability criteria add another layer of discrimination against them (Kent and Kinsella 2015a: 215). Based on my interviews and collection of data, my intent is to contribute to their argument and raise additional layers of discrimination. I examine not only the laws, but also the process of implementation and even the private dynamics that have an effect on the access to and distribution of the veterans' pensions. More specifically, this section focuses on law and policy requirements and is divided into three sub-sections: (1) division of labour, exclusive dedication and a witness requirement; (2) exclusion of sexual violence, exclusion of sexual violence as part of torture, and detention criteria; and (3) the treatment of women who remarry and of 'bush wives'. They have all hindered women's access to the veterans' pensions.

A. Exclusive Dedication, Division of Labour and a Witness Requirement

To apply for the veterans' pensions a person has to demonstrate a specific job/task in the resistance towards which there was an exclusive dedication. More specifically, the law requires a full-time service which involve (a) an 'exclusive dedication to the national liberation struggle, upon a decision by the leading structures of the resistance, without accumulation with student activities or regular waged labour'; and (b) a 'period of imprisonment and deportation suffered by the National Liberation Combatant as a result of participation in the struggle.'[18] As Kent and Kinsella (2015a: 217) explain, this means that a combatant's years of service are considered to be the sum of all periods of deportation, detention and work in 'exclusive dedication' to the resistance, meaning that individuals were not supposed to be engaged in study or regular paid labour.

However, if in applying for the veterans' pensions a person has to demonstrate an exclusive dedication to the resistance, ie full-time work, then this clause discriminates against those working in the clandestine front. Leach (2017: 98) has argued that by the 1990s the clandestine front would become a leading element of the resistance. Fernandes (2011: 125) claims that the civilian clandestine resistance has to date been relatively neglected by historians and I further add intentionally so by some Timorese politicians. Although by 2002 there was an equal recognition of the three different factions by the Constitution, I argue

[18] Law 9/2009, Article 10.

that this shared recognition would change progressively through time: today we are seeing that while the armed front has become the controlling voice and thus its members the main recipient of the post-conflict benefits, the clandestine, and also the diplomatic fronts have not been recognised as they should have been. Why is this relevant for women? Because there are allegations that the clandestine front was 60 per cent women (Cristalis and Scott 2005: 38). This also corresponds to the data gathered during my interviews: out of all the 43 women interviewed who said they had participated in the resistance, only one of them participated in the armed struggle. Women did not have many possibilities to belong to any other front than the clandestine one because there was a deep division of labour between men and women during the Indonesian occupation. To show this, I will revert to the historical record.

After the Indonesian occupation in 1975, people in the villages fled into the mountains. The Indonesians would then respond by contaminating their crops in order to force them to return to the villages. As a result of the bombings and use of starvation as a weapon of war, as many as 200,000 people, out of a pre-invasion population of less than 700,000, died during the first five years of the occupation (CAVR 2005: 219–20, 2642). Because of this unsustainable situation, in November 1979, Fretilin's leadership agreed to allow civilians to surrender, and families and those who could not be part of the armed front would then come down to live in the villages under the control of the Indonesians (Wandita, Campbell-Nelson and Pereira 2006: 285). The Timorese warfare strategy would then be adapted to this new reality and the clandestine front would assume a predominant role in the early 1980s. Leach (2017: 84–85) refers, for instance, to a communiqué in 1982, in which Xanana argues that 'the "patriotic consciousness" of the Maubere people was now consolidated in clandestine organisations in the Indonesian-run camps, and in towns and villages, having been transferred from the mountains … we are an entire people at war!'.[19] It was thus conceived that the power of the clandestine front was not violence, but the fact that they were living with the enemy and working behind the scenes (Siapno 2017: 81–82).

This also corresponds to the interview with MP David Ximenes. According to him, in the 1980s, there was a higher participation of women as female combatants in the armed resistance. However, men in the armed resistance realised that once women were captured, the Indonesians sexually assaulted and tortured them. He said that because women were 'easier to sing', meaning more likely to reveal confidential Falintil information, and because women's rape in the detention centres lowered the confidence of their male counterparts, women began to be targeted by the Indonesians.[20] Consequently, according to him, from the 1980s women were not allowed to participate in the armed struggle. Women's low participation in the armed front was thus deliberately decided by their male colleagues. This information was also confirmed to me

[19] Leach (2017) cites Xanana (2000b).
[20] Interview with David Ximenes in Dili, Timor-Leste, 6 September 2016.

by a very brave woman whom I met in a village, and who was a combatant in 1994. Not only did her family disapprove of her actions joining the fighting for being contrary to the normal behaviour of a decent woman, but she also told me how, against her will, she was requested by her superiors to go down to her village since the mountains were not a place for women. Once she reluctantly came down, she was captured by the Indonesians, tortured and raped because of her participation in Falintil.

Although the woman wanted strongly to be a combatant, her case denotes gender stereotypes about the 'appropriate' roles and behaviours that are expected of men and women as well as the social role attached to the effects of the traditional division of labour (Cook and Cusack 2010: 25–28). But it also means that although there were some women combatants in the armed struggle, they were discouraged, if not prohibited, from participating in the armed front from the 1980s. There was also the diplomatic front but it involved a small number of people living abroad. With some exceptions, women's participation in the resistance was therefore, by default, through the clandestine movement. Among the activities in the clandestine front, because of their gender women were expected to perform specific activities for the subsistence of the men in the armed front. Interviewed women mentioned, for instance, having worked as spies, weapons smugglers between the guerrillas, porters, messengers, but also on a daily basis as cooks, having performed tasks such as harvesting, washing clothes, sewing, making traditional containers, collecting money, clothes, medical supplies and goods for the male subsistence in the mountains.

I met a woman, for instance, who was a nurse in Liquiçá, and besides her daily activities she also treated injured members of the resistance. She submitted her application for the pension, but the years she had served were not sufficient. How was she supposed to do that as an exclusive dedication? Owing to the nature of their undercover activities, women could not show they had been working actively for the resistance, neither could they show that their functions were an exclusive activity.[21] In Mauchiga, a woman said that she contributed to the resistance with her cooking. In fact, she had to cook for the Indonesians during the day, and for the resistance during the night. She applied for the pension and she was recognised for working between 4 and 7 years – she had been registered with the OPMT since 1975. Although she received a lump sum, she ended the interview by saying 'we also fought for independence, us women, not only men … once we got independence they forgot us.' There was still a feeling of lack of recognition for what she did.[22]

Although women's activities were essential to effecting and maintaining the operations of the armed front, as is also often seen in domestic family law, 'womanly' activities do not count as work so the tasks that are assigned to women

[21] *cf* CEDAW GR 30 2013: para 67.
[22] Interview with Participant 15, Mauchiga, Ainaru, Timor-Leste, 11 November 2016.

during a conflict are later devalued.[23] This obviously has an effect on women's access to social security and therefore contributes to their low status in society in times of peace (Banda 2012: 365).[24] The issue is that while there is an idea that in order to have access to social security the beneficiary must be shown to have contributed, women are disadvantaged because their income frequently is irregular and unrecorded (Banda 2012: 369). Moreover, based on how 'productive' labour is defined, women's economic contributions can be overlooked: they are classified as inactive despite working on a daily basis (Plan International 2016: 21–22).[25] In this regard, Plan International (2016: 21) proposes a redefinition that takes into account as productive labour 'the time spent cooking, cleaning and caring for children, the ill and the elderly, doing housework or doing voluntary community work'. Vastapuu (2018: 54) also advocates the use of the term 'combat service support' for the non-armed girl and women soldiers – a term that is widely used in military discourse around the world: 'in the US Army, military cooks are not just "cooks" or "camp followers", but "Culinary Specialists" entitled to the same war veteran benefits as any other armed or non-armed soldiers'.[26]

There is also an issue of invisibility regarding how women's work and specific roles led to the commission of violations against them. As shown by the example of the woman combatant, on several occasions women described how they were targeted owing to their activities in support of the resistance. For instance, I heard of several cases where they were detained and/or raped because they were caught sewing or carrying Timorese flags – this was a symbol of leadership so people of the resistance could trust the resistance member. This takes me to my next point. Besides females who worked in the armed, clandestine and diplomatic fronts, there were women who participated exclusively with their bodies, for instance those who became sexual slaves and were forcibly married to Indonesians. While it can be argued that sexual slavery and forced marriage

[23] Reflecting on logistical support, the SCLS Trial Chamber in the AFRC case held that 'to participate actively in hostilities is not limited to participation in combat' and that 'any labour or support that gives effect to, or helps maintain, operations in a conflict constitutes active participation', *Prosecutor v Brima, Kamara and Kanu*, Case no SCSL-2004-16-T, 20 June 2007, para 737.

[24] On states' obligations to provide social security without discrimination, *cf* CESCR GC 16, 2005; CESCR GC 19, 2008; CEDAW GR 16, 1991; CEDAW GR 17, 1991; CEDAW GR 27, 2010. See also the dissenting opinion in *BJ v Germany*, CEDAW Communication No 1/2003.

[25] There is a data gap and a lack of state coverage on women's participation in the unpaid domestic labour force and little knowledge about their access to social protection (Plan International 2016: 15, 19). According to Plan International (2016: 19), this is produced by labour force surveys that ask only about a person's primary economic activity, underestimating the economic contribution of women as 'housewives', which can be considered a secondary activity. As a result, women and girls remain invisible in programmes and policies and there is little understanding of how they add value to the economy (Plan International 2016: 13–19). Banda has showed a similar concern: 'women are seen as economically weak, not least because of the way national statistics are produced. These often leave out of the calculation of "work generated value" the work done by women in subsistence agriculture and in private family enterprises. This in turn reinforces the idea of women as economically unproductive and renders them socially powerless' (2005: 308).

[26] In the US, only 15 to 20% of military personnel take part in combat activities, while the majority of military employees serve in combat service support tasks (Vastapuu 2018: 54).

were not jobs and that women should not get compensation,[27] these crimes were committed for political reasons – these women were targeted for being part of the struggle and/or because of their affiliation. The fact that many of these women were targeted and sexually assaulted because they were family members of resistance fighters has also been recognised by several of the reports, including Chega!. If a man was not found at their home, the Indonesians would suspect that he was in the mountains so they would take revenge against the woman instead. While women's kin were in the mountains, women were thus alone and vulnerable to the actions of the Indonesians and their Timorese collaborators.

During the interview process, I met numerous women who said that they would not have been assaulted if they had had a man next to them, and in many cases, they tried to marry rapidly in order to stop abuses from other men. In Mauchiga, a woman said 'the Indonesians used to come and pick up the young women and the married women without children to rape them.' At the age of 14, she started being subjected to sexual violence along with her sisters.[28] A woman in Los Palos said 'I understand in war, women without husband will be raped … If your husband was in the Indonesian army, then you were protected.' She had been tortured through electrocution and sexual violence, for cooperating with the resistance. In order to get out of the situation, she 'had to fall in love' with a Timorese working with the Indonesians for protection. She was released from detention, where she had been for a year. She said 'to lose our virginity is through marriage, but in this case it is through rape in a war'.[29] Another woman in the same village said that because she was constantly being sexually assaulted, she decided to marry a Hansip to protect herself. She said that they are still together today, but that he beats her and that when he gets drunk, he says to her 'without me, you would be a prostitute'.[30]

These are histories of resistance that are different from the experiences of armed men in the mountains. This also explains why women who were known as the 'mistresses of the *bapas*' say that thanks to their sacrifice, people in their families and community were saved. However, not only did they not have access to reparations, but they also could not opt for the veterans' pensions. This highlights the particular sexual division of labour within law and policy: clauses concerning exclusive dedication not only fail to valorise the uniqueness of women's experiences, but they also deny those who participate through sex. As this happens through the crime of enslavement and its exclusive applicability to women, by denying these women their access to the pensions' schemes, their political agency – and social security – is disregarded.

Rothschild (2017: 455–56) claims that part of the reason why the veteran category is only associated with stereotypical masculine traits like bravery and strength and why veterans are predominantly male, is also the 'exclusive

[27] *cf* MacKinnon (2017: 173).
[28] Interview with Participant 5, Mauchiga, Ainaru, Timor-Leste, 11 November 2016.
[29] Interview with Participant 65, Los Palos, Lautém, Timor-Leste, 12 January 2017.
[30] Interview with Participant 6, Los Palos, Lautém, Timor-Leste, 12 January 2017.

dedication' clause, which means that in order to qualify as a veteran a person needs to have been a guerrilla or involved in the formal structures of the clandestine or diplomatic fronts. Kent and Kinsella (2015a: 216–17) also claim that although pension eligibility was initially based upon a 'vulnerability' criterion, in which elderly and disabled veterans were prioritised while widows, orphans, elderly parents, or tortured siblings of deceased veterans were eligible for a 'survival pension', later revisions to the law have raised pension amounts and shifted the criteria emphasis to the length of service and rank within the resistance structure. This has raised the armed front over the others, producing a discriminatory effect against women: not only were women less able to prove an uninterrupted, full-time period of service, but also were far less likely than men to have held formal positions within the resistance hierarchy (Kent and Kinsella 2015a: 219). This takes me to my next point: recognition by the resistance leadership, which translates as a requirement for a witness to certify a person's work during the occupation.

During the interviews, Timorese women explained that in order to apply for the veterans' pensions, they must provide a witness of their actions in support of the resistance. The issue is that the goods that were sent to the guerilla fighters in the mountains were usually through a third person called '*estafeta*' (clandestine messengers). Women, in particular, relied on these intermediaries to send the product of their work, which means that in practice it is more difficult for women to supply a reliable and sufficient witness to corroborate their contribution. For example, many of the women said that they cooked on a daily basis for the fighters. A messenger was then in charge of taking the food to the fighters, who may never have seen the woman's face. There were also cases in which women were married and both spouses participated in the clandestine movement by, for instance, collecting and providing money and goods to the fighters. However, Timor-Leste being a patriarchal society, it was usually the male spouse who had more direct contact with the members of the armed resistance. The male spouse was, for instance, the one who picked up the phone or dealt with the person who was later to be the 'witness'.

Ximenes also said that in order for women to access the veterans' pension, the natural step was to show their connection to the OPMT.[31] Although the OPMT's dual purpose before the invasion was to participate in the anticolonial struggle and to oppose all forms of violence and discrimination against women, they later theoretically coordinated women's participation during the resistance, both in the armed and clandestine fronts (Wandita, Campbell-Nelson and Pereira 2006: 289–90). There may be a correlation explaining that those who managed to be part of the OPMT registration in the beginning of the war were more likely to have access to a pension – regardless of the exclusion dedication requirement. This may exclude those who did not support the Fretilin political

[31] This was a women's organisation co-founded in 1975 by Rosa 'Muki' Bonaparte Soares, a member of the Fretilin National Committee, later executed by the Indonesians.

party in early 1975, as well as younger generations of women who supported the resistance afterwards without belonging to an OPMT cell.

Moreover, despite the formal structure provided by the OPMT, there were issues of registration, which may also have had an impact on women. I met one woman in Dili whose husband was a prominent figure in Fretilin and who was killed at the beginning of the occupation. She told me how she worked with the resistance between 1975 and 1999 and suffered from sexual violence, particularly because of her political connections at that time. When she submitted her papers to obtain the pension in Dili, the committee told her that because she was from Osu, Viqueque, she had to submit her papers there. She then told me 'I grew up in Dili, I don't live there anymore, I don't know anyone there so I could not provide a witness.'[32] With some matrilineal exceptions, such as the Bunak in Bobonaro, most of Timor-Leste's communities are patrilineal, which means that women move to the family – and local area – of their husbands.

Finally, because of the specificities of the resistance structure and organisation, keeping files and/or records was not allowed and this could have affected the provision of the pensions to semi-autonomous clandestine cells and non-formal community support for the resistance (Silva 2015: 3). In Maliana, I met Domingas Monis and her case confirmed the inconsistences concerning the recognition of clandestines. She said that although her husband was working for the Indonesian army, he was also a clandestine: he was smuggling weapons to his house to be provided to guerrilla fighters. Then, when the violence escalated in September 1999, her husband was stabbed and killed by his colleagues, after he helped some Timorese to escape from the military base. She submitted the papers to obtain the pension for her husband – she never received an answer and she was left alone with her kids. Because her family-in-law thought that she had ordered the killing of her husband, they did not take into account her opinion when choosing where to bury him. She said, 'I want to obtain his pension to support our children who are studying and bring back his bones to Maliana.'[33] Siapno (2017: 80) claims that there is a paradox of being asked to examine 'the truth' when the methods used during the clandestine period meant they were supposed to leave no trace or historical records. Thus, because women's activities were not recorded, the system for eligibility in the veterans' pension law does not help them.

B. Exclusion of Sexual Violence, Exclusion of Sexual Violence as Part of Torture, and Detention Criteria

Different groups of women said that while men were tortured, women were sexually assaulted. This was also confirmed by the MP Ximenes when he indicated

[32] Interview with Participant 32, Dili, Timor-Leste, 27 January 2017.
[33] Interview with Participant 21, Maliana, Bobonaro, Timor-Leste, 24 January 2017.

that rape was used in Timor-Leste to undermine the enemy and described how while he was detained and tortured, his female colleagues were raped in Indonesian custody. The problem is that while torture is an aggravating factor taken into account in the provision of veterans' pensions, sexual violence is not. There are two points that are worth mentioning. If the pension system only recognises torture that is linked to men and does not take into account sexual violence that is linked to women, there is a direct discrimination against women. But also if torture and rape are looked at in a totally separated way, there is also an error of law. Rape under certain circumstances can amount to torture or inhuman treatment according to international law.

As explained by the SR on violence against women there are three main conceptual avenues to frame rape as a human rights violation:

> (a) as a specific form of gender-based violence against women and girls under the women's anti-discrimination framework; *(b) as torture under the torture framework*; and (c) as other human rights violations, such as trafficking, sale of children, slavery, forced marriage and early and child marriage (emphasis added) (UN 2021a: para 20).

Indeed, SGBV may be directly committed against a woman for being a woman and it may include acts that inflict physical, mental or sexual harm or suffering, threats of such acts, coercion and other deprivations of liberty (CEDAW GR 19 1992: para 6). If SGBV is committed under deprivation of liberty by state actors, it may amount to torture. In this regard, the elements that are constitutive of the crime of torture are: the perpetrator inflicted severe physical or mental pain or suffering upon one or more persons, inflicted in custody or under the control of the perpetrator, for the purpose of obtaining information or a confession, punishment, intimidation or coercion (International Protocol on the Documentation and Investigation of Sexual Violence in Conflict 2014: 78–79).

According to the Rome Statute, in the Elements of Crimes, detention is one of the situations where a victim cannot freely consent to sexual contact, and rape in detention by a state official is always a form of torture (*cf* International Commission of Jurists 2016: 204–5). Sexual violence amounting to torture has also been raised by the jurisprudence of the ICTY and ICTR. In the *Mucić* case at the ICTY, for instance, rape was recognised by Trial Chamber II as a form of torture, violating the Geneva Conventions and the laws and customs of war (Fournet 2013: 106).[34] The CAT Committee (GC 2 2008: para 22) has also stated that 'the contexts in which females are at risk [of torture or ill-treatment] include deprivation of liberty, medical treatment, particularly involving reproductive

[34] The Trial Chamber stated that: 'The condemnation and punishment of rape becomes all the more urgent where it is committed by, or at the instigation of, a public official, or with the consent or acquiescence of such an official. The psychological suffering of persons upon whom rape is inflicted may be exacerbated by social and cultural conditions and can be particularly acute and long lasting. Furthermore, it is difficult to envisage circumstances in which rape, by, or at the instigation of a public official, or with the consent or acquiescence of an official, could be considered as occurring for a purpose that does not, in some way, involve punishment, coercion, discrimination or intimidation. In the view of this Trial Chamber this is inherent in situations of armed conflict.' *Prosecutor v Mucić et al*, Case No IT-96-21-T, Judgment, Trial Chamber II quarter, 16 November 1998, para 476.

decisions, and violence by private actors in communities and homes'. While the IACtHR has stated that 'rape can constitute torture even when it only consists of one act or when it occurs outside of state installations, if there is intentionality, severe suffering, and an end on the part of the perpetrators' (IACHR 2015b: para 40).[35] Most of the violations, including SGBV, against the women interviewed were committed under Indonesian control, even in military bases and detention centres, which means they may have amounted to torture.

The Timorese government should have known this, given that even before the drafting of the veterans' pensions law there were already accounts of women being tortured through sexual violence. For instance, the UN SR on violence against women noted in her 1998 report how rape was used as an instrument of torture and intimidation by certain elements of the Indonesian army and how women relatives of political opponents were raped by the military as a form of revenge and/or to force their relatives out of hiding (UN 1999b: paras 43, 78, 81; UN 1999a: para 46). SGBV was thus not only a mean of intimidating and attacking the civilian population, but also, as explained by some Timorese women, it was a means of reprisal by the Indonesians against women for the actions of the resistance. SGBV may be committed for political reasons as shown in other conflicts. In Sierra Leone, for instance, rape was not aimed at a woman personally, but was used to undermine the rebels, as an act targeting a group and the nation (Coulter 2009: 133). As mentioned above, sexual violence as torture does not need physically to occur inside a state installation, but if it does, this crime becomes easier to prove. In this regard, if detention centres are places where enemies are taken, what are the reasons for the exclusion of sexual violence committed against women in them? The issue is that, as Nesiah (2011: 142) argues, from popular culture to human rights policy, the iconic victim of international crimes such as disappearances and torture is male, while those females who may suffer the same injuries as innocent civilians are not seen to be targeted for their political actions but just conceived as collateral damage. Women's political agency is therefore stripped away.

The UN SR also emphasised that the torture of Timorese women detained by the Indonesian security forces was widespread and that besides rape, other methods of torture included electric shock treatment to ears, nose, breasts and vagina, submerging in water tanks, burning with cigarette butts, detention in a room full of water and sewage, severe beating, being stripped and paraded naked, being tied by the thumbs from the ceiling, and forced intercourse with other detainees (UN 1999b: para 44). In fact, some of the women interviewed were just 12 years old when, in Indonesian custody, they suffered rape and electrocution as part of torture. In Mauchiga, a woman said that as a consequence of the revolt in Kablaki, the Indonesians started interrogating everyone. She was taken twice during daytime out of the school where she was taking refuge. She was raped, electrocuted, beaten by the Indonesians. She fainted and almost died.

[35] IACtHR, *Fernández Ortega et al v Mexico*. Preliminary Objection, Merits, Reparations, and Costs, Judgment of 30 August 2010. Series C No 215, para 308.

'There was blood everywhere … and I still have scars, she said'. She submitted her documents for the pension, but she received only one payment, because she was too young to fight – the Indonesians were asking information about her brother who was in the mountains. She was 12 years old at the time and because of what she suffered she wants to be granted the monthly pension.[36]

We are thus not talking solely about rape and violent physical assault against the victim's body, but also about other crimes of a sexual nature that can amount to torture. This reminds me of several women who described rape and/or forced nudity after they were relocated to a school under Indonesian custody close to Mauchiga in Ainaro. These women emphasised not only the act of sexual violence inflicted by the Indonesians, but also the psychological terror attached to the crime that was committed against them. They were subjected to torture. Moreover, CEDAW has also stated that violations of women's sexual and reproductive health and rights (eg forced sterilisation, forced abortion and forced pregnancy), depending on the circumstances, may also amount to torture or cruel, inhuman or degrading treatment (CEDAW GR 35 2017: para 18). Nevertheless, there seems to be a denial, and perhaps ignorance, about the connection between the two – torture and SGBV – crimes in Timor-Leste. But even if there is a continuous denial of the link between the two, the issue keeps re-emerging. The CAT Committee (2017: para 9(b)), for example, stated that the Timorese state should continue with prosecution for crimes in 1999 involving allegations of 'crimes of torture, including sexual violence'.

The point is that the crime of torture can be inflicted through sexual violence, committed by a state agent – even outside of state facilities – and it is independent of a formal registration in a specific organisation. In other words, these women and girls did not need to have been a formal member of the resistance to have been subjected to torture. However, by excluding SGBV victims from the veterans' pensions and endorsing a fault-line between SGBV and torture, women are being denied a social benefit that has been granted to men, downplaying women's political agency. Hence, to the dichotomy of male/resistance and female/victims in Timor-Leste, I would add male/resistance/torture and female/victims/sexual violence. Duggan and Jacobson (2009: 136) have an illuminating suggestion regarding how, by using broader terms, such as tortured and/or bodily injured as opposed to sexually abused, women may be allowed to be identified as part of the resistance, avoiding social stigma and all of its consequences. This conception could be helpful in a post-conflict society in order to avoid a denial of the fact that women have been politically targeted.

I will now focus on how the particularities of the criteria of detention that were chosen within the pensions system are also discriminatory against women. While Article 10 of the Law 9/2009 takes into account a 'prolonged detention' – meaning that the person cannot escape and he/she is in prison for a long time – as full-time dedication, preventive detention is not. This focus on prolonged

[36] Interview with Participant 49, Mauchiga, Ainaru, Timor-Leste, 11 November 2016.

detention as a criterion in order to be recognised as a veteran is discriminatory against women. We know by now that many of them were subjected to nightly deprivation of liberty for years, usually in Indonesian military facilities, and how during those detentions they were tortured and suffered sexual violence. The focus on prolonged detention matters and again, we see that how the crime is defined discriminates against women. Something similar happened in South Africa. Ross (2003: 61) argues that a larger number of women and children than available figures suggest were detained, but that they were not necessarily recorded as arrested or detained since no charges were laid and they were released from police 'custody' after a relatively short period of holding or interrogation. Ross (2003: 61, 106) wisely further insists that 'the length of time they were held does not, of course, bear any necessary relation to the treatment endured during that time' and that it cannot be assumed that the treatment was any less brutal or the effects on family and community less destructive than if they had been held for longer periods. She further highlights that because of this definition, women, particularly the young, could have been ignored in the findings of the Commission for Truth and Reconciliation Report and the Trauma Centre (Ross 2003: 106). The detention for long periods requirement therefore excluded women who were detained every night over several years, who were gang-raped and tortured at Indonesian facilities.

In Timor-Leste, the Director of the Ministry of Solidarity working on the veterans' pension scheme said that, in practice, there are some members of the clandestine movement who because they did not have service of exclusive dedication, only had the right to a medal, for instance, 'in the case if they were detained.'[37] But the exclusive dedication and prolonged detention criteria add barriers for the equal access of women to the veterans' pensions, which may not do justice to their experiences. I heard cases where women obtained less than they deserved. Some women complained, for instance, that despite having worked for the resistance for many years, they were recognised for between 4 and 7 years of work, which meant that they were given a lump sum, instead of the monthly pension (for between 8 and 14 years of work). I met a woman in Ermera, who said she was caught carrying a Timorese flag. The Indonesians thought she was a leader so they beat her and raped her in front of her husband. She was detained for a year and while in detention, she had a child as a result of the sexual violence she suffered. 'All the women detained were raped', she said. She also separated from her husband out of shame. She submitted her application for a veterans' pension in 2003 and she was only recognised on the 4–7 scale, meaning a lump sum, which she received in 2015. She described her frustration about the fact that she was detained owing to her resistance activities, that the veterans pension administrators tried to reduce the number of years she truly worked for the resistance, and that she should have been granted a monthly pension instead.[38]

[37] Interview in Dili, Timor-Leste, 19 November 2017.
[38] Interview with Participant 3, Emera Vila, Ermera, Timor-Leste, 8 November 2016.

Not surprisingly, the same director at the Ministry of Solidarity acknowledged that the complaints received from Timorese women are usually related to: (1) the exclusive dedication clause, (2) the requirement of detention for a long period, and (3) the reduction of the years they truly worked for the resistance. The interviewed Advisor also recognised that there were allegations that women were not being recognised for the years of service that they should be. A woman from Lalerik Mutin who submitted her application in 2009 said 'we helped them with food to survive, but we feel that our efforts to fight for independence are not appreciated.'[39]

C. Women Who Remarry are Excluded But Also the Bush Wives

There is a provision in the veterans' scheme which prohibits spouses of deceased veterans from receiving a pension if they have remarried. According to Kent and Kinsella (2015a: 219), there is an implicit assumption that women are 'not independent persons but the property and responsibility of their husbands' and that they 'should have been "loyal" wives awaiting the return of their men from the battlefront'. During the parliamentary debate on the 2006 Statute, women parliamentarians raised a motion to amend the law, arguing that in many cases these women were left vulnerable to sexual abuse by the Indonesian security forces and their militia after their husband disappeared or died in the mountains and remarriage was often the only way to avoid this abuse (Kent and Kinsella 2015a: 219). However, the motion was defeated with the argument that these women should have been loyal to their deceased husbands and should have demonstrated the same strength as other women who had not remarried (Kent and Kinsella 2015a: 219). I now want to show how women experienced this.

In Bua Nurak, Viqueque, I interviewed a woman whose husband had been in the mountains fighting with the resistance. The woman had been living alone with their children. One day the Indonesian army came to her house and gang-raped her. This lasted for a month and a half. She was then taken to prison in Osu for two weeks, where the Indonesians blamed her for the killing of one of the '*bapas*', saying that it may have been her husband who did the killing. She was then released but had to report in every day. She was sexually assaulted again '*loron loron kalan kalan*' (every day every night) when the Indonesians were coming to her house.[40] That was 1983 and by 1987 she would have a child born out of the rapes. Someone told her husband, who was a platoon commander in the mountains and because the woman was completely alone, he came down in 1988 to be with her. That particular child would die from an illness. She did not know about the Special Panels or the CAVR, but she submitted her papers for the pension in 2009 because she had worked with the OPMT from 1975 to 1979 and also because of what she had been through. The woman also described how she was discriminated against, not only for having a husband in Falintil but also for having had a

[39] Interview with Participant 24, Lalerik Mutin, Viqueque, Timor-Leste, 03 February 2017.
[40] Interview with Participant 30, Bua Nurak, Viqueque, Timor-Leste, 3 February 2017.

son by the Indonesians. She never received a response to her submission. When I asked her husband about his own pension, he said that he submitted his papers after being so many years in the mountains but because he decided to come down to be with his wife, he was not considered to be trustworthy by the guerillas. Other members of the armed front were denying the pension to him, he said. What was he supposed to do? To leave his woman alone? Both spouses were ostracised by the system.

In my interview with the Director of the Ministry of Solidarity, he confirmed that a woman cannot remarry. He further said that, 'if a woman gets a new husband, then the brother or niece of the first husband can ask to get the pension back.'[41] This means that the family-in-law, meaning the family of the deceased husband, may also request to have access to the pension. This clause promotes women's dependency towards men and denies their own right to inheritance.[42] If dignity is the notion that people have equal worth and a right to live as autonomous beings not under the authority of another, this is against women's dignity (Atuahene 2014: 45). A woman in Mauchiga whose first husband's pension was taken away wanted to make sure that I wrote down her case word-for-word so that this would not happen to other women. She said:

> I was tortured and raped because of my husband, and after I did all the paperwork in order to get his veteran's pension, my family-in-law is the one who is receiving the money … But I was the one who suffered because of my husband's participation in the resistance.

When her former family-in-law found out, they took the pension away from her because she had remarried years later. In addition, they told her that her new husband had his own pension since he was another former member of the resistance so she should rely on that one instead.[43] The woman felt frustrated because she felt that after all the suffering that she had endured owing to her connection to her first husband, she was the one entitled to get recognition and a benefit from the state. The mere existence of this type of clause may lead families-in-law to expose women to even more vulnerability for their own benefit. By the institutionalisation of this stereotypical distinction concerning spousal rights and duties within the veterans' scheme, wives have been left subordinated and economically dependent on their husbands, which denies their autonomy as individual human beings (Cook and Cusack 2010: 67).

With this prohibition against remarriage, the veterans' pension not only follows the example of the UN, but it goes a step further in that it is applicable 'only to women'. Here are two points worth elaborating on. First, if local justice conceptions are created through complex and contested relationships between national and international actors, this practice shows the detrimental effects of the power of global rights activists in trying to apply 'universal' norms, as well as the efforts of local agents to replicate their social worlds in their own terms

[41] Interview with Director, Ministry of Solidarity in Dili, Timor-Leste, 19 November 2017.
[42] *cf* Chinkin (2012: 106).
[43] Interview with Participant 70, Mauchiga, Ainaro, Timor-Leste, 11 November 2016.

(Clarke 2009: 229, 236). Second, Cook and Cusack (2010: 117) would argue how this type of clause makes women's 'promiscuity' morally blameworthy, while male 'promiscuity' is seen as an indication of male virility.[44] Not surprisingly in the inverse case, that of men having mistresses, the mistresses are also the ones affected. Besides the 'mistresses of the *bapas*', there were also the '*feen ailaran*' (bush wives, *mulher do mato*), who were described pejoratively as women from the mountains who could engage in sex everywhere. As Pereira told me, it is known that male members of the resistance had second wives in the mountains. However, the veterans' legislation also neglects them because it only recognises first wives. Kent and Kinsella (2015a: 220) argue that 'in the event that multiple wives come forward to present their claims only the legally married spouse is entitled'. As the 'mistresses of the Indonesians', the 'bush wives' could also not apply for the veterans' pensions. These women, with their children, were therefore abandoned after the conflict.

IV. THE IMPLEMENTATION: LOCAL COMMITTEES OF VETERANS AND THE PRIVATE DYNAMICS

A Homage Commission for the resistance was created by the Timor-Leste parliament and was divided into regions, sub-regions and areas of 'popular resistance' corresponding to the clandestine front. Because the process to apply for recognition as a veteran was supposed to take place at the national, municipal and local levels, teams from the Ministry of Social Solidarity were sent from Dili to visit the localities. They would do so together with representatives of the Homage Commission, since the latter were the ones who knew their communities and 'their people'. Among the requirements, a veteran had to show concrete details of his/her participation in the resistance and his/her application would later be validated by a commander. Similarly to the electoral system, the process was supposed to be very participatory. After a decision was taken, a list of beneficiaries was published in houses of the local authorities and the local public could validate and/or complain about the decisions concerning the designation of a specific person as a veteran. According to the World Bank, the veterans' pension was 'a carefully crafted process which included community verification and consultation' (World Bank 2004: 3). I will, in contrast, show how gender stereotyping by members of the local committees of veterans may have limited women's access to a veterans' pension. Moreover, interviewed women alleged corrupt practices and something they called '*sistema familia*' (family system), which deals with family connections, and claimed both were important variables in receiving a favourable outcome. Finally, other intersectionality issues, including literacy levels, access to information and where a person lives, seem also to have had an influence.

[44] Cook and Cusack (2010) cites Bonthuys (2006).

A. Patriarchal Gender Stereotypes

According to a source who formerly worked at the Ministry of Solidarity and was involved in the veterans' pension programme, while Xanana wanted the four commanders of the resistance to be involved in the process, not all of them recognised the role of women during the resistance. That person told me the following story: in 2011, the government organised a national ceremony in order to celebrate the peace achieved through the demobilisation of the military. Xanana was present, surprising the audience by wearing a typical Indonesian shirt showing a message of reconciliation towards the former enemy. Taur Matar Ruak, former army chief and current prime minister also participated. However, prior to the national event, organised mainly by men, there was allegedly an internal battle to allow women to participate. The General Chief of Staff of the Armed Forces, Lere Anan Timur, allegedly threatened to withdraw his participation if women were invited because he did not consider them to be veterans. It is alleged that he said that 'women were there only to serve at the table and in the bed.'[45]

Consequently, according to one of my interviewees, 205 combatants with the highest rank were invited. The participation of a few women was reluctantly accepted, but there were allegations that they were not treated with the highest respect and were seen as 'second class veterans'. The same interviewee said that there were allegations that the case of the Los Palos region was different because the commander, Aluk, recognised the role of women. Because of the difference in treatment, the interviewee claimed that possibly women in Los Palos may have even received more benefits than women under the control of other commanders. Nancy Fraser (2007: 28) has advocated the recognition that a major feature of gender injustice is the institutionalised pattern of cultural value that privileges traits associated with masculinity and which devalues everything coded as feminine, and that this injustice has distribution effects. But even in the cases of female combatants, because of patriarchal gender stereotypes, the recognition of those women who went through a similar experience to male combatants is overlooked, and women are still marginalised. The woman interviewed who was a former combatant in the mountains, said that although she managed to obtain a veteran's pension, her family and community still discriminate against her, saying that she is only a woman and a rape victim, not a veteran.[46] She further expressed her disappointment about how, despite being a former combatant and fit for military service, she found herself without a job after the conflict. 'Nobody listened to me', she said.[47]

[45] Reflecting on the ambivalent treatment towards former combatants, Cock (1991: 184) mentions that while the men of the Zimbabwe African National Liberation Army (Zanla) were seen as national heroes, the spouses of former female guerrilla fighters and people in their communities preferred women who fitted into the traditional image of a 'feminine' woman.

[46] Afrikaner women who supported the ANC were insulted 'by the suggestion that, as women, they could not have been acted autonomously' or by 'making allegations of their "immorality" and portraying them as "failed women"' (Cock 1991: 173–74).

[47] Interview with Participant 46, Bobonaro, Timor-Leste, 24 January 2017.

As Enloe (1988: 15) argues, 'women may serve the military, but they can never be permitted to be the military'. Even in the execution of the most 'masculine' of the professions, the law and society undervalue female activities and characteristics because they are seen as a source of women's subordination, perpetuating notions of their stereotyped roles. In this regard, Ní Aoláin argues that ending violence should not mean decommissioning weapons and militaries and taking away the physical manifestations of violent masculinities, but it should be about engaging with what it means to 'be a man' in a violent society so as to create the conditions conducive for non-violent masculine identity to emerge and be socially validated, including the symbols of self-worth in relation to community, family, and others. She highlights that 'work remains to be done in addressing the gender order that has enabled and sustained certain kinds of masculinity to be privileged through conflict, repression, transition, and the resistance to exposing the privilege' (Ní Aoláin 2019: 167).

If there was sexism at the national level, we can easily imagine what may happen at the local, and more hidden, level. As explained above, national authorities would rely on local veterans' committees. These were mainly composed of men, and there were allegations that in some cases they disregarded women's applications based on stereotyping to the point where those collecting the applications prevented women from registering.[48] During the interviews, I met women who were not allowed by the local Homage Commission to submit their papers.

'Who is a veteran, because I did not hold a gun?' This question was posed to me by a woman who was challenging the lack of recognition towards the clandestine front, and particularly its female members. The same woman said that she was working in the Central Committee of Fretilin before the Indonesian invasion. In 1976, she was caught and detained for one month. While in detention, she was beaten, sexually assaulted and tortured with electroshocks. She was then detained in the prison of Balide for 18 months. They even put the dead body of a man in her cell for eight hours. She was then released, but the Indonesians would come to her house at night in order to rape her. This continued for years and her family could not do anything. She got pregnant in 1980. She continued, though, providing guns, food, clothes and cigarettes to the resistance up to 1999. In 2003, she said 'I was trying to submit my papers, but the man in the community house who was collecting the data told me that I did not hold guns. I felt ashamed and left.' In 2009, she decided to submit her papers again but, because she did so in the second process, she is still waiting for an answer. She submitted her papers too late. She added 'when we were fighting, and I became a political prisoner, it was not about money, but now the people only think about this.'[49] In Baucau, another woman said that she was forced 'to get married' to an Indonesian. The man then left her. She was assaulted in another location. Then she married for protection a Timorese who passed away

[48] MacKinnon wisely asserts that 'men's differences do not make them "different" because men have power; they set the standard. What it means to set the standard is not to have inequality problems. What is means to set the standard is to be on the top of a hierarchy' (2017: 118).

[49] Interview with Participant 35, Dili, Timor-Leste, 27 February 2017.

in 1993. She did the paperwork for another husband that she had, but the local Homage Commission told her that he belonged to UDT and not Fretilin, so her husband could not apply for a veterans' pension. But she said that her husband was Fretilin, not UDT. The resistance fighters then told her 'these mistresses of *Bapas* are lying, no trust'. She, herself, had also supported the resistance with her planting and farming, including through the OPMT, during the 24 years of occupation. That was also not recognised.[50]

My final point is of a more technical nature. Although a veteran must be able to show concrete details of his/her activities in the resistance to the local Homage Commissions, the application form that people fill out and provide to these commissions does not ask about the *activities* carried out by the veterans, but instead about the *duration of support* to the resistance. What counts as work then? Because the activities were not required to be specified in the form to be filled out by the applicants, this also offered a greater margin for local commissions to decide on who is a veteran and what is to be recognised as proper activities for the resistance. As a result, this may also have contributed to local actors arbitrarily reducing the number of years people, particularly women, worked in the clandestine front. Social security in most countries is linked to contribution, and women's exclusion from the veterans' pensions shows how, although women were convinced that they were contributing to Timorese independence and exposed to gross violations, their roles were later not taken into account.[51] What was then the value of their sacrifice and suffering? Because of all this gender stereotyping in the law and its enforcement, women may have been denied a public recognition and equal treatment to men.

B. Corruption and the Family System

Transitional justice may coexist with corruption practices. For instance, in Rwanda, Palmer (2015: 145–46) noticed how there were allegations of corruption, particularly in Kigali, which aimed to exercise pressure on or threaten the witnesses or the members of the gacaca court. Accordingly, corruption has also permeated the provision of veterans' pensions in Timor-Leste. In the different communities visited, it was explained to me how local members of the veterans' committees, who were in charge of receiving the documents, offered their help with the submission of papers on condition that once an application was approved,

[50] Interview with Participant 71, Baucau, Timor-Leste, 13 January 2017.

[51] CESCR GG 19 on the right to social security establishes that states must take steps to cover part-time workers, casual workers, the self-employed, homeworkers and those working on the informal economy (2008: paras 28, 33, 34). While CEDAW Article 14(2)(c) establishes that states shall ensure the right of rural women to 'benefit directly from social security programmes', its GR 34 states that in order to eliminate discrimination against rural women in their access to social security, states should 'ensure that those engaged in unpaid work and/or in the informal sector have access to non-contributory social protection …' and adopt gender-responsive social protection floors to ensure their access to essential health care, childcare facilities and income security (CEDAW GR 34 2016: para 41).

women needed to give a percentage of their monthly pension to them. A woman in Mauchiga said, for instance, that the person in charge of the authorisations could even charge half of the amount to the victims. She further said that 'chiefs of the local Homage Commissions became powerful people with big houses.'[52]

In a patriarchal society, where being represented by a man matters, women, especially singles and widows, may be more vulnerable to this form of abuse of power. Besides corruption, I also heard around all the municipalities in Timor-Leste and on numerous occasions the term '*sistema familia*'. Another woman in Liquiçá was more specific when she said, 'if your family is at the top, they would put your name on the list.'[53] Women meant that who they have as a family member and who they know matters in the decision to grant a veterans' pension. Thus, people with better connections to higher military rank may have had a better chance of a veterans' pension. For instance, how important their husbands were and their rank are things that seemed to have mattered in obtaining a fast and favourable answer. Conversely, if a woman's husband was of lower rank, they had less chance to prove the criteria and therefore to obtain the pension. I myself found inconsistencies in different municipalities.

For instance, one woman in Viqueque said that she worked in the OPMT for a year preparing food and making traditional containers. She received the monthly pension corresponding to 8–14 years of service. When I asked her why she received such a high pension despite only working for a year, she revealed that her husband was a Falintil commander and that both received the monthly pension. She said, 'if your husband is a commander, you are considered to be working as a clandestine as well.'[54] In fact, it was even explained to me in several of the municipalities that wives of high-ranking officers had an automatic right to access the pensions. But it also seemed to extend to other family members. In another case in Viqueque, a woman told me that from 1990 to 1999, she participated in the conflict by selling soaps, cigarettes and cooking oil and obtaining medicines and that she received the 8–14 pension. Again, when I asked why she received that specific pension, she answered that her uncle was Commander Ula. I found similar cases of inconsistencies in Mauchiga as well. I argue that the local Homage Commissions may have privileged specific individual applications and that not all women had equal access to the pensions. The whole system in place may have therefore become perverted and may have reinforced power hierarchies within communities. This has long-term socio-economic consequences for those women in a more disadvantaged position.

When I interviewed the Director of the Ministry of Solidarity, he acknowledged that he had heard of cases of corruption, but insisted that no complaints had been filed. He said that if they had, he would have sent them to the police. The director also recognised that there were lots of falsifications in the

[52] Interview with Participant 23, Mauchiga, Ainaru, Timor-Leste, 10 November 2016.
[53] Interview with Participant 54, Liquiçá, Liquiçá, Timor-Leste, 25 January 2017.
[54] Interviews with Participant 66, Lalerik Mutin, Viqueque, Timor-Leste, 04 February 2017.

applications and the 'family system' must surely have had an impact on this. He recognised that there were rumours of local Homage Commissions making up data but had not received formal claims. According to him, so far only three cases had been submitted to the police concerning falsifications and he was still waiting to see results as of November 2017, when the interview took place. It is worth mentioning that the veterans' pensions system has official forms and procedures established for the filing of complaints and grievances, including a deadline of 30 days for reporting irregularities. The public official explained that this complaint mechanism is the first and only programme of this nature in the whole public administration in Timor-Leste. I acknowledge that this is a positive first formal step but, in practice, it may be difficult to submit formal claims if people are not used to making formal complaints about the injustices entrenched within their public system.

C. Other Intersections: Illiteracy, Access to Information and Rural vs. Urban Dynamics

I found a correlation of veterans' pension grants not only with who the women were connected to, but also with their level of literacy and access to information. Those women better connected to Dili may also have had an advantage over those living in isolated rural communities, which reveals the impact of urban/rural dynamics. These may be intersectionality factors that contributed to a successful veteran's application.

Members of the Ministry of Solidarity and local Homage Commissions were supposed to provide guidance during the whole process of applications. More specifically, because of the high level of illiteracy in the country, members of these institutions were in charge of filling out the declaration forms themselves during the interviews with the applicants. It is possible that in practice, local employees of the Ministry gave the forms away and illiterate people did not know how to fill in their applications. I met several illiterate rural women in very isolated villages, who told me that they did not know how to gather and prepare the necessary documents required to submit their applications. This means that they faced a situation where there were poor records of the clandestine front, combined with the fact that they did not know anyone who could guide them through the process. A rural woman shrewdly pointed out that a system that was initially supposed to help and recognise the actions of the '*maubere*', meaning the people, the masses, turned out to be only accessible to those with better education.[55] Hence, women belonging to the illiterate peasantry who live in the most isolated areas may have been discriminated against in the implementation of the pension system. As Coulter (2009: 73) argues in her recollection of women's experiences in post-conflict Sierra Leone, 'being literate includes being

[55] Interview with Participant 76, Boboró, Liquiçá, Timor-Leste, 26 January 2017.

in the flow of information and being able to read and write means that one does not have to rely on others for writing or reading letters'.[56] This leads me to my next point about the importance of access to information.

While those who submitted their applications in the first registrations process were effectively considered, those who submitted their applications in the last round of registrations are still waiting for a decision. There is then a correlation between those who submitted their documents in the early years of independence and those who obtained a pension. While the World Bank (2004: 3) claims that for a post-conflict benefits programme it is important that a timely and accurate registration takes place, I argue that in the case of Timor-Leste, a system that was supposed to be accessible for everyone who contributed to independence and endured sacrifices may, in practice have been provided more easily to those with better personal connections to Dili. Indeed, I heard several cases of how people in/or connected to Dili managed to apply rapidly for the veterans' pension. They were the first ones to have access to information about the life-long pensions and knew better how to compile the required documentation. In this regard, the Director at the Ministry of Solidarity accepted that access to information has been different in urban and rural areas so, for instance, he said women from Los Palos and Viqueque may have had greater difficulties.[57]

A woman in Los Palos described how she worked in the clandestine movement, together with her brother and father. The three of them were captured, later tortured and spent the same number of years in detention. After independence, her brother started working for an NGO in Dili and soon found out about the life-long pension. She said, 'my brother was in Dili and a friend told him to prepare the documents quietly.' He rapidly and secretly submitted his papers and those of his father, and they both obtained the monthly pension. The woman found out about the pension process years later. Since she worked and experienced the same as her brother and father, she submitted the papers with the hopes of obtaining the monthly financial recognition. However, years have passed, and she is still waiting for a positive answer. This case therefore is about three members of the same family having the same role in the resistance and suffering the same consequences, but those who managed to have access to the pension did so because they were better connected to Dili. The same woman said that an MP of Fretilin in the first elected parliament also told family members in their village to apply rapidly for the pension. They did so and obtained a favourable answer. 'In my case, nobody told me', she said.[58] Therefore, those who were more geographically and personally isolated may have faced additional barriers in accessing the veterans' pension.

As soon as the information spread through the local communities and the provision of the life-long pensions in Timor-Leste became more and more

[56] This would also be in contrast to Article 14 of CEDAW and its GR 34 on the rights of rural women. See also Banda (2012).

[57] According to CESCR GC 20 on non-discrimination, disparities between urban and rural areas, localities and regions should be eliminated (2009: para 34).

[58] Interview with Participant 65, Los Palos, Lautém, Timor-Leste, 12 January 2017.

evident when recipients started to receive their monthly payments, there may consequently have been an increase in the number of applications from people alleging to be veterans. The veterans' pensions became increasingly difficult to obtain for those who only accessed the information at a later stage. Access to information is therefore access to power. It is only in recent years that we have seen more clearly the importance of access to information for the protection of human rights from a gender perspective.[59] When I asked a woman in Liquiçá what women's rights meant to her, she said

> It is to have information about this country, to say that we are veterans too and not only men ... Right now they look after young educated generations, but they forget about us, that we fought for independence. The process of accessing justice should come from the base, but in contrast they did not ask people in the rural areas that also participated in the clandestine movement. It makes us become victims and victims over again. I have the right to know the veterans' law and policy and be asked for our opinions, but they just pass the laws without us knowing the content. It is not coming from the base.[60]

Unfortunately, inequalities in the implementation of transitional justice mechanisms may be more common than expected, as shown by the examples of other states. In the case of the TRC in South Africa, Goldblatt (2006: 74) argues that many people were not aware of the implications of not approaching the TRC and the connection to their access to reparations, and that poor women in rural areas who lacked information and education about these issues were particularly affected. Atuahene makes a similar argument in the case of the Commission on the Restitution of Land Rights in South Africa. She claims that although the commission facilitated, in general, dignity restoration, there were issues of power: 'since there were about 80,000 claims filed, respondents who had the power to demand the attention of commission officials had their voices heard while those who could not were silenced' (2014: 19). In contrast, millions of people missed the deadline of the commission and did not have an opportunity to lodge claims and receive compensation (Atuahene 2014: 104–5). Those whose dignity was not restored – remaining invisible to the state – were the ones often overwhelmed and unable to navigate the complicated land restitution process due to a lack of financial resources, knowledge, networks, or assistance (Atuahene 2014: 18–19, 104–5).

V. GETTING MORE PRIVATE: THE PENSIONS WITHIN THE FAMILY

As is the case with the other mechanisms of transitional justice, women's silence was also mentioned as a reason why women did not apply for the veterans' pensions. The Director of the Ministry of Solidarity said, for example, that

[59] See CEDAW about access to information about rights (GR 28 2010: para 27). The Inter-American system has also emphasised that access to information is closely linked to women's enjoyment of other fundamental human rights (IACHR 2015a).

[60] Interview with Participant 54, Liquiçá, Liquiçá, Timor-Leste, 25 January 2017.

many women may have preferred to remain silent about their experiences during the occupation and not to apply for the pension in order to avoid being discriminated against in their communities. Although I do agree that this may have been the case in the first years after the conflict, I suspect that the comparative effect of seeing people receiving their pensions encouraged people to speak up about their own experiences. In the following section, though, I focus on those women who obtained the pension, what happens afterwards and what the effects of family and community dynamics in the context of the distribution of the pension are. My intent is to show women's real access to and power of decision over the pensions granted to them.

There are informal norms and customary practices that, owing to their social consequences, should be taken into account in policy making. According to Timorese culture, the concept of family is extended and collaboration and solidarity are core values within it. Pensions are therefore distributed among the members of the family in particular ways. I observed that for those women who receive a pension for their own actions, the veterans' pension is their own recognition and entitlement to a benefit because of their actions in the past. They usually distribute the money among their children and other members of the family, but if they did not have children, they could support their own projects. Tia Kasian, for instance, said that she did not want to marry again because she did not want to have a man that beats her, that the pension was hers and that she wanted to have the freedom to decide what to do with her own money. She decided to create a school for children in Liquiçá. I thought that Tia Kasian's point revealed the importance of taking into consideration to what extent men in the family have a role in the money decisions.

If the pension that a woman receives is awarded on the grounds of the actions of her deceased husband during the resistance, then her effective access to and decision over this funding becomes more constrained. We may remember that all pensions are legally established as life-time benefits, which means that beneficiaries are entitled to receive the pension until their death, particularly the survival and martyrs' pensions. This monthly Pensions for the Martyrs can range between US$276 and US$345, which is a comparatively high income in Timor-Leste, and provided according to rank as explained above. It is received in this order: (1) widow, (2) children, (3) parents, and if there are none of the above, (4) siblings, of the member of the resistance who died. In other words, if the widow was not alive, the children were the recipients of the pension, and if the martyr did not have a wife or children, his/her parents were to become the recipients, and so on. The Pensions for the Martyrs resulted in a family strategy that did not necessarily favour women themselves and focused on the family as a whole.[61] There are allegations that widows pretended to have died in order to

[61] Concerning women's access to justice, Banda argues that women's lack of education and independence also often interfere 'in the acceptance of decisions that may suit their families or other interested parties but not themselves' (2009: 144).

have their children assigned as the inheritors of the pension to ensure, thereby, that the family could count on the pension for longer. In other words, women themselves may have participated in and agreed with this decision because it was more financially convenient for the family in the long-term. In one of my interviews with a former employee of the Ministry of Solidarity, because of the complaints received, further legislation was passed to deal with this. However, members of the local population claimed that the widows were too old and that if they passed away, the children were not going to receive any help from the state. This explains why I met many women in the different municipalities who were not the recipients of the pension, which instead was being paid to one of their children.

I also observe that the chosen child was usually male and tended to be the eldest. This child then assumes charge of distributing his father's pension to the rest of his brothers and sisters. In the majority of cases, the pension money is usually given to those children who are studying, while those who get married no longer receive a share. Daughters are not chosen as main beneficiaries because they may get married and, according to Timorese traditions, they are usually expected to live with the family of their male spouses. However, the widow may be excluded as well. I found cases of women who did not receive any sum of money from their children. One old woman in Maliana said, for instance, that her son distributed the pension money to her other children in Dili and that it was too complicated for him to send money to her in Maliana. In another case in Lalerik Mutin, a woman who was married to a commander and who received a monthly pension for 8–14 years of service said that her husband's pension was being received by her son. They also had a daughter, but 'she can only ask her brother for an amount of money when she really needs it', the woman said.[62]

I also find it interesting that the distribution of the veterans' pensions followed the same logic of customary inheritance. In a Universal Periodic Review (UPR) report, for instance, there is an observation of how 'customary practice led to the inherited property usually being passed on to the eldest surviving male heir if the surviving spouse is a woman' (OHCHR 2016b: para 45). The veterans' pension law and practices remind us of the interpretation of family and inheritance laws and how they can be gender-manipulated. Finally, not only can sons get control over pensions, but also depending on the personal circumstances of the widow, as mentioned above, the family-in-law may be entitled to decide over the recipient of the pension of the deceased husband if she remarries. Moreover, because there are cases where a martyr has had several wives, and therefore several families, the pension may also, subject to negotiation, be shared by all.

To sum up, the pensions acquire a communal sense and because of family dynamics, many members can have expectations and claim a right to a part of it. What is certain is that widows may not have absolute control over this sum of money.

[62] Interview with Participant 66, Lalerik Mutin, Viqueque, Timor-Leste, 4 February 2017.

VI. (UN)EXPECTED EFFECTS OF THE TIMORESE VETERANS' PENSIONS

Because, after a conflict, former combatants may become the new socio-political force in a country, their benefits may put pressure on public finances to the point of becoming unsustainable (World Bank 2004: 7). In this regard, there are several reasons that may explain why Timor-Leste, a poor country, decided to provide massive life-long pensions for veterans. Because of their sacrifice during the Indonesian occupation, a life-long pension was supposed to help former members of the resistance to live a life which they would have otherwise had, given the opportunity to study and gain a profession and/or work. Initially thought to be part of a DDR package for the armed combatants, the veterans' scheme was meant to reassure combatants that after giving up their weapons, they would have an income. 'Peace was bought' were the words used by an international adviser.

However, the 2006 crisis may have had an effect. In 2006, the same year when the Statute on the veterans' pensions was enacted, more than one-third of the country's armed forces were discharged after a mutiny linked to claims of poor service conditions and biased promotion (Harris Rimmer 2010: 337). There are allegations that some veterans with links to the leadership might have been behind that. A current minister mentioned to me once that the 2006 crisis was the response of Xanana to limitations on his power as President compared to the Prime Minister at that time, Mari Alkatiri. He said: 'Xanana burned the house down'. The Statute therefore may have been rapidly adopted in a moment of political tension and military crisis. This may also explain why the second campaign of registration was carried out in May 2009, the year after the assassination attempt on Ramos-Horta. The current pension system may guarantee peace in the country, but at a very high price.

Rather than promoting peace, the veterans' pensions sustain militarism and patronage in the new state. If patronage is defined as the government's reward to a specific group for political support received, in Timor-Leste the trade-off meant the veterans receiving the benefits of the pension and the politicians ensuring their electoral support. The veterans' lobby has already achieved an expansion of the veterans' pension scheme and today Timorese politicians are constrained by what their lobby may say (Rothschild 2017: 450). Patronage is creating not only serious political distortions in the state, but also socio-economic imbalances among the population. Aspinall et al (2018: 154–55) claim that this new politics of patronage and distribution in Timor-Leste has emerged over the last decade, facilitated by oil wealth and veterans whose views are a powerful influence on voters in many villages. Why do the veterans have so much local power? Aspinall et al (2018: 163) argue that thanks to their liberation-struggle credentials, many of these veterans have transformed themselves into construction contractors and entrepreneurs, which means that they control local-level development projects and thus have the power to dispense jobs. As the former President and current Prime Minister, Taur Matan Ruak, said in his 2016 speech to the National Parliament on the State of the Nation, 'there are few employment opportunities, especially in rural areas, where 70% of the population live.' The fact that the majority of the Timorese people do not have a job and that the veterans' pension can help them to cover their necessities explain why the system today has become chaotic, with colliding allegations of false submissions from people who did not participate in the resistance, rumours of corruption, and selection bias regarding those who received the pension.

This takes me to my next point. Veterans' pensions do cause harm with all the imbalances that they create within a society and their distortions may be found in several post-conflict contexts, including Guinea-Bissau and Zimbabwe, where there was a higher number of registered fighters, decades after, than at independence (World Bank 2004: 3). This not only speaks of the failure of the state to guarantee socio-economic rights for all citizens, but also shows how these models of direct cash are not sustainable if they are not designed sustainably for the population. This money may arrive in families and local communities and be distributed in small amounts with limited sustainable impact on the society. This money may also have altered family and community dynamics, in particular the psyche of the younger generation. Family members may accommodate themselves to the pension money and the need to secure their share. Taur Matan Ruak, in the same 2016 speech, recognised that

> this law created a system that sets a poor example for the citizens. The Lifelong Pension Law, in some cases, is liable to create parasites, who receive large sums of money from the State each month, even if some of those individuals offer nothing to society in return for the generous support they receive.

Although some policy makers may argue that there should be studies to explore how veterans' pensions are distributed within families and communities and how they have helped to release people from poverty, other experiences of direct cash to specific groups may not be so encouraging. Exploring views about money and its meaning, Duggan and Jacobson (2009: 142) indeed claim that the lump-sum payments that were granted to aboriginal survivors of the government-sanctioned Indian Residential Schools in Canada, were often viewed by the recipients as collective and that large sums of money entering communities were frequently spent quickly and conspicuously. The system seems to be unsustainable and the political parties do not dare to challenge it because the veterans' lobby is too powerful.

Taur Matan Ruak recognised in the same speech how some veterans have received aid, while others still have not, and how this has caused divisions among them. At that moment in time, his speech was considered to be courageous because the political parties did not dare to oppose the system. However, when Taur Matan Ruak tried to ensure for himself the position of

Prime Minister for the 2017 elections (which he later obtained after another election) his political party, PLP, agreed a coalition with Xanana's party, the CNRT. The political campaign of their coalition called Alliance of Change for Progress (AMP) was then based on calling the armed front the 'real legitimate veterans', while minimising the work of the clandestine and diplomatic fronts. There was so much uproar that the historical leader (and current President) José Ramos-Horta, whose internationally-known diplomacy and advocacy led to his becoming a Nobel Peace Prize co-recipient in 1996, had to publicly comment on, if not justify, all the work that he did throughout the years for the Timorese cause. Of great concern is the fact that the young generation of politicians is participating in the exacerbation of this cult for the members of the armed resistance for their own political advantage.

Elites and politicians may not like the truth, but by supporting this idea that the armed front were the main actors of the resistance, they are strengthening not only a patronage system, but also a patriarchal political system that upholds and perpetuates artificially constructed masculine values, in which a relatively small number of men use their privilege and power to exert authority over other men (Rees and Chinkin 2016: 1216–17). Rees and Chinkin (2016: 1216–17) argue that in order for this patriarchal system to survive, it needs a particular form of masculine identity and the support of women encouraging men to identify with it. I see in Timor-Leste the construction of this masculine identity entrenched within the military. We should not be surprised though. Enloe (2004: 217) claims that persistent militarisation in a post-war society serves to entrench the privileging of masculinity, in both private and public life, and that there are subtle ways in which the democratic rhetoric of masculinity is the currency for domination and exclusion. She further conceives militarised masculinity as a 'model of masculinity that is especially likely to be imagined as requiring a feminine complement that excludes women from full and assertive participation in postwar public life' (Enloe 2004: 217–18). My concern in this regard is that the whole dynamics particularly affect the continuum of violence and discrimination against women. MacKinnon (2017: 119), for instance, identifies several traits which characterise inequality: (1) it defines its victims as less than human, less than a full member of society, a second-class citizen; and (2) it excludes people from resources, respect, credibility and power, and materially deprived people translates into poverty. Not only were Timorese women's experiences during the Indonesian occupation not recognised, and not only did they face additional barriers to participation in the transitional justice system, but they also currently live under a great socio-economic disadvantage compared with their male counterparts. This reminds me of Mills's statement in *The Racial Contract* that when white people – and I add male elites – say 'Justice', they mean 'Just Us' (1997: 110).

If we wish to learn about the long-term impacts of warfare and the numerous post-war reintegration programmes, systematic inquiries about the realities of female veterans after the end of the conflict are necessary – currently these are extremely rare (Vastapuu 2018: 2).[63] It is therefore of great concern that Timor-Leste is not the only country that has focused resources on supporting veterans, while retreating from reparations to be provided to victims. In Rwanda, for instance, there was a disproportionate amount of money spent on DDR as against a lack of reparations for survivors (Evans 2012: 98).[64] In Sierra Leone, not only were survivors of SGBV de-prioritised in the reparation process compared to survivors of other conflict-related abuses who received full reparations, but also during the DDR process, male combatants received five times the amount of money as was paid in reparations, suggesting that the provision of recovery resources benefited men much more than women (What Works 2018: 33).[65] Gender stereotyping thus not only affects women's recognition, through their denial of individual dignity and worth, but also affects their access to economic redistribution, by denying them equal access to a fair allocation of public goods (Cook and Cusack 2010: 59–60; Fraser 1997: 11–39). Women's exclusion from reparations and post-conflict social benefits is thus not a matter of chance but framed within a logic of patronage where a select group is controlling the system. Attention should therefore be paid to this dichotomy between benefits for male veterans on the one hand and reparations for women victims on the other hand. If these post-conflict dynamics are not addressed, transitional justice may thus fail to address the socio-economic structures that contribute to the subordination of women.

Finally, because the access to pensions has been equated to access to power and prestige, those who managed to obtain the veterans' pensions may see themselves as the legitimate subjects of public entitlements. And even for those who receive the pension, it is never enough. A woman in Liquiçá who receives both the veterans' pension and the state old age pension described how she was unhappy that other people receive the same amount as her for their old age pension. She said 'the government should have different old age pension for those of us who were veterans.'[66] In other words, even in a pension to which everyone at a specific age should be entitled, she thought there should be a scale that favours the veterans. I thought that her answer reveals the extent to which those who have managed to be legitimised as 'veterans' may be the privileged ones within their communities. The answer of this woman illustrates her sense of entitlement and her perceived right to have more than others. We may therefore be in the presence of the adaption of a neo-liberal discourse of international human rights framework to a local context, bringing negative results for their population as a whole and the future of their nation.

[63] In Liberia, while education, professional dreams and housing were the wishes of the women war veterans, many women still suffered from sexually transmitted diseases as well as from physical damage to reproductive organs: more than 10 years after the war, they were still in need of acute medical assistance (Vastapuu 2018: 75–76, 163).

[64] Evans (2012) cites Waldorf (2009).

[65] *What Works* (2018) cites Williams and Opdam (2017).

[66] Interview with Participant 5X, Liquiçá, Liquiçá, Timor-Leste, 25 January 2017.

VII. THE LIMITS OF THE DISCOURSE ON RIGHTS

Kapur (2018) warns about a conception of human rights that does not lead to lasting freedom but is tied to a specific and narrow understanding of happiness and the 'good life', and aligned with liberal individualism and human freedom – defined in market terms – in which the failed subject must aspire to become successful through an imposed script of freedom. She encourages a shift in the conceptualisation of freedom to one 'addressed not as an explicit, imposed process but as a modality of self-transformation that functions as a catalyst for external emancipation' and based on 'truly mindful, equitable and inclusive strategies of rights deployment' (Kapur 2018: 232–39). Kennedy (2004: 15–16) also observes the tendencies of the human rights movement to focus on individuals, 'one is what one is and has what one has' rather than participants in a shared life, and to focus on right-holding identity, in which human rights consolidate people into 'identities' on the basis of which rights can be claimed. The sense of individual entitlement promoted by the human rights movement is also at great cost to collective political life (Kennedy 2004: 15–16). Similarly, Moyo (2012: 266) cautions that almost all the key concepts associated with transitional justice, such as democratisation, liberalisation and rule of law, imply the transformation of certain values that must be embraced to make a 'successful' transition to a liberal democracy. These values are entrenched in a Western view that 'the individual is the principal holder of rights in tandem with its marginalization of economic, social and cultural rights' (Moyo 2012: 267). Attention to the collective, though, is not enough. The Eurocentric masculine notion of transitional justice cannot adequately account for the diversity of group and individual rights in a post-colonial state because 'women are the conventional care givers who are more directly affected by a state's failure to respect, protect and fulfil its citizens' economic, social and cultural rights' (Moyo 2012: 267–68).

What does it mean then to share a world? While Arendt would be concerned about plurality in the public space, Kennedy (2004: 15–16) talks about how these tendencies of individual entitlement inhibit diversity and the sense of being part of a community. Pluralism is connected to equality and if the state does not recognise the diversity of women's agency within the provision of post-conflict benefits, this may have an impact on the protection of their rights and their participation in the new state. Equality is not about treating women as second-class citizens and inferior to men, but about treating them with the dignity they deserve: as equal participants in the political community that emerges after mass violations and in a re-founding moment of the state. If the Timorese leadership and, I would say, the youth, admire revolutionary leaders, the recognition of women in the public imaginary should come to the fore and they should be given equal benefits and entitlements.

In the meantime, when the UN programmes for women's access to justice after a conflict are examined, the current Women Peace and Security (WPS) agenda still focuses on outcomes around women's protection and political participation.

As part of the implementation and monitoring of the WPS agenda, Timor-Leste started to implement its National Action Plan (NAP) in 2017 and by 2020, with the support of the UN and Japan, ACbit published a training manual called 'Chega! Women for Peace' in order to contribute to delivering the principles of two important documents on post-conflict peace-building in Timor-Leste: The NAP and the Chega! Report.[67] While this initiative seeks to familiarise trainers – and the Timorese population – with the Chega! Report, these types of measures are not enough if women are still invisible in the narrative of the country and subjected disproportionately to poverty in their daily lives. By neglecting their access to post-conflict socio-economic benefits, as indicated by Timorese women, a form of discrimination that affects their livelihoods in the long-term may be sidelined by this international initiative. Moreover, I agree with Ní Aoláin when she claims that the prioritisation of economic justice should further include

> the regulation of the care economy, addressing the formal, and informal barriers to women's participation in the workplace, connecting familial responsibility with market participation, and viewing economic decision-making as a deeply gendered terrain in which women's voices … are rarely heard (Ní Aoláin 2019: 150–71).

There are also the Sustainable Development Goals (SDGs) which deal with women's access to justice. Although there has been much discussion in Timor-Leste about the SDGs, in a visit of the SR on indigenous rights, she urged the government to assign adequate resources to its 2017 SDG Roadmap so that they are truly implemented (UN 2019a). As this book has shown, plans will lack any meaning if they are not assigned resources to be adequately implemented. Rather than placing the focus on prescriptions, the focus should be on the results after implementation.

In summary, a system that is based on life-long veterans' pensions illustrates a poisoning notion of rights entitlements as compatible with the idea of a paying and deserving consumer/client relationship in the market, where some are more successful than others. The community should nevertheless be concerned. Arendt (2006a: 227–28) argues that the opposite of truth is opinion and that in fact favourable opinion is a prerequisite of power, since in order to keep it, governments must rely on the support of those who are like-minded. The disturbing transformation of factual truths into opinions and illusions may put at stake factual reality itself and this is indeed a political problem, even for free countries (Arendt 2006a: 232). In the case of Timor-Leste, women face evident disparities, a lack of recognition of their heterogeneity and of participation in the public space. The armed front may have initially excluded women, but there are trends that indicate that the contributions of the clandestine and diplomatic fronts may also be at risk of being deleted from the history of Timor-Leste.

[67] *cf* ACbit (2020).

VIII. CONCLUSIONS

This chapter analysed women's access to veterans' pensions in Timor-Leste. The law on veterans' pensions and the policies and community practices surrounding their implementation have created additional layers and barriers of accessibility for women, to which men are not necessarily, or are less, exposed. The Timorese veterans' system is therefore discriminatory against women. Issues in the legal framework to determine entitlements – such as the conception of division of labour, the requirement of exclusive dedication, ie full-time service, and the need to provide a witness – not only devalue women's work and contributions, but also serve to deny the different modes of women's participation during a conflict. The exclusion of both sexual violence itself and of sexual violence as part of torture are also features that foster women's exclusion. The fact that only 'prolonged' deprivation of liberty is taken into account in calculating dedicated service, and not preventative or temporary detention, excludes for example the nightly detentions that were suffered by many women during the occupation. Moreover, the withdrawal of the pension from a woman who decides to remarry and the exclusion of the 'bush wives' is also discriminatory. The law has therefore been designed to exclude women. But women's access to veterans' pensions is also being affected throughout its implementation by local power dynamics. During my interviews, I collected information on how patriarchal gender stereotypes imposed by members within local Homage Commissions obstructed women's submissions so that they were not considered veterans. There were also allegations of corruption and of a system that women called the 'family system', which means that who they had as family members could have an impact on obtaining a favourable pension outcome.

Taking into account other forms of intersectionality in the design and implementation of these programmes, we can see how issues such as literacy, access to information and rural/urban dynamics may have affected those women who were in a more disadvantaged position. Within family and community dynamics, there are practices and behaviours concerning income distribution which also affect women's real access to, and power of decision over, the veterans' pensions. All these factors contribute to the creation of higher thresholds for women in the application process for the veterans' pensions. Owing to the constructions of the law, but also to policy and community and family practices, women who because of their gender participated mainly by doing clandestine work, are systematically disqualified from the pension arrangements. The Timorese government's focus on the veterans' pensions has also created a dichotomy between the male/veteran/pensions against the female/victim/reparations, according to which the first became the selective right-holder group, the winner, and the second became a diffuse mass that exists but may be better ignored. The danger of this dichotomy is that it perpetuates women's silence and inequality. On one hand, women's violations may be perceived as collateral damage and to be connected to a denial of their diverse participation during the conflict. As a result, those women who suffered from SGBV because of their part in the struggle and/or their affiliation were denied any form of reparation. On the other hand, by exalting the three components of the Timorese resistance – the armed, clandestine and diplomatic fronts – the dominant narrative of the state seems to have shifted to mean that the armed front, whose main leaders, mostly men, occupy key political roles in the government today, were the main resistance force against the Indonesian occupation.

There is a lack of attention within the literature of transitional justice to veterans' pension programmes. However, international experiences show that these systems may have large and long-term consequences for the enjoyment of human rights by specific groups within a society. The veterans' pensions are designed to support a specific category of men, their alliances and militaristic attitudes, while rejecting everything related to femininity: there is a reinforcement of a patriarchal narrative that connects the independence of Timor-Leste solely to the sacrifice and bravery of armed Timorese men – the heroes – while women's recognition may be silenced. These systems may lead to patronage and a militarised masculinity, while reinforcing the cycle of violence and discrimination against women in times of peace. Moreover, because the life-long pensions are very high compared to the average salary in Timor, women's exclusion from this post-conflict socio-economic benefit is creating socio-economic structural imbalances that put women and their children at a disadvantage in society. This chapter, however, does not argue that all should have access to life-long pensions: it is not about unsustainable cash for a wider sector of society, but about the recognition of women's agency as citizens of the political community during and after the conflict. In the case of Timor-Leste, the system in place puts into question the future of the new state: it is draining its economy and the lobby of the veterans has become too powerful for politicians to change the status quo. Ultimately while those of the armed front seem to be the privileged, even over the clandestine and diplomatic fronts, the veterans' pensions ultimately reinforce women's inequality and socio-economic dependence on men. Curiously, the veterans' pensions may be constructed upon a neoliberal discourse of human rights that is framed within a logic of individual payments and entitlements. The last chapter presents the conclusions.

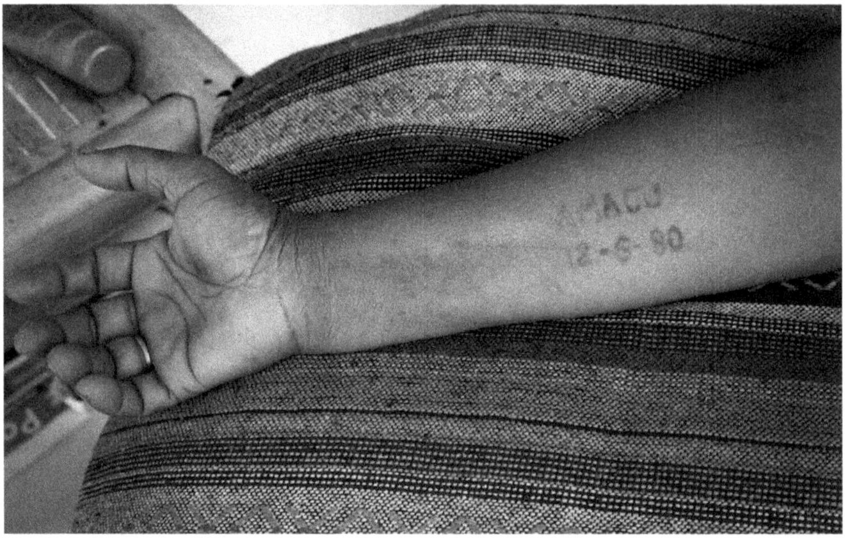

In Dili, Maria Inmaculada Vilejar showed her detention number tattoo on her arm. © Carlos Oviedo.

The National Parliament in Timor-Leste. © Noemí Pérez Vásquez.

8

Conclusions: 'So it Does Not Happen Again'

Seeing transitional justice as a site of contestation, this book has offered a panoramic assessment of the access to this justice from a gender perspective: it deals with conflict, justice and women, it contains a post-colonial theoretical component, and it bases its findings on a deep analysis of a case study. Moreover, not only is there a general lack of in-depth fieldwork analysis on how women have interacted with transitional justice, but also there is no another competing publication which highlights Timorese women's experiences in dealing with the full account of transitional justice. With gender lenses, I therefore reviewed cases at the Special Panels for Serious Crimes, evaluated the participation of women in the CAVR and analysed reparation laws and policies as well as the veterans' pensions. This book also involved archival work, on-site observation and in-depth interviews with women, government officials, UN employees, civil society activists and other officials in Timor-Leste. The starting point of my research was women's views and experiences through the range of possibilities that transitional justice visibly offered them at the local level. I then tried to make sense of the information women gave me – on the gap between their experiences during the conflict and the justice received, and their evaluation of their contributions and the institutional failure to give weight to those contributions – by following the traces between what the law prescribes and how policy implementation evolved. I also engaged with different perspectives of justice, which may be shaped by a person's position on the social ladder and intersectional forms of marginalisation. In addition to carrying out fieldwork, I drew on examples from other jurisdictions to illustrate in a global context the structural barriers that women face when accessing transitional justice.

This book demonstrates that discriminatory practices embedded in the justice process constrain women's participation and their later recognition when benefits are being distributed. The book first shows how the different barriers and discriminatory layers in the laws, policies, community and family practices that affect women in their access to trials, truth commissions and reparations hamper women's ability to participate in these gendered justice processes. By including veterans' pensions as part of the mechanisms of transitional justice, the book also argues that the boundaries of transitional justice need to be re-thought: transitional justice leads to new socio-economic structures that downplay recognition of women's rights and produce long-term consequences in peace time. Transitional justice may thus exacerbate the invisibility and discrimination against women during both its process of implementation and later in the country's reconstruction and development phase.

More specifically, because in Timor-Leste women faced additional barriers to access prosecutions, truth commissions and reparations, I began this book with the metaphor of the blind letters to explain that although transitional justice may be there, it is only accessible to a few. Transitional justice is not an innocent construction: its mechanical implementation may ignore either the different intersections of discrimination, the public and private divides that exist in the local context, or the stereotypes and values of international and national actors. Hence, the law, but also patriarchal values and gender stereotypes, practices of traditional male dominance, the importance of connections and geographical location, corruption, people's level of education and access to information, among many other factors, all had a disproportionate impact on women's access to transitional justice mechanisms.

As a result, although the violations committed against Timorese women were widespread and systematic, my data shows the myriad ways in which women are locked out of the justice system at all stages, from the investigation and prosecution of crimes, judicial decision-making and participation in public hearings, to the provision of urgent reparations. The laws concerning transitional justice, for instance, are modelled on the interests and experiences of men: the imaginaries of sub-categories of crimes and a false scale of gravity may contribute to the invisibility of women's violations. Prioritising murder prosecutions led SGBV crimes to be perceived as crimes of lesser gravity. Furthermore, although during the interviews women and policy-makers made an implicit de facto division between sexual violence and torture, women were wise enough to point out elements that, according to international jurisprudence, show that crimes committed against them may amount to torture. The same is applicable to the false distinction between enslavement and sexual slavery and the idea that men are the only ones who can be enslaved while women are stripped of their political agency. The division between the crimes of forced marriage and sexual slavery appeared sometimes to be blurred in the local context of Timor-Leste.

There are further questions concerning those who are hired to work in the transitional justice cascade: from international investigators who may have posed specific questions that excluded women's experiences, to local leaders who could decide who was a member of the resistance and/or who may have been involved in the commission of violations against women and later had decision power to choose representative cases for the CAVR. A society is based on individual actors and structural relationships and because transitional justice may reinforce selectivity, we should be suspicious of who gets to participate. This also has implications for evidentiary practices and the provision of legal advice. In this regard, despite the fact that reproductive rights have long-term physical and psychological consequences for women, they remained largely invisible throughout all the mechanisms of transitional justice in Timor-Leste. Rather than uniquely focusing on the transfer of international legal standards, policy-makers and designers of transitional justice mechanisms should treat international and local dynamics as a main consideration.

But silence was also highlighted throughout the different mechanisms of transitional justice: revealing the suffering, including of SGBV, is not an individual decision, but one where the family and community interferes. Hence, women themselves may also avoid turning to transitional justice. As a result of a system of legal rules and procedures that is conflated with the enforcement of silence created by private dynamics, women, because they were women, were affected in their equal access to the different mechanisms of transitional justice. All of these factors belonging to the public and private spheres may have therefore contributed to make women's violations less reported and therefore invisible in Timor-Leste. This means that despite the apparent gender neutrality of transitional justice, there are structural and practical barriers that impede women from participating at early stages and disparities that are hidden in these processes. Without women's participation, their perspectives are excluded and their needs are unmet. In this regard, the low number of women participating in transitional justice processes despite multiple UN initiatives speaks to the limits of standard-setting if there is no political will on the side of former combatants and the UN itself. Unless barriers and discriminatory layers in the administration of transitional justice are understood and addressed, the different mechanisms that are implemented in a post-conflict situation may thus set a higher threshold for women's participation and the recognition of their agency.

I further argue that transitional justice may also be used as a tool to support the interests of those in power, while contributing to women's experiences being under-reported and exacerbating the invisibility of and discrimination against them. In the Timorese case, there is a strategic selectivity of transitional justice by the government that may be explained by Timor-Leste's economic dependency on Indonesia, and which may be beneficial to some men, particularly those connected to the armed front. While for the CAVR, reconciliation aimed at dealing with lesser crimes, apology and acceptance by the community, for the government, it has been all about amnesty and oblivion, including for crimes against humanity. Reconciliation therefore has been praised. This shows the co-existence of different meanings of reconciliation that have been used in parallel throughout the years. In contrast, there is an exclusion of everything related to accountability and reparations: trials, the follow-up to the truth and reconciliation commission and the reparations were initially supported by the authorities but were progressively sidelined.

In this regard, I also expand on the usual mechanisms typically considered within the scope of transitional justice, to include, at the women's request, the veterans' pensions, and I argued that this scheme may have the greatest political and socio-economic impact in a post-conflict society in the long-term. There is a tendency by post-conflict states to focus their resources on supporting veterans through pensions, while retreating from court initiatives and refusing to provide reparations to victims. On the one hand, women's violations may be perceived as 'collateral damage' and be connected to a denial of their diverse participation during the conflict. On the other hand, by exalting the three components of the Timorese resistance, the armed, clandestine and diplomatic fronts, the dominant narrative of the state seems to have shifted to promote the idea that the armed front, whose main leaders occupy key political roles in the government today, were the main resistance force against the Indonesian occupation. This is explained by the fact that power competitions come to the surface and they tend to be related to patronage and hyper-militarisation: former members of the armed resistance and politicians may have personal political and financial interests in sidelining accountability and reparations for victims while exalting their own image as heroes. This led to a political opinion according to which women did not fight and thus their contributions in the struggle are deliberately excluded and disregarded in the laws and policies. The veterans' pensions discriminate against women because the framing of military and political participation favours armed combat, while devaluating and failing to take into account women's roles and conditions.

This has also created a dichotomy between male/veteran/pensions and female/victim/reparations. While the former became the selective right-holder group – the winner – the latter became a diffuse mass that exists but may better be ignored. As a result, women's denial of reparations and their restricted access to the veterans' pension perpetuates their silence and discrimination. While the ability to talk about traumatic experiences may be related to an individual's capacity to drop his or her own shield, women may have been prompted by a feeling of abandonment by the welfare system that has been so prominent in the country. Because there were no reparations, women are therefore starting to associate their harms with the veterans' pensions, which is the only mechanism that has received the support of the Timorese leadership. This may explain why many women have become outspoken about their experiences – some women may be forced to abandon their silence in their search for a post-conflict socio-economic benefit. This reveals how a relationship between the violations and post-economic justice may continue within the welfare structures that are reproduced after a conflict, even more so in cases of women heading households.

The implementation of transitional justice in Timor-Leste also shows how this type of justice plays a fundamental role in the creation of the post-colonial identity of the new state – based on a single version of history. While the narrative that was chosen elevates a hyper-masculinisation of the society, promises of equality and of social change made during the times of the resistance were rendered superfluous and treacherous: peace, after all, did *not* make a difference in the lives of many Timorese women and they continue to suffer from violence. By further avoiding the recognition of women's experiences of resistance, we may forget that men and women may suffer and experience a conflict in different ways. As a consequence, the case of Timor-Leste shows how, relatively soon after a conflict, people can be alienated by a dominant narrative, leading to a risk of losing the factual truth. In this regard, across the different mechanisms of transitional justice implemented in Timor-Leste, there have been allegations of evidence being lost: from the actions of the militias when they burned evidence and made their crimes disappear, through the messiness faced by the UN in a post-conflict situation, to – perhaps on a more manipulative ground – the negligence and destruction of evidence by the Timorese government. We usually hear 'justice delayed is justice denied', but justice denied through time and the lack of public recognition towards women's experiences may lead to the oblivion of agency and crimes. As a result, specific categories of Timorese women have been left with a lack of space of appearance in the public space: from the 'comfort women', to the women who suffered gross violations under the Indonesian occupation, to women's situation of disadvantage today, there is a continuum in the cycle of violations against women.

Women's restricted access to the veterans' pension also creates new and hidden forms of political and socio-economic violence in the aftermath of a conflict. Scholars and humanitarian actors have not sufficiently considered the internal distribution of resources and the welfare structures that are produced after a conflict, neglecting the fact that a relationship between violations and post-conflict socio-economic justice may have longer-term consequences for women and their children, since it perpetuates their inequality and lack of recognition in times of peace. In this regard, although the Timorese government has promoted itself as an example of reconciliation, many women interviewed think that the children of the militias have been treated better than their own children. I also observed feelings of unfairness against those who obtained the veterans' pensions. The decisions surrounding transitional justice, and in particular, the denial of post-conflict socio-economic benefits to women may generate further discrimination against and marginalisation of certain groups within society. If resentment is a feeling concerning a past wrong that has not been righted, structural inequalities leading to intergenerational discriminatory cycles could further contribute to producing situations of political instability and to creating a new generation of extremists, therefore fuelling the possibility of future conflicts.

There are also post-colonial elements entrenched within transitional justice. I argue against the mechanical implementation of transitional justice. Truth commissions require the victims to participate in a specific place within a short time-frame, ignoring the reality that some individuals may need more time to be ready to talk. If they do not obey, they are excluded. Some women also stated that to assist in a reconciliation session did not mean that they were ready to reconcile, even though their presence may be counted as a 'success'. I also show how a timid intervention of transitional justice may indeed reinforce the continued invisibility of and discrimination against women after a conflict. What does it mean, then, for a woman to talk publicly about deep traumatic experiences and then 'nothing happens afterwards'? Because of the expectations created by transitional justice, women felt they needed to participate and disclose their violations, but without justice or recognition their situation may contribute afterwards to further discrimination against them. Rather than being empowered, victims, particularly women who suffered SGBV, may be left with increased feelings of vulnerability and stigma. There should thus be a clear commitment from actors and structures before a process begins, given that without proper closure, transitional justice may leave open wounds within the communities. A paradigm shift within transitional justice is needed.

Access to transitional justice presumes the participation of women and that their needs are taken into account. It should also be about a state's recognition and acknowledgement of the harm and wrongdoing that an individual suffered but also of their participation, roles and duties during a conflict. Women in particular will have a better understanding of their agency and the structures in which they were immersed, and recognition of women will help to raise their moral status within the public space. There is so much misunderstanding and knowledge gaps in Timor-Leste that it may be difficult for some to understand their own experiences in context. Some violations were considered unimportant within transitional justice, such as the simple, but very powerful, stories of women being requested to dance. These women, some of whom were children, know that there was something wrong about it, but they, and their communities, seem not to associate it with the crime, for instance, of sexual slavery. The same is applicable to their activities during the Indonesian times. They were performing the activities that they were assigned to do. If there are silences imposed by the authorities, passivity will lead to the reinforcement of stereotypes of women over time and the discrimination cycle may continue for their dependents. Women interviewed, though, continue to raise the wrongdoing, showing how human dignity and self-reflection are at the core of understanding evil. These women are survivors and they did not need a gun to show their resilience and active participation. This is why participation and recognition have been at the core of this book.

Women do not only have a more limited access to transitional justice, but also, by excluding socio-economic benefits from concepts concerning post-conflict justice, their views on justice are not taken into account. Justice for women goes beyond courts and is also related to economic justice. A focus on the delivery of socio-economic rights may thus be of greater use than rhetorical participation in legal processes that do not yield practical solutions for the problems facing them. Taking into consideration women's desires, there should be a stronger connection between justice and social and economic rights, and for that purpose long-term development and economic analysis should be allowed to infiltrate the policy-making of transitional justice. In the meantime, the international community insists on an idea of justice equivalent to criminal law, and budgets may primarily be allocated to courts aiming at the best international standards. There seems therefore to be a false line that divides past atrocities and victims as against an understanding of basic needs and development. In contrast, an international stimulus to see the human rights agenda in terms of individual entitlements has acquired a Timorese dimension, producing adverse results for women. An over-focus on individual compensation, both by international and local actors, may have indeed complicated women's access to reparations. The protection of economic and social rights cannot be a matter of cash injection that disappears and creates dependency, inequality, corruption and political patronage, where some have more advantages than others. Moreover, the idea of so many people having access to life-long pensions and reparations conceived mainly as individual monetary compensation is not only too close to neoliberalism, but also not sustainable. Other types of reparations, such as rehabilitation, satisfaction and non-repetition may be more aligned to women's genuine desire for justice and could help to eliminate the fault-line between reparations and development.

Although the Timorese government discontinued the UN-led trials and the UN-supported reparations programme, many of the norms and policies implemented by the UN did not necessarily facilitate the protection of women's rights after the independence anyway. In addition to local and private variables that affected the prosecutions, substantive and procedural issues also played a role in limiting women's participation and visibility at the trials. As a result, when it comes to the prosecutions of gender-related crimes, out of all the violations committed against Timorese women, there were only two persons convicted. But there are also cases that may reveal a complicity, if not direct participation, of the UN in the commission of human rights violations. The families who claimed compensation for the killing of former UNAMET employees seemed to have faced gender-biased rules and practices. Moreover, the support of international organisations in the provision of contraceptive methods during the Indonesian occupation also seems to have facilitated the commission of SGBV crimes against women. There are further concerns about the domestic legacy and power imbalance within hybrid tribunals, which may translate into the imposition of practices that do not necessary lead to the best results. Moreover, not only did the Timorese government not assume the financial responsibility to provide a reparations programme for victims, but also the UN seemed to have reparation practices that do not follow its international discourse. Although the UN advocates for the rule of law and access to justice, the reality is that the responsibility and accountability of international organisations remains an ill-defined area of international law. What is certain is that the proactive participation of international actors does not necessarily lead to effective access to justice for women.

Although gender mainstreaming has been considered a part of transitional justice mechanisms, the experience of Timorese women shows that in practice this may be more part of a project checklist that focuses on a small number of people and on the production of reports, than a contribution to a transformative momentum for women. Therefore a justice system that has widely been implemented by both the UN and states and that may be presented as a package solution, could go hand-in-hand with discriminatory practices and stereotypes from its legal inception to its implementation, causing women to remain in a lose–lose situation concerning their violations. On the one hand, some feminists argue that there is an over-focus on SGBV violations when it comes to exploring women's experiences after a conflict. This has obscured other issues which are also of the utmost importance for women, such as economic and social rights. But on the other hand, even crimes of SGBV are not duly taken into consideration in the implementation of transitional justice. I see, then, a gap between what transitional justice promotes and the expectations that it creates, what women receive and what women want. In this regard, international policy-makers may present transitional justice as the key to resolving former mass and grave violations of international human rights law and international humanitarian law, while 'the negatives are discussed privately, often cynically, but rarely strategically' (Kennedy 2004: xiii). However, not only policy makers, but also scholars have a role in the widespread mechanical implementation of transitional justice. I read so many books whose arguments were based on policy prescriptions that did not reflect factual realities, what truly happened. This made me think about the scholars' role and contributions to the replication of a system that reinforces ideas of male paradigms of power and domination and that is fundamentally discriminatory against women.

Finally, at a policy level, in order to improve women's equal access to this type of justice, a refocusing of this debate is needed: rather than thinking that the ultimate output is the drafting of legal and policy documents, we should think therefore about the qualitative aspects, including the structures and individual experiences. Moreover, rather than just formal engagement, what it is needed is a change in language to highlight the importance of substantive participation of women in these justice processes. There should be a balance between what transitional justice aims for and how effective justice public policies are implemented. To ensure this, policy makers should make sure that they understand how transitional justice works and constantly review the chain of justice in these mechanisms: not only the laws and policies that were set up, but also the powerful interferences of community structures and family practices. Transitional justice should thus be a critical process in which preventive measures are well-thought-out and in which there are real checks and balances in order both to correct discriminatory laws, policies and practices and to tackle structural differences that impede equal access to its mechanisms. If not, rather than protecting women, we may exacerbate their invisibility and the discrimination against them. There is always possibility for hope.

'I want to tell the story to future generations, so it does not happen again.'[1]

Maria de Fatima, Baucau.

[1] Interview with Participant 56, Baucau, Timor-Leste, 13 January 2017.

Girls performing a traditional Timorese dance in Gleno, Ermera. © Noemí Pérez Vásquez.

Appendix

Questionnaire for Semi-structured Interviews with Timorese women

Information on interviewee:

1. Name.
2. Age.
3. Place of living.
4. Clan.
5. Marital status.
6. Level of education.

Experience during the conflict, including on human rights violation:

7. Could you tell us about your experience during the Indonesian occupation?
8. Did you support the resistance?
9. If so, how?
10. For how many years?
11. Were you a member of the OPMT?

Women's interaction with transitional justice mechanisms:

1. When, how and to whom did you report the crimes committed?
2. Was your case (or the one of your relative) taken to the Special Panels for Serious Crimes?
3. Were you interviewed by the Investigators?
4. If you did, how was the interaction with them?
5. Did you receive any feedback on the progress of your case?
6. Did you participate in the CAVR activities?
7. How was the interaction? Could you explain it to me?
8. Why did you (not) participate?
9. Did you receive an assistance (compensation, rehabilitation, etc.) from the CAVR?
10. What happened after the recollection of testimonies?
11. Do you know about the Chega! report?
12. Do you receive a veterans' pension?
13. How was the process of application?
14. If you do not receive the veterans' pension, why is it so?
15. If you did, are you in charge of its distribution?
16. If you did, how did receiving a pension change family dynamics?

Women's perceptions of justice and wishes for the future:

1. Did your participation in any of the transitional justice mechanisms have a positive impact in your life?
2. Are you satisfied with your participation and with what you received afterwards?
3. What is justice for you?
4. What would you like to have received as justice after the conflict?
5. What does women's rights mean for you?

Bibliography

Abdenur, AE (2018) 'In Colombia, Female Ex-Combatants Still Face Risk of Stigmatization', *Passblue*, www.passblue.com/2018/03/13/in-colombia-female-ex-soldiers-still-face-risk-of-stigmatization/

Aboueldahab, N (2017) *Transitional justice and the prosecution of political leaders in the Arab region: a comparative study of Egypt, Libya, Tunisia and Yemen* (Oxford, Hart Publishing).

ACbit (2019) *Improving the Lives of Women Survivors in Timor-Leste*, https://chegabaita.org/wp-content/uploads/2020/01/Relatoriu-Par-Ingles.pdf

—— (2020) *Chega! Women for Peace. Manual to Understand National Actional Plan on Women, Peace and Security*, http://chegabaita.org/wp-content/uploads/2020/01/Chega-for-Peace-3-1.pdf

Ainley, K (2015) 'Evaluating the success of transitional justice in Sierra Leone and beyond' in K Ainley, R Friedman, and C Mahony (eds), *Evaluating Transitional Justice: Accountability and Peacebuilding in Post-Conflict Sierra Leone* (London, Palgrave Macmillan).

Al Jazeera (2008) 'Indonesia "regrets" Timor violence', *Aljazeera*, www.aljazeera.com/news/asia-pacific/2008/07/20087154370143951.html

Almeida, B (2021) 'The Law and Its Limits: Land Grievances, Wicked Problems, and Transitional Justice in Timor-Leste' 15 *International Journal of Transitional Justice* 128.

Amnesty International (2017) *"Wounds that burn our souls": Compensation for Kosovo's wartime rape survivors, but still no justice*, www.amnesty.org/en/documents/eur70/7558/2017/en/

—— (2018) *Timor-Leste Report 2017/2018*, www.amnesty.org/en/countries/asia-and-the-pacific/timor-leste/report-timor-leste/

Anonymous (2005 [1954]) *A Woman in Berlin* (London, Virago Press).

Arendt, H (1971) 'Thinking and Moral Considerations: A Lecture' 38 *Social Research* 417.

—— (1972) *Crises of the Republic* (New York, Harcourt Brace & Company).

—— (1998) *The Human Condition* (Chicago IL, The University of Chicago Press).

—— (2006a) *Between Past and Future* (New York, Penguin Books).

—— (2006b) *Eichmann in Jerusalem* (New York, Penguin Books).

—— (2007) *The Jewish Writings* (New York, Schocken Books).

—— (2016) *On Revolution* (London, Faber & Faber).

—— (2017) *The Origins of Totalitarianism* (London, Penguin Random House).

Arthur, P (2009) 'How 'Transitions' Reshaped Human Rights: A Conceptual History of Transitional Justice' 31 *Human Rights Quarterly* 321.

Article 19 (2005) *Freedom of Expression and the Media in Timor-Leste*, www.Article19.org/data/files/pdfs/publications/timor-leste-baseline-study.pdf

Asia Justice And Rights (AJAR) (2015) *Enduring impunity. Women surviving atrocities in the absence of justice*, www.asia-ajar.org/files/ENDURING%20IMPUNIY%20final-23%20Nov-press.pdf

Askin, K (2013) 'Treatment of sexual violence in Armed Conflicts: A Historical Perspective and the Way Forward' in AM de Brouwer, C Ku, R Römkens and L Herik (eds), *Sexual Violence as an International Crime: Interdisciplinary Approaches* (Cambridge, Intersentia).

Aspinall, E and Hicken, A, Scambary, J and Weiss, M (2018) 'Timor-Leste Votes – Parties and Patronage' 29 *Journal of Democracy* 187.

Atuahene, B (2014) *We Want What's Ours. Learning from South Africa's Land Restitution Program* (Oxford, Oxford University Press).

Ašimović Akyol, R (2019) 'For Bosnian Women, No Justice – and No Seats', *Foreign Policy*, https://foreignpolicy.com/2019/10/03/bosnian-women-balkan-war-no-justice-and-no-political-power/

Bafo, S (2019) 'Three reasons why an intersectional approach to women's peace and security agenda is important', *Oxfam Policy & Practices: Views & Voices*, https://views-voices.oxfam.org.uk/2019/11/three-reasons-why-an-intersectional-approach-to-womens-peace-and-security-agenda-is-important/

Balibar, E (1991) 'The Nation Form: History and Ideology' in E Balibar and I Wallerstein (eds), *Race, Nation, Class: Ambiguous Identities* (London, Verso).

Banakar, R (2013) 'Can Legal Sociology Account for the Normativity of Law?' in M Baier (ed), *Social and Legal Norms. Towards a Socio-legal Understanding of Normativity* (Aldershot, Ashgate Publishing Limited).

Banda, F (2005) *Women, Law and Human Rights: An African Perspective* (Oxford, Hart Publishing).

—— (2009) 'Women and Access to Justice' in AK Dias and GH Welch (eds), *Justice for the Poor, Perspectives on Accelerating Access* (New Delhi, Oxford University Press).

—— (2012) 'Article 14' in M Freeman, C Chinkin and B Rudolf (eds), *The UN Convention on the Elimination of All Forms of Discrimination against Women: A Commentary* (Oxford, Oxford University Press).

—— (2016) 'Gender, Religion and Human Rights in Africa' in F Banda and L Fishbayn Joffe (eds), *Women's Rights and Religious Law: Domestic and International Perspectives* (New York, Routledge).

Barnes, S and Palmer, L, Kakuma, R and Larke, B (2019) 'Towards an integrated and accessible mental healthcare system in Timor-Leste' in A McWilliam and M Leach (eds), *Routledge Handbook of Contemporary Timor-Leste* (London, Routledge).

BBC Mundo (2016) 'Colombia: qué quieren cambiar de los acuerdos de paz con las FARC los promotores del "no" y cuán factible es que lo consigan', www.bbc.com/mundo/noticias-america-latina-37582078

Bell, C (2009) 'Transitional Justice, Interdisciplinarity and the State of the "Field" or "Non-Field"' 3 *International Journal of Transitional Justice* 5.

Bennett, T (2012) 'Access to Justice and Human Rights in the Traditional Courts of Sub-Saharan Africa' in T Bennet, E Brems, G Corradi, L Nijzink and M Schotsmans (eds), *African Perspectives on Tradition and Justice* (Cambridge, Intersentia).

Bentzon, AW and Hellum, A, Stewart, J, Ncube, W and Agersnap, T (1998) *Pursuing Grounded Theory in Law, South-North Experiences in Developing Women's Law* (Harare, Mond Books).

Bernstein, A (2009) 'Tort Theory, Microfinance, and Gender Equality Convergent in Pecuniary Reparations' in R Rubio-Marín (ed), *The Gender of Reparations. Unsettling Sexual Hierarchies while Redressing Human Rights Violations.* International Center for Transitional Justice (New York, Cambridge University Press).

Bernstein, R (1986) 'Rethinking the Social and the Political' 11 *Graduate Faculty Philosophy Journal* 111.

Bianchini, B and Rubert, S (2020) 'A Sustainable Psychosocial Model to Support the National Investigation and Prosecution of Conflict-related Sexual Violence Crimes' 18 *Journal of International Criminal Justice* 425.

Bistoen, G (2016) *Trauma, Ethics and the Political Beyond PTSD: The Dislocations of the Real* (Basingstoke, Palgrave MacMillan).

Bonthuys, E (2006) 'Women's Sexuality in the South African Constitution' 14 *Feminist Legal Studies* 391–406.

Braithwaite, J (2002) *Restorative Justice & Responsive Regulation* (Oxford, Oxford University Press).

Brammertz, S and Jarvis, M (2010) 'Lessons Learned in Prosecuting Gender Crimes under International Law: Experiences from the ICTY' in C Eboe-Osuji (ed), *Protecting Humanity: Essays in International Law and Policy in Honour of Navanethem Pillay.* (Leiden, Brill).

Bull, C (2008) *No Entry Without Strategy: Building the Rule of Law under UN Transitional Administration* (USA, United Nations University Press).

Burgess, P (2004) 'Justice and Reconciliation in East Timor. The Relationship between the Commission for Reception, Truth and Reconciliation and the Courts' 15 *Criminal Law Forum* 153.

Burt, J-M (2019) 'Gender Justice in Post-Conflict Guatemala: The Sepur Zarco Sexual Violence and Sexual Slavery Trial' 4 *Critical Studies* 63: https://genderandsecurity.org/sites/default/files/Burt_-_G_Justice_in_Post-Con_Guatemala_-_The_Sepur_Zarco_SV_Sexual_Slavery_Trial.pdf

Byrnes, A (2012) 'Article 1 [The Definition of Discrimination]' and 'Article 2 [State obligations]' in M Freeman, C Chinkin and B Rudolf (eds), *The UN Convention on the Elimination of All Forms of Discrimination against Women: A Commentary* (Oxford, Oxford University Press).

Cambodia Defenders Project (2012) *Asia-Pacific Regional Women's Hearing on Gender-Based Violence in Conflict*, www.gbvkr.org/wp-content/uploads/2013/01/Asia-Pacific-Regional-Womens-Hearing-on-GBV-in-Conflict-2012-Report.pdf

Cameron, I (2008) 'Individual Responsibility under National and International Law' in O Engdahl and P Wrange (eds), *Law at War: The Law as it Was and the Law as it Should Be* (Leiden, Martinus Nijhoff Publishers).

Campbell, K (2007) 'The Gender of Transitional Justice: Law, Sexual Violence and the International Criminal Tribunal for the Former Yugoslavia' 1 *The International Journal of Transitional Justice* 411.

Carrascalão, C (2021) *Open Letter to the President of Indonesia*, 13 August 2021, ETAN.

Cassel, D (2005) 'The Expanding Scope and Impact of Reparations Awarded by the Inter-American Court of Human Rights' in K De Feyter, S Parmentier, M Bossuyt and P Lemmens (eds), *Out of the Ashes: Reparations for Gross Violations of Human Rights* (Oxford, Intersentia).

CAVR (2005) *Chega! Report*. The Commission for Reception, Truth and Reconciliation in East Timor, http://chegareport.net/Chega%20All%20Volumes.pdf

Chappell, L (2016) *The Politics of Gender Justice at the International Criminal Court: Legacies and Legitimacy* (New York, Oxford University Press).

Charlesworth, H (2014) 'Two steps forward, one step back?: The field of women's human rights' 6 *European Human Rights Law Review* 560.

Charlesworth, H and Chinkin, C (2000) *The boundaries of international law. A feminist analysis* (Manchester, Manchester University Press).

Charlesworth, H, Chinkin, C and Wright, S (1991) 'Feminist Approaches to International Law' 85 *The American Journal of International Law* 613.

Chinkin, C (2001) 'Women's International Tribunal on Japanese Military Sexual Slavery' 95 *The American Journal of International Law* 335.

—— (2012) 'Article 3' in M Freeman, C Chinkin and B Rudolf (eds), *The UN Convention on the Elimination of All Forms of Discrimination against Women: A Commentary* (Oxford, Oxford University Press).

Chinkin, C and Kaldor, M (2013) 'Gender and New Wars' 67 *Journal of International Affairs* 167.

Chinkin, C and Paradine, K (2001) 'Vision and Reality: Democracy and Citizenship of Women in the Dayton Peace Accords' 26 *The Yale Journal of International Law* 103

Chinkin, C and Rees, M (2019) 'Commentary on Security Council Resolution 2467: Continued State Obligation and Civil Society Action on Sexual Violence in Conflict', *Centre for Women, Peace and Security*, www.lse.ac.uk/women-peace-security/assets/documents/2019/reports/WPS-Commentary-Report-online.pdf

Chopra, J (2000) 'The UN's Kingdom of East Timor' 42 *Survival* 27.

Clark, P (2008) 'Establishing a Conceptual Framework: Six Key Transitional Justice Themes' in P Clark and Z Kaufman (eds), *After Genocide: Transitional Justice, Post-conflict Reconstruction and Reconciliation in Rwanda and Beyond* (London, Hurst Publishers).

—— (2010) *The Gacaca Courts, Post-Genocide Justice and Reconciliation in Rwanda: Justice without Lawyers* (Cambridge, Cambridge University Press).

—— (2018) *Distant Justice. The Impact of the International Criminal Court on African Politics* (Cambridge, Cambridge University Press).

Clarke, KM (2009) *Fictions of Justice. The International Criminal Court and the Challenge of Legal Pluralism in Sub-Saharan Africa* (New York, Cambridge University Press).

CNN, *Prabowo gives awards to Eurico Guterres, thousands of ex-East Timor militia*, 16 December 2020, www.cnnindonesia.com/nasional/20201216075707-32-582690/prabowo-ganjar-ribuan-eks-pejuang-timor-timur-piagam-patriot

Cock, J (1991) *Colonels & Cadres. War & Gender in South Africa* (Cape Town, Oxford University Press).

Cockburn, C (2004) 'The Continuum of Violence: A Gender Perspective on War and Peace' in W Giles and J Hyndman (eds), *Sites of Violence: Gender and Conflict Zones* (Berkeley University of California Press).

Cohn, C (2013) 'Women and Wars: Toward a Conceptual Framework' in C Cohn (ed), *Women and Wars* (Cambridge, Polity Press).

'Comfort Women' Justice Coalition (2020) *About CM*, https://remembercomfortwomen.org.
Cook, R & Cusack, S (2010) *Gender Stereotyping: Transnational Legal Perspectives* (Philadelphia PA, University of Pennsylvania Press).
Corcoran-Nantes, Y (2009) 'The Politics of Culture and the Culture of Politics – a case study of gender and politics in Los Palos, Timor-Leste' 9 *Conflict, Security & Development* 165.
—— (2011) 'The Politics of Culture and the Culture of Politics: A case study of Gender and Politics in Los Palos, Timor-Leste' in V Harris and A Goldsmith (eds), *Security, Development and Nation-Building in Timor-Leste. A Cross-sectoral Assessment* (London, Routledge).
Corradi, G and Schotsmans, M (2012) 'Introduction' in T Bennet, E Brems, G Corradi, L Nijzink and M Schotsmans (eds), *African Perspectives on Tradition and Justice* (Cambridge, Intersentia).
Coulter, C (2009) *Bush Wives and Girl Soldiers, Women's Lives through War and Peace in Sierra Leone* (Ithaca NY, Cornell University Press).
Crenshaw, K (1989) 'Demarginalizing the Intersection of Race and Sex: A Black Feminist Critique of Antidiscrimination Doctrine, Feminist Theory and Antiracist Politics' 8 *University of Chicago Legal Forum* 139.
Cristalis, I and Scott, C (2005) *Independent Women. The story of women's activism in East Timor* (London, Catholic Institute for International Relations).
CNRT (2000) Outcomes of the CNRT National Congress 21st–30th August 2000. *United to Liberate. United to Construct.*
CTF (2008) *Per Memoriam Ad Spem. Final Report of the Commission of Truth and Friendship (CTF) Indonesia – Timor-Leste*, www.chegareport.net/wp-content/uploads/2014/10/CTF-report-English-Version.pdf
Cunha, T (2017) 'Beyond the Timorese nationalist orthodoxy: The 'Herstory' of Bi-Murak' in S Niner (ed), *Women and the Politics of Gender in Post-Conflict Timor-Leste. Between Heaven and Earth* (Oxford, Routledge).
Cusack, S (2014) 'Eliminating Judicial Stereotyping: Equal access to justice for women in gender-based violence cases', *Office of the High Commissioner for Human Rights*, 9 June 2014.
Das, V (2007) *Life and words: violence and the descent into the ordinary* (Berkeley CA, University of California Press).
Da Silva, K (2012) *As Nações Desunidas: Práticas da Onu e a Estruturação do Estado em Timor-Leste* (Brasil, Humanitas/UFMG).
De Araújo e Corte-Real, B, Cabasset, C and Durand, F (2014) *Timor-Leste contemporain: l'émergence d'une nation* (Bangkok, Irasec).
DeLargy, P (2013) 'Sexual Violence and Women's Health in War' in C Cohn (ed), *Women and Wars* (Cambridge, Polity Press).
Denov, MS and Drumbl, MA (2020) 'The Many Harms of Forced Marriage: Insights for Law from Ethnography in Northern Uganda' 18 *Journal of International Criminal Justice* 349.
De Sousa, C (2021) 'Around 856 Indonesian companies operate in Timor-Leste', *Tatoli*, www.tatoli.tl/en/2021/06/17/around-856-indonesian-companies-operate-in-timor-leste/
De Vos, D (2020) *Colombia's Constitutional Court issues landmark decision recognising victims of reproductive violence in conflict*, https://ilg2.org/2020/01/11/colombias-constitutional-court-issues-landmark-decision-recognising-victims-of-reproductive-violence-in-conflict/
Dias, AK (2009) 'International Law and Sources of Access to Justice' in AK Dias and GH Welch (eds), *Justice for the Poor, Perspectives on Accelerating Access* (New Delhi, Oxford University Press).
Dias, AK and Welch, GH (2009) 'Introduction' in AK Dias and GH Welch (eds), *Justice for the Poor, Perspectives on Accelerating Access* (New Delhi, Oxford University Press).
Dicker, R and Keppler, E (2004) *Beyond the Hague: The Challenges of International Justice, Human Rights Watch World Report 2004*, http://hrw.org/wr2k4/10.htm
Dogopol, U (2011) 'Crimes against the Comfort Women in the Tokyo Trial' in Y Tanaka, T McCormack and G Simpson (eds), *Beyond Victor's Justice? The Tokyo War Crimes Trial Revisited* (Leiden, Martinus Nijhoff Publishers).
Dowds, E (2019) 'Children Born of Sexual and Gender-Based Violence in Conflict: The International Criminal Court, Ecological Environments and Human Development' 33 *Children and Society* 226.

Duggan, C (2010) 'Editorial Note' 4 *The International Journal of Transitional Justice* 315.

Duggan, C and Abusharaf, AM (2006) *Reparation of Sexual Violence in Democratic Transitions: The Search for Gender Justice* (Oxford, Oxford University Press).

Duggan, C and Jacobson, R (2009) 'Reparation of Sexual and Reproductive Violence: Moving from Codification to Implementation' in R Rubio-Marín (ed), *The Gender of Reparations. Unsettling Sexual Hierarchies while Redressing Human Rights Violations* (New York, Cambridge University Press).

Du Toit, F (2018) *When Political Transitions Work. Reconciliation as Interdependence* (New York, Oxford University Press).

Ellickson, RC (1998) 'Law and Economics discover social norms' 27 *The Journal of Legal Studies* 537–52.

Elster, J (2004) *Closing the books: Transitional Justice in historical perspective* (Cambridge, Cambridge University Press).

Engle, K (2015) 'Anti-impunity and the Turn to Criminal Law in Human Rights' 100 *Cornell Law Review* 1069.

Enloe, C (1988) *Does Khaki Become You? The Militarization of women's Lives* (London, Pandora Press).

—— (2004) *The curious feminist: searching for women in a new age of empire* (Berkeley CA, University of California Press).

—— (2014) *Bananas, beaches and bases: making feminist sense of international politics* (Berkeley CA, University of California Press).

Evans, C (2012) *The Right to Reparation in International Law for Victims of Armed Conflict* (Cambridge, Cambridge University Press).

Evrard, E, Mejía Bonifazi, G and Destrooper, T (2021) 'The Meaning of Participation in Transitional Justice: A Conceptual Proposal for Empirical Analysis' 15 *International Journal of Transitional Justice* 428.

Favali, L and Pateman, R (2003) *Blood, Land, and Sex. Legal and Political Pluralism in Eritrea* (Bloomington IN, Indiana University Press).

Fernandes, C (2021) 'Indonesia's war against East Timor: how it ended' 32 *Small Wars & Insurgencies* 867.

Firchow, P and MacGinty, R (2019) 'Indivisibility as a Way of Life: Transformation in Micro-Processes of Peace in Northern Uganda' in P Gready and S Robins (eds), *From Transitional to Transformative Justice* (Cambridge, Cambridge University Press).

Fournet, C (2013) 'The adjudication of sex crimes under international criminal law' in L Yarwood (ed), *Women and Transitional Justice. The experience of women as participants* (Oxford, Routledge).

Fraser, N (1997) *Justice Interruptus: Critical Reflections on the 'Postsocialist' Condition* (New York, Routledge).

—— (2007) 'Feminist Politics in the Age of Recognition: A Two-Dimensional Approach to Gender Justice' 1 *Studies in Social Justice* 23.

—— (2008) *Scales of Justice. Reimagining Political Space in a Globalizing World* (Cambridge, Polity Press).

Friedman, R (2015) 'Restorative Justice in Sierra Leone: Promises and Limitations' in K Ainley, R Friedman and C Mahony (eds), *Evaluating Transitional Justice, Accountability and Peacebuilding in Post-Conflict Sierra Leone* (London, Palgrave Macmillan).

Fundasaun Mahein (2019) *Martial Arts Groups: Risks, Threats and Opportunities*, www.fundasaunmahein.org/2019/03/05/martial-arts-groups-risks-threats-and-opportunities/

Galtung, J (1969) 'Violence, Peace and Peace Research' 6 *Journal of Peace Research* 167.

Ganguly, M (2014) *Silenced and forgotten: Survivors of Nepal's conflict-era sexual violence* (Human Rights Watch).

Gilmore, S, Guillerot, J and Sandoval, C (2020) *Beyond Silence and Stigma: Crafting a Gender-Sensitive Approach for Victims of Sexual Violence in Domestic Reparations Programmes*, https://reparations.qub.ac.uk/assets/uploads/QUB-SGBV_Report_English_Web.pdf

Gluck, C (2007) 'Operations of Memory' in S Jager and R Mitter (eds), *Ruptured Histories: War, Memory, and the Post-Cold War in Asia* (Cambridge MA, Harvard University Press).

Goldblatt, B (1997) 'Violence, Gender and Human Rights: An Examination of South Africa's Truth and Reconciliation Commission', paper presented at the annual meeting of the Law and Society Association, May 29–June 1, 1997, St Louis, Missouri.

—— (2006) 'Evaluating the Gender Content of Reparations: Lessons from South Africa' in R Rubio-Marín (ed), *What happened to the women? Gender and reparations for human rights violations* (New York, Social Science Research Council).

Granville, D (2012) 'Self-Inflicted Genocide and State- and Nation-Building in post-Soviet Russia' in N Palmer, P Clark and D Granville (eds), *Critical Perspectives in Transitional Justice* (Cambridge, Intersentia).

Graybill, L (2012) 'Gender and Transitional Justice: Experiences from South Africa, Rwanda and Sierra Leone' in A Schnabel and A Tabyshalieva (eds), *Defying Victimhood: Women and Post-Conflict Peacebuilding* (Tokyo, United Nations University Press).

Gready, P (2019) 'Introduction' in P Gready and S Robins (eds), *From Transitional to Transformative Justice* (Cambridge, Cambridge University Press).

Gready, P and Robins, S (2019) 'From Transitional to Transformative Justice. A New Agenda for Practice' in P Gready and S Robins (eds), *From Transitional to Transformative Justice* (Cambridge, Cambridge University Press).

Guillemin, M and Gillan, L (2004) 'Ethics, Reflexivity, and 'Ethically Important Moments' in Research' 10 *Qualitative Inquiry* 261.

Guillerot, J (2006) 'Linking Gender and Reparations in Peru: A Failed Opportunity' in R Rubio-Marín (ed), *What happened to the women? Gender and reparations for human rights violations* (New York, Social Science Research Council).

Habermas, J (2001) 'Constitutional Democracy: A Paradoxical Union of Contradictory Principles?' 29 *Democracy, Law, Founding* 766.

Hale, S (2001) 'The Soldier and the State Post-Liberation Women: The Case of Eritrea' in M Waller and J Rycenga (eds), *Frontline Feminisms: Women, War, and Resistance* (London, Routledge).

Halley, J (2018) 'Varieties of Governance Feminism' in J Halley, P Kotiswaran, R Rebouché and H Shamir, *Governance Feminism. An Introduction* (Minneapolis MN, University of Minnesota Press).

Harhoff, F (2008) 'Sense and Sensibility in Sentencing' in O Engdahl and P Wrange (eds), *Law at War: The Law as it Was and the Law as it Should Be* (Leiden, Martinus Nijhoff Publishers).

Harris Rimmer, S (2010) *Gender and Transitional Justice: The Women of East Timor*, www.researchgate.net/publication/228195121_Gender_and_Transitional_Justice_The_Women_of_East_Timor

Hasegawa, S (2006) 'The Development Perspective: Three Imperatives for Sustainable Peace and Nation-building in a Post-Conflict Country' in N Azimi and CL Lin (eds), *United Nations as Peacekeeper and Nation-Builder: Continuity and Change – What Lies Ahead?* (Leiden, Martinus Nijhoff Publishers).

Haugbolle, S (2005) 'Public and Private Memory of the Lebanese Civil War' 25 *Comparative Studies of South Asia, Africa and the Middle East* 191.

Hayes, N (2016) 'Investigating sexual and gender-based violence', *Investigators Manual of the Institute for International Criminal Investigators* (IICI).

Hayner, P (2010) *Unspeakable Truths: Transitional Justice and the Challenge of Truth Commissions* (London, Routledge).

Heathcote, G (2018) 'Security Council Resolution 2242 on women, peace and security: progressive gains or dangerous development?' 32 *Global Society* 374.

Hicks, D (2007) 'Community and Nation-State in East Timor: A View from the Periphery' 23 *Anthropology Today, Royal Anthropological Institute* 13.

Hobsbawm, E (1983) 'Introduction: Inventing Traditions' in E Hobsbawm and T Ranger (eds), *The Invention of Tradition* (Cambridge, Cambridge University Press).

Hobfoll, SE et al (2007) 'Five Essential Elements of Immediate and Mid-term mass Trauma Intervention: Empirical Evidence' 70(4) *Psychiatry* 283.

Hohe, T (2003) 'Justice without judiciary in East Timor' 3 *Conflict, Security & Development* 335.

Hollis, B (2015) 'Evaluating the Legacy of the Special Court for Sierra Leone' in K Ainley, R Friedman and C Mahony (eds), *Evaluating Transitional Justice: Accountability and Peacebuilding in Post-Conflict Sierra Leone* (London, Palgrave Macmillan).

Holocaust Encyclopedia (2019), 'Jewish Councils (Judenraete)', *United States Holocaust Memorial Museum*, https://encyclopedia.ushmm.org/content/en/article/jewish-councils-judenraete

Holtmaat, R (2013) 'The CEDAW: A Holistic Approach to Women's Equality and Freedom' in A Hellum and H Aasen (eds), *Women's human rights: CEDAW in international, regional, and national law* (Cambridge, Cambridge University Press).

Hopgood, S (2017) 'Human Rights on the Road to Nowhere' in S Hopgood, J Snyder and L Vinjamuri (eds), *Human Rights Futures* (Cambridge, Cambridge University Press).

HRAP (2016) *Annual Report 2015/16, Kosovo Human Rights Advisory Panel*, M Nowicki, C Chinkin and F Tulkens, www.europarl.europa.eu/meetdocs/2014_2019/documents/dsee/dv/09_hr_advisory/09_hr_advisoryen.pdf

Human Rights Watch (2014) *Silenced and Forgotten: Survivors of Nepal's Conflict-Era Sexual Violence*, www.hrw.org/report/2014/09/23/silenced-and-forgotten/survivors-nepals-conflict-era-sexual-violence

—— (2004) *Indonesia: Justice Denied in East Timor Church Massacre*, www.hrw.org/news/2004/03/11/indonesia-justice-denied-east-timor-church-massacre

Hunt, J (2017) 'FOKUPERS – The East Timorese Women's Communication Forum: The development of Timor's first women's NGO' in S Niner (ed), *Women and the Politics of Gender in Post-Conflict Timor-Leste. Between Heaven and Earth* (Oxford, Routledge).

Hägerdal, H and Kammen, D (2017) 'The lost queens of Timor' in S Niner (ed), *Women and the Politics of Gender in Post-Conflict Timor-Leste. Between Heaven and Earth* (Oxford, Routledge).

IACHR (2015a) 'Access to Information, Violence against Women, and the Administration of Justice in the Americas', *Inter-American Commission on Human Rights*, www.oas.org/en/iachr/reports/pdfs/Access-information.pdf

—— (2015b) 'Legal Standards related to Gender Equality and Women's Rights in the Inter- American Human Rights System: Development and Application', *Inter-American Commission on Human Rights*, www.oas.org/en/iachr/reports/pdfs/LegalStandards.pdf

ICC (2019) 'ICC Trial Chamber VI declares Bosco Ntaganda guilty of war crimes and crimes against humanity', International Criminal Court Press Release, 8 July 2019, www.icc-cpi.int/Pages/item.aspx?name=pr1466.

ICRC (2004) 'How "grave breaches" are defined in the Geneva Conventions and Additional Protocols', *International Committee of the Red Cross*, www.icrc.org/eng/resources/documents/faq/5zmgf9.htm

—— (2005) 'Customary International Humanitarian Law, Volume I: Rules', JM Henckaerts and L Doswald-Beck with contributions by C Alvermann, K Dörmann and B Rolle, *International Committee of the Red Cross* (Cambridge, Cambridge University Press).

—— (2008) 'How is the Term "Armed Conflict" Defined in International Humanitarian Law?', *International Committee of the Red Cross*, www.icrc.org/eng/assets/files/other/opinion-paper-armed-conflict.pdf

—— (2014) 'The Geneva Conventions of 1949 and their Additional Protocols', *International Committee of the Red Cross*, www.icrc.org/en/document/geneva-conventions-1949-additional-protocols

ICTJ (2006a) 'Truth Commissions and Gender: Principles, Policies, and Procedures', drafted by V Nesiah et al, *International Center for Transitional Justice*, www.ictj.org/sites/default/files/ICTJ-Global-Commissions-Gender-2006-English_0.pdf

—— (2006b) 'The Serious Crimes Process in Timor-Leste: In Retrospect', drafted by C Reiger and M Wierda, *International Center for Transitional Justice*, www.ictj.org/sites/default/files/ICTJ-TimorLeste-Criminal-Process-2006-English.pdf

—— (2008) 'Too Much Friendship, Too Little Truth: Monitoring Report on the Commission of Truth and Friendship in Indonesia and Timor-Leste', drafted by M Hirst, *International Center for Transitional Justice*, www.ictj.org/sites/default/files/ICTJ-Indonesia-Commission-Monitoring-2008-English.pdf

—— (2010) 'Unfulfilled Expectations victims' perceptions of justice and reparations in Timor-Leste', *International Center for Transitional Justice*, www.ictj.org/publication/unfulfilled-expectations-victims-perceptions-justice-and-reparations-timor-leste

IDLO (2013) 'Accessing Justice: Models, Strategies and Best Practices on Women's Empowerment', *International Development Law Organization*, www.idlo.int/sites/default/files/Womens_Access_to_Justice_Full_Report.pdf

—— (2016) 'Linking formal and informal justice', *International Development Law Organization*, www.idlo.int/news/highlights/linking-formal-and-informal-justice

International Commission of Jurists (2016) *Women's Access to Justice for Gender-Based Violence – A Practitioners' Guide*, www.icj.org/wp-content/uploads/2016/03/Universal-Womens-accesss-to-justice-Publications-Practitioners-Guide-Series-2016-ENG.pdf

—— (2018) *The Right to a Remedy and Reparation for Gross Human Rights Violations. A Practitioners' Guide*, www.icj.org/wp-content/uploads/2018/11/Universal-Right-to-a-Remedy-Publications-Reports-Practitioners-Guides-2018-ENG.pdf

IPU (2019) 'Women in national parliaments', *The Inter-Parliamentary Union*, http://archive.ipu.org/wmn-e/ClaSSif.htm

Jackson, M (2015) 'A Conspiracy to Commit Genocide: Anti-Fertility Research in Apartheid's Chemical and Biological Weapons Programme' 13 *Journal of International Criminal Justice* 933.

—— (2019) 'Virtuous accomplices in International Criminal Law' 68 *International & Comparative Law Quarterly* 817.

JSMP (2002a) 'Timor serious crimes panel – first rape conviction', *Judicial System Monitoring Programme*, Press Release, 12 September 2002, https://etan.org/et2002c/september/08-14/12seriou.htm

—— (2002b) *The General Prosecutor v Joni Marques and 9 Others*, (The Los Palos Case), *Judicial System Monitoring Programme* (Case Report), https://jsmp.tl/wp-content/uploads/2012/05/The-Los-Palos-Case-2002.pdf

—— (2003) 'Lolotoe Militia Commander Sentenced To 12 Years', *Judicial System Monitoring Programme*, Press Release, 7 April 2003, www.etan.org/et2003/april/04/07sculol.htm

—— (2021) 'JSMP is disappointed with the amendments to the Law on Pardons and Commutation of Sentences', *Judicial System Monitoring Programme*, Press Release, 5 October 2021.

Justino, P, Cardona, I, Mitchell, R and Müller, C (2012) 'Quantifying the Impact of Women's Participation in Post-Conflict Economic Recovery', *Households in Conflict Network, The Institute of Development Studies, University of Sussex*, https://opendocs.ids.ac.uk/opendocs/bitstream/handle/123456789/3221/HiCN-WP-131.pdf?sequence=2&isAllowed=y

Kakuma, R, Barnes, S, Seixas dos Santos, H and Palmer, L (2015) 'Towards an integrated and accessible mental health care system in Timor-Leste', *Swinburne Press*, www.academia.edu/38524177/Towards_an_integrated_and_accessible_mental_health_care_system_in_Timor_Leste_Kakuma_R._Barnes_S._Seixas_dos_Santos_H._and_Palmer_L._

Kapur, R (2018) *Gender, Alterity and Human Rights. Freedom in a Fishbowl* (Northampton, Edward Elgar Publishing).

Katzenstein, S (2003) 'Hybrid Tribunals: Searching for Justice in East Timor' 16 *Harvard Human Rights Journal* 245.

Kelsall, M and Stepakoff, S (2007) ''When We Wanted to Talk About Rape': Silencing Sexual Violence at the Special Court for Sierra Leone' 1 *The International Journal of Transitional Justice* 335.

Kennedy, D (2004) *The Dark Sides of Virtue: Reassessing International Humanitarism* (Princeton NJ, Princeton University Press).

—— (2006) *Of Law and War* (Princeton NJ, Princeton University Press).

Kent, L (2008) 'Truth Seeking and Memory Politics in Post Conflict East Timor', 17th Biennial Conference of the Asian Studies Association of Australia, http://citeseerx.ist.psu.edu/viewdoc/download?doi=10.1.1.532.3800&rep=rep1&type=pdf

Kent, L and Kinsella, N (2015a) 'The Veterans' Valorisation Scheme: Marginalising Women's Contributions to the Resistance' in S Ingram, L Kent, and A McWilliam (eds), *A New Era? Timor-Leste after the UN* (Canberra, Australian National University Press).

—— (2015b) 'A Luta Kontinua (The Struggle Continues)' 17 *International Feminist Journal of Politics* 473.

King, J (2006) 'Gender and Reparations in Sierra Leone: The Wounds of War Remain Open' in R Rubio-Marín (ed), *What happened to the women? Gender and reparations for human rights violations* (New York, Social Science Research Council).

KPP-HAM (2000) 'Executive Summary Report', *The Commission for Human Rights Violations in East Timor*, Jakarta, 31 January 2000, www.unsw.adfa.edu.au/school-of-humanities-and-social-sciences/sites/default/files/documents/KPP-HAM.pdf

Komakech, D (2012) 'Reinventing and Validating the Cosmology and Ontology of Restorative Justice' in T Bennet, E Brems, G Corradi, L Nijzink and M Schotsmans (eds), *African Perspectives on Tradition and Justice* (Cambridge, Intersentia).

Koskenniemi, M (2008) 'Occupation and Sovereignty – Still a Useful Distinction?' in O Engdahl and P Wrange (eds), *Law at War: The Law as it Was and the Law as it Should Be* (Leiden, Martinus Nijhoff Publishers).

Kouvo, S (2011) 'Taking Women Seriously? Conflict, State-building and Gender in Afghanistan' in S Kouvo and Z Pearson (eds), *Feminist Perspectives on Contemporary International Law: Between Resistance and Compliance?* (Oxford, Hart Publishing).

Kristjánsdóttir, E, Nollkaemper, A and Ryngaert, C (2012) 'Concluding Observations' in E Kristjánsdóttir, A Nollkaemper and C Ryngaert (eds), *International Law in Domestic Courts: Rule of Law Reform in Post-Conflict States* (Cambridge, Intersentia).

Kumar, K (2012) 'Mass crimes and resilience of women: A cross-national perspective' in A Schnabel and A Tabyshalieva (eds), *Defying Victimhood: Women and Post-Conflict Peacebuilding* (Tokyo, United Nations University Press).

Laakso, J (2007) *Justice, Order and Peace: Transitional Justice and Peacebuilding in Timor-Leste* (PhD Thesis, University of Queensland), https://espace.library.uq.edu.au/view/UQ:133342

La'o Hamutuk (2010) *Maternus Bere indicted for Crimes Against Humanity in Suai Church Massacre and other Laksaur Militia activities*, www.laohamutuk.org/Justice/99/bere/09MaternusBere.htm

Lawry-White, M (2015) 'The Reparative Effect of Truth Seeking in Transitional Justice' 64 *International and Comparative Law Quarterly* 141.

Leach, M (2017) *Nation-building and national identity in Timor-Leste* (London, Routledge).

—— (2021) 'East Timorese politics in flux', *Inside Story*, https://insidestory.org.au/east-timorese-politics-in-flux/

Lee, RM (1993) *Doing Research on Sensitive Topics* (London, Sage).

Leebaw, B (2008) 'The Irreconcilable Goals of Transitional Justice' 30 *Human Rights Quarterly* 95.

Leimbach, D (2019) 'At the UN, the US Darkens Women's Right to Abortion', *Passblue*, www.passblue.com/2019/04/23/at-the-un-the-us-darkens-womens-right-to-abortion/

Lemarchand, R (2008) 'The Politics of Memory in Post-Genocide Rwanda' in P Clark and Z Kaufman (eds), *After Genocide: Transitional Justice, Post-Conflict Reconstruction and Reconciliation in Rwanda and beyond* (London, Hurst).

Lestari, K (2021) 'Outrage as Indonesia honors massacre-tainted militia leader', *UCA News*, www.ucanews.com/news/outrage-as-indonesia-honors-massacre-tainted-militia-leader/93699#

Lewin, M (2014) 'Putas y guerrilleras', *Página 12*, www.pagina12.com.ar/diario/elpais/1-245499-2014-05-05.html

Linton, S (2001) 'Cambodia, East Timor and Sierra Leone: Experiments in International Justice' 12 *Criminal Law Forum* 185.

Lixinski, L (2021) *Legalized Identities Cultural Heritage Law and the Shaping of Transitional Justice* (Cambridge, Cambridge University Press).

Loney, H (2014) "And I started to understand:' moments of illumination within women's oral narratives from Indonesian-occupied East Timor' 36 *The Oral History Association of Australia Journal* 61.

Lundy, P and McGovern, M (2008) 'Whose Justice? Rethinking Transitional Justice from the Bottom Up' 35 *Journal of Law and Society* 265.

Lusa (2008) *Government honors fifteen leading figures of the struggle of liberation*, www.etan.org/et2008/8august/16/11fifteen.htm?fbclid=IwAR2sNBJLZOxJ5RKy5KoXCcJRMg6eif8JYjEOiyHpaem-lyHMZh-IC9fT-Aw.

MacKinnon, C (2006) *Are Women Human? And Other International Dialogues* (Cambridge MA, Harvard University Press).

—— (2017) *Butterfly Politics* (Cambridge MA, Harvard University Press).

Maddox, S (2013) 'Lessons from the field. The inclusion of refugee women in transitional justice initiatives' in L Yarwood (ed), *Women and Transitional Justice. The experience of women as participants* (Oxford, Routledge).

Magalhães, F (2016) *Where is Nicolau Lobato?*, http://fidelismagalhaes.blogspot.com/2016/02/v-behaviorurldefaultvmlo.html

Maloney, K (2021) 'Ending Impunity for Forced Marriage in Conflict Zones: The Need for Greater Judicial Emphasis on the Human Rights of Girls' 19 *Journal of International Criminal Justice* 327.

Mamdani, M (2000) 'The Truth According to the TRC' in I Amadiume and A An-Na'im (eds), *The Politics of Memory: Truth, Healing and Social Justice* (London, Zed Books).

—— (2001a) 'Beyond Settler and Native as Political Identities: Overcoming the Political Legacy of Colonialism' 43 *Comparative Studies in Society and History* 651.

—— (2001b) *When Victims Become Killers: colonialism, nativism, and the genocide in Rwanda* (Princeton NJ, Princeton University Press).

Mannell, J, Ahmad, L and Ahmad, A (2018) 'Narrative storytelling as mental health support for women experiencing gender-based violence in Afghanistan' 214 *Social Science and Medicine* 91.

Martin, C and SáCouto, S (2020) 'Access to Justice for Victims of Conflict-related Sexual Violence: Lessons Learned from the Sepur Zarco Case' 18 *Journal of International Criminal Justice* 243.

Martin, I and Mayer-Rieckh, A (2005) 'The United Nations and East Timor: from self-determination to state-building' 12 *International Peacekeeping* 125.

Martins, F (2021) 'CNC organizes national conference to celebrate International Archives Day', *Tatoli*, www.tatoli.tl/en/2021/06/09/cnc-helds-national-conference-to-celebrate-international-archives-day/

Mazurana, D and Cole, L (2013) 'Women, Girls, and Disarmament, Demobilization and Reintegration (DDR)' in C Cohn (ed), *Women and Wars* (Cambridge, Polity Press).

McAuliffe, P (2011) 'UN Peace-Building, Transitional Justice and the Rule of Law in East Timor: The Limits of Institutional Responses to Political Questions' 58 *Netherlands International Law Review* 103.

McEvoy, K (2007) 'Beyond Legalism: Towards a Thicker Understanding of Transitional Justice' 34 *Journal of Law and Society* 411.

Meffert, SM, Shome, S, Neylan, TC, et al (2016) 'Health impact of human rights testimony: harming the most vulnerable?', *BMJ Global Health*, https://gh.bmj.com/content/bmjgh/1/1/e000001.full.pdf

Menon, V (2019) *Rising from the Ashes: UN Peacebuilding in Timor-Leste* (Singapore, World Scientific Publishing).

Merry, SE (2011) 'Measuring the World: Indicators, Human Rights, and Global Governance' 52 *Current Anthropology* S83.

Mills, C (1997) *The Racial Contract* (Ithaca NY, Cornell University Press).

Moyo, K (2012) 'Feminism, Postcolonial Legal Theory and Transitional Justice: A Critique of Current Trends' 1 *International Human Rights Law Review* 237.

Ndahinda, FM and Muleefu, A (2012) 'Revisiting the Legal and Socio-Political Foundations and (Western) Criticisms of Gacaca Courts' in T Bennet, E Brems, G Corradi, L Nijzink and M Schotsmans (eds), *African Perspectives on Tradition and Justice* (Cambridge, Intersentia).

Nesiah, V (2011) 'Missionary Zeal for a Secular Mission: Bringing Gender to Transitional Justice and Redemption to Feminism' in S Kouvo and Z Pearson (eds), *Feminist Perspectives on Contemporary International Law: between resistance and compliance?* (Oxford, Hart Publishing).

Niner, S (2011) 'Women in the post-conflict moment in Timorese society' in V Harris and A Goldsmith (eds), *Security, Development and Nation-Building in Timor-Leste. A Cross-sectoral Assessment* (Oxford, Routledge).
Ní Aoláin, F (1997) 'Radical Rules: The Effects of Evidential and Procedural Rules on the Regulation of Sexual Violence in War' 60 *Albany Law Review* 883.
—— (2019) 'Transformative Gender Justice?' in P Gready and S Robins (eds), *From Transitional to Transformative Justice* (Cambridge, Cambridge University Press).
Ní Aoláin, F and Turner, C (2007) 'Gender, Truth & Transition' 16 *UCLA Women's Law Journal* 229.
Ní Aoláin, F, and Valji, N (2019) 'Scholarly Debates and Contested Meanings of WPS' in S Davies and J True (eds), *The Oxford Handbook of Women, Peace, and Security* (New York, Oxford University Press).
Ní Aoláin, F, Haynes, DF and Cahn, N (2011) *On the frontlines: gender, war, and the post-conflict process* (New York, Oxford University Press).
Nino, CS (1991) 'The Duty to Punish Past Abuses of Human Rights Put into Context: The Case of Argentina' 100 *Yale Law Journal* 2619.
Nouwen, S (2006) '"Hybrid courts", the hybrid category of a new type of international crimes courts' 2 *Utrecht Law Review* 190.
Nouwen, S and Werner, W (2011) 'Doing Justice to the Political: The International Criminal Court in Uganda and Sudan' 21 *The European Journal of International Law* 941.
Nowicki, M, Chinkin, C and Tulkens, F (2017) 'Final Report of the Human Rights Advisory Panel' 28 *Criminal Law Forum* 77.
Oakley, A (1998) 'Science, gender, and women's liberation: an argument against postmodernism' 21 *Women's Studies International Forum* 133.
Oette, L (2009) 'Bringing Justice to Victims? Responses of Regional and International Human Rights Courts and Treaty Bodies to Mass Violations' in C Ferstman, M Goetz and A Stephens (eds), *Reparations for Victims of Genocide, War Crimes and Crimes against Humanity: Systems in Place and Systems in the Making* (Leiden, Martinus Nijhoff Publishers).
OHCHR (2005) *Rule of law tools for post-conflict states: Reparations Programmes* (Geneva, United Nations Publications).
—— (2006) *Rule of law tools for post-conflict states: Mapping the justice sector* (Geneva, United Nations Publications).
—— (2008) *Rule of law tools for post-conflict states: Maximizing the legacy of hybrid courts* (Geneva, United Nations Publications).
—— (2009) 'Analytical study on human rights and transitional justice', *Annual Report of the United Nations High Commissioner for Human Rights and Reports of the Office of the High Commissioner and the Secretary-General*, 6 August 2009, A/HRC/12/18.
—— (2011a) 'Interviewing' in *Manual on Human Rights Monitoring*, www.ohchr.org/Documents/Publications/Chapter11-MHRM.pdf
—— (2011b) 'Trauma and Self-Care' in *Manual on Human Rights Monitoring*, www.ohchr.org/Documents/Publications/Chapter12-MHRM.pdf
—— (2011c) 'Integrating Gender into Human Rights Monitoring' in *Manual on Human Rights Monitoring*, www.ohchr.org/Documents/Publications/Chapter15-20pp.pdf
—— (2014a) *Transitional Justice and Economics, Social and Cultural Rights*, www.ohchr.org/Documents/Publications/hr-pub-13-05.pdf
—— (2014b) *Sexual and gender-based violence in the context of transitional justice*, www.ohchr.org/documents/issues/women/wrgs/onepagers/sexual_and_gender-based_violence.pdf
—— (2015) *Commissions of Inquiry and Fact-Finding Missions on International Huma Rights and Humanitarian Law. Guidance and Practice*, www.ohchr.org/Documents/Publications/CoI_Guidance_and_Practice.pdf?fbclid=IwAR3Icvwlt_mI6uN-xhVSD36FyToMsXN6ZYbfv2hJFxfqKg2PH48Pu721nBU
—— (2016a) *Compilation of UN information. Working Group on the Universal Periodic Review*, 22 August 2016, A/HRC/WG.6/26/TLS/2.

—— (2016b) *Summary of stakeholders' information. Working Group on the Universal Periodic Review*, 17 August 2016, A/HRC/WG.6/26/TLS/3.

—— (2018) *Integrating a Gender Perspective into Human Rights Investigations. Guidance and Practice*, www.ohchr.org/Documents/Issues/Women/Publications/GenderIntegrationintoHRInvestigations.pdf

—— (2020) 'Justice for past crimes can build a shared future. Peacebuilding and sustaining peace: Transitional justice in conflict and post-conflict situations', *Statement to the Security Council*, www.ohchr.org/EN/NewsEvents/Pages/DisplayNews.aspx?NewsID=25552&LangID=E

Okello, MC and Hovil, L (2007) 'Confronting the Reality of Gender-based Violence in Northern Uganda' 1 *The International Journal of Transitional Justice* 433.

Okin, SM (1999) *Is Multiculturalism Bad for Women?* (Princeton NJ, Princeton University Press).

Oliveira, B, Gomes, C and dos Santos, R (2015) *Os direitos fundamentais em Timor-Leste: Teoria e prática* (Porto Alegre, Simplíssimo).

Olsen, T, Payne, A and Reiter, A (2010) 'Transitional justice in the world, 1970–2007: Insights from a new dataset' 47 *Journal of Peace Research* 980.

Ostowar, D (2020) *Transitional Justice in Peacebuilding: Actor-Contingent and Malleable Justice* (London, Routledge).

Palmer, N (2012) 'Understandings of International Law in Rwanda' in E Kristjánsdóttir, A Nollkaemper and C Ryngaert (eds), *International Law in Domestic Courts: Rule of Law Reform in Post-Conflict States* (Cambridge, Intersentia).

—— (2015) *Courts in Conflict. Interpreting the layers of justice in post-genocide Rwanda* (New York, Oxford University Press).

Parpart, J and Parashar, S (2019) 'Introduction: rethinking the power of silence in insecure and gendered sites' in J Parpart and S Parashar (eds), *Rethinking Silence, Voice and Agency in Contested Gendered Terrains* (Oxford, Routledge).

Peake, G (2013) *Beloved Land: stories, struggles, and secrets from Timor-Leste* (London, Scribe).

Pereira, M (2017) 'Chega! for Us: Socializing a Living Document' in D Webster (ed), *Flowers in the Wall: Truth and Reconciliation in Timor-Leste, Indonesia, and Melanesia.* (Calgary, University of Calgary Press).

Plan International (2016) 'Counting the Invisible. Using Data to Transform the Lives of Girls and Women by 2030', *State of the World's Girls report*, https://plan-uk.org/file/because-i-am-a-girl-2016-counting-the-invisiblepdf/download?token=u2So9CKR

—— (2017) *Timor-Leste's proposed family planning policy will deny girls their rights*, https://plan-international.org/blog/2017/08/timor-lestes-proposed-family-planning-policy-will-deny-girls-their-rights

Post-CAVR (2008) *Timor-Leste. As Mulheres e o Conflito*. Audiência Pública Nacional, 28 e 29 de Abril de 2003 (Berlin, BMZ).

Rahmani, B (2020) 'Timor-Leste's New Kingmakers', *The Diplomat*, https://magazine.thediplomat.com/#/issues/-M8FAQGYM4DzL1ar5rXG/preview/-M8FATCVRHR8VjnKqrl8

Reading, A (2019) 'The Restitutional Assemblage: The Art of Transformative Justice at Parramatta Girls Home, Australia' in P Gready and S Robins (eds), *From Transitional to Transformative Justice* (Cambridge, Cambridge University Press).

Reilly, N (2009) *Women's Human Rights. Seeking Gender Justice in a Globalizing Age* (Cambridge, Polity Press).

Rees, M and Chinkin, C (2016) 'Post Conflict Transition: The Transformative Power of Economic and Social Rights' 48 *Journal of International Law and Politics* 1211.

Richards, E (2017) 'A gender perspective on the Catholic Church and reproductive health rights in Timor-Leste' in S Niner (ed), *Women and the Politics of Gender in Post-Conflict Timor-Leste. Between Heaven and Earth* (Oxford, Routledge).

Ricouer, P (2004) *Memory, History, Forgetting* (Chicago IL, The University of Chicago Press).

Robins, S (2012) 'Challenging the Therapeutic Ethic: A Victim-Centred Evaluation of Transitional Justice Process in Timor-Leste' 6 *The International Journal of Transitional Justice* 83.

—— (2019) 'Conclusion: Toward Transformative Justice' in P Gready and S Robins (eds), *From Transitional to Transformative Justice* (Cambridge, Cambridge University Press).

Roht-Arriaza, N (2019) 'Measures of Non-Repetition in Transitional Justice: The Missing Link?' in P Gready and S Robins (eds), *From Transitional to Transformative Justice* (Cambridge, Cambridge University Press).
Ronen, Y (2012) 'The Use and Abuse of International Law' in E Kristjánsdóttir, A Nollkaemper and C Ryngaert (eds), *International Law in Domestic Courts: Rule of Law Reform in Post-Conflict States* (Cambridge, Intersentia).
Ross, F (2003) *Bearing Witness. Women and the Truth and Reconciliation Commission in South Africa* (London, Pluto Press).
Rothschild, A (2017) 'Victims versus Veterans: Agency, Resistance and Legacies of Timor-Leste's Truth Commission' 11 *International Journal of Transitional Justice* 443.
Rubio-Marín, R (2006) 'Introduction: The Gender of Reparations: Setting the Agenda' in R Rubio-Marín (ed), *What happened to the women? Gender and reparations for human rights violations* (New York, Social Science Research Council).
—— (2009) 'The Gender of Reparations in Transitional Societies' in R Rubio-Marín (ed), *The Gender of Reparations. Unsettling Sexual Hierarchies while Redressing Human Rights Violations* (New York, Cambridge University Press).
Rubio-Marín, R and de Greiff, P (2007) 'Women and Reparations' 1 *The International Journal of Transitional Justice* 318.
Sánchez Parra, T (2018) 'The hollow Shell: Children Born of War and the Realities of the Armed Conflict in Colombia' 12 *International Journal of Transitional Justice* 45.
Sannerholm, R (2012) *Rule of Law after War and Crisis: Ideologies, Norms and Methods* (Cambridge, Intersentia).
Schabas, W (2008) 'Post-Genocide Justice in Rwanda: A Spectrum of Opinions' in P Clark and Z Kaufman (eds), *After Genocide: Transitional Justice, Post-Conflict Reconstruction and Reconciliation in Rwanda and beyond* (London, Hurst).
Schömer, E (2013) 'Norms and Normality – Framing Normality: An Eye-Catcher on the Swedish Labour Court' in M Baier (ed), *Social and Legal Norms. Towards a Socio-legal Understanding of Normativity* (Aldershot, Ashgate Publishing).
SDG16hub (2019) 'Enabling the implementation of the 2030 Agenda through SDG 16+: Anchoring peace, justice and inclusion', *Summary of key trends on peace, justice and inclusion*, www.sdg16hub.org/system/files/2019-07/GA%20SDG16%2BReport%20-%20SUMMARY%20OF%20TRENDS.pdf
Sellers, P (2011) 'Wartime Female Slavery: Enslavement?' 44 *Cornell International Law Journal* 115.
Sen, A (2010) *The Idea of Justice* (London, Penguin Books).
Shaw, R (2005) *Rethinking Truth and Reconciliation Commissions: Lessons from Sierra Leone.* United States Institute for Peace. Special Report no 130.
Siapno, J (2017) 'Politika Taka Malu, Censorship, and Silencing: Virtuosos of Clandestinity and One's Relationship to Truth and Memory' in D Webster (ed), *Flowers in the Wall: Truth and Reconciliation in Timor-Leste, Indonesia, and Melanesia* (Calgary AB, University of Calgary Press).
Sikkink, K (2017) *Evidence for Hope: Making Human Rights Work in the 21st Century* (Princeton NJ, Princeton University Press).
Sikkink, K and Booth, C (2007) 'Errors about Trials: The Emergence and Impact of the Justice Cascade', *Paper presented at NYU Law School*, www.iilj.org/courses/documents/Session11.Sikkink.pdf
Silva, S (2015) 'Multi-country review on Veterans programs. The case study of Timor-Leste', *Document prepared for the World Bank.*
Skaar, E, and Gianella Malca, C, (2015) 'Transitional justice alternatives: claims and counterclaims' in E Skaar, C Gianella Malca and T Eide (eds), *After Violence: Transitional Justice, Peace and Democracy* (Oxford, Routledge).
Solnit, R (2017) *The Mother of All Questions* (London, Granta Publications).
Steele, J (2002) 'Nation Building in East Timor' 19 *World Policy Journal* 76.
Strating, R (2019) *The Post-colonial Security Dilemma: Timor-Leste and the International Community* (Singapore, ISEAS Publishing).

Strohmeyer, H (2001) 'Making multilateral interventions work: the UN and the creation of transitional justice systems in Kosovo and East Timor' 25 *Fletcher Forum of World Affairs* 107.

Svensson, M (2013) 'Norms in law and Society: Towards a Definition of the Socio-Legal Concept of Norms' in M Baier (ed), *Social and Legal Norms. Towards a Socio-legal Understanding of Normativity* (Aldershot, Ashgate Publishing).

Tamale, S (1999) *When Hens Begin to Crow: Gender and Parliamentary Politics in Uganda* (Boulder CO, Westview Press).

Taur Matan Ruak (2020) *Speech of the Prime Minister in occasion of the 2021 General State Budget Law Proposal*, 30 November 2020, http://timor-leste.gov.tl/wp-content/uploads/2020/11/ENG-Speech-of-H.E.-the-Prime-Minister-of-Republic-Democratic-of-Timor-Leste-Taur-Matan-Ruak_ENG.pdf

Teitel, RG (2003) 'Transitional justice genealogy' 16 *Harvard Human Rights Journal* 69.

The Asia Foundation (2016) 'Understanding Violence Against Women and Children in Timor-Leste: Findings from the Nabilan Baseline Report', *Report*. Report prepared by the Equality Institute, https://asiafoundation.org/wp-content/uploads/2016/05/UnderstandingVAWTL_main.pdf

The Guardian (2016) *Congo politician guilty in first ICC trial to focus on rape as a war crime*, www.theguardian.com/world/2016/mar/21/icc-finds-ex-congolese-vice-president-jean-pierre-bemba-guilty-of-war-crimes

The Washington Post (2003) *Most Suspects in East Timor Violence*. Written by Sipress, A., www.globalpolicy.org/component/content/Article/163/29181.html

Torgovnik, J (2019) 'Rwanda's Children of Rape Have Come of Age', *The New York Times*, www.nytimes.com/2019/03/30/opinion/rwandas-children-of-rape-have-come-of-age.html

TPO (2015) 'A Study about Victims' Participation at the Extraordinary Chambers in the Courts of Cambodia and Gender-Based Violence under the Khmer Rouge Regime', *Transcultural Psychosocial Organization Cambodia*, https://tpocambodia.org/wp-content/uploads/2014/06/TPO_GBV-under-the-Khmer-Rouge_Report_20151.pdf

Trindade, J and Castro, B (2007) 'Rethinking Timorese Identity as a Peacebuilding Strategy: The Lorosa'e – Loromonu Conflict from a Traditional Perspective', *The European Union's Rapid Reaction Mechanism Programme*, www.indopubs.com/Trindade_Castro_Rethinking_Timorese_Identity.pdf

UN (1998) *Report of the Secretary-General on the question of integrating the human rights of women throughout the United Nations system*, 25 March 1998, E/CN.4/1998/49.

—— (1999a) *UN General Assembly, Situation of human rights in East Timor.* Report on the joint mission to East Timor undertaken by the Special Rapporteur of the Commission on Human Rights on extrajudicial, summary or arbitrary executions, the Special Rapporteur of the Commission on the question of torture and the Special Rapporteur of the Commission on violence against women, its causes and consequences, in accordance with Commission resolution 1999/S-4/1 of 27 September 1999, 10 December 1999, A/54/660.

—— (1999b) *UN Commission on Human Rights, Report of the Special Rapporteur on violence against women, its causes and consequences, Ms. Radhika Coomaraswamy, Mission to Indonesia and East Timor on the issue of violence against women (20 November-4 December 1998)*, Fifty-fifth session, 21 January 1999, E/CN.4/1999/68/Add.3.

—— (2004) *The rule of law and transitional justice in conflict and post-conflict societies*, 23 August 2004, S/2004/616.

—— (2006) *Report of the Secretary-General on Timor-Leste pursuant to Security Council resolution 1690*. 8 August 2006, S/2006/628.

—— (2008a) *Country mission report on the Democratic Republic of Congo*. Report of the Special Rapporteur on violence against women, its causes and consequences, Yakin Ertürk, 28 February 2008, A/hRC/7/6/Add.4.

—— (2008b) *Report of the Special Rapporteur on the independence of judges and lawyers*, Despouy, L. *on the Promotion and Protection of all Human Rights, Civil, Political, Economic, Social and Cultural Rights, including the Right to Development*, 13 May 2008, A/HRC/8/4.

—— (2010) *Thematic report submitted to the Human Rights Council by Rashida Manjoo that focuses on the topic of reparations to women who have been subjected to violence in contexts of both peace and post-conflict*. Report of the Special Rapporteur on violence against women, its causes and consequences. A/HRC/14/22.

—— (2014) *Sexual Violence: A Tool of War. Background Note*, www.un.org/en/preventgenocide/rwanda/assets/pdf/Backgrounder%20Sexual%20Violence%202014.pdf

—— (2018) *A Practitioner's Toolkit on Women's Access to Justice Programming*, www.unodc.org/pdf/criminal_justice/WA2J_Consolidated.pdf

—— (2019a) *Timor-Leste's commitment to customary justice and conservation sets examples for other countries*. UN Special Rapporteur on the rights of indigenous peoples, Victoria Tauli-Corpuz. Press Release, www.ohchr.org/SP/NewsEvents/Pages/DisplayNews.aspx?NewsID=24493&LangID=E

—— (2019b) *Report of the Special Rapporteur on the right of everyone to the enjoyment of the highest attainable standard of physical and mental health on the right to mental health*, 12 April 2019, A/HRC/41/34.

—— (2020) *The gender perspective in transitional justice processes*, Report of the Special Rapporteur on the promotion of truth, justice, reparation and guarantees of non-recurrence. A/75/174.

—— (2021a) *Thematic report on Rape as a grave, systematic and widespread human rights violation, a crime and a manifestation of gender-based violence against women and girls, and its prevention*, Report of the Special Rapporteur on violence against women, its causes and consequences. A/HRC/47/26.

—— (2021b) *Transitional justice measures and the legacy of human rights violations in colonial contexts*, Report of the Special Rapporteur on the promotion of truth, justice, reparation and guarantees of non-recurrence. A/76/180.

UNDDR (2006) Introduction to the IDDRS (Module 1.10) and Glossary: Terms and Definitions (Module 1.20), *The Integrated Disarmament, Demobilization and Reintegration Standards (IDDRS)*, https://unddr.org/uploads/documents/IDDRS%201.20%20Glossary.pdf

UNDP (2011) *Customary Law and Domestic Violence in Timor-Leste. Approaches to Domestic Violence against Women in Timor-Leste: A Review of the Literature*. Drafted by Kovar, A. Justice System Program. UNDP Timor-Leste, www.undp.org/content/dam/timorleste/docs/JSP%20docs/TL_JSP_LitReview%20DV_CL_FINALJan2011.pdf

—— (2013) *Breaking the cycle of domestic violence in Timor-Leste, Access to Justice options, barriers and decision-making processes in the context of legal pluralism*. Justice System Programme, UNDP Timor-Leste, www.undp.org/content/dam/timorleste/docs/reports/DG/Domestic%20Violence%20Report%20_with%20cover%20FINAL.pdf

UNFPA (2017) 'Teenage Pregnancy and Early Marriage in Timor-Leste', *Secretariat of State for Youth and Sports, UNFPA and Plan International. Drafted by D Cummins*, https://plan-international.org/tpem-report

UNTAET (2001) *East Timor: Backgrounder – Justice and serious crimes, UN Transitional Administration in East Timor*. 9 July 2001, https://reliefweb.int/report/timor-leste/east-timor-backgrounder-justice-and-serious-crimes.

UN Women (2015) 'Guidebook on CEDAW General Recommendation No. 30 and the UN Security Council Resolutions on Women, Peace and Security', *drafted by A Swaine and C O'Rourke*, www.unwomen.org/-/media/headquarters/attachments/sections/library/publications/2015/guidebook-cedaw-general-recommendation-30-women-peace-security-en.pdf?la=en&vs=1850.

UN Women (2018) 'Women's multiple pathways to justice: Alternative Dispute Resolution and the impact on women in Timor-Leste', *drafted by D Cummins*, http://asiapacific.unwomen.org/en/digital-library/publications/2019/03/multiple-pathways-to-justice

—— (2019) *Statement by UN Women Executive Director Phumzile Mlambo-Ngcuka on the conviction of Bosco Ntaganda by the International Criminal Court*, www.unwomen.org/en/news/stories/2019/7/statement-ed-conviction-of-bosco-ntaganda-by-the-international-criminal-court

US Department of State (2018) 'Timor-Leste 2018 Human Rights Report. Bureau of Democracy', *Human Rights and Labor*, www.state.gov/documents/organization/289331.pdf

—— (2021) '2020 Country Reports on Human Rights Practices: Timor-Leste. Bureau of Democracy', *Human Rights and Labor*, www.state.gov/reports/2020-country-reports-on-human-rights-practices/

Utas, M (2005) 'West-African Warscapes: Victimcy, Girlfriending, Soldiering: Tactic Agency in a Young Woman's Social Navigation of the Liberian War Zone' 78 *Anthropological Quarterly* 403.

van Boven, T (2009) 'Victims' Rights to a Remedy and Reparation: The New United Nations Principles and Guidelines' in C Ferstman, M Goetz and A Stephens (eds), *Reparations for Victims of Genocide, War Crimes and Crimes against Humanity: Systems in Place and Systems in the Making* (Leiden, Martinus Nijhoff Publishers).

Vastapuu, L (2018) *Liberia's Women Veterans* (London, Zed Books).

Vice (2017) 'The Lost Children of East Timor', *Vice*, www.vice.com/en_asia/Article/53q7mn/the-lost-children-of-east-timor

Vinjamuri, L (2017) 'Human Rights Backlash' in S Hopgood, J Snyder and L Vinjamuri (eds), *Human Rights Futures* (Cambridge, Cambridge University Press).

Waldorf, L (2009) 'Goats and Graves: Reparations in Rwanda's Community Courts' in C Ferstman, M Goetz and A Stephens (eds), *Reparations for Victims of Genocide, War Crimes and Crimes against Humanity, Systems in Place and Systems in the Making* (Leiden, Martinus Nijhoff), 515–39.

—— (2019) 'Between Transition and Transformation: Legal Empowerment as Collective Reparations' in P Gready and S Robins (eds), *From Transitional to Transformative Justice* (Cambridge, Cambridge University Press).

Walsh, A (2013) 'International criminal justice and the girl child' in L Yarwood (ed), *Women and Transitional Justice. The experience of women as participants* (Oxford, Routledge).

Walsh, P (2011) *At the Scene of the Crime. Essays, reflections and poetry on East Timor*, 1999–2010 (Victoria, Mosaic Press).

—— (2017) 'Shining Chega!'s Light into the Cracks' in D Webster (ed), *Flowers in the Wall: Truth and Reconciliation in Timor-Leste, Indonesia, and Melanesia* (Calgary, University of Calgary Press).

Wandita, G, Campbell-Nelson, K and Pereira, M (2006) 'Learning to Engender Reparations in Timor-Leste: Reaching Out to Female Victims' in R Rubio-Marín (ed), *What happened to the women? Gender and reparations for human rights violations* (New York, Social Science Research Council).

Weill, S and Jovanović, I (2012) 'War Crimes Prosecution in a Post-Conflict Era and a Pluralism of Jurisdictions: The Experience of the Belgrade War crimes Chamber' in E Kristjánsdóttir, A Nollkaemper and C Ryngaert (eds), *International Law in Domestic Courts: Rule of Law Reform in Post-Conflict States* (Cambridge, Intersentia).

What Works (2018) 'Intersections of violence against women and girls with state-building and peace-building: Lessons from Nepal, Sierra Leone and South Sudan', *What Works to prevent violence against Women and Girls in Conflict and Humanitarian Crises*, a report drafted by A Swaine, M Spearing, M Murphy and M Contreras, https://globalwomensinstitute.gwu.edu/sites/g/files/zaxdzs1356/f/downloads/P784%20IRC%20What%20Works%20Report_LR.pdf

Wittkopp, S (2012) 'Article 7' in M Freeman, C Chinkin and B Rudolf (eds), *The UN Convention on the Elimination of All Forms of Discrimination against Women: A Commentary* (Oxford, Oxford University Press).

WLSA (1999) *Botswana, Chasing the Mirage: Women and the Administration of Justice* (Gaborone, Women and Law in Southern Africa Research Trust).

Women's Initiatives for Gender Justice (2018) *Gender Report Card on the International Criminal Court*, http://4genderjustice.org/pub/Gender-Report-Card-on-the-ICC-2018.pdf

Women's Link Worldwide (2019) *Convictions and pending prosecutions for sexual and reproductive violence committed against forcibly recruited, civilian, and combatant women and girls in the armed conflict of Colombia*, www.womenslinkworldwide.org/en/files/3100/convictions-and-pending-prosecutions-for-sexual-and-reproductive-violence-committed-against-women-and-girls-in-the-armed-conflict-of-colombia.pdf

World Bank (2004) *Veterans – Pensions and other compensation in post-conflict countries*, https://documents1.worldbank.org/curated/en/795621468319558367/pdf/333910rev0PRPNoteVeterans.pdf

—— (2019) *The World Bank in Timor-Leste: Overview*, www.worldbank.org/en/country/timor-leste/overview

WSD Handa Center for Human Rights and International Justice (2017) *Documentary Co-Produced by Handa Center Screens in Cambodia, Stanford University*, https://handacenter.stanford.edu/news/documentary-co-produced-handa-center-screens-cambodia

GENERAL COMMENTS, GENERAL RECOMMENDATIONS AND CONCLUDING OBSERVATIONS

CAT (2008) *General Comment No 2, Implementation of article 2 by States parties*, Committee against Torture, 24 January 2008, CAT/C/GC/2.

—— (2012) *General Comment No 3, Implementation of Article 14 by States parties*, Committee against Torture, 13 December 2012, CAT/C/GC/3.

—— (2017) *Concluding observations on the initial report of Timor-Leste*, Committee against Torture, 15 December 2017, CAT/C/TLS/CO/1.

CEDAW (2006) *Concluding comments of the Committee on the Elimination of Discrimination against Women: Bosnia and Herzegovina*, 2 June 2006, CEDAW/C/BIH/CO/3.

—— (2015) *Concluding observations on the combined second and third periodic reports of Timor-Leste*, Committee on the Elimination of Discrimination against Women, 24 November 2015, CEDAW/C/TLS/CO/2–3.

—— (1991) *General Recommendation No 16: Unpaid women workers in rural and urban family enterprises*, A/46/38.

—— (1991) *General Recommendation No 17: Measurement and quantification of the unremunerated domestic activities of women and their recognition in the gross national product*, A/46/38.

—— (1992) *General Recommendation No 19: Violence against women*, Committee on the Elimination of Discrimination against Women, A/47/38.

—— (1997) *General Recommendation No 23: Political and Public Life*, Committee on the Elimination of Discrimination against Women, A/52/38.

—— (1999) *General Recommendation No 24: Article 12 of the Convention (women and health)*, Committee on the Elimination of Discrimination against Women.

—— (2004) *General Recommendation No 25, on Article 4, paragraph 1, of the Convention on the Elimination of All Forms of Discrimination against Women, on temporary special measures*, Committee on the Elimination of Discrimination against Women.

—— (2010) *General Recommendation No 27 on older women and protection of their human rights*, 16 December 2010, CEDAW/C/GC/27.

—— (2010) *General Recommendation No 28 on the core obligations of States parties under Article 2 of the Convention on the Elimination of All Forms of Discrimination against Women*, 16 December 2010, CEDAW/C/GC/28.

—— (2013) *General Recommendation No 30 on women in conflict prevention, conflict and post-conflict situations*, Committee on the Elimination of Discrimination against Women, 18 October 2013, CEDAW/C/GC/30.

—— (2015) *General Recommendation No. 33 on women's access to justice*, Committee on the Elimination of Discrimination against Women, 23 July 2015, CEDAW/C/GC/33.

—— (2016) *General Recommendation No 34 on the rights of rural women*, Committee on the Elimination of Discrimination against Women, 4 March 2016, CEDAW/C/GC/34.

—— (2017) *General Recommendation No 35 on gender-based violence against women, updating general recommendation No 19*, Committee on the Elimination of Discrimination against Women, 14 July 2017, CEDAW/C/GC/35.

—— (2017) *General Recommendation No 36 on the right of girls and women to education*, Committee on the Elimination of Discrimination against Women, 16 November 2017, CEDAW/C/GC/36.

CERD (2000) *General Recommendation No 25 on gender-related dimensions of racial discrimination*, Committee on the Elimination of Racial Discrimination, 20 March 2000, A/55/18.
CESCR (2005) *General Comment No 16 The Equal Right of Men and Women to the Enjoyment of All Economic, Social and Cultural Rights (Art. 3 of the Covenant)*, Committee on Economic, Social and Cultural Rights, 11 August 2005, E/C.12/2005/4.
—— (2008) *General Comment No 19 The right to social security (art. 9)*, Committee on Economic, Social and Cultural Rights, 4 February 2008, E/C.12/GC/19.
—— (2009) *General Comment No 20 Non-discrimination in economic, social and cultural rights (art 2, para 2, of the International Covenant on Economic, Social and Cultural Rights)*, Committee on Economic, Social and Cultural Rights, 2 July 2009, E/C.12/GC/20.
—— (2009) *General Comment No 21 on the right of everyone to take part in cultural life (art 15, para 1 (a) of the International Covenant on Economic, Social and Cultural Rights)*, Committee on Economic, Social and Cultural Rights, 21 December 2009, E/C.12/GC/21.
—— (2016) *General Comment No 22 on the right to sexual and reproductive health (article 12 of the International Covenant on Economic, Social and Cultural Rights)*, Committee on Economic, Social and Cultural Rights, 2 May 2016, E/C.12/GC/22.
CRC (2013) *General Comment No 14 on the right of the child to have his or her best interests taken as a primary consideration (art 3, para 1)*, Committee on the Rights of the Child, 29 May 2013, CRC/C/GC/14.
—— (2015) *Concluding observations on the combined second and third periodic reports of Timor-Leste*, Committee on the Rights of the Child, 30 October 2015, CRC/C/TLS/CO/2-3.
—— (2016) *General Comment No 20 on the implementation of the rights of the child during adolescence*, Committee on the Rights of the Child, 6 December 2016, CRC/C/GC/20.
CRPD (2016) *General comment No 3 (2016), Article 6: Women and girls with disabilities*, Committee on the Rights of Persons with Disabilities, 2 September 2016, CRPD/C/GC/3.
HRC (1984) *General Comment No 13 Equality before the courts and the right to a fair and public hearing by an independent court established by law (Art. 14)*. UN Human Rights Committee, 13 April 1984.
—— (2000) *General Comment No 28: Article 3 (The Equality of Rights Between Men and Women)*. UN Human Rights Committee, 29 March 2000, CCPR/C/21/Rev.1/Add.10.
—— (2004) *General Comment No 31: The nature of the general legal obligation imposed on States Parties to the Covenant*. UN Human Rights Committee, 26 May 2004, CCPR/C/21/Rev.1/Add. 13
—— (2007) *General Comment No 32 on Article 14: Right to equality before courts and tribunals and to a fair trial*. UN Human Rights Committee, 23 August 2007, CCPR/C/GC/32.

HUMAN RIGHTS AND CRIMINAL LAW INSTRUMENTS (IN CHRONOLOGICAL ORDER)

The Charter of the United Nations (UN Charter), San Francisco 26 June 1945.
Universal Declaration of Human Rights (UDHR), adopted by General Assembly on 10 December 1948.
International Covenant on Civil and Political Rights (ICCPR), adopted by General Assembly on 16 December 1966.
International Covenant on Economic, Social and Cultural Rights (ICESCR), adopted by General Assembly on 19 December 1966.
Convention on the Elimination of All Forms of Racial Discrimination (CERD), adopted by General Assembly on 21 December 1965.
Convention on the Elimination of All Forms of Discrimination against Women (CEDAW), adopted by General Assembly on 18 December 1979.
Convention against Torture and Other Cruel, Inhuman or Degrading Treatment or Punishment (CAT), adopted by General Assembly on 10 December 1984.

Basic Principles on the Independence of the Judiciary (BPIJ), adopted by the Seventh UN Congress on the Prevention of Crime and the Treatment of Offenders held at Milan from 26 August to 6 September 1985 and endorsed by General Assembly resolutions 40/32 of 29 November 1985 and 40/146 of 13 December 1985.

Declaration of Basic Principles of Justice for Victims of Crime and Abuse of Power, adopted by the 96th plenary meeting of the UNGA, 29 November 1985, A/RES/40/34.

Convention on the Rights of the Child (CRC), adopted by General Assembly on 20 November 1989.

Basic Principles on the Role of Lawyers (BPRL), adopted by the Eighth UN Congress on the Prevention of Crime and the Treatment of Offenders, Havana, Cuba, 27 August to 7 September 1990.

Guidelines on the Role of Prosecutors, adopted by the Eighth UN Congress on the Prevention of Crime and the Treatment of Offenders, Havana, Cuba, 27 August to 7 September 1990.

Declaration on the Elimination of Violence against Women (DEVAW), adopted by General Assembly on 20 December 1993.

International Criminal Court Statute (Rome Statute), adopted at a diplomatic conference on 17 July 1998.

Draft Articles on the Responsibility of States for Internationally Wrongful Acts (ILC Articles), adopted by the International Law Commission (ILC) at its fifty-third session, 2001.

Rules of Procedure and Evidence, International Criminal Court (ICC), UN Doc ICC-ASP/1/3, 2002.

Updated Set of principles for the protection and promotion of human rights through action to combat impunity (the Impunity Principles), adopted by UN ECOSOC on 8 February 2005, E/CN.4/2005/102/Add.1.

The Basic Principles and Guidelines on the Right to a Remedy and Reparation for Victims of Gross Violations of International Human Rights Law and Serious Violations of International Humanitarian Law, adopted by General Assembly on 16 December 2005, A/RES/60/147.

Protocol on the Prevention and Suppression of Sexual Violence against Women and Children, International Conference on the Great Lakes Region, 30 November 2006.

Convention on the Rights of Persons with Disabilities (CRPD), adopted by General Assembly on 13 December 2006.

Resolution on the Right to a Remedy and Reparation for Women and Girls Victims of Sexual Violence, African Commission on Human and Peoples' Rights (ACHPR), Res. 111 (XXXXII) 15–28 November 2007.

International Convention for the Protection of All Persons from Enforced Disappearance (ICCPED), adopted by General Assembly on 6 February 2007.

The Council of Europe Convention on preventing and combating violence against women and domestic violence (the Istanbul Convention), adopted by the Council of Europe on 11 May 2011.

International Protocol on the Documentation and Investigation of Sexual Violence in Conflict (2014) Basic Standards of Best Practice on the Documentation of Sexual Violence as a Crime under International Law, First Edition.

LEGISLATION OF TIMOR-LESTE

Indonesian Penal Code art 64 art 285

Indonesian criminal procedure code art 185

Constitution of the Democratic Republic of Timor-Leste (2002), adopted in March 2002.

Decree Law No 3/2005 on *The Restructuring of the First Constitutional Government*, 28 June 2005.

Decree Law 15/2008 on *Pensions of the Combatants and Martyrs of the National Liberation*, 08 May 2008.

Decree Law No 5/2012 on *Single Lump Sum for National Liberation Combatants and families of Martyrs*, 15 February 2012.

Law No 10/2003 on *the Interpretation of Article 1 of Law 2/2002 of 7 August on the Sources of Law*, 20 November 2003.

Law No 1/2006 on *Freedom of Assembly and Demonstration*, 16 January 2006.
Law No 3/2006, *Statute of the National Liberation Combatants*, 13 March 2006.
Law No 9/2009, *First amendment to Law No 3/2006 of 12 April (Statute of the National Liberation Combatants)*, 29 July 2009.
Law No 2/2011, *Second Amendment to Law no 3/2006 of 12 April (Statute of the National Liberation Combatants)*, 23 March 2011.
Law No 13/2017 on *Lands* (Regime Especial para a Definição da Titularidade dos Bens Imóveis), 5 June 2017.
UNTAET Regulation 2000/11, *On the Organization of Courts in East Timor*, 6 March 2000, UNTAET/REG/2000/11.
—— 2000/15, *On the Establishment of Panels with exclusive jurisdiction over serious criminal offences*, 6 June 2000, UNTAET/REG/2000/15.
—— 2000/30, *On Transitional Rules of Criminal Procedure*, 25 September 2000, UNTAET/REG/2000/30.
—— 2001/10, *On the Establishment of a Commission for Reception, Truth and Reconciliation in East Timor*, 13 July 2001, UNTAET/REG/2001/10.
—— 2001/25, *On the Amendment of UNTAET Regulation No 2000/11 on the Organization of Courts in East Timor and UNTAET REGULATION No 2000/30 on the Transitional Rules of Criminal Procedure*, 14 September 2001, UNTAET/REG/2001/25.

TABLE OF CASES

ACERWC, *Michelo Hunsungule and Others (on behalf of children in Northern Uganda) v The Government of Uganda*, Decision, Communication No 1/2005, African Committee of Experts on the Rights and Welfare of the Child, 15–19 April 2013.
CCPR, *Melleh v Ireland*, Com No 2324/2013 (CCPR/C/116/D/2324/2013), Views adopted by the Human Rights Committee under article 5(4) of the Optional Protocol to the ICCPR, 11 November 2013.
CEDAW, *BJ v Germany*, Communication No. 1/2003, UN Doc CEDAW/C/36/D/1/2003, 14 July 2004.
CEDAW, *Jallow v Bulgaria*, Communication No 32/2011; UN Doc CEDAW/C/52/D/32/2011, 28 August 2012.
CEDAW, *LC v Peru*, Communication No 22/2009, UN Doc CEDAW/C/50/D/22/2009, 18 June 2009.
CEDAW, *Vertido v Philippines*, Communication No 18/2008, UN Doc CEDAW/C/46/D/18/2008, 16 July 2010.
ECtHR, *El-Masri v The Former Yugoslav Republic of Macedonia* (Application No 39630/09), European Court of Human Rights, 13 December 2012.
ECtHR, *MC v Bulgaria* (Application No 39272/98), European Court of Human Rights, 3 December 2003.
HRAP, *Bogoljub Kostić and Others against UNMIK*, Case 111/09 and others, Kosovo Human Rights Advisory Panel, opinion of 23 October 2015.
IACHR, *Paloma Angélica Escobar Ledezma et al v Mexico*, Case 1175-03, Report No 32/06, Inter-American Commission on Human Rights.
IACtHR, *Aloeboetoe et al v Suriname*, Judgement (Reparations), The Inter-American Court of Human Rights, 10 September 1993.
IACtHR, *Fernández Ortega et al v Mexico*, Preliminary Objection, Merits, Reparations, and Costs, Judgment, The Inter-American Court of Human Rights, August 30, 2010.
IACtHR, *Gelman v Uruguay*, Merits and Reparations, Judgment, The Inter-American Court of Human Rights, 24 February 2011.
IACtHR, *González et al ('Cotton Field') v Mexico*, Judgment (Preliminary Objection, Merits, Reparations, and Costs), The Inter-American Court of Human Rights, 16 November 2009.
IACtHR, *Gudiel Álvarez (Diario Militar) v Guatemala*, Merits, Reparations and Costs, Judgment, The Inter-American Court of Human Rights, 20 November 2012.

IACtHR, *Plan de Sánchez Massacre v Guatemala*, Judgment, The Inter-American Court of Human Rights, 29 April 2004.

IACtHR, *Zambrano Vélez et al v Ecuador*, Merits, Reparations and Costs, Judgment, The Inter-American Court of Human Rights, 4 July 2007.

ICC, *The Prosecutor v Dominic Ongwen*, 'Prosecution application for the Pre-Trial Chamber to preserve evidence and take measures under article 56 of the Rome Statute', ICC-02/04-01/15-256-Conf, 26 June 2015.

ICJ, *Advisory Opinion on the Legal Consequences for States of the Continued Presence of South Africa in Namibia (Namibia case)*, International Court of Justice, 21 June 1971.

ICTR, *Prosecutor v Jean-Paul Akayesu (Akayesu case)*, Case No ICTR-96-4-T, Judgment, Trial Chamber, International Criminal Tribunal for Rwanda, 2 September 1998.

ICTY, *Prosecutor v Dragoljub Kunarac, Radomir Kovac and Zoran Vukovic (Kunarac case)*, The International Criminal Tribunal for the former Yugoslavia, 22 February 2001.

ICTY, *Prosecutor v Dusko Tadic USKO TADIC a/k/a 'Dule' (Tadić Case)*, Appeal Chamber, The International Criminal Tribunal for the former Yugoslavia, 2 October 1995.

ICTY, *Prosecutor v Mucić et al*, Case No IT-96-21-T, Judgment, The International Criminal Tribunal for the former Yugoslavia, 16 November 1998.

SCSL, *Prosecutor v Brima, Kamara and Kanu*, Case No SCSL-2004-16-T, AFRC Trial Judgment, Special Court for Sierra Leone, 20 June 2007.

Special Panels for Serious Crimes, *The Deputy General Prosecutor v Manek and 13 Others (Maternus Bere/ Suai Church massacre case)*, Timor-Leste, Case number 09/2003.

Special Panels for Serious Crimes, *The Prosecutor v Gonsalves et al (The Atabae case)*, Timor-Leste, Case number 8/2002.

Special Panels for Serious Crimes, *The Prosecutor v Jose Cardoso and 4 Others (The Lolotoe case)*, Timor-Leste, Case number 04/2001.

Special Panels for Serious Crimes, *The General Prosecutor v Joni Marques and 9 Others (The Los Palos case)*, Timor-Leste, Case number 09/2000.

US District Court (Southern District of New York) *Kadić v. Karadžić*, Order Entering Default on Liability, 93 Civ. II63 (PKL) (S.D.N.Y. June 13, 2000).

Index

www.ingramcontent.com/pod-product-compliance
Ingram Content Group UK Ltd.
Pitfield, Milton Keynes, MK11 3LW, UK
UKHW020242290926
15470UKWH00002B/682

9 781509 957637